THE ROCK RABBIT AND THE RAINBOW

The Rock Rabbit
and
The Rainbow

Laurens van der Post
among Friends

"In the time of the early race, the Bushmen,
the first people of Africa, said that their god-hero,
Mantis, was married to the Rock Rabbit
and the Rainbow was their son."

edited by Robert Hinshaw

DAIMON
VERLAG

The Rock Rabbit and the Rainbow, Laurens van der Post among Friends,
edited by Robert Hinshaw.

Front cover art and design by Frances Baruch, London; back cover photograph of Sir Laurens at Oberer Heller, Willerzell, Switzerland, 1988 by
Robert Hinshaw; jacket flap photo by Frances Baruch. All other credits are
listed to the extent they are known, on the List of Illustrations p. 389.

ISBN 3-85630-512-2 (hardbound)
ISBN 3-85630-540-8 (paperback)

© 1998 Daimon Verlag, Einsiedeln, Switzerland

Contents

Index of Authors

Note:

The written contributions in this collection have been minimally edited; that is to say, the original spellings and the individual styles of the authors have been retained whenever possible, which results in certain inconsistencies, for example, with regard to references and footnotes. Some of the material by Sir Laurens was transcribed from recorded conversations with the editor and subsequently edited, with the approval of Sir Laurens.

Illustrations and photographs came from a variety of sources, not always identifiable; as far as possible, they are provided in the list of illustrations on page 389.

Sir Laurens in Boulder, Colorado, September 1996

Editor's Foreword

Robert Hinshaw

I had always thought of departure and return as the deepest pattern of human life. I had always thought of them in terms of an origin and a destination, and yet in the emotions of this image, which still arises as clear and undimmed as it seemed when it first came into my awareness, beginnings and end, origin and destination, had all along been one.

Laurens van der Post, *The Voice of the Thunder*

The life of Sir Laurens van der Post, encompassing the greater part of the Twentieth Century, unfolded like one of his own fascinating stories, and it would seem that an appropriate beginning here might be, "Once upon a time …" While living out his incredible personal story to the full, he also dedicated his life to the spirit of story by sharing his entire bagful with us, making it highly appropriate that his last works should appear in the form that you see before you: as a collection of his stories and reflections, together with those of his friends and fellow travelers, to be shared by one and all.

Laurens Jan van der Post was born in the Orange Free State of South Africa on December 13, 1906, and he died almost exactly ninety years later in London. His was a long life of departures and returns, of patterns old and new: a never-ending quest for meaning.

The Rock Rabbit and the Rainbow began as a *Festschrift*, or celebratory collection of writings, by some of his friends as a surprise birthday gift to him some years ago. He was touched and deeply gratified; however, he resisted the idea of the manuscript being prepared for publication at that time, ostensibly because he felt there were other more urgent tasks to be completed first. With that, the idea of making the *Festschrift* into a published book was put on hold – but not forgotten.

In subsequent years, as the work on other projects progressed, Sir Laurens gradually became aware of another possibility: he needn't merely 'receive' this gift, but could also respond in kind, by making his own contribution. Once this was evident, he came to embrace the idea of publication wholeheartedly, seeing it as an opportunity to make a statement together with his friends about things deeply meaningful to them all. Thus, the *Festschrift* idea was superseded by a further-reaching one with a greater purpose, as reflected in the subtitle: *Laurens van der Post among Friends*. Delighted with this plan, he enthusiastically began to prepare his own gift.

It was characteristic of Sir Laurens that he felt moved not only to reciprocate by making his own contribution to the collection, but also to further enhance it by inviting a wider circle of friends to join in. In this way, the relatively modest original collection grew to become something far more: a mosaic of shared experiences and stories, while also a testament to a spirit and attitude Sir Laurens both lived and taught. Eventually, it was ready to go out into the world.

To celebrate the occasion of his ninety earthly years in December of 1996, Sir Laurens and several of his friends gathered for what would be the last time, and a bound volume of the printer's proofs for *The Rock Rabbit and The Rainbow: Laurens van der Post among Friends* was placed in his hands. He was overjoyed on this occasion to know that the project he had been working on with so many of them would soon be complete. In his spontaneous response that evening, he spoke from the heart of the importance of love and of friendship, as reflected in that gathering and in these pages, and without which life has no meaning. Physically exhausted, yet deeply content, he then retired to his home, his beloved 'spaceship' in the skies above Chelsea, to sleep the longest of sleeps.

In our final conversation shortly before his death, I told Sir Laurens that I had been deeply moved by his message in a recent talk in Zürich (at a testimonial honoring his life and work), when he addressed the essentiality of eros in our personal lives and in our work – of love for humanity and one's fellow human beings – and then, at his birthday party, when he had spoken, tears in his eyes, of his realizing ever more as he grew older, that what really matters in life is our friendships and our capacity to be loving, in all ways. As we talked, and he reaffirmed this, I was struck to the depths, not only by his message, but also by a sense of his role as a messenger of that meaning.

Disappointed as he was at his weakness and, at that moment in particular, the reality of having to cancel a journey to New York City, where he was to have delivered the sermon for the final Advent Sunday at the Church of St. John the Divine, as he had done regularly in recent years, he understood it as the ending of a pattern. "And patterns," he reflected, "are meant to be broken. We'll create new patterns – there is still so much to be done." Forward ever, backward never: his focus was on the path ahead.

In fact, his final months had been lived at an incredible pace, in spite of his ever frailer physical condition. There was a major event in September in Boulder, Colorado, a 'Laurens van der Post Festival' extending over four days and evenings, featuring his films: he responded generously, giving lengthy talks each day, sometimes twice a day, to audiences of nearly a thousand. It was here, too, that a sensitive new documentary film of his life, *Hasten Slowly*, by Mickey Lemle, had its U.S. premiere.

No sooner was he back in London than his last full-length book, *The Admiral's Baby*, was launched with a new publisher, John Murray, with all of the many accompanying events, and there was no opportunity to even consider such indulgences as, for example, jet-lag!

Though physically weak and tortured by deteriorating bones, he also managed to travel to Zürich to address a full house at the E.T.H. (Federal University), where his friends, C.G. Jung and C.A. Meier, had both been professors, as he noted to the young students. They listened raptly and awarded him a thundering standing ovation – as did a second large Zürich assembly when he was later presented with a citation for his life of devoted service.[1]

But his mortal energy was spent and he was in tremendous pain, though he would never reveal the true extent of it, even to his closest friends: "Every cell in my body is exhausted," was the most I ever heard from him in this regard, and that, only once. Asked if he didn't wish to slow the pace, however, his reply was: "I will just soldier on." And soldier on he did, right to the end.

***

Some, but certainly not all, of the many fields in which Sir Laurens was active are represented in this collection, and of course only a selection of friends could take part; of those who did, some chose to be very personal, relating something of themselves and their relation-

---

[1] See the *Laudatio* by Prof. Theodor Abt on p. 339 of this volume.

ships to Sir Laurens, while others chose to concentrate on writing essays in his spirit. In reading through the proofs one last time, I was particularly touched by what, in several cases, are final messages, written shortly before death. What all of the contributors to this volume have in common is a meaningful relationship with Sir Laurens, the man as well as his work.

For me, too, friendship with Sir Laurens van der Post was, and continues to be, something very special, and yes, life-changing. We first met in the early Seventies, but a decade was to pass before a personal relationship began to develop. Through our many common friends in Zürich, London and elsewhere, and interests – psychology, publishing, ecology, diverse cultures, including, perhaps most of all, Africa – we found our paths crossing ever more frequently, and with growing friendship, collaborative projects began to emerge: the book conceived for his old friend, Fredy Meier, *A Testament to the Wilderness*; recording his views on the occasion of Earth Day[1]; his recollections of the Eranos Conferences; occasions for storytelling, and so on. Our working together was formalized, to a certain degree, when his participation in *The Rock Rabbit and the Rainbow* became a reality, and there followed numerous other publishing projects, such as preparing an additional section for his biography of C.G. Jung, a revised edition of *The Dark Eye of Africa*, Forewords and Postscripts to new editions of his works and, most challenging and meaningful for me, a long-term endeavor we called "Conversations in Chelsea." Some of these works have since been realized and others are forthcoming; yet others, including the last-mentioned, were only in the early stages at the time of his death and thus will never be completed. But rather than grieve what will not be, I simply feel extremely grateful for all that he gave us: deep and true and ever-loyal friendship, and a wealth of story and wisdom that lives on, ever nourishing.

What did Laurens mean to me? First and foremost, he was a true friend, unflinching in his loyalty. He broadened my horizons while touching my heart. The quality of his friendship explains why he had so many friends, from so many different lands, cultures and generations: he genuinely met them in friendship and respect and they responded in kind. True to the depths, he was for me one of the few strong examples of a good 'way to be' as a human being, even while, or perhaps just because, his 'shadow' was also discernible. By this, I

---

[1] See "Our Mother Earth" on page 301 of this volume.

mean that he had his flaws, his prejudices and blind-spots, just as we all do; but he didn't allow these ever so human qualities to interfere with the greater values that guided his life.

Much of what has been publicly said and published about him over the years would seem to fall into one of two categories: 'sainthood' or 'devilry.' Would the possibilities really have to be so limited? Perhaps we could attempt to take a slightly different focus and see that this man indeed possessed extraordinary and admirable qualities, and that, in being of the stature he was, he very naturally also threw quite a sizeable shadow. But rather than concentrate only on his gifts or his shortcomings, as so many have done, why not back off by a step or two and try to see the phenomenon 'Laurens van der Post' as more of a whole, with brightness *and* shadow? The present volume, written by friends and in a spirit of celebration, consists, by its very nature, primarily of the stuff for which he has been admired and loved. In other places, some commentators have not hesitated to find – and in some cases, to exaggerate or even invent – other qualities. I would hope that, with the passage of time, a more balanced view of this man, including his context, might emerge – perhaps with the help of a well-researched biography.

He was a person who truly 'made a difference', both personally and collectively; he was a builder of bridges: among cultures, religions, continents. I repeatedly experienced how he would drop whatever he was doing, no matter how important, for a friend or a cause in need: this I will never forget.

He said in his talk at the Eranos Conference in 1956, and repeated many a time in subsequent years: "There is a part of our spirit to which (the) voice of Mantis, speaking from our age of stone to an age of men with hearts of stone, commands as with the authentic tone of eternal renewal: 'You must henceforth be the moon. You must shine at night. By your shining you shall lighten the darkness for men until the sun rises again to light up all things for men.'"

Laurens van der Post saw in this an image of what is wanting in the contemporary spirit: living in a sunset hour of time, we need encouragement and development of that aspect of ourselves represented by the moon. The moon and our intuitions that walk by the light of the moon need protection and support, and in his attitude and his generous sharing, Laurens van der Post has given us help to find our own moons.

He served the Moon, we might say. Not only did he revere that object in the heavens, keeping a watchful eye on it wherever he was in the world, and loving to point it out to whomever he was with, often with a story; but he also carried what might be called 'moonliness' within; that is to say, he embodied the qualities most associated with the moon; in a word, perhaps, the feminine: reflective, soft, intuitive, receiving, as contrasted with the brightness of the harder, more penetrating sun.

Foreign as this way of being is in most of the world of today, it is what so often leads to misunderstanding, criticism and derision. He was himself very aware of this; indeed, it was an inherent part of the highly-valued advice he was time and again able to impart to some of the leaders of his lifetime, sung and unsung, and of course to us all in his writing, his storytelling, his films and his friendships.

He served the causes he believed in to the end, never betraying or compromising them: this was his way of trying to make a better world. Perhaps more than anything else, he was a great lover of stories, of course, "the most precious container of the spirit of 'primitive' man, and the meanings that they carry": food for the journey. In this sense, he has provided for us well.

His words in the 'Preamble' to *A Mantis Carol* might inspire us to reflect on the spirit he carried among us:

> ... *the truth unhappily, from the point of view of those who try to serve it, is always more than literal or statistical fact. The writer who would warm ... cold, literal and statistical clay with life finds himself inevitably involved in some sort of alchemical approach to his subject, since life and the living of it for all our knowing, is still as great a mystery at its end as it was in its beginning. As fast as our knowledge expands to the rim of the unknown, the mystery at heart forms another horizon compelling the known to keep to the same respectful distance again.*

A year before his death, Sir Laurens, speaking as the 'soldier' that he was, anticipated his own earthly departure in the following way:

> *I think that, through life, we have this tremendous privilege of being in partnership with creation and time. So when I sail with the Ferryman, it will be, as we used to say in the war, 'under sealed orders.' To be opened only at the destination.*[1]

Hamba Ga'hle![2]

[1] *Sunday Times*, London, 10 December, 1995.
[2] "Go in peace and happiness."

In Acknowledgment

We are deeply indebted to the many collaborators who have given of themselves to make this volume a reality. It would not have been possible without the generous support of countless individuals, in spirit and in so many other ways, but most tangibly in the rich and varied contributions that comprise this collection. There were numerous friends who were of invaluable assistance 'behind the scenes,' as it were, providing connections, suggestions or vital pieces of information: Jane Bedford, Tom Bedford, Catherine Berthaud, Lela Fischli, Anne Imhoff, Robert Imhoff, Jean-Marc Pottiez, Valerie Solheim and Louise Stein are remembered here with particular gratitude. Heartfelt thanks are also due to those who offered financial support: George T. Page, Ronald Cohen, Carolyn Grant Fay, Katharine Graham, Aniela Jaffé, Mrs. Frank N. McMillan, Mr. and Mrs. Frank N. McMillan III, Eva Monley, Lloyd Phillips, Mario Schiess, Claire Townsend and Candice van Runkel, along with unnamed others.

Last but not least, thanks are due to Laurens van der Post himself, the original recipient of this work in its conception, who gratefully accepted it and then honored the gift of giving in his own generous fashion to help create a beautiful collection of stories that will live beyond our time.

Laurens: snapshot taken on his thirteenth birthday

And from my own experience of living I came to realize that, even if one accomplished the full round of one's allocated span, the best of us would have added little to what life and creation had already invested within us as children.

Laurens van der Post
The Voice of the Thunder, p. 7

Introduction

A Word from Laurens van der Post

I remember many snatches and fragments of stories from far back in my beginning in Africa that left a feeling as of a rainbow arched over the darkening clouds of time behind me, but the first really coherent story that I can recall was told to me by my old nurse, who was one of the last survivors in my part of Africa of the first people in the country. She it was who told me, "in the days of the people of the early race, our father Mantis, the snatcher of fire, was married to the Rock Rabbit and they had a son who was to be seen in the Rainbow."
– Laurens van der Post, BBC radio interview

They order these things better in Europe than in Britain as Sterne already observed in his remarkable "sentimental journey" to France. Nowhere else do they order them better than in Switzerland. Something which illustrates this most graciously for me is the observance of the ritual of the *Festschrift*. It seems to me to be one of the most civilised conceits of intimate human relationships, and since I encountered it first in Switzerland, I thought my encounter, and what came out of it, would do well to introduce this *Festschrift* which some dear friends of mine had decided to compile on the occasion of my birthday.

It happened soon after the end of my War. My war had gone on for just over ten years, and when I came back in winter, 1948, I came back utterly to a world estranged from myself. I was rather lost, bewildered; I had just resigned my commission in the army to which I had felt for the first time enclosed in a very fateful and closely knit community, almost like a monastic order. I walked out of it, and walked for the first time into the post-war world. I didn't like it, and I didn't feel I belonged to it. I had to go to Switzerland to join Ingaret Giffard, to whom I am married today. She had suffered as a result of the war, particularly under the great blackout, which came down over England when the war broke out, a blackout also of the human spirit. She felt this so deeply that she renounced her own calling of becoming a playwright. One of her plays had been compared to Chekov when it was first performed in London, but she abandoned all that. She did her war service and, already looking for something beyond the blackout, encountered Alan McGlashan, a remarkable Jungian-orientated analyst and doctor working in London. At the end of the war, she decided to go to Zürich. She already knew about C.G. Jung through an acquaintance of her mother with Godwyn Baines and everything she heard made her feel that the answer, the penetration of this blackness, was to be found in the world around Jung.

I arrived there just before Christmas in 1948 and not only found Ingaret very happy, but with a new sense of purpose, working with Dr. C. A. Meier and Toni Wolff, to whom she had been referred by Jung himself. And they had just newly created what is today the premier Jungian Institute in the world. It had only just begun with Dr. Meier as the president-founder and with the remarkable and incomparable Aniela Jaffé as secretary.

Through Ingaret's introduction and the experience of that circle that was growing around Jung, I suddenly felt as if I was in the presence of a small renaissance court of the human spirit. There was a sense of discovery, of the reawakening of it. I went to talks at the Institute and ultimately met Jung himself. We instantly clicked and became friends, and our friendship grew and was even more deep and lasting and permanent for myself at the time of his death. In this sense of getting my direction again, what was very important was that, through the Jungian way of looking at life, through Jung himself and what he had achieved, I found that already I was being confirmed, almost as if one is confirmed in a great new church. As a result of talking to Jung about the Africa I had within myself, I was re-confirmed into a new area of the human spirit which had been singularly mine intuitively ever since I was born. Nothing seemed to me more wonderful than the prophetic observation by Sir Thomas Browne, the intuitive alchemist figure of Norwich in the Elizabethan age, "We seek the wonders without that we carry within us – we have all Africa and its wonders within us."

I had all these wonders within me, but they were strange in the world in which I grew – nothing could have been more foreign to the war, and suddenly I found that Jung not only was already there in that

Africa, but had actually made the journey to it – a journey which confirmed him in his own seeking of additional evidence for the great transforming hypothesis of the collective unconscious to which we owe so much today – to which we shall owe very much more in the future. I got a sense of personal confirmation through him, through this great man of the science of spirit – this great religious phenomenon that he was.

I found that he was singularly moved by my own experience of Africa, particularly of the first people of Africa, when I told him about them, how I was going back into the desert to live with them and how important I found their spirit was. I could only illustrate it to him by telling him stories. He said to me, "Look, these are frightfully important, these stories are an immense expansion of the light in which we should look at the human psyche and human soul, because in the beginning, it's pure, uncluttered by the rationalism and materialism of all these civilisations that defeated themselves and perished behind us. These are products of the natural psyche – for God's sake, spread it about, tell them, give them these interpretations you've given me."

He felt that so deeply that he got in touch with Olga Froebe Kapteyn at Ascona in Switzerland. Now, Olga, as you probably know, had started there a remarkable *Tagung* called Eranos, where scholars came from all over the world to talk on a common theme. Jung himself had been approached by her during the dark days of the war. She said to Jung, "You've told us about these horrible visions that had haunted you where you saw Europe as a flooded field of mangled corpses and other horrors of the human flesh torn to bits; you saw a rising tide of blood which came to the rhythm of these mountains, and intuitively I already felt that these mountains of Switzerland constitute a natural expression of a safeguard of the mandala pattern in the human spirit which is designed to protect it from chaos. We are keeping our Eranos world going – let's keep it going during the war, and please come and help us." Jung went there, and every year for a long period, he made some of his most important pronouncements at Eranos, and he said to me at a certain point, "You, too, must go and talk about these things at Eranos."

It is so much part of our beginning, so constantly with me, that period of illumination, of readjustment that I was painfully doing myself and which led me back to Africa to the first spirit; this all became clarified and purposeful in Zürich. It is not that I look back to that period in Zürich in the way mythology says we must not look back. It is dangerous to look back; look at Orpheus, look at Lot. Never do it. Never look back. That is true – it is a command we must never transgress. When I talk about a period, it's not looking back, it's what I think a *Festschrift* is so uniquely designed to do: you can talk about the past and the common experience, not as a looking back, but as a common remembrance. And so, I would like to root this *Festschrift* which these dear friends of mine have thought has been deserved, into my first experience in Zürich. Seeing that many of my friends who have contributed to it come in any case from Zürich, seeing that they do it so graciously and with such intimacy, I hope that this command of Jung's which I fulfilled at Eranos will naturally join in and particularly fit in with the pattern of *The Rock Rabbit and the Rainbow*, which is the title of this *Festschrift*.

God's Spies

For Laurens van der Post on his ninetieth birthday

Kathleen Raine

Life lived, lives, yours, mine,
All who have been, all who will be
Outlive ourselves into memory –
But who the rememberer? As if we were another
Than this transient traveller
From day to day, inexhaustible world's epiphany,
Arriving, passing, yet always
Here and now, though now as far
From those once present presents as most distant star, whose ray
Shines from long light-years away

In the beginning, father, mother,
All the loved and known of then –
That sunny wall where our golden tabby
Basked in a long-ago summer, the garden
Where mint and pansies grew, loaves rising on the kitchen fender
Now under Keilder loch, whose bright surface mirrors
Always and only timeless sky;
The way home leads to the water's edge, then under.
And though no lake submerges, no demolition
Has brought down houses, libraries, colleges, gardens,
                cities and wildernesses
Change has carried them away,
And we who remember are not those who were,
Awaited, hoped,
who looked into the eyes of the beloved,

This world the place of meeting, place of parting.

Times and places, far and near,
Familiar and dear faces, voices,
Earth's marvels we have known, but could never find again
What is, like landscape in a dream, once only.
Times past were futures once, infinitely desired,
And all those futures past of the ceaseless world.

'Beyond sorrow' I have heard that country called,
Beyond beginnings and endings, world's times and places
For recollection is not remembrance of things past:
The unborn undying
Travels the field of earth, gathering fragrance,
The one life, in which we are one another
Lives in all who were, all who will be;
Undying joy is who we are,
What love has gathered remains, the rest was never.
Lovers, toilers, mourners, endurers, enactors of the one story,
We have imagined into being.
We live, weave and interweave each our one thread
In the seamless texture of the world, our one note utter
In the music of the spheres, drop in unbounded ocean, boundless
Here and now, here and now at heart and for ever.

A Synchronicity Out of Space

From conversations with a comet
months before Kathleen Raine wrote her poem.

Laurens van der Post

Our comet is on the way out, and in its Cometese sent a farewell message to all of us who have watched it with delight every evening when the clouds permitted. These are its last words on its dropping-in visit within human vision, which will not be repeated for some 20,000 years.

Remember (it said) at the end that we comets are not like other heavenly bodies, even supposing that we have such things as the word "bodies" conveys, and which is an "Earth" term and not listed in the Cosmic dictionary available to us comets.

We are solitary "bodies" doing our own thing – and that is to bring light to places in the outer darkness of unfulfilled creation where no light as yet has been before. We are not part of any system, solar or otherwise. We are not joined to any of the many-splendoured belted constellations that you all admire night after night. We do our own thing, and before we are launched on our role in creation and given our tails, we take a vow. Please remember this vow because it cannot be improved upon

It is simply this: We vow to take upon our-selves the mystery of things and be one of God's spies – as your Shakespeare (who is much quoted by all comets) put it, as if he were a comet himself.

Marking Time

Laurens van der Post

1. The Voice of Crusoe – A Letter to Sonia Marjasch[1]

My dear Sonia,

Out of Africa, we see you and I greet you and write to say they tell me that you are just about to have a very special birthday. Of course I know what they mean and fully join in with what such a diversity of friends are doing to celebrate the "specialness" of the occasion, but for me it can only be extra special as the latest ambassador of all the special birthdays that you have had since birth.

I do not propose to put any statistics forward as a measure of the special nature of the occasion, as we are normally compelled to do. I think there are quite a long line of ancestors who would be whirling around in their graves in protest if I put years to the life of a great lady like you. It is somehow, somewhere, not manly decency to put public emphasis on this. The right manner for man, in whatever dimension he chooses to deal with the feminine, must be different – or should I coin a word and say "deferent"? Happily, I do believe that I can join in the salute which we all owe you in a manner that does not offend any valid scruples either of immemorial past or strident present.

Your many friends and admirers, who share a fixed place on earth with you, can mark the occasion by raising flags and draw on all the rich and colourful means they have for rejoicing in such a lucky day. They can even, as they should if it were not against the law, fire a 21-gun salute for you and proclaim in sound what they feel about you. They can feast, and wine and dine, and sing, as I am certain they will

---

[1] Sonia Marjasch is a Jungian analyst and friend of many years of Laurens van der Post, living in Forch, near Zürich, Switzerland ... and everywhere.

all do with a new fervour. You all can orchestrate that part of the birthday theme better than I can do.

But even so, there will be a quintessential Sonia who might feel left out and feel she could have done with something extra. It is, I believe, the Sonia who is of no fixed locality, the Sonia who is always on a journey, who is always traveling far and fast, and is on and out of fixed vision before her incursion can be recorded: Perhaps only someone who has traveled on a parallel course, even though not to so great a purpose, can maintain a sighting of her. I believe Robert Louis Stevenson spoke for her as well as for himself when he wrote: "It is better to travel hopefully than to arrive."

This is the Sonia of nowhere in particular but at home everywhere. You can see, of course, where the feeling is taking me, because we have talked about it on several occasions in the past. It is the Sonia who cannot have just a fixed geographical root, a Sonia of a variety of provisional roots, and above all, a "portable tap root." They are hard to come by, and then can only fulfill their role in the spirit of those who contain the paradox of reality and who, in the midst of their being and doing, discover an element of becoming which adds to the being and enriches the doing with moving the whole on, as it were, into new country to explore another pattern of creation.

It is something, of course, of which artists, particularly poets, have been intuitively aware. There is, for instance, Baudelaire. I choose him because he is so much nearer to our time and so full of the unease of the failed traveler because his baggage, although it included the richest of gifts, did not contain any portable roots. And yet he set out with the authentic vision which made him write to the effect – I translate from memory – of: "The real travelers are those who go for the going, hearts light as ships of air, and always with a call of, 'Onward, there!'"

With it, too, he is profoundly aware of the meaninglessness of traveling only in one lateral dimension and in a spirit at most nourished by regional roots – again, a translation from memory:

> For the child in love with his maps and his stamps
> The world is big enough for an appetite so vast
> But, oh! how small it is in the light of lamps
> With eyes looking back at last.

It is a conclusion, alas, in which there is no "Onward, there!", and I am certain – whether you were ever in love with maps and stamps or not, and do indulge in looking back in the light of lamps – that on this special occasion the world will be enlarged for you, as you, through your traveling in your own paradoxical way, have enlarged it for so many of us.

Since you are such a traveler, therefore, and with all this and more that we feel about you in mind, the image I have of your birthday is that it is a blaze on a tree marking a place where you have camped on a journey – I wanted to say a journey almost without an end, but that would have diminished the dimension in which you are traveling, for this journey is one in which end and beginning are one, destination and departure are one, and the movement which seems to separate one from the other is but an enlargement of awareness and the thrust into new areas of meaning.

In this dimension, there is no normal measure of time. There is no difference of size or weight or distance, because all within it are one. It is not an infection of sophistication that calls for this differentiation aimed at realising a oneness. It is the most profound intuition of the natural traveler that demands it, the traveler whose most profound pattern is precisely this oneness of departure and return.

I have, as an example, a hunter who accompanied me through nearly five years of explorations of a vast desert. At our last camp of all, when I went out early in the morning to mark our camp on a tree as I had done at all our other camps over the past five years, and in the centre of the blaze wanted to put a name to each one of them for no explicit reason except that the manner of the journey demanded it of me, I found him already standing on a dune, smoking his pipe and looking at the swift expansion of a red dawn. For a moment, his silhouette made me think of some Red Indian hunter, with the dawn wrapped like a scarlet blanket around him, breathing fire and smoke as an offering to the light. But then I realised we had an image native to the occasion and born of the earth of the desert, far more apt. It was *Heitsi-ebib* dawn, for *Heitsi-eibib* was the god-hero of the aboriginal Hottentots who always fought the darkness in the night to bring the light of day to the world, and the red of the dawn was the blood from the wounds inflicted on him in the struggle.

When I had done my blaze, he was still there, but heard me coming and looked as if he wanted to speak to me. I climbed up to him, and already the red had turned to gold. He took his pipe in his hand and waved the stem at the light, and said: "Special, this, isn't it?"

I nodded but did not speak, and we stood there in silence for quite a while, and then he said: "You know, wherever one camps, one leaves something of oneself behind, but most of all at the last camp, like this one. And the older I get, the more difficult I find it to take."

I offer this example of how instinctive this pattern is in life, especially for you because of the profound way in which you have traveled with your mind and spirit in perhaps the oldest and the greatest desert of all, which lies in the heart of Asia and out of which so much life of man and mind has poured. In doing so, you have done something which is very relevant to our time, something which T.S. Eliot did for the English-speaking world in "The Wasteland." You have understood, not only through this journey of your mind and spirit, why wastelands and deserts are fundamental in the great scheme of things and why we now, who have explored and traveled so much of the world so badly and brutally, and even turned the physical scene inside out to observe it with strangely irreverent eyes, we have done so without knowing it, as the great act of preparation for exploring the vast desert in the heart of contemporary man.

Inevitably, this brings me back to this matter of how one observes birthdays in time. This also has much to do with the sort of traveler you are, and the kind of traveling that is thrust on us by the nature of things and somewhere confronts one with an apparent disaster of great proportions. I say 'apparent,' because it is a disaster in the provisional sense only for those like you who do not lose heart, because the disaster provides the material out of which one repairs and re-equips oneself for traveling on again. It represents itself in the imagination like a kind of shipwreck, a shipwreck that stands for our collective selves that abandon us and perish, and only the lone and now singularly vulnerable part of ourselves survives because it still maintains the heart, one day, to travel on. For the moment, there the journey seems to stop, but the image of the shipwreck moves on, and out of the deep sea of the soul arises the image of the island.

I think I knew this importance even as a child. I remember that, in my first class of geography, when I was taught the definition of an island as "a piece of land surrounded by water," the hair at the back of my head tingled; and I thought it the greatest poetic statement I had ever heard. For me, instantly the association was, of course, Robinson Crusoe.

I wonder if you have wondered, as I have wondered, and perhaps can give me an answer, as I cannot give it to myself: What has happened to Robinson Crusoe? When I was a boy, I knew no one, even among the children of the bush with whom I played in the heart of Africa, who did not know about Robinson Crusoe and could listen to his story over and over again. I remember that just after the war, men like Cocteau and Hans Wedderkopf of *Querschnitt* found his appearance in the European imagination of such significance that they wrote about him at length. But I no longer see him mentioned. I no longer hear about him, and it is a long time since I have seen a child with its nose in an illustrated edition of *Robinson Crusoe*, whereas, in my own childhood, no child ever had a birthday which did not include among the presents another book on Robinson Crusoe.

There is so much to be said in this regard, and I wish I had several days to discuss it with you, but here, as you are about to blaze the tree of another momentous camp in order to get on with your journey, I can only throw a few amplifications at you in such a hurry and lack of considered order that they may seem totally unconnected with what I have been trying to say.

The heart of the matter is that Robinson Crusoe's story is a great island story. No matter what happened before and after, it is this island experience that gives it such a wealth of meaning. It is just as well to pause and think of what the symbol of the island has been trying to tell us. The stories of the great journeys of the past that have meant most to me are all island stories. There is, right at the beginning, even before Robinson Crusoe, Ithaca and Odysseus, Penelope and Nausica. Even long after the story had been told by Homer, in what seemed for so many centuries the final and absolute form, it took the explorer spirit in its most inspirational measure of Dante's *Divine Comedy*, where we rediscover Odysseus in Hell. There he gives an account of how, even after the return to Ithaca and reunion with Penelope, the journey still had to go on, and how he exhorted his men (and I quote again from memory): "Oh, my brothers, you who have come 20,000 leagues, look to the West, to that unpeopled world beyond the Sun! You were not meant to live like beasts, but men of intellect and spirit!"

He came to grief because he traveled on in a way that was not traveling on. He took to the sea again with a full crew of men. It was in a very profound sense a repetition of what he had already done heroically and well. In the process, he was violating one of the cardinal laws of creation, a violation against which all mythology and primordial wisdom warns: Never look back, never repeat a journey already done. After the island, abandon the sea, seek no collective support: journey on alone. Journey, in fact, in a way which the blind seer Tiresias, in the *Odyssey* itself, foretells when he meets Odysseus among the spirits of Hades. It is for this reason that in Dante's account of the journey, he fails, and his heroic spirit is in Hell.

We who know you have no fear that your island self, in the midst of all your traveling, will look back and just attempt to repeat your splendid but spent yesterdays, and that your traveling self will have to be sought on another kind of island which was also a preparation for traveling on.

I think of Shakespeare's *Tempest*. It is the last of Shakespeare's plays. For me, Shakespeare's journey is, from his first great play, *A Midsummer Night's Dream*, to *The Tempest*, not a series of separate pieces, but one continuous work. They are a profound process of self-conducted individuation. On this island, he discovers at last his own objective self. It is on this island where, after all the long hard years of labour and journeying with infinite resource and courage, he achieves a differentiated totality; so that Caliban and Ariel, the brother who betrayed him and even on this magic island was still conspiring to kill him, the King. The highest value of all, his son Ferdinand – the royal future self – and Miranda – his own feminine self – and all that is light and dark and even collective, are contained in a harmonious whole; and Shakespeare can go back to the world again fulfilled, knowing that we are all "such stuff as dreams are made on," and all of that which lies in the future and is beyond all our knowing, is a matter for prayer.

Then, of course, there is Robinson Crusoe – and with all that I have experienced of the order of three in fairy tales and myths and my own life, I will not try and improve on the three. It is enough to show what I am after, and that is how, at heart, the traveler is something of which the island is the most complete and precise symbol.

When the great poet, Donne, says that, "No man is unto himself an island, we are all part of the Main," much as I love him and know, I think, what he is trying to say, I do not think he has got it quite right. I think that every man unto himself, in the deep within himself, is an island – but joined to other islands by The Main, which is the sea.

So, dear Sonia, there I must leave it and hasten back to this matter of your birthday which is approaching so fast, at a speed perhaps which may be more to your liking than it is to someone so rationed in time as myself.

I would just like to say that it is also the Robinson Crusoe in your self, the Robinson Crusoe who may or may not yet be on his island – only you can tell – whom I want to salute particularly on this day. You can imagine how I can amplify the imagery of the story: the cannibals of the collective world that invade this island of the self would devour Man Friday – the individual shadow on which Crusoe's progression depends – the shipwreck, the raft, and all the incidents that I remember still as though I had read the story only yesterday.

There is enough material in this for a very long psychological treatise, but there is one outstanding event that seems almost designed for what is about to happen to you, and that is the moment when Robinson Crusoe discovers that he is forgetting the passing of the days, that time is about to rush by him as a nameless, unobserved torrent of life. He knows that this must not happen, that whatever his fate, he must remember his days, he must remember – because life is not complete if it is only of today and the future: it must be also remembrance. It is a recognition of what I have called to myself the Great Memory, the memory which remembers us when all else has forgotten us. In marking the days, he is latching his memory onto the procession of time wherein remembrance is not only of our yester-days, but of the days and seasons to come.

So please, mark the day, blaze the tree, and I wish that I could have been with you to add my sense of delight to that of you all. The conventional greeting says it all: "Happy Birthday, and Many Happy Returns." And I say 'returns' here, on condition that the last remem-brance demanded is that the returns I have in mind include an equivalent amount of departures, so I would add, "Happy Depar-tures" to the overall wish, as well.

And since I began in my African self, so out of it, too, I wish you a good good-bye and a fair farewell, for which the primitive idiom is: "Yes … no; *Hamba ga'hla; Sahlahle ga'hla.*"

P.S.: This in no way needs a reply. It is a kind of giving in the hope that it will stop there, but should you know where Crusoe is, would you please send me a telegram?

2. The Whisper

A Letter to Robert Schwartz[1]

2 January, 1990

Dear Bobs,

One of the many qualities I've learned to love about you is your many-sidedness. I think you know this, because in order to complete my vision of you and the joy I take in it, I have for many years addressed you as two Bobs, both valid, both immensely important, and both far from suggesting any hint of a split nature.

They are, in fact, as easily integrated as the two sides of the moon, and like the moon, inclined to show us only one face and to keep the other invisible as part of the essential mystery of the individual, as hiding the face directed towards eternity and the infinite. Yet it does play for me a great role, always fueling the glow which the side directed to the earth reveals to us.

But I must confess that the striking photograph, with which the imminence of your birthday was announced to me, surprised me because I did not visualise your diversities, including an aspect of a modern Diogenes in a tub. Diogenes, as I know him from my inadequate brush with the Classics, was a cynic. You are not a cynic because you are that rare phenomenon who finds that cynics, far from being realists, miss out on the ultimate reality by not including faith, trust, hope, and the infinite capacity for invention and an unending intuition of great new vistas of creativity and opportunity and renewal of life stretching out before the human race.

Judging by the expression on your face in the tub, I think it does show one great thing in Diogenes which I had always admired: the courage of his questioning convictions, the will and capacity to live them, and above all, the total independence of spirit and of vision.

I think the photograph is splendid in that it shows you, as it were, without clothes, without the civilised habit – *habit* in Old English as "dress" or "clothes" meant a part of ourselves which was necessary for investing life with grace and the order of the spirit called good

[1] Robert Schwartz is a contributor to this volume, p. 269

manners and measured communication. But here you are shown as you are naturally within yourself: a long-distance look in the eye, and all your senses focused on evaluating something that others cannot see, with determination not only to perceive it in its totality, but the resolution to bring it to others and to live it through.

I think that, if at that moment, which comes so often in your days, Alexander the Great himself were to reappear and say to you, as he did to Diogenes, who had impressed him greatly: "What can I do to help you?", you would answer, as Diogenes did, naturally and curtly and without aggression but firmly: "Remove your shadow from my light."

For here, through the intermediary of the two Bobs, who in their partnership and union are more than the sum of themselves, we have a glimpse of the profoundly intuitive person you are, intuitive about the past, about the present and about the future.

Bach was once asked where he got his tunes from, and he said: "My dear fellow, when I get up in the mornings and get out of bed, I have to take great care not to tread on them." I think that is your situation, too, because of the abundance of hunches and major intuitions and endless possibilities of creation and re-creation that are always within you.

I know a lot of intuitives, and their trouble is that they like intuition so much that once they've had an intuition, they want to press on to the next and leave others to carry out the labour which legitimate intuition demands. But I've never known you to walk out on your intuitions in such an indulgent way. I've never known you not to accept the hunch which, after the examination shown in the photo, has not passed the test always. You have lived what is so painful to the intuitive: to make intuition a reality before you take on the next one. And for this, you have been a great source of enrichment in all your friendships, and with it all, you've not only added to our interests of life, but to our fun and to our laughter and, when necessary, also to our compassion and our need to breathe, which this world of ours increasingly, in its dislike of spiritual discomfort, finds impossible to do.

Perhaps, as I am a storyteller, I can sum up all that I and my friends feel about you in a story. You may be startled because it's a story about a mouse and to dispel any initial alarm, I must tell you that I do not know any culture – and I know a few, exceedingly primitive or exceedingly civilised – which has not got a good mouse story. Even today the United States has given us Mighty Mouse, and the English have their elegant and refined mouse story in Beatrix Potter's *Tailor of Gloucester*. And even the Bushmen, the oldest people in the world, have theirs, too long to tell.

But one of the greatest mouse stories I know is the one which I think speaks for you. I am sorry that I cannot tell it in its entirety because it would make a small novelette, but in essence it is about a little mouse who lived in the large mouse community in a very large and dense forest. It was an extremely busy mouse community, and all day long the mice were busy doing mouse things, their noses to the ground, busy rushing back and forth, getting food, establishing maternity wards, and getting ready for the winter. There seemed to be nothing else in their lives.

But there was this one little mouse who was conscious that whenever there was a lull in the hullabaloo around him, there could be heard a strong whispering noise coming from beyond the forest. He could get no other mice interested in the whisper, so one day he went with a beating heart to explore the land in the direction of the whisper.

After a long, eventful journey in which ultimately he had to sacrifice both his eyes, one after the other – that is, he had to lose all common earthly seeing he came high up in the mountains to a most beautiful place, the source of a great river. Suddenly he discovered that he was no longer a mouse and had become an eagle, and he saw the world spread out below him with the eyes of an eagle, shouldering a far cloud.

It is this story I would like to pass on to you as an unredeemed mouse myself, still following, I think, the same whisper and almost exactly thirteen years longer on the trail than you, as testimony of how you are for me someone who has never failed to follow the whisper, and who will certainly not fail to find it, with the total vision, through the two Bobs, represented by the eagle at the end of the road.

Much love and
an hamba ga'hla to both Bobs,
yours ever,
    Laurens

Mr. Shirakawa ('cup-of-coffee journalist'), Sir Laurens and Captain
Mori in Tokyo at the Yasukuni Shrine (May 1960)

3. The Blessed Hundred

A Letter to Hiroaki Mori[1]

15th August, 1989

My dear Hiroaki,

Thank you for coming to see us in London, and thank you for all the years in which you have kept me linked to your father, your mother and yourself, and for continuing it in our deprived present. And thank you also for all the lovely things you brought us to give substance to the memories we have of you all. I hope one day still to come to Japan and pay my respects to the graves of your father and your mother. In the meantime, let us keep in the closest touch possible.

You ask me for some words to be read at the memorial gathering for your father. This is difficult because he is almost everywhere in all my writing to do with Japan, particularly in *Yet Being Someone Other*. But to sum it up, I would say overall that he was a great man. One of the confusions of our times is the belief that only big things, "muchness" and great positions make men great. The truth is, and the tragedy is, that very often the great offices in places of power in life are occupied by small men, and as a rule – and at the most – by men who just get by. The really great people of our time come from somewhere else. They are people who are great because within themselves they lived truthfully and did the thing for which their natures destined them to the best and fullest extent of their capacities. People who do this live a life full of meaning for themselves and for others with whom they come into contact. In this world of meaning, the importance of the office, the physical extent and bulk of the work, are unimportant – only the truth and the meaning matter. It is from this that nations and periods of time derive their singular qualities – the undismayed numbers of anonymous human beings who do what is on their doorstep without complaint in a dimension of life where they keep company in which everyone is equal, from captains and kings to peasants and priests and streetsweepers.

[1] Hiroaki Mori is the son of Captain Mori, who is a contributor to this volume, p. 81

Your father was great in that he lived to the full a life of meaning. In this sense, he represented the best of the whole of a tremendously fateful era in the life of Japan and the world. There is a saying in England that those whom the gods love die young. That, in history, has often proved to be so. But I also believe that those whom the gods love most live longest of all, so that for me, all that I say about your father is confirmed by the fact that the gods made him live to celebrate his 100th birthday, still so conscious and alert that he could recognise men around him whom he had not seen for forty years.

We should look no further for signs of the fact that your father was "not two." We are blessed to have known him, and I perhaps most blessed of all, because we started from such remote and far away places that all the odds were against our meeting. Yet we met and we remained friends to the end, despite many things that divided other men and, in a sense, your father proved that deep down in all our natures there is a hunger everywhere in the world for an increase of bonds such as these. I feel myself singularly blessed not only to have known him, but to be still alive to go on knowing him and speaking about him to one and all who did not, as my memorial of him.

Yours ever,
Laurens

An African Tale

Frances Baruch

This is a tale from Africa. There are several versions of it among the indigenous peoples of South Africa, and this version was told to me by a friend who heard it in the kraal of a great African prophet in 1927. He heard it at a moment when the emergence of a new prophet was still an unrivalled spiritual event in the lives of primitive peoples in Africa, far more than that of governors.

The moment the news came to my friend, he went to see the prophet and the prophet asked him why he had come to see him, and he replied: "To talk to you about the great first spirit of your people, Umkulunkulu."

The prophet had looked at him sadly and said, "How strange, because people no longer talk of Umkulunkulu. His praise names are forgotten. They talk today only of things that are useful."

I mention this because it illustrates the natural spiritual background in which this story was told.

Once upon a time, among the people who had their kraals near a certain river, there was a girl called 'nKogilidane who was very beautiful and who kept herself well, and who roused the envy of all the other girls in her generation. They therefore tended to be rude to her and to push her aside. She was very sensitive, and she felt this to be hurtful and did all she could to appease her critics, but the more she tried, the more they seemed to reject her.

One day when she discovered that all the girls had already gone down to the river, she decided to follow them and join them. When they saw her coming, their jealousy became more powerful than ever. They quickly hid all their jewels and headbands in the sand, and when she joined them, they said to her: "Why do you walk about always dressed like that? Why can't you be like the rest of us? Look, we've thrown all our ornaments into the river." The girl immediately undid her jewelry and finery and threw them into the river, whereupon the other girls laughed at her and said things like: "You're not only vain, but stupid. We would never have done anything so foolish. Look, here are all our things." And the girls laughed mockingly at her, gathered up their jewels, and fetched the water.

The stricken girl thereupon went to the river alone and in tears, and she cried out: "River, show me please, show me the beads that must have passed this way." But the river merely said in a firm, commanding voice: "Pass on." She went along, calling out in this way to the river, until she became tired and increasingly despairing.

She came to a large deep pool, and she called out the same question she'd asked of the river: "Oh pool, please show me the beads that must have passed this way." The pool was silent. She spoke even louder a second time, but again the pool was silent. Then she spoke more loudly than ever a third time, and there was a great swell of water in the pool, so dark with the deep blue of the day, and it opened completely and said to her: "Enter. Your beads are here."

She immediately obeyed the voice and without hesitation entered the pool and went deep deep down until she came to the bottom, where there was hardly any light to see by. But in this light, she saw a horrendous old lady covered with the most terrible sores. The old lady called out to her and said without further ado: "Come and lick my sores." The girl was so moved by the plight of the old lady that she completely forgot about her own mission, and went over and licked the old lady's sores.

When she had done so, the old lady told her that, although she was young and beautiful, she had something more important: a compassionate heart. "You have shown such pity for an old thing like me. I shall from now on protect you. I am living here with the monster, Dimo. He is away at the moment because he's gone out hunting human beings so that he can eat them. You will know when he's on his way back here by a light wind that will blow and a few drops of rain that will fall. So, for the moment, quickly take some of my food and eat, and when you have finished, I must hide you behind this wall of mine. But you must be quick, because he won't be long."

When the girl had eaten, the old lady took her behind the wall and hid her in such a way that she couldn't possibly be seen by anyone. She'd hardly done so when, as so often happens in Africa when there is a false rainfall and all the hearts of people stricken by drought are grievously disappointed, a swirl of wind took all the clouds away and only a few drops of rain fell, and Dimo appeared.

He looked awful. He had nasty long hair and a great big red mouth with bulging lips, and teeth that were more like the tusks of wild pigs than that of any human being. He immediately confronted the old lady in a most belligerent manner and said that he could smell there was a human being about somewhere. He went over and stirred the fire, and made it throw a light all around the place, and kept on sniffing, saying, "I can smell a human being. What have you done to hide it from me? Tell me at once or I'll kill you."

And indeed, he looked as if he were about to kill her and devour her. But instead, he took out a stick, glowing with fire at the end, and tortured the old lady with it, carefully putting its burning end into all her sores. Again he said he would devour her, because although he'd hunted all day, he had been most unsuccessful. He'd found no human being to eat and was very hungry. In the end, what stopped him from eating her was the realisation that, if he did, he would no longer have anyone to keep his place and cook for him. So he had to content himself with the food that the old lady had already prepared for them. When he had eaten, and done another sniffing session all around the house, still muttering about the smell of human being, he was so tired and full of food that he went to sleep.

The old lady quickly darted behind the wall and took the girl out. To the girl's amazement, from somewhere the lady produced her beads, but not only her beads: she added to them beads and decorations of the most beautiful kind. In addition to all these lovely bracelets and beads, she anointed the girl's head and rubbed in it the finest hippopotamus fats and finally put some lovely brass rings around her ankles and some lovely bracelets on her wrists. She undressed the girl, and in the place of the clothes she'd worn, produced a most beautiful skirt made of the finest duiker skin and stitched with drawn copper wire which glowed even in the dim light of her place. She gave her a cape made of the finest skins of mature young silver jackals.

Finally, last of all, the old lady instructed her, saying: "This is the most important of all the things to do. When you come out again on the banks of the river, promise me, whatever happens, you will not look back. Find a round stone which you can just hold in your hand. When you've had time, you must pause, remember not to turn your head round, and rub the stone well under your armpits. When you've done so, without looking back, throw the stone over your left shoulder into the pool so that it will come back to me. You must walk on steadily until you will meet someone who will give you some water to drink. Drink deeply, and when you've done so, you can look about you normally. Dimo will never again get a whiff of you and be able to spoor and follow you. You will be absolutely safe from then on. Go slowly, my dear little friend. May the rain always come upon you. Hamba Ga'hla."

The girl did as she had been told. When she got back to the place where she'd first thrown the beads into the river, she found one of her younger sisters crying. She said: "We have been searching for you. Where have you been? We all thought you had been lost forever, that some wild beast might have devoured you. We've called out loudly and searched for you, and thank heaven you are back with us."

The girl calmed her, saying: "Please, quick, give me some water to drink." And they went on quietly together to their home. When they got back again among the kraals, they found the whole place in turmoil. Everyone was amazed to see the girl and questioned her, wanting to know where she had gotten those lovely things she was wearing.

As always, the girl was as truthful as she was beautiful, and she told them the whole story. A few of the nicer girls were pleased, but most of them were more jealous and angry than ever, and quite a number of them went back to the river and followed the way she said she had gone.

They came to the pool where a voice again said: "Enter." But when they saw the old lady, just as the girl had seen her, covered with sores and truly a sorrowful and horrible sight, and she called out to them to lick her sores, they were so repulsed that they said things like: "You horror of a thing, you must be mad to think we would do anything so awful. We've just come for some beads and bracelets and ornaments. Give them to us quickly and we will go."

The old lady, therefore, did not warn them about Dimo, and took no trouble to hide them. When Dimo came back, he had a great feast devouring them all.

I would like to begin my commentary with a quote from Helen Luke, a distinguished English-born writer and Jungian therapist. It is from her book, *The Inner Story*. She says: "All those stories that deal with basic human themes draw their power from the archetypal world that is common to people of all cultures and of all times, but the images in each culture will, of course, differ greatly and it is for us to penetrate these varying pictures to the universal wisdom that underlies them ..."

Now we will look psychologically at the various elements in our story and see what we might discover. Although it is really rather spare and unembroidered, every part of the story is meaningful. There is almost nothing accidental or irrelevant in it. There are several possible ways of looking at a story and this is only one of them, as we try to become aware of the many levels on which one can respond to it.

Many stories begin by describing a situation which is unsatisfactory and needs to be changed, as does this one. There is a beautiful girl who is not being allowed to be happy and to enjoy her special gifts and particular beauty because all the other girls are jealous of her and nasty to her. She only wants to be one of them, to stay and be accepted in the group, to be part of the current and collective view of what is feminine. But there are a lot of them and only one of her, and so, of course, she thinks that makes them right! Naturally they hate her because she is different, and the collective hates that which is different because it challenges the collective norm. This challenge is vital, however, because the collective needs the individual who is different for its own renewal and increase, but it still hates change and feels compelled to reject the opportunity and the individual at the same time.

As such, these jealous girls resort to trickery, to try to take away the special qualities of 'nKogilidane. They take off all their jewelry, hide it in the sand and pretend to have thrown it into the river.

Jewelry one might see as a value and that which enhances, part of a woman's adornment and attraction, but in this case, it specially stands for valuable feminine qualities.

In a wonderful book, *Africa Adorned*, Angela Fisher writes: "Bead jewelry virtually takes the form of costume for the Bantu of Southern Africa. There it is worn permanently, in marked contrast to the practice in the equatorial forests where its appearance is mainly restricted to festival times and rites of passage." Hence, the beads and bangles are really integral to the personal expression of the girls themselves; it is not just worn for special occasions, but is really an expression of how they experience themselves in their everyday lives. Also, a special feature of Zulu bead necklaces is the creation of "colour-coded messages" in the tab pendants worn by Zulu girls. These necklaces, often referred to as "love-letters," are given to their young men, who value them greatly. About the message in the pendant, Angela Fisher says, "Messages of love, longing, hope and disappointment, or invitation to courtship are interpreted from the patterns and colours of the beads used. White beads symbolise purity of love: 'My heart is pure and white in the long, lonely days,' and Black says, 'Darkness prevents my coming to you.' Pink stands for poverty, and Green for coolness ... and so on. Beads of Royal Blue symbolise rejection: 'You are a wandering, roving bird ...'"

As such, in the context of this particular story, beads and necklaces represent all the loving, feeling and erotic values both of the women who wear them and the men who receive them.

'nKogilidane is a trusting and naive person, qualities which are often attributed to a bearer of new values. She falls rather easily for the trick which the other girls play on her as they bury their necklaces, sure that they will be easily recovered, while at the same time, equally sure that 'nKogilidane's cannot be recovered. Without her jewelry, they feel she will no longer threaten them. Like a dismal Greek chorus, they then stand and jeer at 'nKogilidane for having believed them and sacrificing her treasures.

Of course, these jealous women, this onslaught of the negative collective, are actually unknowingly doing 'nKogilidane a favour. As so often is true, it is only through conflict, inner or outer, that we are driven, when there is no apparent solution, to dive into the unknown depths in search of our lost precious belongings; all that we had valued, expressing the person we were.

At this moment in the story, with her jewelry having been swept away by the current, 'nKogilidane has seemingly lost all her personal value and is also ridiculed by her community. She faces what is called loss of soul.

It is a time of great danger. What does she do? She follows the river, lets her own natural instinctive self follow the stream of life. Wherever the water runs deepest, she asks it for news of her lost beads, until she comes to the largest and deepest pool, this unknown and mysterious place which mirrors the sky but is not the sky. Why the deepest and largest pool? Because, in the world of stories and legends, the deepest water, whether it be a well or lake or the sea itself, is that body which contains that vast reservoir of unknown potential and richness.

According to De Vries' *Dictionary of Symbols and Imagery*, water is related to the moon and the emotions. Venus was born from water. J.C. Cooper says: "The waters are the source of all potentialities in existence; the source and grave of all things in the Universe; the undifferentiated; the unmanifest; the first form of matter." Plato called it "the liquid of the whole verification." All waters are symbolic of the Great Mother and associated with birth, the feminine principle, the universal womb, the *prima materia*, the waters of fertility and refreshment, the fountain of life. To dive into the waters is to search for the secret of life, the ultimate mystery.

The prophet Shembe, in whose kraal this story was told, spoke of how he heard it when he was young. Shembe, as a young man, began having strange intimations of a presence in himself which, in the eyes of the ordinary person, would make him do things that seemed stupid and dangerous. He felt impelled or called to dive from a high cliff into a pool in the river formed between two sharp and pointed rocks. He had to dive absolutely accurately into the centre to survive, and did! For him, his survival was proof that the voice spoke truly.

As in so many stories, 'nKogilidane first questions the waters in vain. It is only after the third time of asking that the pool opens and a voice responds, "Enter. Your beads are here." Why does it have to be three times? Perhaps partly because this is the minimum it takes to show perseverance in the quest: there are no instant answers. The number three turns up again and again in fairy stories and myths. Von Franz in *The Interpretation of Fairy Tales* says: "In number symbolism the number three is considered a masculine number (as all odd numbers are) ... to put it briefly, the three is generally connected with the flow of movement and thus with time, because there is no time without movement. There are the three Norns in Norse mythology, which represent past, present and future. Most of the demons of time are triadic. The three had always the symbolism of movement in it because for movement you need two poles and the exchange of energy between them, for instance the positive and negative electric poles and the current which equalises the tension ..." Cooper, in his *Illustrated Dictionary of Traditional Symbols*, says that three can mean "multiplicity, creative power, growth, also forward movement overcoming duality, a synthesis." Aristotle said, "Three is the first number of which the word 'all' has been appropriated and the Triad is the number of the whole inasmuch as it contains a beginning, a middle and an end."

'nKogilidane shows no hesitation when the summons comes and she dives into the pool. She shows immense courage in doing so because, according to Frazer, of *Golden Bough* fame, "The Zulus would not even *look* into a dark pool because they thought there was a beast in it which would take away their reflection, so that they would die." We, too, might be equally afraid to look, let alone dive into such a dark pool because of the fear that the lurking demons in it could easily kill the image we have of ourselves or change it beyond recognition!

When 'nKogilidane reaches the bottom of the pool, the person she encounters is very strange indeed! An old woman in an extreme state of disrepair! Covered in wounds and sores, with only one arm and one leg, truly a horrific sight, she taunts the girl to laugh at her. Instead, 'nKogilidane is filled with pity for her and, seeing this, the old woman begs her to come and lick her sores, an alarming request. However, 'nKogilidane instantly does as she is asked. By licking the old woman's sores, she not only shows extreme compassion, using that most instinctive and intimate part of herself, her mouth, but she also establishes a very close bond with the old woman, one of the closest, as animals do when they lick their newly born offspring as soon as they emerge into the world.

Saliva can have manna properties, like sweat and other body essences which early man believed had magical and sometimes healing powers. De Vries says about spittle that it is the "centre of soul power (like blood) and the life substance (like breath)." In some creation myths, the creator makes man of dust and spittle. Christ used spittle to heal, to open a blind man's eyes.

Jung also refers to these things in his account of his African journey in 1925. In *Memories, Dreams, Reflections*, he writes about his visit to the Elgonyi people in Kenya. They had a ceremony at dawn where they would spit into their palms and then hold their hands up to the rising sun. Though they gave Jung no explanation of this, he says, "Evidently the meaning of the Elgonyi ceremony was that an offering was being made to the sun divinity at the moment of its rising." If the gift was spittle, it was the substance which, in the view of primitives, contains the personal mana, the power of healing, magic and life.

By doing this seemingly repulsive act of licking the raw open sores of this horrific apparition, 'nKogilidane not only saves herself from the monster Dimo, but also sows the seeds of her own redemption and future wholeness. In showing compassion and offering a healing bond with the ravaged old woman, 'nKogilidane releases the old woman's own protective powers, whereupon she is able to both feed and protect the girl from the returning monster. 'nKogilidane instinctively befriended and lovingly helped what psychologically represents her own darkest and most repulsive side. The old woman is perhaps an image of the age-old neglected and wounded aspect of the feminine, both inner and outer, which is in danger of losing its protective powers and hence its ability for self-renewal.

The cause of all this horror is Dimo. He represents the masculine element in the story, and a pretty brutal one at that! He is hairy, has a large red mouth and tusks of a wild pig or boar. The wild boar appears in various mythologies as an image of great and negative masculine destructive strength. Linda Leonard, in *The Wounded Woman*, says of the dominance of masculine power over the feminine: "When the masculine is cut off from feminine values, when it does not allow the feminine principle to manifest itself in its own way. ... when it does not allow the feminine its manifold number of forms but reduces it only to those which serve masculine ends, it loses its relation to the values of the feminine realm. It is then that the masculine becomes brute-like and sacrifices not only the outer woman but also its inner feminine side."

Dimo is a brutal character, not far removed from a wild animal; in fact, he behaves just like an animal when he returns to the pool, running about and sniffing and saying he can smell a human being. Just like the ogre in *Jack and the Beanstalk*: "Fee, Fi, Fo Fum! I smell the blood of Englishman!" Animals use their sense of smell before any other sense, to detect food or friends or enemies, and so does Dimo. But, like all dark and neglected elements in the psyche, somewhere in him is the need to become more human, though the only way he can attempt this is to hunt and *eat* humans. So, on one level, he is trying to destroy human life, out there on land, in the daytime world, and on another, he is perhaps trying to *become* what he eats, by assimilating human beings, to be more like them, to take on their qualities.

Although here we are looking at "people-eating" symbolically, for the African, this was, in fact, a very real fear, based on real experience. Although some modern anthropologists are apparently casting doubt on the reality of cannibalism, I think most people accept that it has existed and maybe still does. Cannibalism is a debased form of ritual slaughter in some cases and in others, is forced on people by starvation. Where it was used ritually, the intention was always to take in the qualities of the people who were eaten. Even among the Zulus themselves, there was once a notorious chief, Matuana, who drank the gall of thirty chiefs whose people he had destroyed, in the belief that it would make him strong. According to Frazer (in *The Golden Bough*, and who provided that last nugget!): "It is a Zulu fancy that by eating the centre of the forehead and the eyebrow of an enemy, they acquire the power of looking steadfastly at a foe."

But, of course, Dimo's efforts are doomed to failure, and the abortive quality of his attempt is symbolised by the thunderstorm that fails to materialise in the upper world. The wind blows, the clouds gather, but only a couple of drops of rain fall before the storm subsides and clears and the relentless sun shines again. The fertilising rain cannot come, the promise is not fulfilled. This linking of Dimo's activities with cosmic natural events stresses the universality of Dimo's negative meaning. His human potential is certainly not apparent here! When he cannot find the food he smells, he attacks the old woman with burning sticks from the fire. He can only use this burning stick, a potential source of light and warmth, to hurt, and would extinguish this poor remnant of feminine life had he not had the realization that, as his slave, she serves his basic needs.

Here is the moment of crisis in the story. Will the old woman be able to protect herself? What are the consequences for the girl, other than sheer survival?

What gives the old woman the ability to protect herself is the new experience she felt of compassion in her life. She has been touched and loved and this releases the great wealth of the old woman's power to protect herself and the girl and to bestow undreamed-of treasures on whomever can relate to her in such a feeling way. She does not respond to Dimo's demands and threats, perhaps for the first time. Upon realizing that she will not sacrifice the girl to his appetite, he also realizes that he cannot sacrifice her to his rage. Thereupon he puts the stick down, eats the food she prepared for them and goes off to sleep. 'nKogilidane emerges from hiding and finds herself almost overwhelmed with new treasures with which the old woman adorns her. Not only does she receive more beautiful jewelry than what she had lost, but she is anointed all over with hippopotamus fat, a very valuable substance. The hippopotamus is an amazing animal, at home equally in both elements of land and water, and, as such, a protective layer of his essence will shield the girl in both of those worlds. In addition, she receives a whole new wardrobe: her visible personality in the outside world is now made of wonderful animal skins which will give her instinctive protection and also refine and enrich her natural beauty. The duiker skin of her apron is the softest and finest leather there is, almost the equivalent of silk for us, and the copper of its hem has the glow of the sun. She wears a shawl of silver jackal skins, silver with the mysterious, diffused and subtle light of the moon. Hence, masculine sun and feminine moon elements are combined in her. And finally, to cover her at night, a rug or kaross made of red jackal skins, whose life-giving and passionate colour will give warmth and protection from cold and damp. Now she is ready to face the upper world again, stronger, more complete and even more beautiful than before.

Only one instruction is given to 'nKogilidane as she sets out for home. She must walk, without looking back, until she finds a round stone and then she must rub it under her armpits and then throw it back over her left shoulder into the river. This curious act makes sense in the context of an African story because, as Laurens van der Post writes in *The Heart of the Hunter*, among the legends of the Bushman, there is one which shows the importance of the armpit and its essence. Among the people of the early race, there was a man who was special because people noticed that, when he raised his arm, a great glow and warmth came out of his armpit. So, when everything was assigned its special role in life, they agreed to throw him up into the sky so that everyone could share in the light and warmth which he bestowed whenever he raised his arm. There was also a Bushman form of baptism which consisted of the father taking the sweat from his armpit and making the form of a cross with it on his son's head. So this special human essence has immense life-giving properties, symbolising light and warmth – perhaps consciousness and feeling?

The stone is a piece of the basic foundation of the earth, solid and enduring, round to symbolise completion and wholeness. As it were, the stone is baptised with 'nKogilidane's own vital essence and is then given back to the world of the river, over the left shoulder, the side of the unconscious. It is a sign of the pact, the continuing relationship with the underwater world, and it is perhaps also the first bit of solid substance from the land which may give the old woman her own lasting link with the outer world, which she so badly needs.

Cooper, in his *Illustrated Dictionary of Traditional Symbols*, says: "Spherical stones depict the moon, hence the feminine principle, and all lunar goddesses." It can stand for stability, durability, immortality, imperishability, the eternal cohesion, the indestructibility of the Supreme Reality. De Vries says that stone-rubbing is a very old activity of mankind: it contains his or her predecessors' soul, and rubbing it perfects it into one harmonious round stone of the Self. ... Stones are often burial gifts. There is a custom among Orthodox Jews to place a stone on the grave of a parent or ancestor when they come to visit it. For Zulus and Hottentots, there is the custom of putting stones on a heap or cairn when they pass a certain place, to appease spirits and avoid danger, like after crossing fords or having just passed a dangerous place on the road.

There is the story about Ian Player (a conservationist friend in South Africa) when he was on trail in the Umfolosi game reserve with his Zulu friend and mentor, Mqubu. Ian was tired and cross. When Mqubu passed a cairn and put a stone on it and told Ian to do the same, Ian couldn't be bothered. Mqubu made him go back and do it. Shortly thereafter, a vast black mamba reared up in front of them. Ian and Mqubu stood stock still and the mamba hissed and went away. Mqubu said: "If you hadn't put that stone on the cairn, you'd be dead." We also know of the cairns left at the tops of mountains by climbers.

Marie-Louise von Franz, in *The Feminine in Fairy Tales*, referring to small children who need a special doll or toy to be there before they can go to sleep safely, says: "It is not yet the child's child like the doll, but it is the child's god." It is like the soul stones of the Stone Age. In those days, people made so-called "caches," some of which have been found in Switzerland. A hole was made in the ground and stones of a special shape were collected and a nest was made in which they were kept. The place was kept secret and was a symbol of the person's individual secret power. Australian aborigines have such "caches." Von Franz goes on to talk of Thor Heyerdahl's experience in the Easter Islands, where families kept secret caches of stone carvings from various places which, being looked after with great care, were magic objects which guaranteed the survival of the clan. She says: "These stones are a symbol of the Self. They represent the secret of eternity and uniqueness and the secret of the essence of the life of the human being." There is also a version of the Parsifal story by Wolfram von Eschenbach in which the Holy Grail is a stone, not a chalice (the Grail is taken as a symbol of the Self). The stone, the lapis in Alchemy, the sought-for goal of the whole Alchemical process, is also a symbol of the Self.

Jung had a great affinity with stones. In her book, *From the Life and Work of C.G. Jung*, Aniela Jaffé writes in the chapter, "Alchemy": "Even as a child Jung had 'his stone' on which he would sit for hours, fascinated by the puzzle of which was, 'Am I the little boy or the stone?' For years, 'it was strangely reassuring and calming' to sit on his stone 'which was eternally the same for thousands of years while I am only a passing phenomenon.' For Jung the stone 'contained and at the same time *was* the bottomless mystery of being, the embodiment of spirit,' and his kinship with it was 'the divine nature in both, in the dead and the living matter.' A cube-shaped stone incised with inscriptions in his own hand, stands like an oracle before his tower in Bollingen, and the last great and solacing dream before his death was of the 'lapis.' He saw 'a huge round block of stone sitting on a high plateau and at the foot of the stone were engraved the words: 'And this shall be a sign unto you of Wholeness and Oneness.'"

If we think of the connection of the stone with the feminine, we talk of Mother Earth, Gaia, the goddess who is the Earth. We talk about the mother lode in mining the Earth, i.e., the main seam of the mineral. Precious stones are set in the matrix (the mother) and apparently the mould in which type is cast or shaped is also called the matrix (one could even talk of the womb of the archetype itself).

In addition to the task of throwing the stone into the pool for the old woman, 'nKogilidane is warned not to look back until she meets someone who will give her water to drink. This is the water of life: given by another human being, it will reconcile her to the everyday world, the land world, and will take away the risk of a dangerous attraction back into the deep waters of the pool from which she might find it difficult to re-emerge. We know of other stories where people have looked back when warned not to, like Orpheus, who lost Eurydice forever when he disobeyed and looked back at her upon emerging from the underworlds, and Lot's wife, who was petrified into a block of salt for looking back at the city of Sodom and its darkness.

With this last instruction, the old woman assures 'nKogilidane that, if she obeys faithfully, she will be safe from the clutches of the awful Dimo; her true feminine self will be protected and shielded from his brutality. The blessing, "Hamba Ga'hla," which the old woman gives 'nKogilidane, means: "Go in peace and happiness," but literally means: "Go slowly," because Zulus and many other African peoples believe that all evil comes from haste, and that evil spirits are always in a hurry.

Indeed, this concept is not confined to Africa. There is a similar belief in Japan. Apparently, in Japanese gardens, which are themselves highly symbolic, the bridges which span the various streams in the garden always had a break in the middle. This was because the belief was that evil was always in a hurry and only traveled in straight lines, and in its rush to cross the bridge, would fail to see the gap, fall through it and drown in the water. There is also the alchemical axiom: "All haste is of the Devil," and, in a letter from Jung, "The devil can best be eaten with patience, having none himself." (*Collected Letters*, Vol. I). "May it always rain upon you," in an African context, hardly needs comment: without rain, nothing can survive.

'nKogilidane does everything she has been told to do and at last meets her younger sister, her newer and younger self, and from this sister, she asks for the protective water to drink. The giving of this water is also a sign that she is accepted back into the community, so she can then return to her family, the village and the kraal. (Incidentally, the word, "kraal," derives from the American/Spanish, "corral," which itself apparently comes from the old Provençale *graille*, the round container.) The kraal is a magic circle protected from the outer world (Holy Grail, etc.).

Of course, only some of the people there are happy about her good fortune; the others are more jealous than ever, since she is more different than ever. They plan to visit the place where 'nKogilidane found her fortune and to try and get some for themselves. They go in a group, and as such, their enterprise is doomed to failure from the start, because, of course, this journey can only be undertaken alone. Having none of 'nKogilidane's compassion and being filled only with greed for the expected treasure, the girls reject the old woman, seeing her only as a repulsive object. Needless to say, their bad behaviour leads where one might expect it to, and they are devoured by Dimo (who, one hopes, might at least have had indigestion afterwards!). Here the collective group approach to the unconscious actually helps to feed, hence increase, the negative elements in that world, while 'nKogilidane's transformation increases the positive.

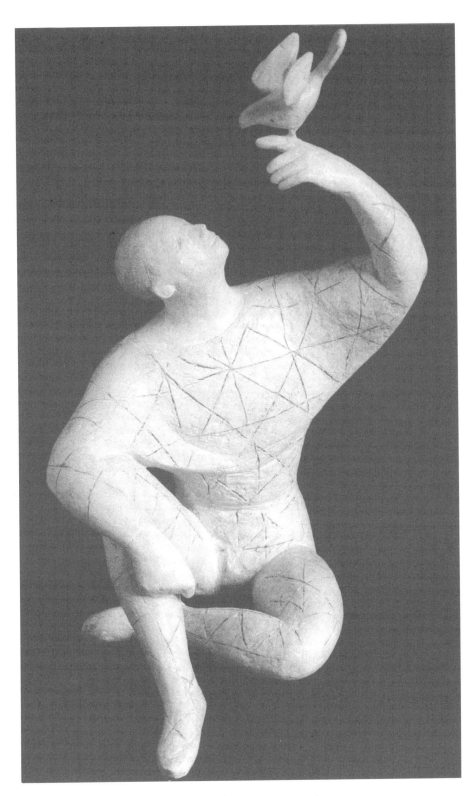

Harlequin by Frances Baruch

A Triad of Landscapes

A Day in the Veld with Laurens

T.C. Robertson

On the day that the holistic nature of the triad of landscapes in Southern Africa first occurred to me, Laurens and myself were headed southwards to the Great River of Elephants. *Themeda triandra* grass (redgrass), heavy with seed, billowed as gently as fields of wheat in the fenced grazing camps. Laurens was mounted on a bay gelding, Vos (The Jackal), while I rode a dappled-grey, Bloubok, named after the extinct antelope of the Cape.

The first white man to cross these *vlaktes* (plains) had also seen them from the back of a horse, for he scouted ahead of the wagon trek, advancing slowly with their cattle and flocks of sheep, until he found fountains or spruits where the stock could be watered and the small barrels, swinging in the shade of the wagon tents, could be filled for the next stage into what was then Darkest Africa.

At one of these outspans, the scout, Karel Trigardt, had seen a cliff of white rocks, eroded by a lost river out of the Ecca sandstones, and from under the lower strata, a clear fountain flowed into the vlei, where arum lilies grew and made snow-white fairy rings to dance round the hippo pools. The valley was like a necklace, which Nature had made for its bride – the golden, virgin veld, unploughed and grazed only by vast herds of game, which ecologists today label, "the greatest biomass of mammals this earth planet has ever known."

Karel Trigardt fell in love with that landscape – deeply, as if for the first time, he had held a physical image of his anima in his arms. When the wagons moved on, like the migrating white storks over-head, Karel made a promise to his beloved landscape with words that have been heard by all women who have ever loved hunters, crusaders or explorers in sailing ships. Softly he whispered: "I will come back to you again."

Now we were tracking a few hoofprints of that Voortrekker spoor. Followed by Laurens, I turned off the gravel road along a wagon track to a sandstone farmhouse, where two companions of my boyhood lived – Karel and Pieta Trigardt, grandsons of Karel Trigardt, who has left to Afrikaners a golden treasury of legends as he traveled the veld, bush, jungles and deserts of Southern Africa. He is even reputed to have seen and heard the thundering mists of the Victoria Falls, and wondered at the play of rainbows in the Rain Forest and down in the gorges of the Devil's Cataract, before David Livingstone did.

As the processes of life moved on and his spoor began to show drag marks, he came back out of the vast darkness of Africa to his first love and called her Koringfontein, the Fountain of Corn, as a tribute to her beauty and the promise of fecundity for the fields of wheat and garden patches of pipe tobacco that he would grow there.

Only two generations of evolving ideas and perceptions separated both Laurens and myself from Voortrekker ancestors, who had come to rest and settle in this plateau country of the Orange Free State and Transvaal. When the family gathered to celebrate her eightieth birthday in Bloemfontein, I had listened to Laurens' mother, still bright-eyed and alert, telling us tales of suffering and bravery as her own parents trekked north and built a laager of wagons near the banks of the Likwa River – tales that Laurens has "spun on a dream thread" into the theme of his early novels.

The night before we set off for the Great River of Elephants, we had listened to my own mother give life and vitality to the Voortrekker history of which, deep down in the unconscious, we were still a part. We felt an inevitable glow of youthful patriotic pride when she recalled a highlight of family history, the story of how her grandfather, Andries François du Toit, had outwitted the "English of the Cape" by smuggling forbidden gunpowder to the Voortrekkers, whose power and rule in Africa was ultimately based on the gun and the speed of their horses – the legendary commandoes of many wars. In modern geopolitical terminology, Oupa du Toit could be described as the first sanctions-buster.

There is another old sandstone farmhouse on Blesbokvlakte (Plains of the Blesbok), once a retreat for Laurens, who was writing his first novel, *In a Province*, and myself, struggling with the monetary theories of Keynes, which sheltered within walls that the British had not pulled down as they scorched the veld during the Boer War, an unusual archaeological collection assembled by my mother and myself from this environment.

The centrepiece was a Matabele rawhide shield with crossed assegais to recall the *Mfekane*, the shattering of the people when the Zulu impis (regiments) began their hunt of death across the open grassveld and slaughtered the Bushman and Iron Age people, who had developed a symbiotic relationship. Mounted below the shield was a heavy *snaphaan* (flint-lock) that had belonged to my great-grandfather – the Voortrekkers' reply to Matabele assegais.

The walls of the long passageway through the house resembled a pictorial genealogy, as stern ancestors gazed blankly at posterity from paintings, daguereotypes and old photographs. The setting was dominated by two lithographs, a fixture in most Afrikaner homes, which were a dramatic portrayal of the battles of Blood River and Veglaer, where Laurens' own grandmother had poured gunpowder into muzzle-loaders. This battle, in the history of our people, has become one of the legends of the resolute bravery of the Boer woman.

But Laurens, like a crystal gazer, had all his attention focused on a rounded dolerite stone with a hole drilled through the centre. It had probably been used by the Bushmen (the San, as they are now named by ethnologists) to add weight to digging sticks and then by Uitkomst Culture hunters on the shafts of assegais that tripped into game traps. Later in life, when my own work involved a study of certain occult mysteries, the image of Laurens staring at the bored stone recurred. It always reminded me of Tom Lethbridge testing divining rods with a pendulum. This was the origin of a belief that my friend, like a dowser, could receive signals to which I was insensitive.

During the next day, as we rode towards the river that was our destination, we saw only scattered relict patches of the physical features of the Voortrekker landscape. It was terminally ill. Soon its epitaph would be the names the first white men gave to the large farms they staked out with stone beacons, their titledeeds to the *vlaktes*. We crossed a hill where they had seen a large herd of wildebeest (Wildebeesbult) and rode down into Seekoievlei (Valley of the Hippos). Ten miles to the north, there was Wolwefontein, where a pack of hyaenas had snarled round a lions' kill, a Blesbok.

But the veld was already being eroded and killed by a new carnivore, the machine. Tractors roared as they dragged mouldboard ploughs to tear the plains and turn the *Themeda* grasses upside down for the planting of huge fields of maize – the gift of the Maya to Africa. The maw of an incline shaft gaped above the valley Karel Trigardt had loved and trains of cocopans, like mechanical ants on an endless pulley wire, crawled under the Ecca sandstones into the coal seams to haul fuel for the boilers and turbines that would help to feed the electricity grid, spreading its steel spider's web over South Africa. Tall smoke stacks would erupt black cumulus, laden with carbon dioxide, into Highveld nimbus to bring the acid rains of doomsday.

Although I was not aware of it then, thirty years of my life would be spent in an attempt to loosen the strangler's grip of the Technological Environment on the Voortrekker Environment of ancestral sagas. I would have to follow the spoor of men like Ian McHarg and show that the builders of the *grootpad* (highway) into a more prosperous future could design with nature.

Ecology belonged exclusively to the discipline of the botanists in the early years, when Laurens and myself unsaddled and knee-haltered our horses on the banks of the river where the elephants had come to drink. Here the stream, in years of peak floods, swerved round a bend to cut an overhang out of the sandstone krans with the outer edge of its hydrolic scimitar.

Today, with the maturer perception of age, I often wonder whether two men, whose youth had followed similar roads, have looked at a landscape and followed such different chains of association. Downstream from our outspan, the Great River of Elephants tumbled over a doletire dyke to stage a *corps de ballet* of droplets in the rainbow dance. We looked into the cone of light rays from an apex where reeds and rushes grew front stage in the black silt of the shallows. For me, a rainbow was a problem of geometrical optics solved by Newton – a mistaken idea which made Goethe exclaim that the analysis of the rainbow's colours would cripple Nature's heart. Such thinking made me wander into the realms of physics to gaze at other rainbows, such as atomic and nuclear ones. Laurens, as shy of "isms" as Jung himself, would follow the path of another culture – that of Goethe, the poet.

We followed one of the footpaths – they have been described as "archetypes of The Way" – which may have been trodden by Late Stone Age hunter-gatherers to reach the shelter of the overhang. Dassies, the rock rabbits which zoologists classify as Cape rockbadgers, resembled tiers of spectators round an arena as they crowded the ledges of the krans above the overhang. The sun, not the rainbow, was the most urgent need in their lives.

The floor of the overhang was piled high with cultural debris, which archaeologists excavate down to the earliest lydianite tools used by evolving man in this valley. Laurens knelt down to examine the rock art on the smooth surfaces of the thin strata of sandstone. Wind and water had eroded the pictures, but ghostlike figures ran, walked and squatted among antelopes that leaped in curves as graceful as that of the rainbow on the river. A steatophygous female waddled along as men with sticks and erect penises danced. Clues to the recent date of the paintings were bovines that came with Iron Age herdsmen and a horseman, symbol of the coming of the white man. As Laurens knelt there, he reminded me of Walter Pater looking at the Mona Lisa or, perhaps more aptly, of a penitent asking his Maker for forgiveness.

We were young, strong and full of earthy vitality during that Highveld summer, so Laurens would not venture to shrive his soul to me. But with those ripening years, I came to realise that he was not looking at pictures in ochre, the pigments used by the first artists to give form to their dawning creative imaginations. He was seeing psychic forces, symbolic figures that unmasked the dawning creative imagination. Like the famous archaeologist priest, the Abbe Breuil, he was looking at "Landscapes of the Soul" – the third and most meaningful of my triad of landscapes.

Our roads forked on Blesbokvlakte, when Laurens and I shook hands and said *Totsiens* (till we see each other again) – all unaware of how great a burden of wanderings, labour and wars we would have to *Abba* (Cape Malay word for carrying a child on the back, now a part of the Afrikaans language). But for me, the record of this quest is starred with asterisks that refer to the Day of the Rainbow, the Rock Rabbits and the Landscapes of the Soul on the banks of the Great River of Elephants. Two of these references will complete my synoptic sketch of "A Day in the Veld with Laurens."

Years ago, weary of the technological tasks of soil and water conservation, I escaped to climb the Bomvu (red) Ridge in the Ngwenya (crocodile) Range of Swaziland, where men mined speculite 21,000 to 28,000 (radiocarbon-dated) years ago. It was not flint for tools, iron or gold that had lured them deep into Mother Earth, which they would later fear as the dwelling place of underground gods, like Inkanyanba, the horned snake.

Raymond Dart contends that the fantastic cultural force of haematite mining was the beginning of Mousterian burial and the late

Paleolithic artistic, religious, trading and bartering applications – a dominant agency in the diffusion of myths, rites and the mysteries of ancient metallurgy and alchemy.

But what was the spiritual awareness that would lead man in the Middle Stone Age to beliefs in deities and life after death – to develop ceremonial occasions and use pigments to paint his body and pictures on the walls of caves? Was this force to be found in the Landscape of the Soul, which Laurens was exploring while I unravelled only the mysteries of geomorphology?

The thought – the second asterisk in my brief sketch – often recurred when our spoors frequently crossed in the Kalahari Desert, where I worked with the famous geologist, E.J. Wayland, to map the distal fading of peneplain rivers and methods of sand-pump storage of runoff from the hills – water that would otherwise be lost in the desert sands. Laurens, too, looked at the hills that milked the clouds, but for him, they were not so much outcrops of igneous rock from dykes and fissures, as features of what he has called the "inscape" within us. Instead of a geological map, he used the myths and dreams of the Kalahari Bushmen to guide his exploration.

I have now become aware that Laurens was probably equally aware of this dichotomy in our synoptic vision of the triad of landscapes in our world view. In the dedication to his book on Jung, he expressed gratitude to me, "for what he has done to make the earth of our native Africa whole again as the example that is the subject of this book exhorts us to be whole within." The rock rabbit and the rainbow, anyhow, were both serving the ecological whole.

And now, already inspanned for the final trek, and in the wisdom of contemplative old age, the rainbow more than the mathematical precision of radio beacons, has become my lodestar. My final task, with the oxen already straining at the trek chains, will be to teach my countrymen to heed the warning of Arnold Toynbee, when he wrote in his last book, *Mankind and Mother Earth,* that an increase in Man's spiritual potentiality is the only conceivable change to the biosphere against the biosphere being destroyed.

When we come to the last outspan of our treks and dreams in the veld, Laurens and myself will find rest in the shade of the same ossewa.

Heavenly Ingredients

Lady Susan Wood

Heavenly Ingredients

You must make room for chaos
The broken vase
The flowers
Upon the ground.

You must make time
For tangled skeins,
The crooked picture
And the jacket torn.

You must begin to love,
The anguish and the night
The death of children
And the fallen star.

You must forgive
The past its burnings,
And the future's
Stalking fear.

Such things are part
Of heaven;
Just like
Perfection.

The Coming of Age

Age is beautiful
Like a basket of flowers
Large fragrant blooms,
Dreams made real.

Age is bountiful
Like a bowl of fruit
Each rounded, smooth shape
Full of seeds.

Age lends distance
To the sharp pains of youth
Giving them
A far-off beauty.

Age is diminishment
It is loss and pain
While a new light grows
In the eyes.

Age is a fullness of spirit
A room full of light
A sea, wide and timeless,
A stillness,
And
The dawn.

A Birthday

A Birthday!
All of your days
Celebrated today.
All of your moments,
Trailing like tendrils
Into the beginnings

Of time,
Here are contained.
All your atoms
Their lineage
And History,
All your moments
When truth was real,
Your days of anguish,
Your dreams,
Your intense joy,
Are here remembered.
I give you all of time
In a single moment,
I give you the Universe
In a single word,
"Now!"

Laurens

Living in cruel times
You have been a healer
Of the world's wounds.

Captive among bitter enemies
You have been able
To forgive.

Sharing a country's strife
You have put out your hand
In understanding.

In praise of you
I send this poem
From the wilderness
Of your beloved Africa,
In praise of you, my friend.

My Friend Nkunzimalanga

Ian Player

Laurens van der Post once told me that no one could claim to really know C.G. Jung, because Jung was a man of so many parts. I believe the same can be said for Laurens, and I often smile to myself when I hear people say that they know Laurens van der Post. They might know something about Laurens the writer, the journalist and newspaper editor, the Shakespearean scholar; or Laurens the Afrikaner, the founder of Capricorn, the captain of the Natal hockey team, or the farmer, the cook, the father and grandfather; or Laurens the soldier, the confidante of royalty, prime ministers, ambassadors and generals; they may know Laurens the prophet, the dreamer, the orator and historian, the ESP intuitive, the initiator and creator of television films; or Laurens the anti-apartheid activist from his teenage years, the defender of the Bushmen and the interpreter of Bushmen paintings; or Laurens the humanist who cut short a visit to Russia to return to London to give evidence on behalf of a friend who had been charged with being a homosexual; or Laurens the psychologist and advocate of Jungian thought. All these are parts of the man called Laurens van der Post, and I do not believe that anyone can claim to know the whole man.

I remember in 1986 being on a fundraising tour for the Fourth World Wilderness Congress in America and we were staying for a time in a house on a beautiful farm in Virginia. Our hostess was a Washington lady who, over the few days while we stayed there, brought a whole range of people – doctors, ambassadors, journalists, army men, experts on Soviet Russia, and scholars of various kinds – to her house. I was amazed, yet again, at the ease with which Laurens conversed with one person after another on his or her subject. Then, in the evening, when everyone had gone, I heard a piano being played and I walked into the lounge and there was Laurens playing: I involuntarily exclaimed, "My God, Laurens, is there nothing you can't do?"

I owe Laurens van der Post two great debts: one is for his help at critical times in the conservation struggles I have been involved in, and the other is for introducing me to the work of Jung, which changed my life.

I first met Laurens in 1969 and until October, 1983, I did not call him by his Christian name: I called him Colonel. I had no other way of expressing the immediate respect he evoked in me. I fell back on the military title because I had spent two years during the Second World War serving with the Sixth South African Armoured Division in the Italian campaign. I had been out of the army for twenty-three years, but, on meeting Laurens, I instinctively used the military idiom. Our friendship grew over the years as he became deeply and actively involved in my conservation battles, and this took us to many parts of the globe together. When we were separated, I would telephone him and almost unconsciously report in military fashion all that had happened since we had last been together. He never asked for this kind of reporting, but again, it was the only way I could convey all that was happening in my world. He was able to respond immediately to the things that mattered and confirm for me the directions I intuitively knew I should follow. Even when we were not in telephonic communication or were for various reasons unable to write to each other, there was some telepathic bond that kept us in touch. When I did get near a telephone, it would often ring at a moment when I was thinking about him, and upon picking it up, it would be Laurens at the other end.

It was for me always a wonderful reunion when we got together, either in his flat in London or in South Africa. We never had to spend hours catching up on news, as one so often does with old friends; we were always up-to-date because of the telephone, the letter and the telepathic connection. We were continually in the present, so to speak. To be in conversation with Laurens was like talking to an encyclopaedia. There seemed to be nothing in the world that he could not talk about.

I remember once in 1970 walking with him along Piccadilly Street in London to a favourite Swiss restaurant of his. Crowds of people were swirling around us, when we passed a beggar sitting beside an upturned hat. Laurens said that most people would say, "But for the grace of God, there go I," but a writer could say, "Thanks to the grace of God, there I can go." He began talking of writers, and as we walked, he spoke about T.S. Eliot, Bernard Shaw, Shakespeare and a host of other English authors. Then I asked him if he had ever heard of Herman Charles Bosman, a South African short story writer. By this time, we had reached Piccadilly Circus, and the crowds were almost shoulder to shoulder as we crossed Lower Regent Street. It was a cold winter day and I remember the wind whistling up the street. Laurens stopped as though I had struck him, and he turned round in the middle of the street with the people brushing past, proclaiming with excitement, "Of course I know Herman Charles Bosman; he is a South African genius. No one can write a short story like he can!"

We began to compare notes about Bosman, both of us almost oblivious of the people rushing by and the cold wind. It was only when the traffic began surging forward and there were irritable blasts from a taxi's hooter that we scuttled to the other side of the street. We talked the whole way to the restaurant about Bosman, the school teacher who had spent a brief period of his life in the Groot Marico district of the Northern Transvaal, a region prone to terrible droughts but filled with wonderful Boer people with a sly sense of humour and a thousand stories of land, the Anglo-Boer War and the struggle to farm. It was for Bosman a literary goldmine. Laurens explained that Bosman had been sent to the Groot Marico by the education depart-ment as a form of punishment, and Bosman had turned it into the opportunity of a lifetime: reverses into verses, as Robert Johnson says. As we continued walking along the streets of theatreland with litter lying everywhere and rubbish bags split open by hungry cats, disgorging indescribable filth, Laurens passed on his detailed knowl-edge of this marvellous South African story writer. Laurens pointed in the direction of Fleet Street, his grey herringbone overcoat flapping in the cold wind and the long streaks of still blond hair blowing about his face: "Did you know that Bosman had spent many years on Fleet Street?" I had no idea.

We reached Leicester Square, descended an escalator, were almost seized by a maître d' and guided to a corner table. Throughout a luncheon of Swiss dishes, a great novelty for me, Laurens continued to feed me with literary food about Bosman's incredible life. Did I know that Bosman had shot and killed his stepbrother and spent three years in gaol, and that when he was released, he was asked by a friend what work he was going to do: "Maybe they will take me on as a musketry instructor at my old school," Bosman had replied with a humour so typical of the man. Laurens spoke as though it had happened the previous week.

I mentioned Bosman's preoccupation with the "veld maiden" and Laurens smiled and said she was his anima. It was the first time I had heard the word and I hadn't the foggiest idea what it meant. Another eight years would have to pass before I would begin to know what the word anima meant. Laurens' intimate knowledge of Jungian psychology would have overwhelmed me at that time, and he knew it intuitively, so he did not elaborate. I know of no man so sensitive and so understanding as to the particular space someone happens to be in. This is part of his amazing genius and his ability to see the inner person. His knowledge and comprehension of the feminine in the masculine and the masculine in the feminine also enables him to work in dimensions that few writers equal. That London winter day in 1970 with Laurens talking about Bosman will always remain in my memory as an insight into an author of seemingly simple Boer stories who was in fact a giant of a short story writer, a man who had had to suffer terrible imprisonment and rejection by society. Laurens understood him because he, too, had been through the same school. In his book, *The Night of the New Moon,* or *Prisoner and the Bomb,* as it was entitled in America, much of Laurens' agony as a prisoner of war under the Japanese is documented, but in such a way that one is sorry for the captors. For Laurens understood them in a way that no one else in the camp did, and because of his understanding, he was able, in a true Christian way, to forgive them, much to the anger of some of his military friends, he once told me. It was the same with Laurens' early revulsion to apartheid. When he was only nineteen, he was writing and campaigning against it. His father had fought against the British in the Anglo-Boer War and the gloom of defeat had affected and given an understanding to the young Laurens of the plight of other rejected and defeated people.

It was in 1954, when, as a young game ranger stationed at the Ndumu Game Reserve in North-east Zululand, I received a book of Laurens. It was *Venture to the Interior*. I have never been sure whether Laurens meant the title literally or symbolically, but the book certainly opened up a part of my interior and synchronized with a sense of Africa that I dimly understood but had not been able to express. Ndumu at that time was a wilderness of small lakes, the habitat of hippo, crocodile and a vast variety of bush and water birds, shrikes, eagles, seedeaters, larks, pipits, scaly-throated honey guides, pelicans and flamingoes. I and my young companion game rangers lived instinctively at one with the rhythm of the land and each day was for us a new awakening of the soul and the senses. It was the African fish eagle's lyrical and prolonged scream echoing across the swift-flowing Usutu and Pongolo rivers that changed the night into day. The hippo returned to the rivers from their grazing grounds on the banks of the lakes and the edge of the Sihangwane forest. We could hear their deep-throated grunting and the loud splashing as they slid down the narrow paths into the water. We were so attuned to the natural world that even one new bird call would make us turn and ask each other, "What's that?"

In the world of natural history, there was a vast literature that we could turn to for scientific enlightenment and my companions used it to further their ornithological or botanical or mammalian knowledge. I learned much from them and from the literature, too, but science lacked a way of explaining satisfactorily to me the soul of Africa: the music of still dawns, bright yellow moonrises and the peculiar scream of Pel's fishing owl in the sycamore fig trees lining the river, on a dark night; the chatter of vervet monkeys, the bark of a suspicious baboon, the whistle of a reedbuck and the smell of the red earth of Africa after the first rains. No scientific writing could explain what this Africa meant to me. I had hungered for years for someone to write with feeling about it and to include the white, black, Asian, Bushmen and coloured people of mother Africa, and to treat the continent holistically. When Laurens' book arrived, I read with mounting excitement and knew that, at last, here was a true man of Africa who could write with feeling about her soul. His knowledge of the feminine enabled him to sense all the moods of desert, plain, mountains, rivers, people and the wild game and draw them into the equivalent of a symphony, and a tribute to the African soul. His book encouraged me to look at myself, too, and had I been recording my dreams at that time, the transforming snake would have been there letting me know that a change was taking place.

On a visit to London in 1969, I met Laurens for the first time. I had, in the meantime, read his *Lost World of the Kalahari* and *Heart of the Hunter* and marvelled once more at how he had not only got into the heart of the fast-vanishing Bushman, but also of Africa.

We met at his Chelsea flat with its splendid 360° view of London and I remember being amazed to see wild geese flying past almost within touching distance and being able to hear the whirring of their wingbeats. It was a fitting home for the man of Africa and Europe. I was never one of those who wondered why a man born in the remote regions of the Orange Free State of South Africa and so attached to Africa would want to live in a metropolis like London. This was the heart of the old British Empire and, in many ways, home to many different nations. It was certainly the literary centre of the world and an opportunity for the writer Laurens van der Post to be exposed to the great writers of the day, and there were few he did not meet, but his advantage as a writer was that he understood many cultures. He had lived amongst the black, the white and the brown people of Southern Africa, traveled extensively in Central and East Africa and assimilated all that the British Empire heritage had to offer. He had farmed, been a journalist and traveled with the whaling and the sugar boats. Few writers in life had come better equipped to the literary world of London, ready to take the world by storm, as he has done. We talked of writing and writers and at great length about the politics of our beloved South Africa. We had both been tarred and tarnished by the same brush, because we had attacked the racialism of fellow South Africans and both of us had been hurt by this. But, as Laurens once said, "South Africa is a microcosm of the world and a victim of its collective shadow. If South Africa sorts its problems out, so will the world."

In 1974, I left the Natal Parks Board, an organisation I had served for twenty years, and I became involved full-time in the International Wilderness Leadership Foundation and the Wilderness Leadership School. When Laurens visited South Africa, he would speak at gatherings we called 'Wilderness Awareness' evenings, and no one could attract a crowd and keep people enthralled the way he did. When he talked, he was immediately in sympathy with the audience, and with his understanding and story-telling ability, the big crowd would be taken on a mental wilderness trail amongst the archetypal realms of ancient and modern Africa. These evenings were valuable not only for the experience that they imparted, but also in the practical sense that they brought much-needed revenue to our Wilderness Leadership School, thus enabling those less privileged people to go out on the walking safaris or trails, as we call them, in the game reserves of Umfolozi and of Lake St. Lucia, and in Bophutatswana and the Eastern Transvaal. Our Wilderness Leadership School was the first conservation organisation in South Africa to bring all the different race groups together in a wilderness setting and away from the pressures, telephones and motorcars of so-called civilisation. Laurens understood my cause from the day I first spoke to him about it, and saw and understood dimensions I was yet to come to, and the healing role the Wilderness Leadership School could play.

I remember sitting in his kitchen in Chelsea one winter morning in the 1970's when the sun was warm against the glass and I could see the snaking line of the Thames in the distance, damp mist rising from it. It reminded me of a canoe journey I and my game ranger companion, Ken Tinley, had undertaken in May of 1956. There is always a river mist in May in the lowveld of Zululand, and the sight of steam on the Thames had triggered off the almost forgotten memory of the canoe trip down the Pongolo River from where it breaks through the Lebombo Mountains and winds its way over the Tongaland flats to its junction with the Usutu River, which in turn becomes the Maputo and spills out into the huge bay on the Indian Ocean. I told Laurens about this expedition and how we had glided and paddled silently down the dun-coloured river in a canoe with gunwales so low that the slightest movement would bring water slopping into the boat. Tiger fish, shining silver in the early morning sunlight, skittered across in front of us, chasing smaller fish and water beetles. Each day was a new revelation of birds that we had not seen before and a sense of discovery of something in ourselves that we did not know existed, nor clearly understood.

Canoeing was not new to either of us. I had pioneered the now-famous canoe race between the cities of Pietermaritzburg and Durban in the early 1950's. And Ken and I had explored many pans, small lakes and humid tributaries of the Pongolo and the Usutu when we were stationed at Ndumu in 1954. But this journey was very different: we knew the river was doomed. There were plans to build a big dam in the gorge where it broke through the Lebombo Mountains, and this would choke the life-giving annual flooding and subsiding that the Tonga people relied upon and that had been part of their lives for generations. In summer, when the river had been at its height, they caught fish in the pans with fonya baskets, which were dropped on the shoals of fish after they had been driven into the shallows by a long line of men, women and children. Often the people would corner a crocodile, which would turn and come charging back. The line would merely part and let it through, then they would continue with their catching. There were, however, occasions when crocodiles did grab a woman or a child, and there would be a terrible fight to kill it and release the victim. We had seen some of the mutilated survivors and helped to take them to mission hospitals on the mountaintop. But the crocodiles were also important for the survival of fish populations and played their part in nature by eating the less palatable fish and catching beetles that preyed upon the eggs of the tilapia or bream the Tongas caught in great quantities. Hippo fertilized the water with their dung and were prey to Tonga hunters who killed them for meat, fat and the making of sjamboks (hide whips), which were decorated with copper wire and beads and then sold as a kind of cash crop. Ken Tinley and I knew that the old way of life was about to disappear forever, and as we paddled down the river, there was a terrible feeling of sadness when the Tonga people greeted us and gave us sweet potatoes, maroela beer and mealies or corn.

We could never have explained to them what was going to happen when the dam wall was complete. They would not have believed us; moreover, how did one explain the methods of modern man where a faceless bureaucrat instructs an obscure engineer to design a dam without taking into account ancient African rhythms?

As I talked on and on, the sun on the windows of Laurens' kitchen grew warmer and I was faintly aware of the sound of traffic in the London streets. Laurens just sat and listened, his head on his hands and an understanding look in his eyes. He was seeing and hearing things that I knew nothing about, because he understood in greater detail the Africa I was trying so hard to describe.

The other important element, related to that particular canoe journey which I tried to explain in detail to Laurens and which he clearly understood, was the realisation of the power of the wilderness, the discovery of rhythms inside ourselves that were beating with the same heartbeat as the Africa without. It was mostly in the quieter moments that this became apparent and it stole upon us unbidden. Each morning, we would cook breakfast over a fire of wood collected from the sandbanks, driftwood washed down in summer floods and dried out by the winter sun. All around us, the African morning was bursting into life: crested francolins cackling out their isikehle calls, Natal robins whistling and imitating the call of the black-crowned tchagra shrike's melancholy song; the rattle of a broadbill and the raucous shriek of the giant kingfisher, as it sped downstream in a blur of red and speckled black. We slipped the canoe into the slow-moving water and, using one paddle as a rudder, steered the boat downstream as the sun's rays pierced the shadows of the bright green fever trees with their glistening white thorns and revealed the thousands of multicoloured butterflies, beetles and bees that hummed above sweet-scented white flowers. Hah-de-dah ibises took off from the tops of sycamore fig trees, shaking the small branches and scattering ripe figs on the damp earth. In the distance, a Tonga woman sang as she pounded maize in her wooden bowl carved from a sycamore fig trunk. Then, as though in unison with her song, a fish eagle screamed from its nest in a fig tree downstream. It was this call that dominated, and cry after cry echoed up- and downstream and across the acacia-covered landscape, taking all other bird and human song with it, turning them into a hymn of the morning. Our ears rang and we could feel the vibration in our sternums. There was the scent of the river and the trees on the banks. This was the Africa of the ancient man, where modern man could find himself. It was a continent like no other, and there was still an unplumbed depth to so much of it, but modern man was imposing his unthinking will upon the landscape, and it was our duty to save a little of the old Africa.

In 1955, when Ken Tinley and I had been transferred from the Ndumu Game Reserve to the Umfolozi Game Reserve, we had been joined by Jim Feely, a young man from the Cape Province, who was extremely well-read in American conservation literature. Jim Feely showed us the fundamentals of the wilderness concept. Instantaneously, I realized the enormous importance of the wilderness concept and what it had meant to ancient man and could mean to modern man. For the last six years, I had been absorbing, almost as a process of osmosis, the wilderness atmosphere of the different game reserves I worked in, such as Umfolozi, Lake St. Lucia, Mkuze and Ndumu. Instinctively, I had grown aware of the healing power of the wilderness experience. I was a living example of its influence.

I told Laurens all this and more as we drank coffee in that warm Chelsea kitchen while the cold English day shook the last leaves from the plane trees in the London parks. He nodded, but said very little at the time.

The canoe journey down the Pongolo in May, the time the Zulus call Nhlangula, for it is the start of winter when the days grow shorter and a great stillness falls on the land, concretized for me the knowledge that the wilderness experience had to be shared. In 1957, I was transferred to Lake St. Lucia and fate sent six young schoolboys from my old school, St. John's College in Johannesburg, to spend a week with me. For five days, I took them with me on my patrols along the eastern shores of this great water wilderness and they saw the pelicans breeding, the mullet shoals gathering and the hippo moving from lake to land – while in the distance, there was the faint surge of the Indian Ocean as waves crashed on pale gold beaches. They smelled the swamps, the scent of ground orchids and the essence of the lake carried on the north wind. When these boys returned home, they wrote one after the other, expressing their feelings about a "oneness" with the world without. "It changed my life," was the common refrain in these letters. This gave birth to the Wilderness Leadership School and the trail system I instituted at the Umfolozi Game Reserve in 1959, and from which has grown so many wilderness trails in other provinces. It was an idea whose time had come.

In 1957, while on a trail in the wilderness of the Umfolozi Game Reserve, we had our usual indaba (discussion) at the end of the trail and, as always, it had been a moving occasion because of the prayer given by Magqubu Ntombela, with whom I had worked from early days as a game ranger. Magqubu and I were talking and we agreed that, for our countrymen to have a better understanding of wilderness, there should be a great indaba where we could bring together all the leading conservationists. This was the birth of the idea of the World Wilderness Congress, a mammoth undertaking that has now taken place three times, once in Johannesburg in 1977, then in Cairns, Australia in 1980, and in Scotland in 1983. Without being able to turn to Laurens for help, I doubt if it would have been possible for me to continue. Organizing the first congress was an absolute nightmare. South Africa had become world headlines with the outbreak of student violence in Soweto, and this put many potential delegates into a state of either funk or antipathy against anything emanating from South Africa, even an apolitical gathering on conservation. Raising money was a torment, but when Laurens came out, he accompanied me to boardrooms for presentations and talked to large audiences, inspiring them to attend the congress. He gave invaluable help in the preparation of the programme and talked to members of the South African government about the dire need for such a congress, to let the world know that there were people in South Africa who really cared for the environment. When my morale was at its lowest possible ebb and disaster seemed to be staring us in the face, Laurens would telephone and give encouragement. The congress was an outstanding success, with international speakers defying their governments and coming to Johannesburg.

Not long after the congress, Laurens came out on trail in the Umfolozi Game Reserve and, together with Magqubu Ntombela, already in his eighties, we walked the rhino paths and other game trails, watching the large mammals and talking about how to involve more people in the wilderness movement. At night, we sat around the fire of acacia and other African hardwoods, drinking coffee and listening to the long drawn-out whooping of hyena, and passing leopard hunting cane rats in the phragmite reeds. After our discussions, Laurens would sit up half the night, staring into the fire or up into the vast, brilliant Southern African night sky, alone with his thoughts. Never had I been with someone who so deeply appreciated the trail experience and who contributed so much to other dimensions of understanding that can only be talked about around an African campfire. It was on the trail that Laurens talked of getting the BBC to make a documentary film. This came about two years later, when he brought his grand-daughter Emma and a BBC film crew. During the three weeks that it took to make the film, we shared a camp with the film crew, Emma, Bridget Duxbury, my son, Kenneth, and Magqubu Ntombela, who befriended Laurens in a way that he had not done with other people. I have only to mention Laurens' name, Nkunzimalanga (he who pushes everything in front of him), and Magqubu instantly wants to know if Laurens is coming again. These two men saw and acknowledged the inner spirit within each other immediately and were able to communicate on that wonderful telepathic level. We all had most enjoyable times around the fire at night, reading from books and telling tales. But the days were hard physical work, carrying packs and being filmed from various angles, setting up scenes and waiting in secluded places for game to arrive. We carried out the normal trail camp duties, which included keeping watch at the fire throughout the night. Again Laurens insisted upon doing the longest watches and would sit until well after midnight on his own. I will always remember lying in my sleeping bag and looking at him dressed in his khaki shirt with old army flashes as he listened and looked into the African night. I was reminded of the title of one of his books, *Face beside the Fire*.

On one occasion, we had walked with heavy packs, as well as film equipment, from Gkiyina, a trail camp, to another camp, called Amatshemhlope (White Rocks). It had been a tiring day of filming and walking. Laurens was on watch at 4 a.m.; I awoke, we began talking, and I told him of a dream. It was a dream of great clarity. It was of a bay with perfect waves rolling in towards a shore of clear, golden-coloured sand, wonderful for surfing. Then I saw a fish swimming in towards the shore. I said to myself that it was a shad, and a big one, too. The fish was perfectly formed except that I noticed there was something wrong with its tail, which was hindering its swimming. It was as though the tail was a lump, grown together. This hindered the movement of the rest of the perfect fish.

Just before dawn, I walked down a bank to the river's edge and I was there staring downstream when the first flash of dawn touched the dark waters. This led to my first and, to date, only peak experience. Without warning, I became part of everything. I was without fear or hate or anger, without thought, just part of the vibrant universe. It was, in a way, like music, but beyond it – a feeling so wonderful and so profound that words would never be able to explain it.

The film was shown on BBC Television on two occasions, which led to a flood of enquiries from Britain by people wanting to go on the trail, proof to me that, despite politics, there were people who instinctively valued the wilderness of Southern Africa and needed the trail to realize something inside of themselves. The film continues to be shown to gatherings all over the world, and there are few people who are not in some, albeit small, way touched by what they see.

In 1980, we had the Second World Wilderness Congress in Cairns, Australia. It involved another long struggle of raising funds, finding suitable speakers, convincing politicians and just making it happen. Laurens again helped in numerous ways and at critical moments. His time in the POW camp in Java made friendships and forged bonds that were as deep as human experience would allow. Laurens' speech at the conclusion of the Second World Wilderness Congress will never be forgotten by all those who were there. It was an incredible achievement towards the uplifting of the human spirit. He spoke not only of wilderness and the value of preserving it if we were interested in the survival of man and our earth, but also of those years in the POW camp and the Australians who shared it with him, their humour, their inner strength and general courage in the face of all the bestialities the Japanese guards could perpetrate. There were very few people in the audience, men and women, who were not weeping at the end of it.

And so we went on to the Third World Wilderness Congress in Scotland in 1983. Raising money and enthusiasm in South Africa and

Australia was extremely hard work. In Britain, it seemed impossible. I was appalled at the malaise that seemed to be creeping over the great island of my forefathers. It was the only time in my life in the cause of conservation that I was prepared to say, "I'm beat." With six months to go we had raised only fifty pounds. But the Findhorn new age community was wonderful, and our friend, Vance Martin, performed near miracles in establishing lines of credit. Again Laurens stumped the streets with me and together we talked to businessmen of every hue and persuasion: in the end, the money was there and the congress was one of the most intimate and moving of all three. Laurens' speech and that of Fredy Meier lifted the banalities of some aspects of conservation work into a new realm of understanding; it was fitting, in this world of the ancient Celts, that homage was paid, because it has been Celts and those of Celtish descent who, worldwide, have made so great a contribution to the cause of wilderness and conservation.

Without Laurens, his contacts, his willingness to participate on the fundraising hustings and his brilliant, moving speeches, the world wilderness congresses could never have been the success they have become. Laurens was always insistent upon the proceedings being published. He said, "The written word will last, it will go out into the world and remain there when all of us are dust once more." All of Laurens' speeches are there, but the atmosphere of the hall in Johannesburg, the town hall in Cairns, the newly built Universal Hall in Findhorn, Scotland, with Finlay MacRae playing the bagpipes, is not there. Nevertheless, that atmosphere will always be carried in the hearts of those fortunate enough to have attended.

At the beginning of this tribute to Laurens, I said that I owed him two great debts: one was for his help in the conservation struggles I have been involved in and the other was for his introduction to the work of C.G. Jung, which brought about a major change in my life.

In the preceding pages, I have outlined some of the conservation work that Laurens has been so helpful with. He has long realized the desperate plight of the earth with its overpopulation, land degeneration and forest destruction, and the steady disappearance in Africa of the once so abundant wild animals of plains, mountains and bushveld. He had seen in my work a contribution being made to tackle some of these problems in the area in which I lived and was involved in. He also keenly appreciated that, apart from my work with wildlife ecology, I knew that the principal key to any solution was to make people more aware of what was happening. Hence, his support for the Wilderness Leadership School, which takes men, women and young people into direct contact with the natural world. Laurens also supported in every way he could the world wilderness congresses, because he saw these international platforms as a selective expression of the deep concern of intelligent modern man. It was the first time that wildlife ecologists, artists, writers, poets, politicians, tribal people, bankers, psychologists and businessmen had been brought together to talk about their own problems and the need for a common action to save the earth from ourselves. Laurens' knowledge and experience made him a most important catalyst for the world wilderness congresses, and it was a platform where he could be understood on many different levels.

In 1976, Laurens sent me his book, *C.G. Jung and the Story of Our Time*. I remember looking at it and wondering to myself, what on earth was Laurens writing about now? It seemed such a different book from the others I had read. I glanced through it and thought to myself, this is not for me: I'm not really interested in what it appears to be about; also, it looked far too intellectual, so I put it aside. In early 1978, with the First World Wilderness Congress just behind me and in an exhausted state from working for the congress, as well as trying to keep the Wilderness Leadership School going and the International Wilderness Leadership Foundation in America a viable concern, reading anything like this proved too much. But, on my way to America to attend a vital board meeting, I had stopped off in London, and just before flying to San Francisco, I saw *C.G. Jung and the Story of Our Time* in a paperback edition in a bookstall in Heathrow Airport. I knew I had a seven hour flight ahead of me, so I bought the book, thinking it would be an opportunity to wade through it. I felt I owed it to Laurens to at least try to read the book.

Morton Kelsey, in one of his taped lectures, says that many people come to Jung when they are on the edge of the abyss. I was certainly in that state, and the book gripped me as little else I had read in the last ten years; throughout the flight, I read it with growing excitement. Here was an answer to so many of the things that had puzzled me over the years. I arrived in San Francisco and continued reading and eventually finished the book in the early hours of the morning. I then tried to phone Laurens, but he was out, so I spoke with his wife, Ingaret, and told her what an enormous impression the book had made upon me. It had saved my life. The insights were quite staggering, so I read the book again, and on the second reading, was made aware of how much I had missed in the first. I began keeping a record of my dreams and embarked in the flimsiest of vessels down the huge interior river with all its dangerous rapids, cascades, waterfalls and unfathomable depths, but at least, I had the Jung model as a map. To describe all I have learned and the people I have met and the knowledge I have gained as a result of reading Laurens' book would require a book in itself. Suffice it to say that my life underwent an enormous change, and a whole bookcase in my house is now a testimony to Jungian thought.

In 1983, Professor C.A. Meier spoke at the Third World Wilderness Congress, and in 1985, Jack and Lynn Sanford, Katie Sanford and Joan Winchell came to South Africa and went on a trail. Dr. Lee Roloff, Dr. Vera Bührmann, Dr. Ian McCallum, Dr. Gloria Gearing, Professor Graham Saayman, Roger Brooke, all interested in Jungian thought, have walked the Umfolozi Trail, met Magqubu Ntombela, and widened my horizons. Very recently, we had a four day meeting in the Drakensberg Mountains of Natal at an old farmhouse acquired on a lease and renovated by the Wilderness Leadership School. Present were Dr. Gloria Gearing, Professor Saayman, Dr. Vera Bührmann and Dr. Ian McCallum, and we debated at great length the establishing of a centre for Jungian studies in South Africa, finally agreeing that it would be in Cape Town. Laurens had been encouraging this idea for years. We agreed, too, that there would be close cooperation between the Centre and the Wilderness Leadership School, and that it was important that those involved in Jungian psychology should walk the ancient trails of wild Africa in a place like the Umfolozi Game Reserve.

A lot had happened since I first knocked on Laurens' door in 1969 with a letter of introduction from his old friend, T.C. Robertson. This essay is an inadequate tribute to one of the most remarkable men of our time, and about how a small glimmer of his great light touched, helped and changed me.

I salute Colonel Sir Laurens van der Post.

Sir Laurens in his lighthouse tower at Aldeburgh, 1973

A Friendship of the Stars

Jean-Marc Pottiez

A friendship which lasts a whole life and ignores frontiers, racial prejudice, time, war and torture, appears to be almost supernatural; it strikes us with awe, but also with wonder, as a comet crossing the sky. A lasting friendship is even more rare than love, of which La Roche-Foucauld wrote in his *Maximes:* "Il en est du véritable amour comme de l'apparition des esprits: tout le monde en parle, mais peu de gens en ont vu" ("True love is like the apparition of ghosts: everyone talks about it, but few are those who have really seen one").

However, those who knew Captain Katsue Mori and Sir Laurens van der Post can bear witness: theirs was a real, a beautiful, and an exemplary friendship.

At the beginning of this friendship comes the parable of the two cups of coffee, which – as described in van der Post's book, *Yet Being Someone Other*, now also available in Japanese, thanks to Professor Yura and his publisher – set in motion the magnetic forces building up a destiny. As a result of two cups of coffee offered by Laurens in a violent racial argument to Messrs. Shirakawa, of the Asahi Shimbun and Hisatomi, of the Mainichi Shimbun, he had been invited to Japan and transported along from Port Natal (Durban today) with his friend, the poet, William Plomer – by Captain Mori, aboard his ship, the Canada-maru. What a graceful ship it was, this Canada-maru! One must say that, in those yesteryears, ships still had a human size, while humans still had ship-sized dreams they could travel with ... It was in 1926; Laurens was then 20, and Captain Mori, 36. Decades later, both of them were still two samurais fighting for their ideas with shining swords for a world to be more human and friendly.

Of Captain Mori, Laurens has written that he was an "upright, clear-cut person" – *mokkosu*, they would say in the Kumamoto dialect of Captain Mori's native region. Indeed, Captain Mori is a real "Meijishin," a person born in the Meiji area. Because of his roaring voice and courage, he certainly deserved his nickname of "Mr. Lion"; but one should not forget that he could also be a talented diplomat, who opened the way for the Japanese in Africa. The reason for his success, I believe, was because he always knew, instinctively, how to deal with men of all races, cultures and creeds – not at the level of their skin or head, but of their heart. Captain Mori had only one love in his life – the sea –, and only one woman in his heart – his wife. Do not ask me whom he loved more …

Laurens van der Post was also in love with the sea, or this ocean which is the Kalahari desert. He, also, was a "bushi," a blue-eyed one, and a lion when it came to hunt for greater meaning. Through Japan, the first country he traveled to, Laurens discovered the world and himself. Japan set in motion – violently but also subtly – his quest, a quest for the White Bird of Truth, which never ended for him as well as every one of us. Laurens felt so close to Japan and the Japanese that he confided to me in the book I had the privilege to co-author with him (*A Walk with a White Bushman*) that, if it were possible, he would choose to be reborn a Japanese … This is not a small compliment if one remembers it is said by someone who fought against the Japanese in Java, had been ambushed, captured, starved, beaten, tortured and nearly died by the sword. But Laurens knew then, and continued to know, the true Japan. He could distinguish the difference between the New Moon Japan, the Black Hole Japan and the bright, warm, sunny, hospitable, fun-loving, peace-loving and civilized Japan; he could distinguish between the sleep-walking Japanese of the Pacific War and the Japan of Captain Mori, of all the Japanese he loved dearly; of Basho, Hokusai or Hiroshige, Kyoto or Nara, zen and Mt. Fuji …

Captain Mori and Sir Laurens van der Post are a lesson to us in bridge-making across continents and great walls of contempt and hate, in wholeness, in forgiveness, out of space and time, of our here and now. Like two dolphins ahead of our rotten raft, aboard which we are drifting desperately on the ocean of our problems, conflicts and wars, they have, in a graceful and friendly manner, showed us the way. Their friendship was indeed a "friendship of the stars," as the Japanese say: it was born many years ago, and long continued to shine strongly before our envious and admiring eyes.

The White Lilac and the Sailor

Captain Katsue Mori

Back in those long-ago days when I was honeymooning more with the sea than spending time at my wife's side, my ship, the *Kanada-Maru*, called at Durban. (This was on our first attempt to establish a regular shipping line between Southern Africa and Japan.) A thick envelope was waiting for me. It contained a letter from two journalists – Mr. Ikai Shirakawa of the *Asahi Shimbun*, and Mr. Tatsuo Hisatomi of the *Mainichi Shimbun* – who had traveled aboard our boat from Japan and had left us at Mombasa, the leading port of Kenya, and the first stop in their reportage about Eastern and Southern Africa.

In their letter, Shirakawa and Histomi mentioned an incident which had happened upon their arrival at Durban: They had gone into a coffee-shop to have a snack, but they had been told in unpleasant terms that they could not be served because they were Asians. Laurens van der Post, then a young journalist, had witnessed this incident and had very kindly taken their side. Then he invited them to sit down at his table and to be his guests. Very grateful for this gesture, the two journalists had wanted to show their gratitude to van der Post, but had not been able to do so because they had to proceed with their reporting mission. So, at the end of their letter, they asked me to substitute for them: "Please, dear Captain, invite this young gentleman on your boat ..." – and that is what I did. I called on van der Post, who was then working at the *Natal Advertiser*, and invited him for supper aboard the *Kanada-Maru*.

During our supper (we had both raw bonito and roast lamb, prepared by our specially trained cook, and plenty of *sake* and wine to drink), I found out that my guest was quite interested in Japan and was eager to visit it. Then I promised him that, since he had helped two fellow Japanese out of a difficult situation, the next time the

Kanada-Maru called in Durban I would give him a passage, free of charge.

Van der Post seemed to really appreciate this invitation, and talked it over with his friend, William Plomer, trying to persuade him to join him on a trip to Japan. However, Plomer was at first reluctant, because he was caught up in a storm unleashed by the publication of his novel, *Turbott Wolf*, which denounced apartheid. He had been invited to London by a group of people who admired his courage; nevertheless, he was very tempted by a trip to Japan on his way to London, and was finally convinced by his friend van der Post.

The following day, the two of them visited me aboard the *Kanada-Maru* and asked if they could make the trip together. While discussing with them, it came to my knowledge that they were fighting apartheid, not only in their books and articles, but also in their literary magazine, *Voorslag*. Couldn't their assistance and talents be put to use by us, the Japanese, to fight racial discrimination? I leapt at this chance, and proposed to them that, rather than wait, they should come to Japan with us now. They accepted without delay ... and the rest of the story has been told, masterfully so, by Laurens van der Post, particularly in his book, *Yet Being Someone Other* – which will to be published in Japan, translated by Professor Yura of Tokyo National University. We do hope that, for this occasion, our friend van der Post may travel to Japan, as he has been invited by his Japanese friends.

Those events took place in 1926 – so many years ago. ... From that moment on, a solid friendship flourished among the three of us, almost a brotherly feeling, I could say. As for the Japanese, they are particularly grateful to Laurens van der Post, because, thanks to his personal action and his articles, they have been able to defeat discrimination and racial prejudice.

This friendship might have been reduced to ashes by the Pacific War, and the three-and-one-half years of internment Laurens van der Post (who was then a Lieutenant-Colonel in the British Army) spent in a prisoner-of-war camp in Java and the considerable amount of torment and hellishness he was subjected to there – a terrible experience related in *The Night of the New Moon*, and somewhat transfigured in *The Seed and the Sower*, which, as everyone knows, inspired the film director, Mr. Nagisa Oshima, and his beautiful and courageous film, *Merry Christmas, Mr. Lawrence*. But, despite – and perhaps because of – the ordeal by fire, our friendship has endured

and prospered, as Japanese swords gain their fine grain and harden-
ing, their beauty and spirit, from repeated beating.

The Japanese, like about everyone else these days, tend to forget
history and its lessons, and how much we need friendship and bridge-
makers like van der Post. In September last year, I was invited by
NHK Radio to reminisce about this period of my life. What a surprise
it was to learn that many listeners called the studio, or wrote letters
afterwards. Particularly moving was the letter I received from a blind
man and written in Braille; he said that there was a time when, in
Japan as elsewhere in the world, the pioneer spirit was strong, and
that what I had done and was doing, with the assistance of Laurens
van der Post, should open the minds of the Japanese Youth.

***

When William Plomer, who became the respected and much
admired writer and poet everyone knows, died of heart arrest in 1974,
I went to London and paid my respects at his grave, on the outskirts
of Brighton, along with our friend van der Post, who later on brought
over some lilac flowers growing on this grave to be transplanted in
our family garden. These English flowers have grown well in the
volcanic soil of Japan, and for me they are the symbol of our
friendship – a friendship which has spanned so many years, survived
so many events, ignored frontiers and space, and can be transplanted
anywhere.

Do you remember, my dear friend? When we first met in Durban
you were nineteen years old, Plomer was twenty-two, and I was thirty-
six. And when we celebrated your 80th birthday, I was in my 96th year.
… Why and how did we live to that age? Well, I believe that only
Kami-sama, only God, has the answer. But something is quite certain:
we had to be friends, and forge this friendship as strong as a sword
made and wielded with the spirit of *Yamato,* or the magic sword
Excalibur, which could help us to fight against the forces of Darkness.
Let us wish for both of us, will you, long life and eternal friendship in
order to be able to fight this neverending battle, and enjoy – you, the
writing of books and the busy bridge- or rainbow-making all over the
world – I, the pleasure of living amongst my seven children, fifteen
grandchildren, five great-grandchildren, and taking care of our lilac
of friendship.

By the way, the winter is so severe that, with the help of my first son, Hiroaki, I have dressed up the stems and shoots of the lilacs with rice straw, making them look like mummies, thereby offending – I am sure – their femininity. But I am just as sure that they will take their revenge next summer, when they will greet us with their best *kimonos*, all silk and smiles.

Captain Mori with Oxon and the white lilac

Good-bye Snail, Hello Mantis!

Satoko Akiyama

The first time I met him was in 1966, when I was studying at the Jung Institute in Zürich. I had already completed two years of study there and was planning to go back to Japan for a period of about two months, because I felt that I had to go back to my native country, to my roots; this was a time for reflection for me, reflection on my work, on my relationship with the Jung Institute and on my own self. Then, at the last moment, somebody told me that there was an interesting lecture scheduled at the Psychological Club in town. But I was supposed to leave for Japan the following day, and I was busy, preparing my baggage, etc. However, since I had some time to spare in the evening, I went to this lecture…

Of course, at the time I had never heard of Laurens van der Post, nor read any of his works. Just before he began his lecture, my analyst, C.A. Meier, arrived with his wife. They exchanged greetings and spoke together, so I thought: "Oh, this lecturer seems to be a very good friend of theirs …" Then van der Post began to speak.

He told us about the Mantis saga. At that time – as I learned later on – he had already published *The Heart of the Hunter* (1961), but not yet *A Mantis Carol* (1975). I should have known this Mantis saga, but in fact, it was the first chance I had to hear such a charming story about this little First Spirit or God of the Bushmen, his wife Kauru, the rock rabbit, their three children and their adopted daughter, the Porcupine, the child of the All-Devourer married to Kwammang-a, who resides in the Rainbow.

In addition, I was struck by his appearance. I had been in Europe two years at that time, and I had never seen or met a man like him, a man who had such… – I don't know – such a strange charm, with his Queen's English and his graceful manner. One should know that in Zürich only a certain kind of English is to be heard, and this was also the first time I could see an old-fashioned gentleman close-up. However, what made the greatest impression of all on me was the Mantis saga itself.

It was Mrs. Meier who wanted to introduce me to the lecturer. She said that I came from Japan, that I was raised in a temple yard and that my father (who was still alive at that time) was a Zen priest. Then van der Post looked at me and said something like: "How nice, I've a few friends in Japan..." The next thing I was saying was: "Will you please count me among your friends?"

Now, this was a very unusual thing for me to have said, because this is not at all typical of Japanese etiquette... Laurens van der Post looked at me in a strange manner. But there were so many people around that our conversation was cut short and we were quickly separated.

After that blunder of mine, I regretted, and regretted, and regretted – all the more, because I knew that the British can be quite like the Japanese: they don't express their opinions so easily, and especially so when they have just been introduced; they prefer to wait, to judge, and to use more indirect ways... What a foolish girl I had been! For years and years, I regretted what I had said. He was perhaps the most attractive person I had met in Europe, I wanted to become a bit better acquainted with him, and this was how I had behaved!

Five or six years later, back in Japan, I obtained van der Post's book, *Jung and the Story of Our Time* – which I have since translated into Japanese, and is soon to be published. When first reading it, I came upon a brief sentence where he was talking about the impor-tance of women in Jung's work, about how they had been, and still are, propagating his ideas. He wrote: "A Japanese woman who trained in Zürich, too, has inspired one of the fastest-growing Jungian schools of all, near the ancient capital of Kyoto and its thousand and one temples of Buddha and Zen..." – to which he added a comment, which, I think, is quite relevant to the situation we are experiencing now between East and West, making a joke of all iron, chrysanthe-mum or bamboo curtains: "To put it in terms of Jung's great dream of transition, the magnolia tree brought back from Europe is in flower again in the Far East, and this interpenetration of spirit and traffic between the East and West is becoming an affair of increasing depth. Without this mobilisation in the world of the feminine, one could easily despair of any resolution to the clash of the opposites and the problem of the shadow which is basic to Jung's approach and the greatest challenge confronting our world."

I thought it over: this Japanese woman could be me – except that I was brought up and working in Tokyo, not in Kyoto or even near Kyoto! Anyhow, it was nice to remember.

***

More than ten years passed again before I heard the rumour that Nagisa Oshima, the movie director, intended to make a movie from Laurens van der Post's book, *The Seed and the Sower*, and that for this reason, the author was in Japan. So I met him a second time, merely to screen some films he had brought along about the Bushmen and Africa (*All Africa Within Us*), and was presenting to the public and a group of friends. I was curious to know whether he would recognize me. I went backstage and – how extraordinary – he did recognize me, and asked if I had come all the way from Kyoto. "No, no," I quickly corrected him, "I am, and always have been, living in Tokyo." We laughed, and he treated me as an old friend.

This is how our friendship started. But is it really a friendship? When I think about it, during all these years, we have met for a total of not more than two or three hours, I should say. Here ten minutes, there half an hour... But still, to me, he is a very, very special person. Perhaps because he is, to me, an ideal person. He can be very tender and nice, but at the same time, very brave and very much of a *bushi*, of a warrior. After all, he is *Colonel* van der Post. Oh, something I love is the way he walks: I'm sure it's almost the way the Bushman walks in the immense desert which is his home, and from which he seems, alas, to have been chased away.

Nevertheless, there is something more that Laurens van der Post brought to me and for which I am very grateful: that is the story of the mantis. For the mantis is a very special creature, and has played a very special role in my dreams.

***

What happened is that, eighteen months before that Zürich lecture, just when I was starting my own so-called training analysis (which is required as part of training to become a Jungian analyst), I dreamed of a mantis and of a snail. This big, poisonous snail was fighting with a mantis, who had a little child mantis with him; he had to fight, in order to continue to feed his little mantis. So I was watching those two insects fighting in my dream. The mantis was black, with a shimmer of gold. The snail was on the right side, partly hidden behind some plant or bush. There are no such snails in Japan, but there are in Switzerland, although they are not poisonous. I must say, I don't like them so much.

In the beginning, I was just watching, but as the fight went on, I somehow sided with the mantis, saying to myself: "Look at this courageous mantis. He has to fight to survive and feed the little one, but sooner or later, he will be devoured by this big, poisonous snail which eats anything…" I say 'he,' because for me, and from the very beginning, it was a male mantis, not a female. Strangely enough, the mantis finally won and started to eat the snail. But then I thought: "How horrible – he will be poisoned!" Fortunately, that did not happen, and the mantis got away with his little one.

In Zürich, at that time, it seemed like everyone involved in Jungian psychology frequently engaged in conversation about his or her dreams. Most of them didn't say, "How are you?," but rather: "What did you dream?" So, although I considered my dream about the mantis and the snail as a little dream, somehow I felt forced to mention it and talk about it. But then they felt sorry for me and said that the mantis is a very cruel insect, especially the female, which has the bad habit of devouring her mate after coupling; but, just before she does so (and this is a good habit and rather sweet of her), she prays – hence, the name 'praying mantis'… I was shocked, particularly when they insisted on giving their own interpretation of my dream by saying: "Ah, ah, so you were eating up your analyst!" Me, a sweet little Japanese, doing such a thing!

But then I began to ponder about this little dream of mine and its significance. What about the snail? The snail is part of the oriental tradition, and I belong precisely to a very traditional family and background. My father was a Zen master, and I was raised in a temple. In fact, when I left for Europe, I was very proud of this tradition, which is very necessary, I think, for every one of us, but which can be also a burden; that is why I felt, at the same time, that I had to break away from it. Therefore, I interpreted this fight with the strange devouring poisonous snail as the fight that I, a mantis, should engage in for survival. However, that interpretation was quite different from the one given by all the good Samaritans around me, who were so quick to give their own interpretation of this little dream of mine. I was crushed by their negative views; no one gave a single positive interpretation.

Of course, I talked about this dream to my analyst, Professor Meier, who just said: "Oh really, a giant snail... uh, uh, a black mantis with a little one... and both fought, and the mantis won..." – nothing else. He was, as usual, very careful and sensitive, in the best Jungian tradition. Jung has always insisted about the rights of the dreamer, and how the analyst should respect them. So my analyst did not interfere; he wanted me to do the main work. What should I do then?

I felt awful, and paralysed; since almost everyone had said that I was eating up my analyst, I could not go on with him anymore. Impossible. All the more because there was some truth, some positive element in their generally negative interpretations; i.e., Jungian analysis can sometimes look very much like the snail of my dream; it can devour you, if... if you don't control it, and if, sometimes, you don't fight back.

I could not stop thinking about this dream, and wanted to forget; but it swirled round and round in my head. A real typhoon, and no eye in the center to hide in. However, I tried to understand the whole meaning of it. First, what is the significance of the mantis? It is true – and they are right in saying so, my good Samaritan friends, the psychologists – that there is nothing more cruel, apparently, than a mantis! Was I not a mantis, deep down? I must confess that I am a typical Oriental girl, for I cannot say 'no'; so there might be in me – and perhaps this is part of my shadow side – a very strong, combative and aggressive spirit like the mantis. Of course, this can be viewed positively, as a counterbalancing element, but can also be considered very negatively. I was very much aware of all that, and that is why this little dream of mine and the mantis stayed so long in my memory.

***

It was in this context that, a year and a half later, I heard from Laurens van der Post that the mantis is a hero, a God or a First Spirit for the Bushman, who is also one of the First Men, a Stone-Age man... And that brought light to me. I began to think that, somewhere in me, something very old, something very original, something which was part of my old self had started to grow, to emerge and to fight with everything which was a menace to it, every devouring snail – be it psychoanalysis itself, or my own tradition, which was not only Zen Buddhist, but also very Confucianist: 'You shouldn't do this, you shouldn't do that, etc. …' Of course, I already knew what this dream meant to me when I heard the saga of the mantis from Laurens van der Post, for it confirmed what the mantis really meant, especially to me: that the mantis' saga is the story of the real beginning of the human spirit.

Now, with my little dream, my life took a strange turn.

***

Two more years passed, and I was due to complete my training at the Jung Institute and take the final examination. But then I went through a very difficult period during which, among other things, my dream of the mantis and a snail were understood – for me! – to indicate that becoming a Jungian analyst was not to be my way. I stayed another six months in Zürich, but was worried about what my next step in life should be. Then someone invited me to participate in an international congress on the History of the Study of Religion, to be held in Jerusalem. So I inscribed, since I had already decided by that time to go back to my beginning, to my own field; i.e., the study of religion. From Jerusalem, I went to Nairobi, where I stayed, vacationing, for about a month. A friend of mine lent me a cottage, where I snugly settled in. It was almost an autumnal season, crisp but sunny, and the scenery was so beautiful. The first thing I wanted to do was to send a letter to my analyst, Professor Meier, to thank him for everything he had done for me and to inform him that I didn't think I could be a Jungian anymore, and that I might go back to my study of religion. So I sat at a table and began to write, but somehow I couldn't finish my letter. Then I looked up at the window, and there it was … a mantis!

Hello, mantis! It was a beautiful mantis, a sort of beige colour, almost gold colour. How incredible, this apparition, at such a moment! I took it as a sign that everything would be all right from now on. The mantis had come back to me. And this time it was golden and not black.

After that encounter, I completely rewrote my letter, and I remember I said in particular: "I don't know what I'm going to do in the future, but I should recognize I learned so much in Zürich, although I also learned about life the hard way…"

Of course, Professor Meier knew all along what was happening, and he really jumped to his guns, but he could not really change the course of events, since he had already retired. He knew, on the other hand, that to try to get my diploma as an analyst was not exactly the objective of my whole life, and that I had so many ways to go. So he did not worry so much about me, but much more about the rest of the students: a certain person who had misinterpreted my dream might inject some real snail poison around him, and from behind his bush.

***

Looking back again at this black and golden past, I feel so grateful.

So grateful to my black mantis, to my black and golden mantis who imposed himself in my dream and helped me, the little one, to survive and grow and fight and find my own self. So grateful, also, to my golden mantis, which popped up at my window, in Kenya, just to say hello to me and to confirm that I was well en route – on my own way. So grateful to Laurens van der Post, because, without his story, I would not have found the whole, the deep meaning of my dream, and the original part of my self represented by the mantis.

Through all those years, full of fury and wonder, the mantis has become a god for me, and Laurens van der Post … a friend, a very special friend, although we only met and spent less than three hours together.

Sir Laurens and Nagisa Oshima in Tokyo during the filming of
Merry Christmas, Mr. Lawrence *in the late 1970's*

The Hearts of Leopards, the Mind of Stars

Nagisa Oshima

"When a baby is born at a Bushman's house …" said Sir Laurens van der Post, a British writer born in South Africa, who is known as the director of a documentary film about Bushmen, the oldest natives in South Africa, "… his father goes hunting to kill a leopard. Then he offers the heart of that animal to God and prays that the baby will be as strong as a leopard."

Fantastic!

Sir Laurens van der Post is a descendant of Boer aristocrats. When he was born, his father was the last prime minister of the Orange Free State. One of the servants at the house was a Bushman. I wonder if someone performed that Bushman's ceremony for his bright future when Sir Laurens van der Post was born. As well as being a writer, he was a brave soldier during World War II; a British colonel, a knight who was conferred the CBE decoration.

"But it's a father's job and mother has another role."

"Does she?"

"At night when the stars are beautiful, she holds her bare baby with both hands and prays to God all night long, so that the baby will have a kind heart like the light of the stars."

When he noticed me listening absorbedly to his beautiful English, he stopped speaking as if he were a little embarrassed. Then he began talking about the *Tenpura* on his dish, moving his chopsticks skill-fully.

Sir Laurens van der Post has been deeply connected with Japan. When he first came to Japan in 1926, he was only nineteen years old.

"At that time *Kanto-Daishinsai* (a disastrous earthquake in 1923) had still left its mark on Tokyo." He and his friend William Plomer (a poet) were taken to Japan by Mr. Mori, who was a captain of the *Kanada-Maru*, the first Japanese ship to sail through the South Africa

route. After staying in Japan for about a year, he went back to South
Africa and published many admirable Japanese papers.

During a recent visit to Japan, after I met him at Narita Airport and
took him to his hotel, he kindly came out to see me off. In front of the
hotel, we noticed an elderly gentleman walking in a dignified manner
with two attendants. When I told him that that gentleman might be
Captain Mori, he laughed and didn't believe it. Next day, however, he
said to me, "You were right. That gentleman was Captain Mori."

He praised the accuracy of my eyes as a film director, which made
me very pleased. I am going to make a new film based on his novel,
The Seed and the Sower. Sir Laurens van der Post had something to do
with Japan when he was in Java during World War II. In 1943, he
moved from North Africa to Java and was working as a commander,
but he was captured by the Japanese and forced to remain in a
concentration camp until 1945. After the war, he wrote about his
experience at the camp. When he published the first part of the novel,
many people criticized it, insisting that his description of the Japanese was too idealized. Nevertheless, despite those criticisms, he
continued to write. Finally his manuscripts were edited by his second
wife, Ingaret Giffard – herself a writer – and became published as *The
Seed and the Sower* (a trilogy).

At the end of his latest stay in Japan, he invited Mr. Jusho Toda, an
art director, and myself to a tea-break at four o'clock. When we
ordered a cup of tea, he urged us to ask for a cake as well as tea. We
felt somewhat embarrassed as, in reality, we were lovers of more
alcoholic beverages.

"Well ..., well, since it's my wife's birthday," said Sir Laurens, his
cheeks slightly blushing. Then at five, he left us to make an international call. He explained that it was 8:00 a.m. in Zürich, where his
wife would now be having breakfast. I hear there is a laboratory
where they study about Jung. He himself once wrote an extensive
treatise on Jung.

Ten minutes later, he came back cheerfully. He had told his wife
that I had a present for her and learned that the flowers he had
ordered in Japan had reached her in Switzerland.

Sir Laurens van der Post was born in 1906 and he continued his
heroic Bushman hunter's journey to the end.

Because Right is Right

Charles Janson

"Because right is right, to follow right
Were wisdom in the scorn of consequence."

Tennyson's words seem to suit Laurens van der Post who, like Tennyson, is a moralist as well as a poet. Profound moralists (as distinct from analysts, tipsters, wits and other shrewd folk) are rare in Britain today, as even fifty years ago, they were not. I have known three: the great Scottish journalist, Darsie Gillie, whose passion for truth was truly religious; Kurt Hahn, the Prussian liberal education-alist; and Laurens himself. The last two, in character widely different, shared one notable characteristic: both were aliens in Britain and both were devoted to the survival of the nation which had conquered their own nation in war. In van der Post's case, this wish to serve Great Britain was the more remarkable in that Boers were perhaps entitled to feel that their David had been suppressed by the British Goliath in the interests of British Mammon.

That a foreigner should best understand the country of his adop-tion or his study is not so rare. Disraeli was by any standard an improbable Victorian prime minister, yet prime minister he became. Even more marvellous was Joseph Conrad, who knew no English until the age of twenty and went on to be a peerless English romantic novelist. In the field of criticism, examples can be multiplied. For instance, Elie Halévy was among the greatest historians of nine-teenth-century England. It is often the racial outsider who most clearly sees the model of a people's mores and institutions. But Laurens has surely done something else: without entering British politics or even establishing himself as a specifically British writer, he has been able to offer a moral message not only to the British, but to all who read the English language.

How has he managed this? For the British he has done it, I suggest, by addressing them not as nationals, still less as nationalists, but as citizens of the world. To do this, one must, naturally, be a world-citizen oneself: which Laurens conspicuously is. As such he is, alas, still a rare and, one might say, an endangered species. One of van der Post's great distinctions, I think, is that the kind of patriotism he himself has, and expects from others, contains no hint of self-congratulation. Moreover, like Kurt Hahn, he holds that a person who doesn't love another's country will not love his own either.

Laurens once told me that one of his *bêtes noires* was Alfred, Lord Milner who at the turn of the century took it upon himself to decide that Great Britain was in danger of becoming imperially decadent and so had better re-forge its virtue in war: the South African War.

In middle-age, Laurens van der Post came to know Carl Gustav Jung through his English wife, Ingaret Giffard. This meeting brought him into Jung's world of depth-psychology, which the great psychologist had been charting for a few decades. But, unlike nearly all Jung's colleagues and patients, Laurens had himself been familiar with visions and myths since early childhood. For he had been brought up among the many races of South Africa, including primitive ones; and the experience had led him to know intuitively their psychic and mythical essences. And, moreover, those of other peoples, too. His books about the Japanese, whom to this day few Westerners understand, shows this remarkable diagnostic ability. Nevertheless, to have been as free as he has been from normal prejudice against other peoples, and other people, is evidence of a rare, earnest and noble nature indeed. Van der Post is a moralist, but he is a poetic one whose message comes from his own depths. His extraordinary first novel, *In A Province*, written when he was twenty-one, already shows the profound loner.

In late twentieth-century Britain, to be naturally profound and at the same unabstruse is highly disconcerting. We are all used to universities serving as National Parks for semi-unintelligible intellectuals, with their extensions in North London and the offices of quarterly periodicals. But to be profound in real life is to risk causing a disturbance. Even in literature, few profound writers have ever penetrated the British middle class. Apart from a few giants, such as Shaw, Wells, D.H. Lawrence: the educated leadership has stuck to the realists, the humourists and the sophisticated crime-writers. In this literary context, Laurens van der Post has been *hors-série:* a spiritual writer with a firm and fairly wide following; and once or twice a best-seller, too.

But if poetic profundity does not easily radiate from the printed word, broadcasts and telecasts can be different. Laurens is, surely, a great and successful telecaster. His monologues, dialogues and voice-over documentaries are almost without rival in the medium. In Britain, it seems, profundity is perfectly acceptable on TV, at least late in the evening.

I remember very well a decade or two ago a telecast done jointly by Laurens and General Sir John Glubb: a legendary national figure vaguely associated with Arabs, daggers, camels and Middle Eastern skirmishes. The interviewer raised immediately the interesting philo-sophical question: why was it that quite a few British people actually wished to live in the desert, amid discomfort, danger and seemingly irrelevant alien peoples? Sir John's response to this fair, and key, question must have gravely disappointed his viewers. A soldier's life in Transjordan, he told us, was a soldier's job like any other. Uncom-fortable it certainly sometimes was, but he had long since learned the knack of making it less so. As to danger, that was much exaggerated. Anyhow he'd come through all right. And so on and so forth. Laurens, having endured this anti-poem of British understatement, then had his turn. He at once stated his answer to the interviewer's question: namely, the British, of all peoples, had the greatest love of adventure and were most willing to cast themselves on the unknown. Like the sea, indeed as a kind of sea, the desert was consequently the natural habitat of such British and other similarly inclined people. So much for Glubb, his saddle-gadgets and his sand-proof whisky-flasks. Equally impressive among Laurens' telecasts was his series on Jung and the two films of the Kalahari desert made at an interval of thirty years. His diction in English, with its most musical phonetics and perfect *andante* tempo, is an ideal utterance of profound themes against visually bewitching settings. Such programmes cast a spell even over professional TV-critics, a class of person not renowned for its suggestibility. (Much less magical, it must be said, was the film made by Laurens and his close personal friend, Prime Minister Margaret Thatcher, in No. 10 Downing Street. For some reason, the Prime Minister found as little to say about her childhood as General Glubb about the desert.)

The well-known symbiosis of Sir Laurens van der Post and Mrs. Thatcher, lately food for the more desperate satirists, is, of course, the symbiosis of two moralists. It seems to have been most fortunate. The most eminent British politician since Churchill grew up looking out of a very Anglo-English window. This could have proved a limitation and a handicap. In Laurens, Margaret Thatcher happened to meet, on her own Chelsea door-step, a citizen of the world, but one who could imagine no world without a positive Great Britain. When all is said and done, they have, between them, steadied a domestically errant nation and re-established in it at least some sense of what the world expects it to be. Their declaration of values, whether Victorian or Kalaharian, has become a kind of public duet culminating in Laurens' latest book and his birthday celebrations.

My colleagues in this appreciation will be writing of Laurens' several functions and facets: in particular, no doubt, of his central tenet that we must regain contact with that ancient part of the human self that we now fail to recognise; and to this end must at the same time conserve enough of the geographical wilderness which has reflected it since the world's beginning. That is the deeper and more poetic side of Laurens' moralism. My theme has been his befriending of the British nation. Nations need friends as much as people do, friends being by definition outside parties. And they need them most when their star is temporarily on the wane.

Quo vadis, Helvetia?

Dieter Baumann

Foreword

When asked to participate in a *Festschrift* for Sir Laurens van der Post, I spontaneously decided to submit an article which I had written in 1989 regarding a plebiscite about an initiative whose goal it was to abolish the Swiss Army. At the end of November, 1989, the initiative was rejected by the Swiss people by a two-thirds majority. My article was never published, but circulated privately, and I had the privilege of talking about it with Sir Laurens while it was in the making, and of receiving his warm encouragement.

Therefore, I dedicate it to him as the soldier who carried heroically and gallantly the spirit of humanity through, and in spite of, many wars, and most particularly so through his Japanese captivity. This spirit (of loving even those who once threatened his life) he generously shares with us through his books and his life. His example in bearing and containing the opposites within himself in the most adverse circumstances has been, and is, a great encouragement for me in my own endeavour.

After due consideration, I have, therefore, come to the conclusion that the present article might reflect some of the spirit for which, dear Laurens, I want to thank you. In bringing us nearer to Africa and to yourself, you bring us nearer to the natural man in ourselves, who desperately needs us.

You mention, in one of your books, that you met in C.G. Jung a man with whom it was possible to talk about Africa because he understood it from his own experience. I think it is not exaggerated to say that C.G. Jung dedicated his life to the inner man, to the Anthropos, i.e., to man within man, to the human and humane within himself, by having the courage and the perseverance to listen to him constantly. It impresses me and fills me with gratitude that, through your books and your life, you generously share with us your own kindred experience of the inner man, especially in as far as it goes through the natural man in Africa and throughout the world.

Maybe the message that the natural man (both within and without) sends and gives us is his religious attitude towards nature, our Mother Earth. A few years ago, you said: rather than to wage wars against each other, we should unite our efforts doing all what we can to save life on our planet. This is the real issue which is at stake.

In the light of this urgent and higher goal, the present article might seem misplaced, and I present it with a certain hesitation. Unfortunately, however, man continues to be wolf to man – *homo homini lupus*. The reality of evil cannot be disregarded, let alone ignored, by those who want and are meant to survive.

As long as we live in a world in which power-madness is raging, the citizen of a predominantly democratic country, however small it may be, will find himself in the uncomfortable paradoxical position of having to defend it and its democratic values of tolerance and compromise, by being armed, trained and prepared to fight on the one hand, while on the other, keeping in mind and heart his solidarity with the whole of mankind and creation, of which he is a responsible part, and which he contains in all its paradoxes.

For those considerations, I now present a somewhat re-modelled version of my original article. Although it is not a verbatim translation, I thought it best not to estrange it from the above-mentioned occasion for which I had written it, and to stick as much as possible to its original wording, in such a way as to preserve its character of actuality and to let it breathe. Although it reflects my concern about a dangerous lack of instinct, in my opinion, in certain people of my own country, I hope that, *mutatis mutandis*, it will be of interest to you, dear Laurens van der Post, and also to some members of your world-wide circle of friends.[1]

---

[1] For the sake of the foreign (in contrast to the Swiss) reader, I must add here that the task of the Swiss Army is exclusively *dissuasive, defensive and protective*, as being part of our armed neutrality, recognized by the European powers since the treaty of Vienna (1815).

Quo vadis, Helvetia?

*Some psychological considerations regarding the initiative
launched for the abolition of the Swiss Army*[1]

In a few days, we shall vote on the survival or the abolition of our
army, and, consequently, decide on the very survival of our Confederation. Every one of us is called to give his opinion: it is a decision of
such weight as to load every single citizen with a responsibility
unknown to us in the course of the 700 years of our history, the very
survival of our State and its values being at stake. The well-known
psychologist Marie-Louise von Franz fears that abolishing our army
would amount to Switzerland's suicide. I agree with her. Here are my
reflections:

First of all, let me remind you of her book on the visions of Niklaus
von Flüe, our national Saint[2], and also of the television film by Guido
Ferrari on the same subject[3], in which she comments upon these
visions in a most earnest and profound way. A number of inner
experiences coming from the unconscious, in particular a terrible
vision of God, led Niklaus von Flüe, a peasant and father of ten
children, to choose to live as a hermit in the Ranft, ten minutes from
his home in Flüeli above Sachseln (Canton Obwalden). Through his
meditation, in secluded loneliness, he managed to bear the terrible
vision of God in himself without being broken and crushed by it. This
gave him such moral authority that, on the occasion of the Diet
(*Tagsatzung*) of Stans in 1481, when the Federation of that time was
on the verge of breaking apart and thus becoming easy prey for
foreign powers, a messenger, Heini am Grund, was sent to ask him
for his advice. He responded: "Stay together!" His advice was followed. This event had such an impact that, in some depictions of this
event, Niklaus von Flüe appears in person at the Diet in Stans.
Subsequently, Niklaus has become the protector and patron of our

---

[1] Slightly revised and adapted translation from the original French and German. Published here for the first time.
[2] Marie-Louise von Franz: *Die Visionen des Niklaus von Flüe*, Zürich 1959/
1980
[3] Swiss-Italian Television, 1987, German and Italian version.

country. He was canonised in 1950. On the mountain of the "Hohe Ronen" (where the Cantons Schwyz, Zug and Zürich meet), there is a wooden cross bearing the inscription: "Blessed Brother Klaus, protect our Homeland" (*Seliger Bruder Klaus schütze unsere Heimat*).

Brother Klaus, as he is often called, is a man who succeeded in bearing and containing in himself the conflict between good and evil. Thus, he avoided projecting these forces onto his fellow beings. Such a capacity for being able to consciously withstand the tension between moral opposites as each of us finds them in himself, enables one to be tolerant with himself and to receive the same tolerance from those who differ from him. On this basis, our Confederation grew in the course of the centuries. In it, we nurse and cultivate our differences. In his book, *La Suisse ou l'histoire d'un peuple heureux*, Denis de Rougemont notes how the old cantons allied themselves, not in order to become identical, but to preserve, defend and protect their own unique characters, and to assist one another in this task. *Tolerance for diversity* (of religion, language, culture, society and point of view) *is unity*. This tolerance becomes possible if a sufficient number of individuals each strive daily to build inner peace by trying to bear the opposites that fight against one another, in a spirit of self-tolerance. The dialogue must be sought in order to reach the so-called democracy of concordance (*Konkordanzdemokratie*), which means etymologically: until "the people rule in unity of the hearts." In such a spirit of speaking with one another, a contrary opinion can be tolerated: it becomes an element of a fertile and constructive on-going discussion. Where such a concordance is lacking, civil war breaks out, at least in the minds of some. But *in extremis*, it seems that now such a discussion could begin from hither and thither in a spirit of concordance. One begins to speak of the future, which, by the way, seems to be the concern of many among those who cherish the initiative in question: so some of them have told me. However, in my opinion, they are risking too much, if, at the poll, we should really shift towards the abolition of our army.

The very principle of (armed) neutrality corresponds to this instinctive need to endure the ethical conflict. The same holds for our armament and training for fighting in case of need. *The paradox of having to build up and keep an army fit and ready for combat in order to avoid as much as possible ever using it, corresponds to this deep-rooted instinct for balance.* In addition to physical training and learning to withstand adverse circumstances, *military service teaches us to withstand consciously the conflict between good and evil and thus to avoid an evil which is still worse.* That, at least, has been my experience.

For this same reason, a man like C.G. Jung could grow on Helvetic soil. He had the courage to look into the depths of his soul to become aware of the darkness in it.

Within the framework of this short article, I must limit myself to those few hints to indicate that, in the course of the centuries, that unique value which is Switzerland grew and developed. This, for me, is worth being defended at all costs, in spite of its failures and vices: haughtiness, arrogance, cold selfishness, intolerance to what is foreign to us, concentration of real estate ownership and money in the hands of the few. Our failures and vices blind us to the demagogic power of the media, while we participate in the destruction of Nature, both in physical and psychical pollution of our environment, and so on.

The adoration of the golden calf on the one hand, and the exaltation of ideology on the other, have become unhealthy exaggerations that go against the needs of the soul. One clings to these pseudo-values out of anxiety for material and spiritual security, without finding a lasting serenity in either. Both, if excessive, become pseudo-securities: they narrow down and imperil the material and spiritual needs of the individual and his very existence; of the individual who is, in the opinion of C.G. Jung, the most precious creation of nature (not to be mistaken for the individualist).

In this general confusion, Switzerland is threatened with the loss of its very *raison d'être*. Feeling values are too much tramped upon. One doesn't talk enough to the other any more, one simply does *do*, i.e., one acts, convinced of his right and of being right, before looking at the shadows our actions are casting and the damage our deeds are doing, and taking heed of this damage. The dire effects of such an unfeeling attitude create an atmosphere wherein we become cold, cynical and greedy; conversely, through the influence of the media, we engage in demagogic agitation against selected scapegoats. In both cases, one is not sufficiently aware of the harmful and destructive aspect of one's actions; or, what is worse, one represses it. But *to repress* is to *murder,* as the language of the dreams clearly expresses it: to kill one's own soul. If one represses the fact that one creates a conflict by acting without consideration, one disregards the existence of whoever happens to find himself in one's way; then one tries to "settle" the "problem" by insinuations and calumnies. This, alas, happens already with us, demoralises us and shatters the trust between our neighbours and ourselves.

If we don't take care, body and soul, of our home earth, if we use nature, physical and psychical, as a garbage-can, if we overrun it, we shall *estrange* ourselves from it. We shall become its foes; but the scapegoat for this deplorable attitude of ours will be and is the *stranger*, the foreigner, hence our xenophobia. If we don't do what is necessary at home, we shall estrange the respect and understanding of other peoples toward us.

The myth and history of William Tell and the origin of our Confederation by the oath of the Grütli (or Rütli) is not understood enough as an interior, intrapsychical drama in the individual, in which good and evil fight against each other. That is why one rationalises it "away;" i.e., into projection. But a people who forgets and loses its stories is doomed, as C.G. Jung and Laurens van der Post have demonstrated. The historical and mythological history of a people has to be retold and reinterpreted for each epoch. It seems that for our turmoiled age (which is the passage from Pisces to Aquarius), this interpretation ought to be psychological, that it ought to explain what the images and facts of tradition mean to the soul of the individual and of the community. Thus, there is a legend of the three Tells who are sleeping inside the rock of Seelisberg (or of the Axen) and will awaken only when our country is in peril. This moment has arrived.

One notices the cracks on the surface of the fragile and delicate structure of our democratic community; one tries to mend them by so-called unificatory measures, such as the goose-step[1] of our trains, although they roll, the synchronisation of the beginnings of the school year (recently unified for all the cantons of Switzerland), and other similar games. But the schematic and inhuman way in which we treat refugees who ask for political asylum bears witness to it: often we send them back to misery, to risking their lives, sometimes even to torture and death. What happened to the parents of the boy who died from exhaustion and cold on the Splügen pass?[2]

---

[1] Taktschritt (milit.) = pas cadencé; allusion to the trains following each other at exactly the same minute every hour.
[2] This refers to a group of Kurd refugees who tried to flee into Switzerland. A boy lost his life. Upon arrival in our country, the father was arrested.

What may keep us united are not so much the measures we take, but Eros; our listening to the voice of feeling. Also the knowledge of being made out of good and evil alike, and of having to ponder and to weigh continuously what is *comparatively* less harmful, in any decision. The practical consequences of such an attitude are greater tolerance, a more humane attitude, broader openness to discussion in a spirit of common search for the truth and its practical application: something which is practical and has been rehearsed in Switzerland for centuries and, although constantly endangered, never taken for granted, yet, always more or less successfully recreated. (Having begun my life abroad, I became attuned to such Swiss values as I should perhaps otherwise have missed.) These values, of which not the least include the sense of compromise and of coexistence, faithfulness and fidelity to oneself, and deep love for our mountains: we have thus far succeeded, with the help of God, in protecting them. It is one of the very tasks of our army to safeguard the possibility of cultivating and deepening them. The enormous problems of this world are also ours. But let us work on them at home as well, in our own limited space! This will also help the world. It is a matter of protecting and defending a way of living together, which, in spite of all its abuses, conveys, as it does so in few other places, to the responsible individual, a possibility of realising himself. Let us unite, as did the old cantons in 1291, in a mutual spirit of respect for the individuality of the other! It is in the microcosm of the free but responsible individual that the destiny of humanity ultimately finds the source of its strength, from which it derives. And it is from this way of living that the latter ultimately is inspired and nourished with trust.

The great problem resides in the fact that the army, too, *is a compromise* with evil, *a pact with the devil*. To abolish it does not mean abolishing evil. Far from that, it means repressing the awareness of Evil. When we abandon evil to the whims of fatality, we shall no longer have any influence over it, whereas *now we keep conscious* and somewhat controllable the evil with which we must reckon and to which we have to deliver our tenth (tribute). If we unburden ourselves of this responsibility, the controlled power (by the will of the people, in spite of everything!) of our army, we will give way to other powers, against which we shall remain defenceless: foreign powers, financial interests, terrorism, subversion, demagogy, increased importance of the police, etc. The well-balanced equilibrium between army and police will be disrupted. If we abolish our army, nobody will prevent terrorists from arming themselves.

Inside our territory, the army contributes to our stability, it being composed of men and women from all parts of the country, all social layers, *and above all, of individuals who see its necessity, and sense in it, without identifying themselves with it.* A human being *who commits himself to a necessary institution and remains critical of it will not become fanatical,* because he keeps his sense of humour. We can learn much from the British in this respect. In such a way, the army is a factor of stability and cohesion. Conversely, the institution should be composed, as much as possible, of individuals who are responsible for, but not identified with it, so as to respect the individual who puts himself at its service, whatever be his rank in the hierarchy. It is thus, in the first instance, a primarily human problem, and not an organisational or "abolitional" one. If feeling is strong enough, one will be better able to withstand the paradoxes of "the army *and* the peace" and of "yes, but. ..." This will render the institution more humane.

One of the psychological causes for war is the accumulation, the heaping-up of the projection of the evil, which is in each of us, upon a fellow being or a group. One can therefore hope to reduce wars if the number of individuals increases who succeed in becoming aware that their shadow, in the first instance, resides in themselves.

But, if good and evil are a part of creation, one must conclude that they represent two poles, two contrary aspects of the inner and outer experience man calls God. C.G. Jung suffered from, and fought with, this terrible problem; he bore witness to it in his *Answer to Job* (see in particular Chapter XV). He stresses the fact that God (i.e., God in us: it is the only one of which he dares to speak as a psychologist) needs man in order to become morally conscious of Himself. In harmony with the author of the Revelation (St. John), he observes that God can be loved, but must be feared: "The fear of the Lord is the beginning of wisdom ..." (Psalm 111:10).

What does this have to do with the Swiss army? Good and evil are in every one of us, *and we have to take into account the reality of evil* within and without us. Swiss introversion began after the defeat of Marignano (1515), and to my knowledge no federated, let alone confederated, army has attacked another country since. The army is the tool and the expression of our will to survive in freedom, as well as a school of tolerance and solidarity with those different from us, who perform their military service together with us. The army is a paradox, as life is: *in order to protect ourselves from being annihilated and to pay our tribute to the stability and freedom of Europe, we have to make a pact with evil, i.e., to recognise and acknowledge its existence as a power in us, and to suffer morally from this attitude.* In view of the misery that reigns on the earth, Jung says, it is a blasphemy to declare that God is only (the supreme) good. In the same sense, I consider it a lack of respect and fear of God to underestimate evil and to think it will disappear if we just behave nicely. The submissiveness of the weaker, with the animal, puts a break on the stronger, but alas!, with humans, this doesn't (often) work, because there is, in the human, too much repressed and accumulated aggression and frustration. (In a restricted space, the weakness of the weaker hen doesn't protect her from being pecked at by the stronger ones.) The price to be paid for lack of respect before the reality of evil is very high. Does a war have to break out to arouse us? The sense of duty and sacrifice, the spirit in which our forefathers, and even we, have tried to perform our military service has nothing to do with the exaltation of patriotism, nor with an apothesis of war; it means: to take seriously the reality of evil, i.e., to fear God.

In the impending vote, it will be for each of us a matter of asking his or her conscience, and to ponder, of what nature and what size the compromise will be that he or she *can* make with evil, and what compromise he or she *will have* to make with it in order to save what is, from the point of view of conscience, *relatively more precious.* C.G. Jung stressed the importance of sacrificing the relatively less to the relatively more precious. Whatever his or her decision will be, it will be questionable from a moral standpoint. Who is able to be 60% on the side of what is comparatively less harmful and less dangerous can deem himself lucky. To know, at the same time, that he is also 40% on the side of the evil and the harmful will protect himself from fanaticism, from intolerance, from cynicism and from the lack of consideration. If he goes on to keep awake this conscience and awareness of having his feet on both sides, he will remain flexible and open, ready for the dialogue with himself and with his neighbour and will be able to perceive better which are the exceptions and the unique cases that make up life and reality.

Even if – thank God! – freedom is in the process of rending the curtains and breaking the walls[1], and a new hope arrives in our

---

[1] Written in 1989.

hearts, our work for peace requires a solid and protected base. The hypothesis of the impossibility of a conventional war which is suggested in spite of the terrible suffering in Lebanon, Afghanistan, Cambodia and elsewhere, and the gratuitous declaration that no danger whatsoever will appear against which we should need our army; these assertions are at least as dangerous as to disregard the so-called "residual" risks of atomic plants, in spite of Chernobyl.

History teaches us that peace has never been attained once and for all, but has always required great and sustained sacrifices. The same holds for the inner peace of the individual; it is, however, the *condicio sine qua non* of the pacific coexistence between people in communities. The construction of inner peace is not in the last instance a goal of many religions; it represents a continuous effort and a difficult task, because it requires from the individual to observe constantly within himself antagonistic tendencies, to listen to their respective voices, to have a dialogue with them; all of this in order to be able to make his practical decisions in due knowledge of its pros and cons, by listening to reason and to his heart. The same holds for life in community at all levels. We need the dialogue, i.e., to speak and to listen to each other, in order not to mistake the other for the whole of the devil (half is quite enough!). The knowledge about one's own devil is most propitious for living together. For generally known reasons, we, the inhabitants of the terrestrial globe, have become a community of destiny, as never before in history. If I understand it well, an important part of those who want to abolish our army are inspired by a feeling of solidarity with the whole of mankind and of creation. However, in criticising justly, but only, our Swiss vices, and fighting them, we run the risk of becoming blind to our values, which, too, are our tasks. To sacrifice our army means, unfortunately, to bereave ourselves of our country, our homeland, and of the possibility of deciding ourselves about our future, in as far as it also depends on human will, in spite of all interdependencies and intertwinings.

Seven hundred years we have needed for the growth and development of the Swiss Confederation, i.e., of a community of human being appertaining to different substrata and bound by different loyalties (linguistic, cultural, religious, local, political, of age, of sex, etc.), which all overlap one another and intertwine in slanted ways, which is a great incentive for the development of the individual (Denis de Rougemont). Almost everywhere, our state-border is *not* a linguistic border. In a very restricted space, and by the will of (almost) all, a subtle balance between diversity and unity has developed; a perpetual, constant school of tolerance. And our army is one of these schools. I had the privilege of living this experience in the recruit school for medical troops, in a mixed company of young men from the Tessin and the Italian-speaking part of Graubünden, Romandy (French-speaking) and from the Alemannic Swiss German-speaking parts of our country. During marches, we learned the ways of the others, and our company song was … English! ("She'll be coming 'round the mountain when she comes") What unites us is thus not linguistic "ethnicity," but something deeper, not in the least a civic sense which also respects individuality (provided it doesn't become too glamorous!). There are material reasons as well. But they are not enough, they alone won't do. What unites us is the attachment to our earth, as well as the will to find and to work out a consensus beyond the aforementioned differences, to bear and support each other in spite of our differences and of getting on one another's nerves. That is an arduous task. In this respect, we are going through a very dangerous period, because feeling and consciousness of the paradox, which we can scarcely bear, are threatened most seriously. In former Yugoslavia, the heroic attitude of those who defend multiethnicity, in spite of everything, arouses my unconditional admiration and gratitude. Dialogue has become difficult.

An example of this is the regrettable fact that, in the course of the discussion about abolishing or keeping our army, false notes are to be heard. Devoted men of great personal integrity, who are in favour of the army, and ranking officers in it, are being personally attacked or used as scapegoats for abuses in which they are not involved. Without producing any proofs, one doubts and questions the integrity of their commitment. These men, and some women, on whom we have conferred a high responsibility, and who have committed themselves, would deserve at least to be listened to; their experiences, knowledge, and their practical conclusions deserve to be discussed *objectively*. In the army, *everyone* is responsible for his post and his function. Of course, there are abuses, as in any institution, and also for selfish purposes. But they can be corrected, as was the case at the beginning of the active service of 1939 to 1945. Even the army of the best of all democracies cannot be democratic in its structure and organisation, which have the purpose of rendering it efficient and fit for fighting. But it can be democratic in the mental attitude of its members, i.e., in the respect for one's fellow-beings, whether they be a superior, an

equal or a subordinate reporting to his superior. The army knows the
right of complaint in various ways, and of being listened to.

Marie-Louise von Franz says that it is by no means difficult to be a
blind idealist, nor a cynical realist, but that it is difficult and desirable
to see, without illusion, reality as it is and yet to nourish the inner
flame and keep it high.

Our armed mentality responds to this claim. It is the policy we have
adopted and followed for almost two centuries, and on which our
neighbours are counting. This policy is our commitment to Europe
and the world. It has contributed to our not having become a theatre
of war and not having had to endure a foreign occupation since
Napoleon. He who wants the good too much calls for the evil. Certain
leaders of the Khmers rouge have studied at the Sorbonne, only to put
into practice their idealistic *vue de l'esprit* in such a direct way that the
result was a genocide whose cruelty is on a scale comparable to the
mass-murder of millions of Jews and half a million Gypsies in
Europe.

If, for idealistic reasons, we make ourselves defenceless by disar-
mament, the subtle and fragile, ever-to-be-recreated equilibrium
between good and evil will be shattered. This equilibrium expresses
itself in our will to defend ourselves and takes shape in our strictly
defensive army. If we abolish it, we put our existence, as citizens of
Switzerland, at stake, and we give up the dialogue and the community
life. Conscious compromise with evil is necessary for our survival; in
a decisive way, such an attitude helps us to avoid the even worse. If
we sacrifice this compromise, evil will appear in much more insidi-
ous, malignant and deleterious guises: blackmail (Who would protect
our airports from terrorists? Who, in an emergency, would prevent a
neighbour from occupying our territory, from imposing his law upon
us, and from re-equipping himself with our own material and troops,
if it pleases him? There would be collaborationists and heroic patriots
fighting for freedom, but there would be bloodshed. All this happened
a few decades ago in Europe; loss of the possibility to settle our own
problems on our own small territory. Switzerland could become
divided between our neighbours. No, thank you. Seven hundred years
were needed for our democracy to develop. Shall we throw it into the
trash can? In spite of all abuses of power, there is probably no country
in the world where the simple citizen enjoys as much freedom and
possibility to influence actively the course of events. If we disarm, our
neighbours will feel cheated, and the moral credit they granted us,

which is already dwindling, would soon be exhausted. One would easily dispose of the "special case" of Switzerland.

To want to "make a beginning to build peace," by abolishing our army would be over-straining the Swiss instinct; as one ends up killing an animal by asking more from him than his forces can yield. Abolishing the army amounts to an excessive concretisation of idealism. It would lead to its contrary. Symbolically speaking, William Tell would aim and shoot too low at his target: too much on the concrete level, too near the earth. But by so doing, he would not only miss the apple, but kill his son, i.e., the future of our descendants and of the Swiss Anthropos (*Menschenbild*), as he expresses himself in Tell (as well as in the three Confederates; *Eidgenossen* means 'fellows in oath,' and in the three women Gertrud Stauffacher, Bertha von Bruneck (with Schiller) and Tell's wife.

All this has nothing to do with a noisy or sentimental patriotism. It is but a reflection on our psychological roots:

- *The individual who acts alone and by himself,* but in solidarity with the others: *Tell*;

- *The commitment by the oath of assistance and solidarity*[1]: *the three Confederates*[2];

- The practical spirit and mind and the realistic evaluation of what is possible: the women.

The three Confederates took their oath in the name of the *masculine divine ideal*: the Father, the Son and the Holy Ghost, on the *sacred feminine earth of the Grütli*[3] which is the limited space of *possible reality* as well as *the symbol of our Swiss earth* (legally, it belongs to the Swiss youth).

There are people who, in a sarcastic way, please themselves to call the army our "sacred cow," which has to be butchered. Well, yes: the cow is indeed sacred, in these modern times in which our fields and gardens become ever smaller and fewer, and in which there are fewer and fewer farmers. She is our totem animal, if we think of the rituals of the cowherds going up to the Alps (*Alpaufzug*) with the cattle in

---

[1] The oath given by the three Confederates or representatives of the three original Cantons Uri, Schwyz and Unterwalden, on the meadow of the Rütli or Grütli, which is the birthplace and shrine of Switzerland to this day. It started in 1291 with this league.

[2] or Eidgenossen = fellows in oath. To this day, the German designation for the Helvetic or Swiss Confederation is "Schweizerische Eidgenossenschaft" = Swiss "community in oath."

[3] Grütli or Rütli = clearing (in a wood).

spring and down again in the autumn (*Alpabzug, désalpe, scargada*) and of all the songs which are inspired by the life of the cowherds. She is for us – we know it only dimly – as sacred as the caribou of the inland Eskimos of Canada[1], or the reindeer for the Lapps of Scandinavia. She gives us the gift of her life with her milk and meat, for which she has to die. As an animal, she symbolises the instinct of our attachment to the earth; the same holds for our purely defensive army. This common root thus explains the assimilation of our army by the sacred cow, sarcastic as it is. The times I have served in the Army in rural districts have helped me to sensitize my "green" conscience, as well as to encourage and further my attachment to people of all parts of Switzerland, who welcomed us with their warm hospitality.

It is by virtue of these considerations, and of the feeling that goes with them, that I shall vote[2] against the abolition of our army. For the same reasons, I wish that the dialogue on the future of our country will go on in a constructive and responsible way. I hope to contribute to it. Let us first attune our tuning-forks! Then our instruments.

Postscript 1996:

Since 1989, many things have changed. Terrible wars have brought infinite suffering to those who didn't have enough means to defend themselves. I am well aware of how conflicted the substance of my consideration is, and how there is another side, a shadow side to it as well. But I hope to have expressed how much the cross of the paradoxes, which every one has to carry for himself, inspired by C.G. Jung, is a central symbol. Thank you, dear Laurens van der Post, for your encouraging example.

---

[1] see Farley Mowat: *People of the Deer*, Michael Joseph Ltd., London, 1952.
[2] 1996: and have voted since.

Prejudice as Self-Rejection

Vernon Brooks

Racism – "The notion that one's own ethnic stock is superior"[1] to all others – was such an accepted norm, so much taken for granted by our more immediate antecedents that it may not have loomed as a great individual problem for most of the inhabitants of the western world before well into the Twentieth Century. As late as 1911, the unsurpassed eleventh edition of the *Encyclopaedia Britannica,*[2] published simultaneously in England and the United States, had no entry at all for "racism" and the seventeen line entry for "prejudice"[3] dealt only with legal prejudices; there was no mention of racial, religious, social or psychological prejudices; they existed, but were apparently not considered of sufficient importance to warrant acknowledgement in the most prestigious of English-language lexicons. Even today, the *Oxford English Dictionary*[4] does not define "racism" – or "racialism," as the word generally occurs in British English – confining the term to a substantive form of the adjective "racial" (hence "Racialism").[5]

Dictionaries and encyclopedias aside, however, racism has flourished, especially since World War I, not more extensively than before, but with a consciousness which had apparently not previously informed its manifestations.

It is not that there were no instances of racism in previous centuries; racial prejudices were as extensive then, if not more so, as they are today. But it was only when the depth psychologists of the

---

[1] *The American Heritage Dictionary of the English Language*, New York, 1969, p. 1075.
[2] *The Encyclopaedia Britannica; A Dictionary of Arts, Sciences, Literature and General Information.* Eleventh edition. New York, 1911.
[3] Volume 22, p. 277.
[4] *The Shorter Oxford English Dictionary on Historical Principles.* London: Oxford University Press. Third edition, 1964.
[5] P. 1647.

early 1900s began to question such attitudes and convictions that the tendencies of our thoughts and feelings toward those who are not exactly identical with us became of a personal concern. Men of good will then began to suspect that racism – along with a lot of other prejudicial afflictions – perhaps represented something not altogether healthy in the psychic life of individuals. Unfortunately, however, there are tens of thousands today who, in spite of the advances which have been made by subjective-oriented psychologies, especially the depth psychology of C.G. Jung, in our understanding of this clouded area of human behavior, are still victims of this subversive mechanism.

For feelings, negative or otherwise, attitudes, convictions, evaluations of the world around us and the people in our world, have their origins in the human psyche. These feelings do not and obviously cannot exist apart from the individuals who nourish them. So we are responsible for our attitudes; they may be activated, encouraged, energized by outer events, but reactions to outer influences and disturbances are inescapably subjective; it is in our psychic life that the causes, the origins of all forms of racism lie. If this problem concerns us in any way at all, then it is only within ourselves that some answers to its unresolved conflicts may possibly be found.

Two varieties of racism are especially abundant in contemporary western life: anti-Semitism and anti-Black prejudice. It is of passing interest to note that the former has a substantive to indicate its existence, the latter only an adjective form which then needs a subject to modify: anti-Black feelings, anti-Black prejudice, anti-Black activities, etc. There are many other racial animosities alive and well and living in the world around us – anti-Mexican, anti-Arab, anti-white, anti-Gypsy, anti-Aboriginal – although most are more or less confined to local areas. Anti-Semitism and manifestations of anti-Black prejudice, however, are general, westernwide, provocative and ugly.

What might these two extreme instances of racism convey to us, not about the rights or wrongs of such attitudes, but about what they might mean subjectively, what they have to reveal to us about ourselves, insofar as we are infected with them? What is their origin, their possible resolution, if any?

"Anti-Semitism," the word itself, is rather a linguistic misapplication. It is used today to specify a prejudicial bias against Jews, who, however, are not the only Semitic peoples extant. The Semites are traditionally believed to have descended from them, the eldest son of Noah, the biblical ancestor of those races and tribes inhabiting the eastern Mediterranean areas. In ancient times they included the Babylonians, Assyrians and Phoenecians, as well as Arabs and Jews. Only Arabs and Jews remain as our twentieth century Semites. However, Arabs are never included in the term "anti-Semitism." An anti-Semite is, in the words of the *American Heritage Dictionary*, "a person who is hostile toward or prejudiced against Jews."[1] Nothing about Arabs is there at all. How have the latter come to be excluded in the almost universal prejudice which we call anti-Semitism?

There are, of course, anti-Arab feelings abroad; Israelis certainly entertain them, and Israelis do not consider themselves anti-Semitic: only Anti-Arab.

The linguistic conundrum is merely of intellectual interest, however. What is more consequential is the psychological relevance of the very prevalent anti-Jewish sentiments in western civilization. What may be responsible for its prevalence, and what has this prevalence to say about the subjective factors which have given rise to it?

Anti-Israel sentiments are not, strictly speaking, anti-Semitic, although anti-Jewish prejudices often hide behind attitudes of criticism, hostility or hatred toward the state of Israel. But anti-Israel attitudes are political, not racist; they are directed toward a government, toward its policies and activities, and sometimes those policies test and try even the most faithful of pro-Israel friends. There are countless similar political or nationalist antipathies toward any number of present-day states and nations: anti-Russian, anti-German, anti-American and so on, all around the globe. But these, like anti-Israel manifestations, tend to be less racial than political.

Anti-Semitism (and although it does misrepresent its own definition, the term will be used, since it has never been applied to anyone but Jews and there is no other convenient noun-term for specifically anti-Jewish sentiments) – is, on the other hand, an emotional, feeling state of mind rather than a thinking event, directed negatively toward a particular race of people. It may lie behind a façade of intellectual arguments (generally untenable) or of social convictions (equally untenable), but whatever its outer face, the prejudicial dynamic is, to

[1] P. 50.

speak colloquially, a "gut" feeling. The anti-Jew individual hates the object of his prejudice, and the emotional strength of his hatred betrays its subjective nature and source.

Throughout many of the earlier centuries of the Christian era, hatred toward Jews was justified, in the eyes of the bigot, by the argument that the Jews crucified Christ, were therefore responsible for the death of the Savior and consequently a justifiable object for rejection. In the eighteenth and nineteenth centuries and well into the twentieth, anti-Jewish feelings shifted from the religious to a social level and were defended on the grounds that the Jew was attempting to gain control of the western world through financial manipulations. This was the familiar argument of the Third Reich; the western world, in the Nazi view, belonged not to Jews but rather to Germany, or at least the European continent, and the British Isles belonged or should belong to the Germans, and any threat to their eventual mastery of Europe had to be exterminated.

Today, toward the end of the 1900s, few hold either of these rather hoary convictions. Yet, anti-Semitism still pervades the civilized areas of the Occident and, even more virulently during the last few decades, the Near East.

Laurens van der Post, writing of the anti-Black phenomenon, isolated the root cause of racial prejudice toward Blacks. "We have the despised Black person in ourselves," he observes in *Race Prejudice as Self Rejection*. "We resent this dark person in ourselves, and then we get it mixed up with the dark person in society."[1] It is, in other words, an outer manifestation of an inner rejection, a rejection of the dark areas of our own psyche. Could a similar form of rejection apply in the case of anti-Semitism?

There are many significant differences between the two phenomena: historical, social and economic. A closer scrutiny of anti-Semitism, however, may suggest that at its roots there does lie an even deeper, more hidden kind of rejection.

All prejudices are directed toward an outer object and represent an inner condition projected onto that object. The strength, the power, the energy in the prejudice discloses the intensity of the projection. And every projection projects a complex in the individual doing the

[1] Van der Post, Laurens. *Race Prejudice as Self Rejection: An Inquiry into the Psychological and Spiritual Aspects of Group Conflicts*. New York: The Workshop for Cultural Democracy, 1957, p. 13.

projecting, an unintegrated complex which throws its image outward onto some available object. Jung, in a rather different context, it is true, refers to the "great shadow which Christianity [has] not assimilated."[1] It is no violation of his observation to say that anti-Semitism is also a shadow which has long gone unassimilated by non-Jewish races, Christian or otherwise.

Overt anti-Semitism is observable. It may express itself only verbally, in derogatory or insulting remarks about Jews in general or an individual Jew in particular, on the one hand, or on the other, in acts of violence directed at the objects of the prejudice. Covert anti-Semitism, however, is oftentimes quite subtle, frequently betraying an inner bias hidden by outer expressions either of neutrality or even of pro-Semitism – of the "some-of-my-best-friends-are-Jews" variety. In some cases, the individual may be consciously convinced that he is not an anti-Semite at all, that he does not have an anti-Semitic bone in his body. Sometimes, however, such bones will out. When the prime minister of France, expressing his outrage at the bombing of a synagogue in Paris, declared that, "They aimed at the Jews and they hit innocent Frenchmen," there is good reason to understand him to have said in effect that the Jews who were present in the synagogue were neither French nor innocent, a type of concealed, perhaps "innocent," prejudice slipping through a public expression of sympathy.

Deep, inherited racial prejudice probably lurks somewhere in the hearts of all of us, the type of prejudice varying according to culture, race, religion. It is something visceral, something circulating in the blood. There is a sentimental song in the Rodgers and Hammerstein musical, *South Pacific*, which melodiously declares that, "you've got to be taught to hate all the people your relatives hate, you've got to be carefully taught." Unfortunately, this does not always seem to conform to reality. One *can* be taught to hate, of course, and many are so taught; such teaching then intensifies the latent prejudice. But from where does the hatred come which is not taught? And, if our relatives hate, who taught them? It must go back to some original hatred which was not taught, but surfaced from somewhere in the cold, uncivilized inner depths.

---

[1] Jung, C.G., *Psychological Types*. Vol. 6 of the *Collected Works*. Princeton: Princeton University Press, 1971, par. 422.

If, in the anti-Black phenomenon, we hate the shadowy dark corners of our own nature, what latent characteristic might we be hating in ourselves where the Jew serves as a "hook" for our projection?

Anti-Black racism clearly has its hook mechanism in two characteristics of Black people: color and so-called primitivity. Color is conspicuously there; all Blacks have some degree of dark skin, and the darkest skins are the more racially pure. Primitivity, however, is a notoriously relative thing. Many Blacks in present-day Africa, such as the Bushmen of the Kalahari Desert, befriended and loved by van der Post, still live to some extent under Stone-Age circumstances, although their isolation from the outer world is fading these days. When Sir Laurens made his second documentary about the Bushmen in 1986, he ended his commentary with the melancholy observation that contemporary Bushmen are being more and more drawn into the demeaning ambience of "civilization." Stone-Age characteristics will inevitably cling, however, and insofar as Black Africans retain them, they may still seem primitive to non-Blacks. Primitivity, however, has its psychological values, its natural insights, its instinctual reverence for the physical world; as Jung frequently makes clear, the psychic health of the primitive, especially his ability to "follow his instinct without difficulty,"[1] and his freedom from "one-sidedness,"[2] are values which men in contemporary white civilizations have surrendered in their mania for technology, for rationalism, for a one-sided psychic development.

Still, the old condescending view of the primitive sticks. He still appears to represent something undeveloped, undifferentiated, unattractive and undesirable – a palpable object for rejection.

Color and putative primitivity prejudice the non-Black against the Black man, however irrational it may be. Both color and primitiveness look backward to a time when all men were equally primitive. Whites have lost the values of such early states – as indeed have many modern Blacks – and something in them knows that they are losers. And something secretly resents observing it in those who still possess some measure of it.

---

[1] Jung, C.G., *Collected Works*, Volume 6, par. 422.
[2] Ibid., par. 346. Cf. also *Collected Works*, Vol. 8, par. 95.

Perhaps the roots of anti-Semitism may also lie in a comparable secret resentment, a resentment which, in the case of the Jew, would not be traceable all the way back to Stone-Age man, but rather to the early history of the Jews themselves, a people who introduced monotheism, the belief in one god, into man's developing image of the godhead.

Traditionally, the religion of the Jews was the result of a covenant with that one god, Jahweh (or Jehovah, as the English version of the Old Testament has it), a covenant which specified that Abraham and his descendants were chosen by Jahweh to carry the message of one god to all mankind. Unfortunately – for the Jews themselves – from the time that news of this covenant reached the gentile world, a secondary aspect (that it was the Jews who were chosen, that they were then God's favored people), rather than the primary element (that the idea of one god, instead of a plurality of gods and goddesses, was the next great step in the formation of the creative deity), became a stumbling block for non-Jews. That the Jew was chosen to introduce a new understanding of the godhead was clouded over by the suggestion that God was only interested in the Hebrew race. A notion which may very well have been encouraged by the Jew himself, in an understandable sense of inflation, as the result of being so chosen.

The imputation that non-Jewish peoples were of secondary interest to Jahweh was one which would inevitably promote a feeling in the gentile that he was considered to be a second-class citizen in the eyes of God, a feeling which would inevitably be resented, resisted and rejected.

It is only too human, when placed in a secondary position of any sort, to turn against those responsible for having placed you there, never mind the fact that consciously you do not feel second-rate at all; on the contrary, the imputation of however relative an inferiority merely fuels a conviction of superiority, and, in a reversal of attitudes, the peoples not chosen by God begin to assemble reasons for believing they are the more civilized, the more humane, the more admirable.

The two ethnic entities in this historical interplay of superiority-inferiority are what are known today as the Semitic and Aryan races – although the two are somewhat inaccurate as racial descriptions, being basically linguistic rather than ethnological terms.[1] The other Semites, the Arabs, remained uninfected by the mushrooming antipathies toward Jewish Semites until the twentieth century, when

political developments gave rise to a growing hostility toward some
Arab peoples. Mohammedans accepted the Jews' Jesus as another
prophet in a long line of prophets, a line in which Mohammed himself
was the last and greatest.

What was – or what soon became – a paradoxical aspect of the
historically developing anti-Semitism of the Christian was the curious but incontrovertible fact that the Christian god was himself a Jew
– simply lending support to the original Jewish conviction that it
would be through the people so chosen to do so that a savior of
mankind, an incarnation of the godhead, would descend into the
human world.

Why, one wonders, did the Christianized nations turn so violently
during some decades of their history against the very people who gave
them their new god, so to speak? The old argument that the Jews
killed Jesus persisted for many centuries, but it was a rather weak
rationalization for the secret reason behind the social exclusion, the
ghettos, the pogroms.

God, the Son, sad to say, was not an Aryan. That strange fact must
have seemed offensive to those Aryans convinced of their superior
status among the races. It would be unthinkable to find God himself
guilty of such a lapse of taste; the hatred must be directed toward the
instrument of his incarnation, the Jews themselves. That this is quite
illogical – as long as one adheres to a literal interpretation of
Christian mythology – seems to have made little difference. Emotional energies are notoriously illogical, however they may express
themselves. Resentment against the Creator for having come down
onto earth as a Jew is an insult to the Aryan – an unconscious insult,
probably, but the unconscious is not so meticulous about such
matters. Consequently, this personal insult must be turned into an
accusation against the Jew of whatever negative qualities come to
mind: greed, deviousness, arrogance, criminality, even murder, especially ritual murder of gentile children.

There seems to be little documentary evidence of this hypothetical
subjective pattern among those who have kept anti-Semitism alive
through the centuries of the Christian aeon until its cataclysmic
eruption in the 1930s. There is one instance, however, of a recorded
remark which does reveal such a pattern – not exactly hidden, in this

---

[1] Bernard Lewis, *Semites and Anti-Semites: An Inquiry into Conflict and Prejudice*. New York/London: W. W. Norton & Company, 1986, pp. 45ff.

instance. The Prince de Ligne was once a guest of Voltaire and was obliged to listen for several days to his host's prejudices, both anti-Christian and anti-Jewish. The Prince noted that, "the only reason why M. de Voltaire gave vent to such outbursts against Jesus Christ is that he was born among a nation whom he detested."

Hitler's anti-Semitism was apocalyptic. But he was also not moved by any great pro-Christian convictions. What he championed was not Christianity, but Aryanism;[1] the god-given (whether God of the Christians or some Germanic pagan god) superiority of the Aryan race, especially that of the Nordic branch, was the driving force behind his program for destroying forms of non-Aryan life in order to make the world – or, at any rate, Europe – clean, healthy and strong for its blonde inhabitants. (That the second object of his determination to eliminate racial impurities was the Gypsies was another example of his irrationality, for Gypsies are in no sense a Semitic people.)

If such a dynamic was – or still is – operative in those who are overtly or covertly anti-Semitic – hatred of the Jew because the Christian god was a Jew rather than an Aryan – then what form of psychic dynamism would have been projected onto the Jew?

Our killer shadow, because the Jew killed the god? This was a conscious operative during earlier periods in Jewish-Christian relations; today, however, this notion that the Jews crucified Jesus is only a clouded historical detail. Pilate may have washed his hands, but his Roman soldiers hung the Nazarine to the cross. Crucifixion was common and frequent throughout the Roman Empire; there is no instance in history of Jews ever having crucified anyone: it was not their style of punishment. They did choose Barabbas instead of Jesus and thereby indirectly decided the fate of the latter. But then his fate had been preordained by the Father himself. So that, from a somewhat deterministic point of view, the Jew had no choice but to choose Barabbas. If they had *not* chosen him, what would have happened to the Father's cosmic plan for mankind's redemption? Could anyone have sidetracked the divine program?

Something rather more far-reaching than a distorted historical event must be operative today, something from an even darker psychic chasm.

---

[1] Ibid., pp. 115-16.

If, with Black racism, the non-Black is projecting his own blackness – that is, his personal shadow – onto the Black man, is the
Christian – and today the Mohammedan – projecting a subjective
Jewish nature onto the Jew? That is to say, projecting those inferior
qualities which he tends to observe in the Jew, whether they are
literally there or not, onto the people who are psychologically as black
for him as is the literal Black. At first sight, this may seem a rather
commonplace mechanism; on closer inspection, it may perhaps not
be so commonplace after all.

As the libel that Jews were god-killers died over the centuries, there
did remain the justifiable observation that the Jew rejected Jesus as
the messiah. Can the Christian be projecting onto the Jew his own
secret rejection of Jesus as the Christ? And to what extent would such
a projection also operate in a non-Christian non-Jew? Such a
dynamic would obviously be no conscious rejection; the acceptance
of Jesus as God is the very essence of Christianity. But throughout the
twenty centuries of its existence, the Christian Church has a troubled
history of betraying the teachings of the man whom it considers to be
its special god. The list of crimes committed in Christ's name are
matters of history. It is as though Christianity were merely a veneer
covering something rather less humane than it appears to be on the
surface.

The shadow pattern projected onto the black is a pattern from the
more available images of the unconscious, from, that is, the personal
layer. The projections of large collective images spring from areas far
less accessible to consciousness; and when it is a matter of gods (or
goddesses, as the case may be), then we are touching the great
archetypal ocean.

If, in our most distant natures, we never really quite became
Christianized, then the old gods would still be lurking within us. As
inheritors of the Judaeo-Christian tradition, Jahweh, with all his
jealousy, vindictiveness and murderous impulses, would be very
much alive in us, not only in the unconscious of the Jew, but also of
the Christian. And behind Jahweh, the more ancient of the darker
deities: Moloch, Set, Teshup, Baal, Ahriman, Esus, Wotan. As Jung
observed, the latter emerged cataclysmically in Germany in our own
century; he was not only still alive, he was healthy and bursting with
rage and suppressed violence.

As Jung also so often noted, our dreams show that the pagan deities
are indeed still with us, in the chaos of the unconscious. We seem to

ourselves to be so civilized, so Christianized, so sane and rational, but we are still generations away from having reached any desirable goal of human behavior. After all, the history of earthly man extends backward into thousands of centuries; in only a recent few can any significant markings of consciousness be observed. It is little wonder that the dark gods who served as carriers of the numinous for countless eons have never vanished from our unconscious selves.

Is our rejection of the Jew as a rejector of the latest manifestation of the godhead, then, a projection of our own rejection of our inner pagan deities? Such a mechanism could be equally true of the non-Christian, who has just as unfathomable a reserve of pagan gods as any so-called Christian.

Van der Post has thrown illuminating beams on our rejection of the Black man as a rejection of our own dark shadow nature. But behind our personal shadow lie the deep collective archetypes, figured sometimes in dreams as pre-historic deities. Perhaps all racial prejudice reflects in some way a form of inner rejection, which twentieth century man may just be beginning to understand about himself. At any rate, it would not be unrealistic to suppose that, if and when we ever withdraw these powerful racial projections, we may find that we are at last free of the need to visit upon others the sins of both our fathers and ourselves.

A Small Word

John Charlton

Laurens van der Post has always been the most appreciative of authors. It was over sixty years ago, in September, 1933, when Leonard Woolf wrote to him offering to publish *In a Province,* his first book, under the imprint of The Hogarth Press, and he replied at once in that unassuming manner that is still characteristically his today: "I am so grateful to you for the trouble you have taken about *In a Province* and gratefully accept your offer to publish it next Spring on the terms you suggested." In that simple, unqualified response lies one of the keys to his sensibility. There, right at the start, may be seen not only his unfailing gratitude to others for any help or support they may have given (and which he has always been wonderfully quick to recognise), but also the basic trust on which his long, fruitful and harmonious association with The Hogarth Press was founded.

Some forty years later, Laurens described how important this bond of trust had been to him:

> *The relationship between a writer and his publisher, like all things worthwhile, is complex, exacting and at its best an art, more than a business – an art moreover which is by the day less well understood and therefore increasingly inaccurate, uncreative and unworthy in practice. At its best it presupposes an act of faith, a common loyalty and continuing trust which enables both writer and publisher to leap as it were without hesitating into the dark of new areas of mind and communication, and unless the publisher has something also of the artist within himself he tends to look too much and leap too little and so fail both the writer and himself in their main function of making their time more aware of itself.*

This was written in 1976, in a privately circulated collection of tributes to Ian Parsons, his long-standing friend and publisher, who, in Laurens' words, "… took over for me where Virginia and Leonard Woolf left off":

I met Ian first in those blind and desperate years between the Spanish Civil War and the Second World War and knew him briefly as a poet without any inkling that he would one day be my publisher. … When I came back from nine years of war, he had not only become a senior partner of Chatto & Windus but had joined forces with The Hogarth Press, who had published my first book, In a Province, *when everybody else for years had rejected it. Although Virginia Woolf was dead, Leonard Woolf, who had founded The Hogarth Press with her, was still alive, and I thought it a vindication of Leonard's exceptionally intuitive perception, as well as poetic justice, that he should have discovered a natural ally in Ian and his firm. Had Chatto's and The Hogarth Press not been made for each other, as it were, I do not think I could have stayed with them both these forty years and more.*

Laurens went on:

Both Virginia and Leonard Woolf were of course considerable artists in their own right and gifted naturally with an acute insight into the aboriginal nature of the writer and his almost primitive vulnerability in the sophisticated and ruthless world wherever his work has to be peddled. The poet in Ian made certain that this rare insight was firmly established and transformed into living tradition in the Chatto-Hogarth condominium.

Eight years later, Laurens was to take up the same theme again, this time in public, in a moving tribute to "the incomparable Norah Smallwood," who succeeded Ian Parsons as Chairman and Managing Director of The Hogarth Press, and who had played a central role in both firms throughout the post-war years. The occasion was a service held in her memory at the church of St. Martin-in-the-Fields on 29 November, 1984, when he gave the address, combining once again the themes of trust and gratitude:

Publishing at its best, as I have found it over some fifty-five years as a writer, is ultimately far more of an art than a purely exact business or economic science. … [Norah] knew that the sense of the artist and the condition of complete trust between writer and publisher is necessary if publishing is not to become a mere repetition of the successful platitudes and writing patterns of yesterday. …

As one illustration of this condition of trust established between The Hogarth Press, Chatto's, Norah and her writers, I would quote from my own experience – and I am certain there are many others who can do so as effectively. It is simply this: I have never had any other publisher except Hogarth. Indeed, I have never even found it necessary to employ an agent. From the beginning, I was more than content to leave it all – translation rights, film rights, television rights, the whole lot – in the hands of my publishers, which ultimately for some twenty-five years meant the hands of Norah. Not only had I no reason ever to regret it, but many to be grateful for it, because it gave me unusual freedom to concentrate solely on my work.

Norah Smallwood had died the month before, Ian Parsons in 1980, Leonard Woolf in 1969. The days of The Hogarth Press as a separate publishing entity were over, the links in that long continuity of trust almost at an end. Would this mean for Laurens the loss of the 'unusual freedom' to get on with his own writing?

That it did not is largely due to Laurens himself. In the first place, his capacity for engaging the loyalty of others, that 'common loyalty' which from the very beginning has meant so much to him as a writer, did not dry up, nor, I believe, will it ever desert him. He will always win the loyalty and goodwill of those who work with him, if only because he himself contributes so much towards the essential bond of mutual trust. Secondly, the confidence which over the years he has felt able to place in his publishers has never been blind or idealised. Laurens is well aware of the practical aspects of publishing and bookselling, and he knows too the limitations and shortcomings of people, including publishers, which are to be found in any human endeavour, even the most creative and worthwhile. And thirdly, along with this understanding and lack of illusion has gone a remarkable degree of tolerance.

He describes his fifty years with The Hogarth Press as "publishing at its best," yet he did not always receive the support he must have hoped for, even from those whose opinions he valued most highly. More than once when he had handed in the typescript of a new book, he was warned that, although it was of great interest, it was "rather difficult" and "may not be easy to sell." After this muted reaction, it was perhaps no surprise that the announcement copy was sometimes less than full-blooded and even lapsing on the side of understatement. Laurens knows this. In fact, it was he who told me about the recurring pattern of low-key response to his new books. But when he did so, in a casual conversation, what struck me most was that he made the remark so lightly, merely in passing, with no sense of grievance or hurt, no blame, just a mild amusement tinged with the faintest trace of resignation. That resignation could so easily have been resentment, and doubtless would have been for many people who do not have his generosity of spirit.

I could cite other examples of that tolerance which has been such a source of strength to him over the years and which, I feel sure, must have eased for him the uncertain transition from fifty years of security with The Hogarth Press to a new era with Chatto & Windus. This began in 1985, when the first four titles in a new collected edition of his writings appeared under the Chatto imprint. It continued in 1986 when, for the first time, a new book of his, *A Walk With a White Bushman,* came out not from The Hogarth Press, but from Chatto. Now, this may not seem a significant departure to anyone who recalls the passage I quoted earlier, where Laurens explained how the two firms had joined forces after the war and, with their matching approach to publishing, had formed 'the Chatto-Hogarth condominium.' Nor did it seem at all drastic to me, who had worked with equal commitment to both firms for the past twenty years, and who knew that they had in effect been operating as one ever since Leonard Woolf's death. He had been the only post-war director of The Hogarth Press who had not also been a director of Chatto & Windus. Ian Parsons, Norah Smallwood, Cecil Day-Lewis and indeed everyone in the office did their daily work for authors of The Hogarth Press exactly as they did for Chatto authors. No distinction was made between them, with the result that, in time, and certainly by the 1980s, it became artificial to maintain the two separate imprints for our new publications.

For Laurens, however, it was not as straightforward as that, although none of us knew it at the time. We knew that he was unwaveringly loyal to The Hogarth Press and ever grateful to the Woolfs for publishing his first book; but given the wholescale integration of the two firms that had long been a fact of our working lives, the idea never occurred to us, or to me anyway, that Laurens might have anything against Chatto. Nor did he give us any cause to think so, even when the switch to the Chatto imprint was made. It was not until late last year, shortly before his eightieth birthday, that I found out. And even then, so brief and slight was his reference that I wasn't immediately sure I had heard it correctly. But yes, on checking our records, it proved to be true: Chatto had indeed been offered *In a Province* the year before it was taken on by The Hogarth Press, and had turned it down.

Not long after this discovery, and as near to Laurens' eightieth birthday as we could, we published *A Walk With a White Bushman;* and then on 12 December, the eve of his birthday, we held a luncheon in his honour at the Garrick Club in London. It was a heart-warming occasion, heightened by the presence of Laurens' American publisher for over thirty years, Larry Hughes of William Morrow, who had flown over from New York specially to celebrate Laurens' birthday – another example of the loyalty that he both gives and engenders. And at that lunch, I took the opportunity of trying to thank Laurens for the rare trust he had bestowed upon us, as upon our predecessors, and in particular to say how greatly we valued the forgiveness that was implicit in his transfer of allegiance to Chatto, the firm which, I now knew, had turned him down when he was a young and unknown writer.

Laurens, appreciative as ever, lost no time in writing to thank us all 'for what you gave me,' and asked me please to tell my colleagues 'how deeply, deeply grateful I am, and encouraged, and shall certainly write more because of it than I could have done without it. Why is gratitude so small a word?'

A small word, perhaps, but one which has always ranked high in his perceptions and in his values. This is no coincidence. Over Christmas, I happened to be reading *A Mantis Carol* and found there, on page 80 of the Hogarth Press edition, a heartfelt credo and ringing confirmation of what gratitude means to him:

> 'Bitterness, resentment, hatred at the end over
> what life has given one, I believe, is defeat;
> gratitude despite all, victory.'

By that measure, and if our experience of Laurens as an author is anything to go by, as I am certain it is, his life has not just been a victory, but a triumph.

*Sir Laurens with Yoyo Ma during preparations for the
latter's documentary film, London, 1993*

Reflecting Upon *Yet Being Someone Other*

Lawrence Hughes

I am examining the front cover of one of Laurens van der Post's books. It is a paperback edition of *Yet Being Someone Other*, which I recall purchasing at Hatchard's in London on the afternoon of the thirteenth of December 1986, a Friday. I remember the date so exactly because I had just come from a luncheon party given by The Hogarth Press in honor of Sir Laurens' eightieth birthday. It had been a warm and nostalgic occasion, a small gathering – mixing members of Laurens' own family with those of his publishing families.

I had arrived by plane from New York that very morning, and I remarked to Laurens that, as a result of my inclusion as a guest, the group now numbered thirteen at table. He immediately put me at my ease by reminding me that his birthday was on the thirteenth day of the month, that he was the thirteenth child in a family of fifteen – and that once, when thrown into a prison cell by the Japanese with the angry shout that he would be executed in the morning, he had taken courage from the fact that the cell number was thirteen.

Upon each occasion that I have seen Laurens, since first meeting him twenty-seven years ago, I have learned something new about his remarkable life. This luncheon had already proved to be no exception.

Later, as I walked down Piccadilly toward Hatchard's, I had thought about the party. Laurens had told about his early attempts to be published, unsuccessfully, until E.M. Forster delivered him into the caring hands of Virginia and Leonard Woolf, founders of The Hogarth Press. Also, Laurens and Elspeth Huxley, the only other author in attendance, talked about the recent film, *Out of Africa,* and whether the portrayals by Meryl Streep and Robert Redford of Isak Dinesen and Denys George Finch Hatton had borne a resemblance to the living persons whom Laurens and Miss Huxley had known. To hear these two great tellers of tales converse on Africa, the continent they know so well and have taught us so much about, had been for me a heady experience.

But I have found that one never gets enough of Laurens van der Post, which of course was why I had headed for a London bookstore. I particularly wanted to reread *Yet Being Someone Other*. As its publisher in the United States, I had read the work prior to publication some four years before. It was the closest Laurens had come to writing an autobiography, although as we know, Laurens' work taken together is the story of his life.

The front cover of the edition I purchased shows a recent photograph of Laurens. He is looking straight on at the reader with those clear eyes that have seen so much of this world – its jungles, deserts, oceans, plains and palaces. His hair is blown by the wind. Obviously the photograph was taken outdoors. I suddenly realized that, although almost every time I have met with Laurens it has been indoors – at his home, in a restaurant, at a reception, or in the offices of William Morrow, where I work. When I think of him, it is always as being outdoors. Then when I think of his books, I know why. He is not the kind of writer one associates with immobility.

On the cover between the author's credit and the title, there is a publisher's blurb that reads, "'There is no one else in whose company I would rather spend five hours,' Auberon Waugh in the *Sunday Telegraph*." As a fellow publisher, I admire the selling quality of the blurb. As someone who has had the privilege of knowing Laurens, I feel the quotation is inadequate. I think to myself, "There is no one else alive whom I would prefer to stand beside me in times of stress or danger or ethical predicament." Somehow, I believe Laurens van der Post would lead me out or show me the right way.

The first person to introduce me to Laurens was his then-editor at Morrow, Frances Phillips, who told me, "You will find that Laurens van der Post has the command presence of a Colonel of the Regiment and the spiritual presence of a saint." Frances was not off the mark.

I leaf through the book until I come to one of a number of pages where I have turned down the corner. Laurens writes:

> *But I had never felt my longing privileged enough, nor my gift suffi-*
> *ciently great, to allow me to be only a writer. There seemed to me mo-*
> *ments in a desperate time when one had also to do and act on the*
> *ordinary everyday human scene. Art and writing, it seemed, ultimate-*
> *ly demanded not only expression in their own idiom but also trans-*

lation into behaviour and action on the part of their begetters. Being and doing, doing and being, for me were profoundly interdependent, particularly in a world where increasingly it seemed to me the 'doers' did not think and the thinkers did not 'do.' But if I had to lay an emphasis on any one of these considerations which faced me as a result of Desmond's cable, it would have been on the 'being.' In the Western World to which I belonged, all the stress was on the 'doing' without awareness of the importance to it of the 'being.' Somewhere in this over-balance of contemporary spirit, there appeared to be an increasing loss of meaning through the growing failure to realise how 'being' was in itself primal action, and that at the core of 'being' was a dynamic element of 'becoming' which gave life its quality and from which it derived its values and overall sense of direction. Because of a lack of such 'being', we were constantly in danger of becoming too busy to live. I longed to 'do' as a consequence of my 'being', but feared the busyness of my day like a plague.

"Constantly in danger of becoming too busy to live." It is the curse of the world in which we as publishers operate. Often too busy to read with understanding and too busy to think with patience. In short: ours is the danger of becoming too busy to live. As usual, Laurens van der Post goes right to the heart of the matter.

I close my book and turn it over, and while I do so I am thinking of the great personal friendship Laurens and his wife, Ingaret, have given to me and my wife, Rose, and of the immense loyalty, often uncalled for, which he has shown to the publishing house of Morrow and to the many people, myself included, who have had the exhilarating honor and pleasure to bring the work of Laurens van der Post to many thousands of American readers.

I am examining the back of *Yet Being Someone Other*. At the bottom of the cover, a reviewer for the *Spectator* writes, "I have no words at my command to suggest the stature of this man ... one cannot risk skipping any page of this book for fear of missing something astonishing." It could not be better said.

A Letter From Rosamond

Rosamond Lehmann

I feel both proud and pleased to be invited to contribute to this volume collected in honour of Sir Laurens van der Post. The idea is a splendid one, and I can only hope that what I have to say will not be thought too inadequate. My dear friend Laurens knows already, I think, that I am hampered nowadays by indifferent health and severely impaired eyesight. I cannot present him with a learned paper or a work of creative imagination, as I should like to. This is simply a personal note commemorating our long, strange and deeply valued friendship: long in terms of earth time, and strange because – owing to the numerous calls upon his energies – we meet but rarely nowadays, and yet, when we do meet, it is as if we were resuming a familiar relationship after only a slight break in it. Perhaps I flatter myself: it may be that his exceptional gift of empathy gives all his friends and acquaintances a similar impression. Be that as it may, here is my letter:

Dearest Laurens,

Do you remember our first meeting? It was at a little dinner party in a London restaurant, soon after your return from the Far East. Ingaret was with you, of course, and another guest was William Plomer. I already knew from him something of the prolonged unimaginable ordeal which you had undergone in Japanese prison camps. I expected to feel the kind of awe and tension one is bound to sense in the presence of one who has endured intolerable suffering. I did feel it. I did see it, like the residue of experiences forever graven in you; but far more potent was the impression you gave of spiritual strength, sanity, humour, wisdom and integrity. It was a delightful social occasion and others must have followed it; but the original essential image of you persisted, and caused me to turn to you during a bad time in my private life; and again, later, in my darkest hour. Once, in a letter, you advised me to "trust my unhappiness." I had not thought of doing so, but I tried it, and found it had a curiously comforting and liberating effect. Much later, in that darkest hour – I mean the death in Java of my beautiful young daughter, Sally –, I rang you up on an irresistible impulse and said: "Please come." You were there, it seemed to me, almost immediately, and I was able to stammer out something of the overwhelming mystical experiences that were lifting me into dimensions of consciousness hitherto undreamed of. You could not stay long, and I don't remember what you said or did; but I know you gave me a moment of complete understanding and re-assurance. You were, in fact, the first witness to the *metanoia* that broke my hitherto unawakened life in two, and enabled me gradually to rebuild it until I could say, as Jung once said of life after death, "I don't believe, I know."

Some years later, I wrote and told you I wanted to write about these experiences but didn't know how to set about it. You suggested a certain shape and pattern for the work, and almost at once, I started to write a book called, *The Swan in the Evening*, a testament presented so warily and anxiously because of the climate of the times, and yet which, over the years, has become almost a best-seller. I think of you always as having been, in a sense, that book's godfather.

Dear Laurens, I am six years ahead of you in earth time, and my great grandchildren tell me I am very old and sure to die soon. This is true, and I look forward to the event. I know very well that old age is a meaningless term because, to put it in a banal way, and in spite of frustrating limitations and handicaps, one goes on feeling "just the same inside." That is because the true Self in each one of us continues to tell us that there is no place for death considered as extinction in the Universe; that we are, each one of us, bound on an immortal journey far beyond human comprehension, but never meaningless. Perhaps you were born knowing this, or perhaps, like me, you learned it the hardest way.

I think of you constantly, Laurens; and though I wish I saw you more frequently, I feel that separation does not matter, because you are a real part of my consciousness, although our activities and destinies have been so different. I wish I had been able to be present at your eightieth birthday party, and I hope it was a joyous occasion.

Your life, I suppose, must be nearing the end of this particular tremendous chapter, but I hope you will stay here a while longer, because you are so badly needed. I dream that we may meet again somehow, in further realms of Being. I cherish a fantasy of meeting you in some Elysian jungle of Africa and going on a safari with you as my guide; and seeing tigers burning bright, not with blood lust but with celestial fire; of lions lying down with lambs and all the magnificent creatures of the beloved land of your birth peaceful, fearless, happily at play. (I am told that there are no crocodiles or snakes in the next world, and I am very glad to hear it.)

To end on a more serious note, your marvellous books are always with me. I want to send you my heartfelt thanks for all of them, but particularly, perhaps, for *Jung and the Story of Our Time*, which is a kind of Bible for me. I see you and Jung standing shoulder to shoulder, two uniquely great benefactors, symbols of hope for humanity in this turbulent century.

God bless you.

> Ever with admiration, gratitude and love,
> your friend,
> Rosamond

A Threesome of Friends

Jessica Douglas-Home

It is well known that Laurens has been an important influence and source of inspiration in our time. What is less well known is the manner in which this influence and inspiration take effect. One person will, of course, differ substantially from another. Nevertheless, I shall offer a few thoughts – inevitably very personal – about two instances of Laurens' influence, and I hope they will serve to suggest a more general picture. The two cases I have in mind are the leaders of the *Times* newspaper, whose impact on the world has been quite considerable, and my own work as a painter, which has involved no comparable attempt to change the world, but only to express my experience of it.

It was in consequence of reading Laurens' books and much later talking to Laurens, that I was first led to C.G. Jung. I began studying the works of the great psychologist, and in due course was guided to those parts of his thought most relevant to my own artistic efforts. At the time I was attending the Slade School of Fine Art. Because it happened to have no central meeting place, the students had nowhere to go for informal discussions during their breaks. I would therefore spend those periods alone, reading – and by no means always about art. It is of course true that painters are influenced by painters, and learn their art from others who also practice it. But it is also true, in painting as in any other form of artistic expression, that the key experiences, the ones which bring with them a vision of order and harmony, often come from outside – and in particular from the work of writers. At heart this is true for me. Certain writers have provided me with a magic key, offering both a clearer understanding of the world, and a sense of its inner coherence. In this way, I have been given many ideas for paintings.

Of the writers who have conveyed such illuminations to me, Laurens has been among the most outstanding. Moreover, it is not only through his writings that he has had an effect. He has also influenced me as a friend, whose counsels and conversations I shall always remember with gratitude. When I think, now, of his writings, they are, for me, inextricably linked with his companionship, which provides indeed a kind of commentary on them. Laurens has also influenced me in a third, and for me surprising way. Although, as I said, I discovered Jung through Laurens, it was not until seeing his film about Jung, made for the BBC, that I felt the full impact of this extraordinary thinker. That film was, indeed, a landmark in my life, as I think it must have been in the lives of many other people.

I later heard Laurens give a talk at the memorial service of the poet William Plomer. This talk made a profound impression on me. I felt that Laurens had built a bridge across what, until then, had seemed to me an impassable gulf between the rational mind and the life of the spirit. Like so much of Laurens' work, it struck me like a homecoming from a place of estrangement. I described the lecture to my husband Charlie, whose interest was aroused. Shortly afterwards, while working on a book about Kenya, Charlie met Laurens for the first time. A deep friendship quickly developed between us and Laurens and Ingaret – a friendship which was enormously important, both for myself and for Charlie.

Between 1976 and 1982, I began to work in a new way and with a new inspiration. And looking back on that period now, through the inevitable changes of style and interest that have come after it, I realize that it is to Laurens, and to Charlie, that I owe the creative energy of that time, when ideas were constantly emerging from the discussions we had together, and when Laurens introduced us to so many of his favourite themes from Jung. Painters are often required to write some notes in the catalogue produced for their exhibitions. In two shows – one in 1977, the other in 1982 – I drew on these discussions, in order to explain what it was that motivated my paintings. I showed the notes to Charlie and Laurens, and they approved them; though for me it was only in the paintings that I had found a language for the feelings which preoccupied me.

Charlie derived as much from Laurens as I did. I was already familiar, when we met, with the works of Jung; Charlie was not. But, tutored by Laurens, he came to know them, and to find in them a spiritual breadth and a sense of the sacred which were to make an enormous impact on his writing, and, through his writing, on the world. Charlie's appointment as editor of the *Times* gave him a unique opportunity to reflect on the condition of mankind, and to convey his thoughts in his own vivid way to the educated public. Often he would discuss his leaders with Laurens, and when he touched on those aspects of the modern world which must be discussed with especial gravity – I think particularly of religion, art and morality, but also of the ever present spectre of communism, with its untiring war against the human soul – the inspiration of Laurens could always be felt. Charlie's interests were broad, but no broader than those of Laurens, who had found in the many diverse things that engaged his attention a unifying thread of consolation. The calm of Laurens can be felt too in Charlie's leaders; even in the midst of terrible suffering, he was able to write with profundity and humour of the many things that demand an editor's attention. It was for this reason that Charlie's leaders were so much appreciated by the readers of the *Times*, who found in them a good sense and authority which are increasingly rare in modern journalism. Without Laurens, Charlie's leaders might never have ranged so widely or so deeply; certainly they would not have possessed such a deep sense of the life of the spirit.

When I heard Laurens speaking in memory of William Plomer, I did not know that I was again to hear him speak in memory of a good man. This time the subject of his talk was Charlie, who was to die tragically in 1985. As I listened to Laurens' words, I thought back to that other talk he had given, and to all the difference it had wrought in my life and Charlie's. And I had reason, then, to be grateful to this extraordinary man who had given to my husband some of the secret of his own spiritual calm.

In his ninth decade, Laurens continues to serve as a conductor and counsellor – one whose insight into man's condition will be a lasting benefit for present and future generations.

Long may he continue.

A Lesson from War

William Pitt Root

… I enclose what I hope may be a fittingly brief nod in the right direction. I wrote it in Viet Nam, where Laurens was never far from my thoughts:

A LESSON FROM WAR
for Laurens van der Post

When men, heavy-booted, thrash
through reeds towards the river, river
offers up its heron, shows us how to fly.

Among the things I had in mind in writing this piece was Laurens' account of the ersatz university he helped establish in prison on Java and the long-term effects it had on those who partook in it.

All best,
William Pitt Root

On Becoming

Harry A. Wilmer

*After much toil and labour, one comes to the summit of the moun-
tain. Now he must descend the mountain with utmost care and return to the ordinary daily life on earth. We call such a person the
'Great Fool.' Rusty [The great Sage Tokuun was described as an old
rusty gimlet. A new gimlet is sharp and useful. An old rusty gimlet is
dull though still a gimlet.] he may look, but a true gimlet without
doubt. Though ordinary and inconspicuous he may remain, he has
a serene, lucid atmosphere around him. Anybody that comes in
touch with him will be enveloped in it. This is the ideal Zen personality. People of the East, from olden days, have had the tendency to
revere such personalities.*

Zenkei Shibayama[1]

When you talk about BEING AND BECOMING
the state of *being* is to be
satisfied with oneself as one is
without having to project into the future
some better state.

To get to this some better state
one must have come through BECOMING.
And now being in that better state
all you have to be is to be
who and what you are right now.

To want to become again is to want too much.
It is to keep growing all one's life

---

[1] *A Flower Does Not Talk*, Charles E. Tuttle Co., Rutland, Vermont, 1972,
pp. 136-137.

in the outer achievement world
when the inner growth is what occurs
with being.

Becoming was how you got here.
Being is where you are.
Being content is not pushing for anything more.
And that means also waiting for what comes
and then you may take that if you wish.

In the times of becoming you were many places
To which you cannot return any more.
You are now being
and being is its own reward.
It is not happiness;
it is not high;
it is not low.
It is somewhere in between.
At the interpenetration of the spirit and the material worlds.

The connection of Becoming-Being
is the reality of the here and now
when past, present and future are
for the time being
the same
Is there any other reality at this moment?
We are in search of a compass of being
which points both/and
east-west
north-south
hot-cold
yin-yang
masculine-feminine
ad-infinitum-ad.

Listen to me, the wounded healer,
learning from the wounded who came my way seeking
another way
to bear the tension
to quest in the ordinary struggle of horrendous life that
which seems to each of us so extraordinary.

Looking inward.

Reflecting in the light of introversion
is not high on the American agenda of ringing
The clarion calls of
outgoing, doing, action, and know-how
Sitting quietly, being alone without being lonely
is being.
Action and doing are forever becoming.

Becoming – Being follow one another.
Becoming more characteristic of the first half of life
The second half is nourished by being.
Yet we are always
both being and becoming.
Each day has a first and a second half.
It is in each indivisible moment
that we are what we are
where we might be in the realm of
the nonbeing.

In the *Tao* Chuang Tsu said,
"Being is without dwelling place.
Continuity is without duration.
Being without dwelling place is space.

Continuity without duration is time.
There is birth, there is death,
there is issuing forth, there is entering in.
That through which one passes in and out
without seeing its form is the Gate of Heaven.
The Gate of Heaven is nonbeing.
All things sprang from nonbeing."

[Ch. XXIII, p. 35, Chang Chung-yuan]

An Australian Tribute
to Laurens van der Post

Edward Dunlop

"The desert shall rejoice and blossom as the rose."
Isaiah XXXV:1

The idea for a celebration of this remarkable man in print under the title, *The Rock Rabbit and the Rainbow,* was originally born in the Year of the Rabbit, which is appropriate. I am aware that in Japan the low-posture, earth-burrowing rabbit is replaced by the larger speedier hare and the term becomes "Year of the Hare." At least the rabbit, whilst a far from popular animal in the antipodes, has not been made a figure of fun as in the fable "The Hare and the Tortoise." Nor is it associated with madness, as attributed to the fictional "March hare."

The rabbit typifies the humble enduring earth spirit, and the rainbow, that luminous many-splendoured arc, raises our thoughts and aspirations to the less attainable world of the spirit itself.

I am often conscious of a nostalgic envy of our Australian aboriginal man living like the Bushman (so dear to Laurens) in close harmony with the earth for which he entertained such reverence, adorning it with the rainbow radiance of "the dreamtime."

The dizzy pace of urban man, dragged behind the chariot wheels of science and materialism, leaves little time for either dreams or their interpretation.

I recall a venerable aboriginal chief of his tribe who summed up one of the impatient peculiarities of European man as:

White fellah plurry funny fellah
always sit down to walk.

My own life spans a period in which there has been an astonishingly rapid intrusion of mechanical power into earth, sea, and sky.

The ringing axes of early days recalled Thomas Gray's imagery:

> *How bowed the woods beneath their sturdy stroke …*

This and the plod of the admirable Clydesdale has been succeeded by the chain saw, and most formidable bull-dozing, earth-moving and chain clearing devices.

I ponder about my devout Presbyterian father walking behind Clydesdale teams and the plough, and at times running the fresh turned fertile soil between his fingers with a sort of reverence for the earth.

I have discerned in the simple peasant people of the earth this same deep reverence. In the Buddhist peoples of South Vietnam and Thailand living close to river, mountain, and jungle, there is an older spiritual concept of the gods of the river and the mountain: the gods of their fathers and mothers, offering kindly security against their becoming "lost and wandering souls" in the hereafter.

I discern in the writings and expressed thoughts of Laurens van der Post a voice and an influence which, shaped without advanced formal education, quite transcends the academics of our day. It speaks with the sensitive insight of a man who drank deeply of a morning of the world atmosphere with an unprejudiced appraisal of the earth, its varied fascinating peoples, and the magical rich stream of life in his beloved Africa.

This accords with my own less developed concept of the Australia Felix of my boyhood, of the smiling earth on the Emu Plains, the Broken River, and the Sheepwash Creek. There was much of horse and hound, the sweet calling of birds, and at night the booming of the bittern across plains beneath the brilliant southern stars.

The somewhat doggerel lines of 'Banjo' Paterson in *Clancy of the Overflow* catches the spirit of those days:

> *And the bush has friends to meet him, and their kindly voices*
> *greet him*
> *In the murmur of the breezes, and the river on its bars*
> *And he sees the vision splendid of the sunlit plains extended*
> *And at night the wondrous glory of the everlasting stars.*

It is true that man was at times tested by fire, flood and drought, fierce contrasts of dust, heat, and frost, and at times plagues of pests: locusts, mice, and, let's face it, rabbits.

For a prudent, patient man there emerged on balance the fullness and richness of the earth. There was the deep satisfaction of hard work in the open air when "the hardest day was never then too hard." (Adam Lindsay Gordon)

To his intimates, Laurens has revealed his San Michele dream, that one day he will recreate for his friends the African ranch life of his boyhood, to be savoured as a magical existence to be enjoyed like the gold at the end of the rainbow.

We did not meet until well after reaching relative maturity. We were serving in World War II. As a boy, I had watched with deep frustration and envy the Anzac's sallying forth to distant lands of epic adventures and romantic overtones of heroism and death. I later met and admired the poet, John Masefield, who wrote:

> *To the Anzacs in the blazing sun and the frost of the Gallipoli night death was a relaxation and a wound a luxury.*

Denied this experience, my schooldays were followed by the study of pharmacy, and later medicine at Melbourne University as a pathway to a surgical career. My tough country boyhood stood me in good stead at international level in rugby union football and as Australian Universities heavyweight boxing champion.

During postgraduate work at St. Bartholomew's Hospital, the British Post-Graduate Medical School, Hammersmith and St. Mary's Hospital, Paddington, I entertained a deep disgust towards the contemporary appeasement of monstrous dictators, especially Hitler. November 1939 found me in the Australian Army in London destined to leave for Jerusalem on New Year's Eve, 1939.

It was during my sojourn in Jerusalem that I learned from that strange, grim, prophetic man of destiny, Ord Wingate (later of Chindit fame), of the difficult Abyssinian Campaign and the invaluable support given by van der Post at that time.

For me, that phase of the War embraced stirring days in the Western Desert, Greece, Crete, and Tobruk.

Eventually, it was my lot to be one of a shipload of Australians on the ill-fated "Orcades" who were landed in Java after the fall of Singapore to contend against hopeless odds whilst denied their usual weapons, which were on other ships.

It seemed a situation such as depicted by A. E. Housman:

The King with half the East at heel is marched from lands of morning
Their fighters drink the rivers up, their shafts benight the air
And he that stands will die for nought and home there's no returning.
The Spartans on the sea wet rock sat down and combed their hair.

I became a prisoner of war of the Japanese whilst commanding the Allied General Hospital hastily improvised in Bandoeng, Java.

There were in hospital 1300 wounded and sick British, Australian, and other nationalities of navy, army and airforce services.

Most of these, along with the majority of my allied staff of similar derivation, soon found ourselves in a greatly over-crowded gaol – the *Landsopvoedingsgesticht.*

The deep sadness of becoming prisoners of war was compounded by the fact that many were obliged to surrender by order of the higher command without firing a shot. Then they suffered the searing contempt and savage treatment of captors who despised those who surrendered, and who themselves followed a code in which surrender deprived them of honour, and shamed them in their society.

Our disorganised mixture of services and units mostly were without their own officers, and frequently they were with officers as confused and bitter as they were themselves.

Further, whilst officers were not segregated from other ranks, they too were treated with brutality and contempt, and had little power to help men for whom they were allotted responsibility.

Successive moves in 1942 found me back at Bandoeng, administering Prisoner of War Command of a motley dressed assortment of races and services consisting of my old hospital population swollen by many other prisoners more recently rounded up.

My first and highly significant meeting with Laurens was recorded in a diary that I maintained precariously at the time:

Fine clear day, Saturday: – all hands out to wash and sun their floor boards (on which they sleep), which are freely bug-ridden. No drill. Arrival of a party of British and Australian troops from Soekabumi by train. Officers include Lt. Col. van der Post, Wing Commander Nichols, RAF, Majors Woods and Wearne, AIF, and a remnant of about 70 of the missing Pioneer Battalion. They consist largely of parties who 'went bush' and were ultimately rounded up by the Japa-

nese. Laurens van der Post is the most impressive character. South African in origin, British in style, he speaks English, French, Spanish, Dutch, German, Russian and Malay, some Japanese and numerous African languages."

The impact of the man's striking personality increased with further acquaintance and the privilege of enjoying his counsel and advice in the difficult task of commanding a large ill-assorted prison camp so full of collective misery and personal distress.

It contained largely British and Australian service-men derived however from army, navy, and airforce, together with a smattering of Americans, British Indians, New Zealanders, and even a couple of unfortunate Black seamen from Portuguese East Africa, who described themselves, to the puzzlement of the Japanese, as "non-combatant Portuguese Gentlemen."

To my surprise and something akin to consternation, Laurens saw value in my continuing to command this medley of services, with many disorganised and disillusioned men, as a combined British and Australian Camp.

It was a tribute to his persuasive powers that such numbers of seasoned combatant officers of considerable seniority accepted command by an Australian noncombatant, a substantive Lieutenant Colonel (temporary Colonel). This highly gifted man who acted in a supporting role as a staff officer, was not merely the standard pattern of brave British Officer, but displayed a mind and intellect like a great Storehouse with many mansions.

His knowledge and interpretation of Japanese attitudes and psychology was of great value to those of us whose only approach was an implacable defiant hostility. It was necessary in the interests of men under our command to at least strive for a working relationship with our captors.

He saw more clearly than most of us that there was a quality of mind and spirit which provided an intellectual escape from captivity, the paradoxical "victory in defeat."

It was revealed to me that this complex man had not only mastered the languages of many countries, but was steeped in their history, literature, and culture. He could quote and debate the merits of Homer, Cervantes, Camouens of Portugal, along with French dramatists and Shakespeare.

His African stories of tribes, hunting, exploration, and adventures had the mystery and wonder of the Rider Haggard stories which I had devoured in my boyhood.

The man himself had an inner reserve which he wore like a cloak of mystery.

He was a great catalyst in the concept of organising the whole camp into a sort of university or school in captivity designed to free and improve the liberated mind.

His linguistic ability and persuasive diplomacy was extremely useful in dangerous negotiations with friendly civilians, mainly Chinese traders, who bravely advanced sums of money against the day of a British victory. He assisted in good relationships with our Dutch allies.

I cannot recall a more exciting and challenging period in my own life than in those few months in which we shared his companionship and enthusiasm in what he has termed "a war for sanity of mind and body."

Against almost insuperable obstacles posed by the vascillations of our captors, the brutal excesses of guards, especially the Koreans, and the shortage of all material aids, we deployed the many talents of individuals into a remarkable educational and recreational programme of lectures, demonstrations, tutorships, arts and crafts classes, debates, theatre, concerts, and organised games.

The personalities of the camp who loomed large were not necessarily officers, but essentially those who gave of richly stored minds.

Two fascinating examples were L.A.C. "Don" Gregory, Fellow of a Cambridge College, who specialised in Ancient and more contemporary Modern History presented with absorbing attraction, like the tales of Homer; and Gunnar Penry Rees who dealt in French and Spanish languages with a lyric professorial competence.

At a lower level, Capt. Pat Lancaster, in the clipped English of his Hussar background, taught one or two men of the "outback" to read and write!

We evolved a magic collectivism for sane survival which was to sustain us during long years of unimagined suffering and the squalid miseries of life and death upon such projects as railway construction in Burma, Thailand and Sumatra, and work in the mines of Japan.

It was during this period that I became aware that Laurens had been captured whilst organising gorilla band resistance in a remote mountain area of Djajasempoer – the "Mountain of the Arrow." The events of his capture were related to me years later by Ingaret, his wife.

This type of irregular activity was scarcely feasible in a thickly populated country with little or no support from inhabitants who were required to put their own lives on the line.

His force contained a number of battle-seasoned Australians eager to continue the fight, but with little knowledge of Indonesian or Dutch or of jungle welfare.

In such circumstances, the leader as the Queen piece on the board should be covered against capture at all costs.

However, this leader was a man given to the acceptance of personal responsibility with a sensitive recoil from sacrifice of pawns.

He was betrayed negotiating with the village head and suddenly surrounded by armed Japanese under circumstances in which his life was forfeit on the spot.

In the exquisite politeness reserved for the highest level of Japanese society, he found himself saying: "Would you please be so kind as to pause an honourable moment, gentlemen." The puzzled Japanese decided to "take him to their leader" for investigation.

This was the beginning of a long battle for his life and that of others, and even when released from Soekabumi to my camp, suspicion must have followed him.

His sensitive insight into the Japanese motivation behind the strange mixture of savage brutality and seeming demoniac fury along with steadfast loyalty and ultimate courage is portrayed by his Sgt. Hara in *A Bar of Shadow*.

Van der Post, with all his unrivalled ability to negotiate for underground money, lived with a spartan simplicity.

He proved quite invaluable to me in helping to establish a contributory pattern by officers and paid other ranks whereby the wretched general ration was supplemented for all, and the sick especially helped. (In the Japanese code their ration was reduced.)

There were those who were shocked by our seeming light regard for the King's Regulations!

When my Australia Force left Bandoeng in the early hours of 6 November, 1942, under the slightly paling stars of what in Australia is sometimes called the "picaninny dawn," he saw me off, and our cheerful demeanour cloaked an intuitive foreboding as to the future.

When we next met, a third of our camp friends had died in the Netherlands Indies, Borneo, Malaysia, Thailand, Burma, Japan, and in the seas about them. Most had been near to death and many would not fully recover.

I found that this unusual man seemed to have gained in mental and spiritual vigour as his body wasted.

So few men have excelled in so many roles: a writer of such sensitive and imaginative prose, soldier, farmer, diplomat extraordinary, explorer, counsellor in high places, ardent fighter for the rights of exploited peoples and threatened species, a visionary thinker, and lucid advocate of Wilderness Preservation.

His voice has been heard in wise counsel as regards preservation of wilderness areas in this country as in many others.

He is a man surrounded by a charmed circle of distinguished friends who still find time for the less distinguished. I suspect that, like me, he has found in harsh adversity that there is quite a lot of God in man.

It would seem that only when mankind is put at full stretch that the full inherent potential can be reached.

Through the years, I have treasured the continuity of our friendship, and the pleasure and inspiration of our infrequent meetings.

He enjoys a most affectionate remembrance and the admiration of many Australians.

I conclude with John Buchan that:

No experience can be too strange and no task too arduous if a man can link it up with that which he loves and knows. (Memory Hold the Door)

All in all, I have yet to meet a man whose feet have been rooted so firmly in the many-splendoured earth, and in practical achievement, yet who articulates so well the passage through the dream world to the gleaming rainbow world of the spirit.

His extraordinary life with its so numerous Himalayan peaks of achievement has at all times been at a level above that of ordinary men.

Nevertheless, he has something of the humility and Elizabethan quality which is reflected by Walter Raleigh's prayer:

Oh Lord God
When thou givest to thy servants
To endeavour any great matter
Grant us to know

That it is not in the beginning
But continuing of the same to the end
Until it is thoroughly finished
Which yieldeth the true glory.

May his next decade know no dimming of the rainbow spirit
linking earth and sky.

Australian coin issued in memory of 'Weary' Dunlop

The Splendor of the Sun

Joseph L. Henderson

I have always admired Laurens van der Post's special sensitivity to the principle of synchronicity, and, above all to its demonstration in his writings. In *A Mantis Carol*, he plays with synchronistic experiences as a master composer plays with the interweaving motifs of the sonata or symphony or string quartet. But there is another theme that seems to me important. Synchronicity is not just the interlocking events that represent its inner and outer forms. Is there not a mysterious, original condition for synchronicity to take place at all? I think this may be so unconscious that we cannot expect to understand it, but rather it seems to understand us at significant moments.

This happened to me in the late nineteen thirties when I was living in London, but still strongly influenced by C.G. Jung, who had been my analyst in Zürich at an earlier period. I knew of his interest in alchemy, and no doubt some of his interest in this rubbed off on me in the way that patients easily pick up interests of their analysts even when they do not know what they are – or at least not fully. Jung had written nothing yet about alchemy except the commentary to Wilhelm's *Secret of the Golden Flower*, and this had never caught my imagination, though I of course was interested in it intellectually. Yet in 1937-38, here came into my dreams colors and color sequences that made me realize that something alchemical was coming to me, and this was certainly not imitation, because it occurred so spontaneously.

I do not remember how I happened to discover the beautiful illuminated manuscript of an ancient alchemical manuscript by Solomon Trismosin, called the *Splendor Solis,* but there it was in the British Library of the British Museum, near where I was studying for my final examinations for graduation from medical school. I was allowed to look at this beautiful book, supervised by someone in the illuminated manuscript department. In it, I found many of the same colors and color sequences I had seen in my dreams. Strangely, the correspondence between these two synchronistic occurrences did not seem at all surprising. I reacted as if it were the most natural thing in the world. One's interest is attracted to what it needs. Does that also mean that what is called forth is also attracted to one's interest? If so, that *is* surprising!

Edward Edinger illuminates this possibility by saying:

> ... *the gods we have lost are descending on us, demanding recognition. Like Baucis and Philemon, modern individuals are visited by and asked to provide hospitality for transpersonal factors with which they have lost connection.*

After I had passed my medical examinations, I gave hospitality to alchemy in a crayon drawing I made of a medieval stained glass window in which the basic alchemical colors, black, white, yellow/ green, red, appeared associated with certain symbolic elements surrounding a central sun. I suspected myself of having contrived this design until I showed it later to Jung, who said, "O yes, this is eleventh century alchemy." How easy it is for us to doubt the messages that come from the deep unconscious! So having unconsciously deepened my awareness of the alchemical images from *The Splendor Solis*, which was painted in the sixteenth century, I had unwittingly descended to a much earlier period, when alchemy was more simply symbolized, and so I could no longer doubt the authority of this message, that I was more subjectively receptive than I thought.

The superficial meaning of my interest in alchemy at that time meant to me that I needed help from this source in getting through my medical examinations and into my vocation as an analytical psychologist. The deeper meaning of my interest chose to wait for a very long time before it took an important place in my life and work, as teacher as well as therapist. In 1968, I found I was able to acquire the whole series of transparencies of the *Splendor Solis* paintings for a moderate sum of money from the British Library. I took them back to San Francisco, where I work, and began to use them for teaching seminars at the C.G. Jung Institute. The series of paintings were not used merely to illustrate the symbolism of alchemy, but provided me with a series of metaphors to express significant stages in the process of self-discovery we find in Jungian depth analysis. Their usefulness was essentially clinical rather than theoretically interpretive.

What about synchronicity in this connection? My personal experience and understanding of what alchemical symbolism means progressed slowly, and I still do not consider myself an alchemical scholar. But there have been many significant inner/outer experiences. One of these occurred when I was asked, in 1977, to contribute a short paper for a symposium on alchemy at the International Congress for Analytical Psychology in Rome. At first, I did not think this was very important, but *Alchemy* seems to have thought otherwise, and this was conveyed to me in spontaneous images and dreams. These brought back the colors, black, white, yellow, red of my earlier dreams and I knew that the same old interest was again being rekindled. For this occasion, I chose the *Frontispiece* of the *Splendor Solis* to "show and tell."

Before I left home, I began to see, not only in my dreams, but also in my house and garden, surprising examples of these colors. The charter flight that took me to Rome to attend the conference along with friends and colleagues was outwardly uneventful for them, but when we landed for two hours at Bangor, Maine, for our plane to refuel, I went into the waiting room and there I saw several parallel rows of plastic chairs neatly covered in successive colors of black, white, yellow and red. I simply laughed aloud at this joke *Alchemy* was playing on me as if it were a living person, and it put me into a wonderful mood which lasted throughout my stay in Rome. It stayed with me until I returned to San Francisco, where I felt confident I could still go on learning and teaching what I knew to my students about that obscure subject.

One thing about this manuscript was not obscure and became for me the central theme from beginning to end: the sun was never allowed to reign supreme as a symbol of rational, masculine consciousness, important as this was. It could only sustain its health and be the symbol of the philosophical gold if it was suitably joined in harmony with, reflected and compensated by the radiance of the moon, a feminine but nonetheless active luminary. And so, I thought, Splendor of the Sun and Radiance of the Moon must be the essential equation to be experienced inwardly and outwardly in the psychological wisdom of *Alchemy*.

A Letter to Laurens about a Painting

C. A. Meier

The kind of instant note at which his great love of the arts excelled.

Laurens van der Post

Beloved Friend,

Your country's National Gallery houses a canvas by Paolo Uccello which has intrigued me for many years. Without claiming to have solved its riddle, I should like to give you an idea of how it strikes me, so as to serve as a starting point for our next *viva voce* discussion. So, please, when you pay your next visit to the Gallery, spend a few more than the usual two minutes looking at and meditating upon this picture.

Strangely enough, they call the picture "St. George and the Dragon," while all the brave knight does is to kill the monster. Now, according to my view, that part of the painting (right side) can quickly be forgotten, as the far more fascinating and far more carefully painted left side carries all the mystery.

You know that, according to the legend, George killed the dragon because he threatened to devour the royal princess. So far, so good, for a Christian knight.

But with respect to Paolo, we have to forget this point, leave the legend alone and see what *he* makes of it on the left side. What do we see there? A beautiful maiden-princess perfectly poised in full regalia, drawn up to her full stately height, holding the dragon on an extremely subtle leash hanging from the little finger of her left hand only, and going round the dragon's neck. We understand at once that the relationship between her and him [the dragon] must be very friendly and that she handles him rather like a lap-dog. The monster might be ever so frightening to others, but certainly not to her. He no doubt functions as her powerful protector, but certainly not as a tyrant. The two of them are apparently just leaving their cave in order to go for a walk, when, out of the blue, lo and behold appears this human monster [the knight] on his high horse in shining armour with a dark whirlwind about him; i.e., he is a highly emotional youth, who then spears the dragon fatally without the slightest provocation, and obviously without the slightest regard for the mysterious relation of maid and dragon. (One cannot help but to think of the unicorn.) The princess consequently remains highly bewildered, if not shocked. The heroic deed must, in reality, have been a tragic mistake! St. George, being a good Christian, fell for it because he has to *écraser l'infâme*, as was advocated by the medieval Church.

If it is not me, but Paolo Uccello, who is responsible for this idiosyncratic rendering of the saga, he must be admired for the liberty with which he treats his subject in such an unorthodox way. But he has always been prone to a great deal of fantasy, which is beautifully testified to by his decorations and frescoes at the cloisters of Santa Maria Novella in Florence, so that my view would be in accordance with his character. It has to be admitted that the girl very naively exposed her animus to a chilvalrous man who equally naively knew nothing else than to kill him. What a shame! She must have had a perfectly good relationship with this magnificent animal, genuinely feminine.

Moreover, Paolo gave the knight's face a rather puerile, if not infantile, expression so that one cannot help immediately recalling the medieval *dumbhe Thor*, who is something of an unpremeditated hero with an abundance of naive aggression. One also cannot help feeling sorry for the beautiful poor monster. There may be more than one reason for this feeling, one being the fact that, on the dragon's wings, we perceive six (3 + 3) discs of red and blue on the lower side and of yellow and green on the upper side. This and the green colour of the dragon's skin (obviously, the *draco viridis* of the alchemists) reminds us immediately of his highly mysterious qualities. He certainly represents the *materia transformationis* of alchemy and, being both of us inveterate Jungians, it becomes clear to us that the Collective Unconscious is here implied. This fact in itself, then, makes us understand that the princess is nothing less than the classical Anima-figure. Doesn't she have this subtle but most effective and decisive relationship [the leash] with the Collective Unconscious?

"Saint George and the Dragon" by Paolo Uccello (about 1397-1475)

Surely, one could go to any length from here, but this short essay
is not meant to be a learned paper. Therefore, I restrict myself, in
conclusion, to the sad hint that, among many other deeply "philo-
sophical" meanings Paolo conveys to us in this painting, Christianity
has, in a brutal way, destroyed our deeply mysterious harmony with
the equally mysterious Unconscious and Nature.

But more of this next time!

Valé!

A final meeting of old friends: Sir Laurens and C.A. (Fredy)
Meier in the latter's Zürich study, September 1995

How to be Haveable

Alan McGlashan

It is only a half-truth to say that we have ideas. The ideas that matter have *us*. That is, if we allow them to have us. The difficulty is, to learn how to be 'haveable.' The business of living makes such greedy demands for ideas – how to deal with friends, relations, sex life, how to keep solvent, how to keep healthy – all these things clamour for ideational solutions. We flog tired minds towards inadequate answers, with a discouraged feeling that we are not making a very good job of it.

Such ideas as these are not so much active as re-active, a hasty response to external pressures. The secret is to give these ideas our *second-best attention*. This is all they are worth. A second-best attention is quite capable of dealing with them successfully. Our best attention is then held in reserve, an unsleeping eye waiting for a Moment which, of course, may never arrive.

A crazy way to live? But this is what everyone does in intimate human relations; behaving more or less amiably to all and sundry until that one appears for whom the unsleeping eye has all the time been waiting. Not infrequently, it must be admitted, the long-awaited encounter has a disastrous outcome, whereupon the inner eye resumes its sleepless search. Or it does not; and then an important part of the individual is already dead, while continuing to go through the motions of living.

But this aspect of human behaviour has a wider application, less generally recognised. It is also possible to hold the inner attention in constant reserve at another level, waiting for that rare and fugitive visitor, a seminal idea. When it arrives and knocks lightly on the door of the mind, it must be instantly admitted with all honour. Nothing is frailer than the life of a new-born idea, nothing so precise as the moment it chooses to try to enter the human mind. If its tentative plea to be admitted is rejected or postponed, it dies within the hour. The door-step of the mind is littered with the corpses of angels.

Where do these seminal ideas come from? No easy answer can be found. There is no spatial image that quite fits. Major discoveries in science often arise simultaneously in widely different parts of the world, which points to the possibility that they are not so much born in an individual as spontaneously generated within the *Zeitgeist* of an era, to which certain lucky researchers have tuned in. But this leaves the mystery of their origin still unsolved. Or they may be thought of as 'bubbles' rising from the fermenting depths of the unconscious. This may be close to the truth. Perhaps the nearest we can get to their point of origin is to regard them as a form of dreaming, about which Jung has also said, "We do not have our dreams – our dreams have us."

Seminal ideas have the same evanescent quality as dreams, and the same transforming power if they are welcomed and worked upon.

It can be doubted if seminal ideas are the sole prerogative of genius. It is equally tenable that the title of genius is the accolade given to any man or woman who is ready to give excited and total attention to an idea of that order. James Watt was no scientific *savant*. He simply allowed the potentialities of steam to possess him instantly and totally. Joan of Arc, an unlettered country girl, gave passionate welcome to her momentary vision. Lindbergh was an ordinary young man with an overmastering idea. In our own time, there is Bob Geldof, a rough-spoken young pop singer, possessed by a simple, numinous idea which carried him in one leap on to the world's stage.

The clearest and most detailed description of the transforming power of an idea is to be found in *The Confessions of Rousseau*. After an adolescence of what would now be called juvenile delinquency, he one day saw by sheer accident in a newspaper that a prize was being offered by the Dijon Academy for an essay on the question: "Has the progress of the sciences and arts done more to corrupt morals or improve them?" "The moment I read this," said Rousseau, "I beheld another universe and became a new man. ... When I reached Vincennes, I was in a state bordering on delirium ... my feelings rose with inconceivable rapidity to the level of my ideas. ..." He won the prize and leapt to literary fame.

The list is endless – of ordinary human beings who have been lifted into figures of world stature by their one-pointed devotion to a single idea. The world then believes that these figures were geniuses from the start, with outstanding but unrecognised abilities. Not so. What is unrecognised is the power of a seminal idea to raise to a miraculous height anyone who will forsake all else and be its faithful servant. The idea carries the man.

But this fact is no panacea for the world's ills. A seminal idea can be destructive, and its servant a monstrous agent of death, as national dictators at one extreme, and leaders of murderous little sects at the other, all too clearly show. The world then shakes its head forlornly, and decides that they must be mad.

The question arises, is it desirable to be completely possessed by an idea? To be single-minded seems all right until it is called 'lop-sided,' when it does not sound quite so good. Should not human beings always be a size larger than their job, whatever that job may be? – a human being first, and only after *that* an expert? To develop a balanced and harmonious personality is an ancient and honourable aim, endorsed by such men as Lao-tse and Plato, among many other thinkers through the centuries. It may seem rash to question such eminent authorities. But one answer to their view is that humanity would then have missed a whole series of world-transforming achievements. Though Rousseau is currently unfashionable, there can be little doubt that four of the typical figures I have quoted have each in their own way altered the course of human history.

There is another answer. Instead of pursuing this middle-of-the-road philosophy, it is possible to reach a balanced personality by totally surrendering to the seminal idea *while it lasts*. Life is long. There is time enough for the individual human spirit to entertain a succession of over-mastering ideas. To cultivate the habit – and the courage – to yield completely to an idea is more rather than less likely to encourage other seminal ideas to enter in at their appointed time. A mind of this temper acquires, as it were, a reputation for hospitality. It draws in new visitants, as a lighted Inn with its ever-open door attracts the foot-sore traveler. In the end such a mind achieves a balance of a different kind – a balance of opposites.

Learning to be 'haveable,' then, is a tricky business. Shall we leave the door of the mind open in starry-eyed welcome to all comers, as if there were no such thing as psychic burglars? Or bolt and bar our minds in neurotic anxiety? Scientists solve the dilemma by opening their doors wide to every idea, and disclaiming all responsibility for whatever good- or ill-use the world – 'the others' – may make of it.

This just won't do. If a scientist is taken over by an immensely important idea, and promotes it for all he is worth, he is entitled to praise, but also is morally responsible for the effect it has on humanity. This uncomfortable fact has surfaced for all to see in modern medicine, where controversy already rages on the morality of assuming so-called brain-death in living donors of organs for transplant surgery. Orthodox religionists claim that the inner door should be open to only one idea, the idea of God, and that He will take care of all the rest. This could be true; but the blood-soaked annals of religious wars make it a dubious solution. In any case what is secular and unscientific Everyman to do?

Perhaps all he can do is to keep his heart as open as his mind – and not allow himself to be too intimidated by grey-beard wisdom.

* * *

I have chosen this contribution to the Festschrift because of its close relevance to an essential factor in the rich and many-sided personality of Laurens van der Post. He is himself the most convincing example of one who understands the secret of 'How to be Haveable.' The quality required – and which he possesses – is a limitless generosity of spirit that impels a man to commit himself instantly and fearlessly to a person or a cause in need of his support, as if nothing else in the world mattered but that need. I am honoured to be the friend of such a man. There can be very few dead angels on the doorstep of Laurens van der Post's mind.

Sir Laurens and Benjamin Britten on the beach at Aldeburgh in the Fifties

Laurens' Sonata

Joseph B. Wheelwright

For many years, Sir Laurens has fought the good fight – always with his ear close to the ground – and lived Polonius' advice to Laertes. This has meant writing and living from the inside out, not the outside in. He doesn't write about Nature – it permeates him and he listens and understands. Reading *Venture into the Interior* is like listening to Yehudi Menuhin playing a violin sonata. It is the only book I have ever read four times. And let us not forget the Kalahari; one scarcely knows where it leaves off and he begins.

In a totally different genre, his account of his imprisonment by the Japanese during World War II reveals his compassion for, and his deep commitment to, humanity.

My last experience of him was totally unexpected. My friend and fellow analyst, Harry Wilmer, recently ran a three-day workshop on evil. This was sponsored by the U.S. Institute for the Humanities. It was launched by Sir Laurens, who spoke to us by means of a ten-minute video-tape. This set the tone for a remarkable meeting, making it possible for blacks and whites from many backgrounds to pool resources in a meaningful way.

Welcome to the 90's, Sir Laurens!

The House

To Laurens:
I greet you with warmth and friendship. May you have a superb
birthday as you savor the fullness of your years. I want to share this
soul-searching piece of my life in recognition of the vital part you have
played in my growth and development. All of us at the Jung Center also
acknowledge with gratitude your contribution to its unfolding and blos-
soming over the years of your coming.
I have a guest room in my new house in the sky to which I invite you
and Ingaret this year and every year. So – see you soon –

Carolyn Grant Fay

The house – my house – our house – my husband's house – my
children's house – and at times, my grandchildren's house. I told it
good-bye three days ago.

My husband and I bought the land for the house the year we were
married, fifty years past. We were at the wedding of a cousin of mine
and, as the champagne flowed, a friend said to us, "We are building
on this farm outside town, and I'd like to buy the farm next to it. How
about buying a piece of it and coming out to live next door to us?" We
enthusiastically agreed to this. He went to the phone right then, called
the owner of the farm next door, and bought the land.

We went to a fine architect in town, showed him our piece of this
farm and asked him to design a house for us. We were young and had
a few ideas, but mostly we left it up to him to design the house. He
chose to pattern it after a Louisiana country house, because my
husband was born and brought up in that state. He drew it long and
low on the ground after the fashion of the early country houses in
Louisiana. To go into the semi-circular front hall, he planned a stoop
with a wide, strong front door. (It was here, Laurens, that we
encountered the praying mantis that year you went on the journey of
A Mantis Carol.)

Downstairs, there was an octagonal dining room with a wide window framing the view over the meadow to the tree-filled bayou. It adjoined all the service area. Next to the dining room was a panelled room which we called the game room in the early years, when we played many card games there. After a while, it became the model room, as my husband's collection of full and half models of sailing yachts grew. Many of these he designed and had built at the yacht-yard that he and his brother owned. He sailed all of them in races, on Galveston Bay, around the United States, in England, and in Europe. His tiny designing room was just off this model room.

The ground floor was completed by a guest room with ample space for sitting to read or write, as well as sleeping. (You remember, Laurens, that was your room when you came to lecture and show your films at the C.G. Jung Educational Center of Houston, Texas, and to visit us.)

We walked up a curving stairway to the upstairs hall and into our living room. This was the most important room in the house to me, where my husband and I spent long hours in front of the fireplace. Together we had collected books, paintings, and some small sculptures which we enjoyed here. He had given me a piano the year we married to encourage me to keep playing, as had my mother and grandmother before me, and it had a special place in this room. However, as the years went by, the music emanated more and more from the records and tapes in the alcove next to it.

Over the years, the only space we added to the house was a small room next to the living room, which served different purposes as our needs changed. At one time, it was our sleeping area, when we used the living room for our room, and later it became my study and dressing room.

Over the dining room was an octagonal-shaped bedroom. When we were building the house, I shyly told the architect that we were going to have a new occupant in the family for that room. In turn, each of our three children used this room after they were born and as small children. The next room was a small bedroom panelled in an exotic wood that was used by our son, or, alternatively, by a baby nurse or governess as needed.

There was a wonderfully large bedroom at the end of the hall with a raised, tray ceiling that always cried out for (and was answered by) interesting wallpaper treatment. It was planned for my husband and me with a large dressing and bath area, and this was where we started our life in the house. During the four years of World War II, my husband was gone on active duty in the Navy most of the time. I kept the home fires burning with the two older children and gave birth to the third child, whom my husband saw for the first time at nine months of age. After the War, our two daughters took over that spacious bedroom, and my husband and I moved into the downstairs guest bedroom and later into the little room off the living room.

When the children grew up and moved away, we made the octagonal bedroom ours; he took the panelled bedroom for his dressing-room, and I, the room off the living room as my special place. So really, we have lived all over the house – and loved it – for almost forty-nine years.

Our son and two daughters gave us an exciting party to celebrate our 50th wedding anniversary. It included balloons, flowers, music, dancing with dinner, and a display of photographs of all of us during the years of the house.

Two weeks later, I fell in the house and broke my hip. As I look back now, I needed this. I had gotten into many outside activities, not the least of which was my practice as a dance/movement psychotherapist and my work at the Jung Center. My husband had had a heart attack on a trip wc took to the Adriatic the Fall before. After we returned, I had a mock heart attack, 'sympathetic,' the doctor said, to which I paid scant attention. I needed to be in the house and aware of the total life situation at this time in our history.

He and I had six weeks of being together at home, a beautiful, caring time. Then he had a heart attack in his boat after rounding the weather mark in a sailing race. Though heroic efforts were made to revive him, he did not survive. I have stayed closely in the house since he died. The memories in it sheltered and comforted me.

My older daughter and I gave a good-bye-to-the-house party as a final celebration. Lots of old and new friends came.

Now, nine months from the day of breaking my hip, June 25th, to the day of moving, March 25th, I have left the house. Nine months is that period of gestation, a time from conception through carrying a developing life to full term and birth: birth at the time of the Vernal Equinox – Spring.

I am building a "house in the sky," as I call it – a condominium on the 29th floor of an apartment building. From it, I can look south and see the place where I grew up as a child. I can walk to the Jung Center and to the house of my older daughter. It is a green area with parks and museums nearby.

There have been weeks of clearing out the attic of the old house with constant help from my older daughter and some from my younger one, who came from her farm out of town to do some of the work with us. It took weeks of sorting: what to keep, what to give, what to throw away – to empty the attic, the whole third floor of the house, of all that we had collected for fifty years. We found photographs of family members of several generations; letters – from my parents, childhood friends, boyfriends, husband, children, grandchildren; old silver; records of family happenings; furniture; clothes of my mother, mine, and my children as babies and tots; and costumes from my childhood dance recitals up through my husband's and my "fancy dress party" costumes. My daughters each found their childhood books, toys, furniture and clothes, and they made a pile for their brother of his things.

The last week, these two young women and I worked all day every day finishing the task of emptying the house. They took a few things for themselves and helped me collect a box of things for each of the five grandchildren.

Our big, woolly poodle is very sensitive and practically glued herself to my heels as the packing and preparations for moving progressed. She missed her master. Every time we went into his room, we found chewed up pictures and papers, and one day, a fine leather frame around a photograph of him had been demolished. I thought this destruction must have been done by an animal from the woods in the back of the house, and I called in a man who catches stray animals in "Have-a Heart" traps and releases them far away. He only pointed to and shook his head at our own canine family member.

Big vans came and hauled away all the things from my life in the house; some to go to a temporary apartment and others to go in storage until the construction of my condominium was finished. I am now installed in the interim place – a place of transition. I feel in limbo.

I went back to the house after everyone had left for a day of being alone there with only the dog. I went around and spent a long time in each room, remembering. I found again that the most important room for me was the living room – "living" is a good name for it. As the dog lay in her usual spot, I lay on the floor, too, and let memories flood through me. I started at the beginning, as I have in this writing, recalling people and events that took place – some brought smiles and others, tears, and I savored all of it. I spent time outside watering the plants and running with the dog.

As it grew dark at the end of the day, I went to each room again to touch it and say good-bye. Out on the grounds, I circumambulated the house clockwise, a direction symbolizing movement into consciousness and outward into life. I wanted to see it and bid it farewell at some distance. I handed the house key to the guard to give to the new tenants.

As I drove out, I stopped at the last curve in the road where I could just see a dark shape and the lamps on either side lighting the front door. With more tears, I said a final good-bye to the house.

This marks the end of an era in my life – the finish of a way of life very special to me. The house becomes a symbol for the fullness of my married time of life. I don't want to leave. I don't want it to end. I feel I am sacrificing something of the utmost value to me, and taking an enormous risk of what might come next.

My temporary quarters seem like a bridge. It is warm and cosy here, but I feel shaky – uncertain of what the future will bring. I am embarking on an unknown course – open and feeling vulnerable and unprotected; but at the same time, feeling stronger than usual.

I often find myself not using my married name, but my own personal name in dealings both business and social.

I seem to be inclined toward more extraversion. My small apartment has been filled with people most of the few days I've been here and I am constantly on the telephone. I am writing this, sharing with many, perhaps, instead of holding it tightly to myself.

I must be in the archetypal experience of death/rebirth. The completion and death of a full period of my life, the time of transition, and the coming into the next stage of my life with whatever it might bring. I thank God that I have immersed myself in the psychology of C.G. Jung so that I can be aware and fully present in the reality of this moment of transition and all it can mean.

On Laurens and Film-Making

Jonathan Stedall

Others more qualified than I have paid and will continue to pay tribute to Laurens van der Post, the writer, the explorer, the unofficial and anonymous diplomat working on behalf of his beloved Africa in the fight against racial prejudice and in his campaign to awaken in us an understanding of, and respect for, the 'primitive' in others and in ourselves. My own particular connection with Laurens came about through a documentary film project for the BBC, and it is about this collaboration that I would like to contribute a few words.

In 1971, I wrote to the author of *The Lost World of the Kalahari*, having been moved, like many others, by the profundity of the book's message. As a young documentary film-maker at the BBC, I said in my letter that I was interested in exploring, through the medium of film, the theme of the Child in Man, and that I would like to discuss the idea with him. What I remember most vividly about that first meeting, which took place in the study of his Chelsea apartment, was that the conversation started in the daylight of an autumn afternoon and that we were still talking long after darkness had fallen. By then, the silhouetted figure opposite me was talking about Jung. I myself had read *Memories, Dreams, Reflections* some years earlier, but otherwise knew very little about Jung. Nor did I know about Laurens' close friendship with that great pioneer in the field of modern psychiatry. By the end of our first meeting, in the mysterious and unexpected way that significant things often come about, we had decided to make a series of films about Jung's life and work. The enlightened and broadminded head of Religious Programmes at the BBC, Oliver Hunkin, for whom I was working at the time, supported our initiative from the start, and by the following spring, I was at Küsnacht on the shores of the lake near Zürich, together with a talented and sensitive BBC film crew.

Laurens was, from the beginning, an extremely easy and helpful person with whom to work. He respected the limitations and the disciplines of film-making, and he really seemed to enjoy the team effort that is necessary on such a project. Writers do not always find this process of working closely with others, each with different disciplines to follow, an easy or even a welcome challenge – particularly when they are also acting, as Laurens was, as presenters on camera. This difficulty that they experience is, I think, very understandable; and it is perhaps even more surprising that a man like Laurens, who is, like so many writers, essentially a 'loner' in the very best sense of the word, should so easily have become just one of the team – albeit, a very crucial one! We were all full of admiration for the way in which he adjusted to the trials and the compromises that filming inevitably involves, and were deeply touched by the interest he took in each person's particular job. Later, when he and I worked together in the cutting-room on the commentary for the films, this attitude of trust, this respect for the disciplines of film-making, was even more in evidence: "We've got seventeen seconds to introduce the subject of the Collective Unconscious" was the sort of absurd but necessary challenge I had to throw at him! Perhaps, in the end, the key to our successful collaboration was simply that Laurens sensed, even knew, that his trust and respect was very definitely mutual.

The films were, I think, a great success in that they interested many people in Jung for the first time. The three programmes have continued to be shown, particularly in America, on college campuses and at small cinemas for over fifteen years.

Some three years later, Laurens and I made another film together, this time in Africa. The subject was the mythology of the Bushmen, and we called the programme, *All Africa Within Us*. It was my first experience of the African continent, and I felt greatly privileged to encounter the magic and the majesty of the bush in the company of someone who loved and knew it so well. Again, Laurens showed the same respect for my task as a film-maker as he had done during the Jung project. He was always willing to try out some idea we might suggest, whether it was standing in the pouring rain to relate a particular legend or lying on his stomach on the hot and dusty earth in order to converse at close quarters with a praying mantis!

In 1986, I was commissioned by the BBC to produce a film portrait: *Laurens van der Post – Eighty*. We talked on camera at his Chelsea home and at Aldeburgh about many aspects of his life and work. I still find it deeply distressing that so little of what we discussed was able to find its way into the final programme. But that is so often the case with television documentaries and is one of the very real limitations of the medium. Nevertheless, I try to comfort myself with the thought that perhaps a number of people, maybe even many people, will have been introduced to Laurens through the fragments I have been privileged to produce, and thus find their way to his actual books. And hopefully, things do not necessarily stop there. Truly great people do not want just to be admired, followed, believed. Their special gift, or rather, their potential gift is, I believe, to inspire each one of us to become a little truer to ourselves. It was Jung himself who said, "Thank God I'm Jung and not a Jungian!" – just one of the memorable quotations I remember hearing on that first evening I spent with Laurens van der Post in the twilight of an autumn evening.

Paul Bellinger and Sir Laurens with camera and soundman during filming of Testament to the Bushman *in the Kalahari, 1983*

Filming with Laurens van der Post

Paul Bellinger

The filming of *A Region of Shadow* was a particular challenge for me, requiring me to adapt my television news cameraman instincts and skills. Covering the wars in both Rhodesia and Angola are very different to the more leisurely disciplines of documentary filming, but I soon embraced this new role with a passion. This was really the ultimate shooting for a programme that would last longer than one minute and thirty seconds, as was the norm for news pieces.

Not having known Laurens' history, I was continually playing catch-up as each day of the filming went by. Steven Cross, the director, suggested a short-cut into the van der Post world: read *The Lost World of the Kalahari*, he suggested; so down to the nearest CNA, the nation's bookstore, I dashed. It was only then that I realised how prolific a writer Laurens had been, and still is. I was amazed to find rows of soft-covers: *Venture into the Interior, Flamingo Feather, Journey into Russia* and *The Lost World of the Kalahari*, and the list continued. What I found and what I hadn't bargained on, was that the book was so proudly displayed. I imagined that, if there were any of his books, one might find them tucked away in a back room, because here in South Africa, Laurens was, after all, the man they (the Government and a good many Afrikaaners) loved to hate. I guess that's what makes the country so bizarre.

Well, that night I lost myself in the Kalahari. I finally put the book down as the sun tried to creep through the crack I had left in my curtain. As with many people, I was immediately transfixed and caught in the van der Post imagination. I knew I had finally arrived. That book, *The Lost World of the Kalahari*, was to play a major part in my next big step in filmmaking.

Most of the filming for *A Region of Shadow* was uneventful, except for the logistics of climbing the Brandburg, a mountain range which rises up out of the desert of Namibia. The idea was to film one of the finest bushmen paintings in the region, The White Lady.

Before we started our trek, Laurens handed out salt tablets to stop us dehydrating, but before we moved off, there was one major obstacle to overcome. As with most film shoots, there was too much gear: How on earth were we to get to the top with all the equipment?!

We each loaded as much as we could carry, but there were still three rather large items lying on the ground, which we needed and which were essential for the shoot: the tripod, a large roll of reflective material and a wide-angle lens. I can clearly remember everyone in unison turning to Laurens for help. It took five hours to reach the painting; the temperature in the shadow of the huge boulders which litter the mountain was 40° C. But, oh my God, was it worth it! The White Lady is a most extraordinarily wonderful painting. It is a painting of a white woman holding a flower, but what struck me in particular about the painting was how fresh the paint looked, almost as if it had been painted moments before our arrival!

The other interesting encounter occurred while filming at a university in Durban. Laurens was talking to some students in an amphitheater on the campus. The talk was about the dark forces of evil that are at work in the minds of many South Africans. Lo and behold, no sooner had Laurens finished the discussion, when, from behind the trees that surrounded the amphitheater, we saw some of those very dark forces skulking around taking pictures, not only of us, but any and all of the students that were in the vicinity.

A Region of Shadow was well-received by the BBC, so much so that, within a year or so, we were back together again making another film for the Corporation. This time, I was to be introduced to another of Laurens' friends, Jonathan Stedall, a film producer for the BBC. Jonathan and I struck up a most wonderful relationship. Almost from the beginning, there was a feeling that we would achieve a remarkable programme. And it was!

The film, *All Africa Within Us*, is the story of Laurens' return to Africa after spending the worst nightmare imaginable as a prisoner of war in those infamous Japanese camps. This film is a celebration of life which is told with great sensitivity and care.

One of the most amusing moments during the filming was in the Kruger National Park while traveling to Pufuri in the north of the park. We traveled in a VW Microbus with the sliding door open, because of the heat. Earlier in the filming, I had told Jonathan a story of the amazing speed a snake called the mamba can travel in order to catch its prey. I told Jonathan that it could reach speeds of 50 mph. I like to think he believed me. Anyway, as the VW cruised around on its journey north, I took this as a cue to demonstrate the snake's extraordinary speed. I slipped out of the open door on the side of the van as it slowed up, and ducked under the passenger window, where Jonathan sat. I ran, half crouching, raising my arm to appear as I thought a mamba would look at this speed, and tapped on the window. Well, Jonathan almost pushed the driver out of his seat to get away from his 'attacker.' That sort of banter was to carry on throughout the shoot.

For me, the next break was to come in 1983, when Laurens agreed to collaborate with me on a series of six films on the Bushmen of the Kalahari. Maybe it was my memories of the book, *The Lost World of the Kalahari*, that generated my curiosity for learning more about the first man of Africa. But I also think that this was a deliberate move on my part, because in 1953, Laurens and an intrepid film crew with 35mm cameras had gone into the Kalahari to document the Bushmen's plight and to show the world how vulnerable the Bushmen were to the onslaught of the 20th Century. The series, *The Lost World of the Kalahari*, was the most successful series BBC Television had ever done, and it paved the way for a new series, *World About* Us, which ran for 10 years.

So, thirty years later, Laurens went back to the Kalahari with me in tow to rediscover and find out just what had happened to those Bushmen. We retraced his earlier journey; what we found was a tattered remnant of those Bushmen on the edge of what we call civilisation. I directed and filmed the series, which was known as, *Testament to the Bushmen*.

Friendship and Film

Eva Monley

FRIENDSHIP AND FILM is based on
coffee and croissants
listen and talk time
questions and answers
agreeing and disagreeing
wit and humour
laughter, wonder and joy,
BUT MOST OF ALL AFRICA.

Film introduced us in 1980, but Africa built our friendship for lasting. Laurens was raised in South Africa, I was raised in Kenya. He wrote books and told stories, I made films, so when we met, we merely combined our talents!

Over the years, one of the best times I remember was our first location survey for the Amblin/Disney adaptation of *A Far-Off Place*. We took off in a small turbojet charter, just the two of us (with a brilliant young pilot who had every van der Post novel in his plane for autographing!!) for a memoryjog of where best to shoot the film. Imagine flying into the sunrise from misty grey and cold Swakopmund, flying up the Skeleton Coast, then into the sunset over miles and miles of pink sand dunes, to land in a blistering sandstorm in Luderitz. Awesome.

We flew over the Kalahari, the Makakari Pan for the Baines Baobabs, and flew on into Maun. Friends everywhere and good talk and good wine from Zimbabwe to Botswana to Namibia. Amazing.

A week later, we picked up our director and writer and showed them our best findings and then the real jigsaw of thought and talk and visual of film-making began.

Many scripts, many surveys and many years later, we eventually made the film, but our first survey remains for me a great magical memory of vast horizons, total awareness and utterly belonging.

And now, there are more van der Post books to adapt for film, and we are working on several of them. Exciting.

P.S. Hasten slowly. The scent of freesias. It must be Sunday.

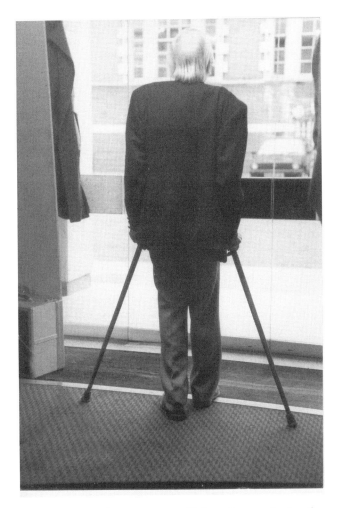

Sir Laurens at the entrance to Chelsea Towers during the filming of Hasten Slowly, *1995*

Hasten Slowly

Richard Osler

In June, 1996, a one-hour film premiered in Calgary, Alberta, Canada. It was called, *Hasten Slowly – the Journey of Sir Laurens van der Post*. I was there with fellow co-producer Eva Monley, Laurens' long-time friend and film-collaborator, and Mickey Lemle, the director and producer. Through the lens of Laurens' life, the movie tells a story of hope – of the deep meaning available to us at the core of our lives if we are prepared to see it. Life often uses meaningful coincidences or synchronicity to wake us to that meaning. For me, my journey to Laurens and ultimately to a movie owed much to such coincidences – owed much to a 36-year-old copy of a book.

My journey to Laurens and that premiere included a lot of curves in the road. As I look back, in spite of the curves, the destination seems to have been inevitable all along. This seems to be one of the lessons I have learned after being fortunate enough to intersect the life of this special man. The most interesting plans and events in our lives seem to be the ones that life plans for us, not the ones we make for ourselves. It now seems clear that the movie was making plans for us years before. The synchronicities that connected me to the life of Laurens in the days leading up to our meeting should have warned me that something was brewing.

I first met Laurens in April, 1991. As soon as we greeted each other, I told him this story: My wife Susan and I had made an unexpected trip to Bath the day before with close friends who had arranged my meeting with Laurens. On arrival, I made all of us drop in to the first bookshop we saw. It was a second-hand bookstore on Chapel Row. As usual for me, I asked the man at the front desk if he had any first editions by Laurens van der Post in stock. The dusty-looking man behind the dusty book-covered desk muttered, "I don't think so."

A few minutes later, the bookseller arrived with a sun-faded red book. "I thought I had an autographed copy of this somewhere," he said. It was all I could do to prevent myself from wrenching it out of his hands. I took the book and opened it as if it were some sacred relic in a temple. Strangely, it was a 1955 Canadian first edition of *Flamingo Feather*. Coincidence? Then I discovered that this bookseller had lived in my home town of Calgary for ten years, about twenty years before. Coincidence?

Then another coincidence became apparent: I was reading *Flamingo Feather* on the way back to London. The hotel we stayed in, just outside of Bath, was called "Petty France." The name of the main character's house in *Flamingo Feather* was "Petite France." Laurens, I found out later, had farmed near "Petty France" in the Thirties.

As I was telling Laurens about finding the book, he asked me if it had come from a man or woman. "It was owned by a woman," I replied. "Was her name Eileen Mahoney?", he asked. "Yes," I said. He turned around abruptly on the narrow stairs and said, "Then she must be dead. She never would have sold the book otherwise." "Yes," I answered, "the bookshop owner said that she had died about nine months ago." Eileen Mahoney, it turned out, had been one of Laurens' producers at the BBC.

I had gone to see Laurens just to let him know how much his books had meant to me. I did not expect to see him again. Life had other ideas. After a radio program where I had been interviewed about my quest to meet Laurens, a former film producer contacted me and suggested that a new documentary be made on Laurens' life. This seemed like a strange idea, since I had no background or interest, at that time, in movie-making. But that suggestion began a correspondence and then a friendship with Sir Laurens. It also led to the making of the movie by Mickey Lemle that premiered in Calgary five years later. The story of the coincidences that led Mickey to the movie is a story of its own.

While remembering the many coincidences that surrounded my first meeting with Laurens, I went to my library for that copy of *Flamingo Feather* I had found in Bath. Almost idly, I read the last page. There Laurens says that, if one lives one's life in pursuit of a "cause beyond himself," then his life will achieve "something which is greater than happiness and unhappiness: and that is meaning."

This is the exact thought with which Mickey Lemle ends his movie on Laurens, who brought up this idea while we were filming in

London without any prompting. Mickey used it as his ending without realizing where it had first come from. Yet there it is already in this book. There it is in this book that seemed to confirm my journey to meet Laurens. Already at the beginning, the book could see the end.

A Peal of Bells

Peter Ammann

It was on a September evening that I went to the cinema to see Oshima's film, *Merry Christmas, Mr. Lawrence*. It made a strong impression on me. The most significant scene, the one in which Celliers, a South African officer of the Allied forces taken prisoner by the Japanese, embraces the camp's most brutal commanding officer during a prison roll-call, remains unforgettable.

I read in the credit titles that the film was based on Laurens van der Post's book, *The Seed and the Sower*. This led me to begin reading his books, starting with *The Night of the New Moon*, which deeply moved me. I had known of van der Post for a long time, in fact, since my studies at the C.G. Jung Institute in Zürich some twenty years previously. I asked myself how it was possible that I had been blind for so long, coming to discover this man and his work only now.

As I continued reading his books, I felt more and more drawn to this man and the remarkable unity of his life and work. Then I also discovered hidden ties related to my childhood. As a boy during World War II, in the comparative safety of Switzerland, I had followed the deadly happenings in the newspapers, as if they were an adventure series. One of my great heroes was the British General Wavell. I cut out magazine pictures of him and pinned them on my bedroom wall next to those of the King and Queen of England. Wavell had become known mainly through his African campaign against the Italians in 1941. And now, here I was reading – decades later – how Laurens van der Post, at that time, had served under him as an officer, first in Abyssinia and later, when the General had taken over the supreme command in the Southeast Asia, in Java; how he had been captured there by the Japanese and held prisoner of war for more than three years. I had been happily attending school at that time and making lighthearted bets with my school friends that the Allies would be sure to win the war. In a rather naive way, I took my sympathies for the Allies as a sufficient assurance of security.

Such parallels could, perhaps, appear presumptuous, if it weren't for the fact that they were, in my opinion, characteristic of the situation of a young Swiss person. Switzerland was, at that time, an island shielded from the harsh reality of worldwide events, a haven of peace, as one can so lightly say. For me as a Swiss citizen, this seemed to describe my situation. For we were *sheltered* from world events, but, at the same time, we were also *cut off* from many aspects of life. A haven of peace can also become an ivory tower.

In any case, I suffered increasingly from being cramped in *my* ivory tower until later, while studying music, I began seeking a way out and started a Jungian analysis. To my great surprise, and thanks to my analyst, I was soon able to meet in person with Jung, who was then over eighty years of age. He had lost his wife only a short time before, and I clearly remember that he was wearing, in accordance with tradition, a wide black band around his jacket sleeve, to show that he was in mourning. I told him that I was studying to be a musician, but added that I had many other interests and did not know if one day these would become more important to me than music. Jung answered, "Yes, that's also my impression," and he began to say that reflecting on music led beyond music itself. Listening to music was only one aspect of hearing. Hearing also meant heeding and obeying a voice, the voice of the spirit.[1]

It was about this time that Laurens van der Post made his Kalahari expedition, which was the source not only of his famous book, *The Lost World of the Kalahari*, but also of his unique film of the same name. I was traversing my own inner desert and had no idea that later I myself would also be making films. "Obeying the voice of spirit" led me to study at the C.G. Jung Institute in Zürich, and a whole new world opened up before me. And yet, upon completing my studies, I could not imagine spending the rest of my life sitting in the analyst's chair. Had, then, my studies at the Jung Institute – i.e., for me, and at that time – perhaps become another sort of ivory tower?

In any case, I had a longing for *adventure;* not just superficially, but in the sense of the original meaning of the word, *adventura:* that

---

[1] German original: "Vom *Hören* führt ein Weg zum *Gehorsam*, zum Gehorsam im Geist."

which draws near, falls upon one, an unexpected incident, a hazardous undertaking, an extraordinary experience.

My dreams led me to Italy, and through my relationship with Federico Fellini, who was strongly influenced by Jung, on into filmwork. In wanting to make my own films, my original goal had been to shoot feature films; however, in the sense of *adventura*, a few 'coincidences' led me to make documentary films and deal closely with events of the *outside* world. I made documentaries about Italian workers in Switzerland and about those extremely conservative Swiss who thought the world was a better place if women stayed at home and left voting and 'dirty' business to the men. Television work led me to a kibbutz in Israel, and to the adventurous routes of drug-smuggling in Colombia and the United States.

But where had my long years of involvement with Jungian psychology gone? They seemed to have receded and faded into the background. Eventually, the turning point came: the true meaning of Jung and his ideas for me gradually reemerged and came clearly and strongly into focus, thrusting through the images that had hitherto dominated the foreground of my life. This happened during some difficult filming in which I was trying to discover direct connections and relationships between my passions for music, filmwork and Jungian psychology. At the same time, I was beginning to read the books of Laurens van der Post. Thus, parallel to my work, came this discovery of a man, of a life and a work, that appeared in the most natural and exemplary way to correspond with my understanding of what a 'Jungian' view of life means. Nothing was acquired theoretically; everything was experienced and suffered in the sense of *adventura*. There was no danger of artificially accumulating psychological associations and interpretations, no actual gap between life and experience, action and reflection, between ability and knowledge, between art and science. The scholar becomes an artist, the artist a scholar: a person who has both the courage and the modesty to say 'I,' and to speak from his own point of view as the only authentic and legitimate one.

In my first letter to Laurens van der Post, I wrote that I was anxious to discover what sort of film a 'Jungian' could and should make. And I expressed my hope that his opinion would enlighten me. Subsequently, as we met frequently and came to know one another better, we never discussed this question directly; indirectly, however, an answer and a certain stimulation arose. The urge to shoot a film in

Africa involving an experience of wilderness – both within and without – grew stronger in me. Laurens suggested that I discuss this idea with his friend Ian Player, a well-known South African conservationist and founder of the Wilderness Leadership Organization in Zululand. In the spring of 1986, the opportunity finally arose: Laurens telephoned me that Ian Player had just arrived in London from the United States and would be spending a few days there before returning to South Africa. Only three days later, Ian and I met, and we spoke together for several hours. During our discussion, Ian threw out an idea which struck me like a bolt of lightning: right from the start, participants in such a film should take careful notice of their dreams. In my immediate enthusiasm, I went a step further: these dreams should, in one way or another, *become part of the film*. Wilderness without – wilderness within: a film which would include the voice of the dream. A risky, but extraordinary *adventura*. The very next day, Ian and I went to see Laurens, who immediately agreed with the idea, and added that *this* film had, as yet, never been made. Laurens thus dispelled my fear that I would be unable to make a film which would convey anything beyond what his own African films had already done. A few days after I returned to Geneva, I had a dream:

> *I found myself at the foot of a volcano and saw enormous piles of white rubbish bags on the steep slopes. Together with other people, I began climbing the mountain alongside a long wide band of these bags. Suddenly, like a landslide, the bags began hurtling down the mountainside. By lying down to the right, in a kind of gutter, I was able to protect myself.*

In Switzerland, white rubbish bags are used for collecting old clothes for charity. Old worn-out pieces of clothing – in other words, a way of showing and conducting oneself – this has become out-of-date. Tons of these bags were sliding down the volcanic slopes, driven by the sheer force of the eruption. It was as if the dream wanted to say: these bags not only contain your own old clothes, but also worn-out things from countless people; this is a problem that concerns *us all*. As I suspected, deep within the volcano *e-motion* was boiling and the first result was the expulsion of the old 'crust,' i.e., the white rubbish bags.

The day after I had this dream, I met E., a friend sharing my enthusiasm for Laurens' books, for lunch. Laurens himself had already suggested that she might take part in the film. As I now sat with E. and enthusiastically told her of my discussion in London with Ian and Laurens, the fantasy of the film project suddenly took on a degree of reality. It seemed to me as if the idea had now entered the realm of feasibility. That night, I had another dream:

> *I was looking up at a church tower, which resembled a mighty skyscraper. Were there people standing up there? I saw the tower swaying dangerously, like a skyscraper in a strong wind. But it was not the wind that was causing the tower to sway so violently: it was the church bells swinging with uncannily powerful movements. Suddenly, disaster struck: the huge church tower toppled over, away from me and onto the nave, which it destroyed.*

In thinking about this dream, I immediately perceived that the vibration of the swinging bells – the movement, the excitation, the emotion – was much too powerful for this tall city church to bear. It was simply not strong enough to contain the intensity of the 'emotion.' It then struck me that the two dreams had something in common: both revealed an intense motion or excitation. First, the image of a volcano with boiling hot lava which then erupts, tearing and bearing away the 'old'; and now the swinging, vibrating, proclaiming bells, causing the 'old' to collapse, and falling to earth themselves. I understood the dream as a kind of echo of my journey to London and of my talks with Laurens and Ian. I remembered the very striking dream Ian Player had had one night beside the campfire, on one of his bush trails.[1] In his dream, Ian had entered a church which had an enormous tree embedded in its left-hand wall. Church and tree, religion and nature – such was the dream's message – are not opposites, but form an inseparable and mutually supporting unity. This reminded me of Laurens' words when he speaks of the wilderness as the original church and cathedral of life, out of which man returns, transformed and healed.

By reflecting in this way, I am actually going beyond the present phase of my own dreams. The 'new,' the future *adventura*, is not – or, at any rate, not yet – their theme. It is the 'old' which will collapse and be cast out. The bells fall to earth, perhaps even into it, penetrating the earth's crust and sinking into the fiery lava, as into the sea. There are tales told of bells that sink or are lost in the earth or in the water; there they secretly ring out and are eventually – in the sense of

---

[1] Cf. *A Testament to the Wilderness*, Daimon Verlag, Zürich / Lapis Press, Santa Monica, 1985, pp. 70-71.

"obeying the voice of the spirit" – found again and must be drawn back into the light.

A bell tolls and its sound creates a bond – of this, there are also many tales. It is a bond between earth and heaven, between the material and the spiritual worlds. This bond is reminiscent of the old image of a string linking heaven and earth and whose vibrations create the *musica mundana*, the music of the world or the harmony of the spheres. This string reminds me of the *cord* in the wonderful African tale of which Laurens is so fond, the cord on which beautiful star fairies come down to earth at night from heaven, to milk a farmer's cows. Having done so, they climb back up to heaven again with their pails full of milk. The farmer wonders why his cows aren't giving milk anymore. One night, he manages to surprise the star fairies at their work and to capture one. She tells him that she would be happy to live with him on the one condition that he never look into the small pail she has brought with her, without her permission. But, one day, he can bear it no longer and lifts the lid of the pail. To his astonishment, he sees nothing at all in the pail. When his wife realizes that he has broken his promise, he makes fun of her, asking: "Why do you make such a fuss about this empty little pail?" At this, his wife is sad beyond words, for it shows that he doesn't perceive the world of the invisible, and she leaves him.

This man, who does not see the heavenly gift of the soul in the pail, resembles modern man, who so often – to come back to the symbol of the world string – has lost the ability to perceive the secret vibrations of the strings and bells in our world.

Let us return to my second dream. On my way into the wilderness, the wildly swinging bells caused the church tower and nave to collapse. At this point, I cannot say more about the meaning of this dream. For now, I can only try to listen patiently for the tolling of the sunken bells, and when I finally hear them, to follow their sound. In this endeavor, my hearing is being sharpened, my patience strengthened, and my faith confirmed by the example and inspiration provided by Laurens van der Post in his life and work, and by the friendship we share.[1]

(In 1992 the author completed his documentary film, Hlonipa, *which addresses the theme of wilderness within and without.)*

[1] I wish to express my particular thanks to Robert Hinshaw, Elizabeth Copson and Jenny Werner for their generous assistance in preparing the English version of this article.

Rainbow Rhapsody

Jean-Marc Pottiez

What happened on the day before the last day of the Year of the Tiger (1986), while I was snorkeling along the reef of the southern tip of the Island of Saipan, one of the Mariana Islands in the Pacific, was altogether a delightful and unusual sort of experience; but I still don't understand fully the meaning of it and wonder if I should.

Let's have the facts first. I was heading back to the beach and my family when I spotted the luminescent green smile of a giant clam. I dived for it, but, as soon as I picked it, the smile vanished, and I was confronted by nothing more than a stony fist. What should I do? Take it back with me, and have it boiled so that we could have its shell as a souvenir, or leave it near its bushy pink coral to grow and illuminate the seascape? I decided to let it slowly plunge back alongside its bushy companion. A little further, I discovered an indigo starfish, which, when I picked it up, started immediately to retract its myriad microscopic orange tentacles and transform itself into a leathery hand with five spread-out fingers. However, perhaps thanks to the exhilaration the experience gave me, the gesture that this rainbow finger had somehow made to me gave me a sense of relief. I said to myself at that time: "Take it easy, from now on everything will be all right. Nothing like a rainbow to cure anyone of the blues. You'll see, wounds will heal, scars will vanish, once again beauty and reason will prevail. … Rest assured, Saipan will again be Saipan."

That's what it was: until the appearance of 'my' rainbow, I had tended to see everything in black, and had got the blues. But why? For some clear, and also for some not so clear, reasons.

First, and quite clearly, Saipan was – and is – no more Saipan.

***

The Death of a Paradise Island

For the first time in the fifteen years we had known her, enjoying her balmy weather, her crystal clear water and fabulous sunsets (is not paradise always an island?), Saipan seemed to be sick, and soon (was it contagious?) we became sick too. One of the clear reasons was the killer, Kim. Just two weeks before our arrival, typhoon Kim had devastated the island; the scars were still visible everywhere: roofs had been hurled away, concrete walls smashed, trees uprooted, gardens and parks annihilated. No more flowers, and hence no more smiles around. Even the ocean – the magic Pacific Ocean – had metamorphosed into a sick and furious dragon, still twisting its tail, fins and thousand-and-one heads, darting its thousand-and-one tongues, flashing its fiery looks, and disgorging endless streams of seaweed onto the glaring white sandy beaches – all aimed in our direction.

Claire-Yumi was stricken with chronic nausea and stomach-ache – some kind of infection, according to the local doctor – but I was sure that the typhoon and the sick and angry island and ocean were responsible; there was, in fact, a recrudescence of bacterial activity, particularly in the water of the swimming pools, and in the sea where, moreover, the islanders had dumped all the food that had spoiled in their refrigerators while the electric power was wiped out. Next was my turn, with a severe cold, something quite unusual for me, especially in tropical weather, which suits me just as well as my own skin. As a result, I felt uneasy throughout the nine days we stayed on the island.

But I knew that sadness, too, not only fever, poisoned this vacation. For Saipan was not only no more Saipan: the Saipan we liked so much was – and still is – dying.

This is not mere nostalgia, but sad reality. Of course, it is the tourists like us, and those who live off them, milking them, who are chiefly responsible for this sorry state of affairs. Just as they are everywhere else in the world, tourists are welcomed in Saipan and considered as a benediction – whereas, they should also be considered as invaders, and sometimes destroyers, and be dealt with accordingly. With them, and for them, there is blaring noise, eyesores of all kinds, hotels, restaurants, bars and discos, mushrooming almost one after the other, money-milking à gogo; pimps, prostitutes, gambling, drugs; more waste, more refuse in the ocean and inland, more pollution, and thus rapid destruction of the fragile ecology. Yes, indeed, it was as if there was a war going on, with airplanes zooming back and forth every-day, air-conditioned tanks – I mean buses –, huge dormitories, blitz missions – I mean tours –, heavy casualties because of napalm – sorry: because of sunburns. … To make it easier and more profitable, one hotel has even constructed a small Christian chapel between the swimming pool and the barbecue corner, so as to offer a complete package to candidates-in-marriage and honeymoon-ers, with the sunset thrown in as a bonus.

I have seen it with my own eyes: the destruction is extensive and seems irreversible; all along the west coast, the corals are dying. An eery sight: the once splendid polyps of all colours, sizes and shapes were now but greyish cadavers, wrapped in shrouds woven with sticky whitish filaments, and looking like butterflies cocooned in spider webs. "All that is the responsibility of the green starfish," was the quick response of the people with interests to protect. But they could not reply to people who pointed out (as I did) that the corals, and thus all the fishes and shells feeding on them or sheltering among them, were disappearing only along the west coast, i.e., along the coast which was developed – overdeveloped, one should say more emphatically – for tourist-trade. Can you imagine the sadness of it all? It is as if all the stars in the sky, the Sky of the Ocean, were dying one by one.

46,900 Angry Ghosts

Inevitably, too, it seemed to us that a negative chain reaction had set in the other world – the invisible world.

Sadness, grief and even despair were shared by those who, nor-mally, would not be moved to wrenching hearts, or crying eyes … We felt – those of us who, like the island, the ocean and the sky, had become sick – that the wounds and graves of the Pacific War were suddenly re-opening, oozing forth pus, as well as bad memories. Suddenly, the rusty skeletons of Japanese tanks or American landing crafts were no more the homes of multi-coloured fishes, birds or insects: they reverted to bloody ruins again and symbols of hate, savagery, absurdity, not of forgiveness. White bones and skeletons, which had become part of the jungle humus, of the sand or of the corals, lullabied into a peace, were now springing back to life. One could not help but feel on the back of one's neck the breath of the angry ghosts of the 46,900 who died in battles or suicides (on just 47 square miles!). Images of the holocaust flashed again and again in memories: the mass suicides at Banzai, or Suicide, Cliffs, the fathers tying themselves up to their wives and children to make sure they would die with them, a mother running back and forth along the edge of the abyss, apparently unable to make up her mind, but who finally leapt with the child, to be swallowed up by the ocean dragon. One could hear the crying on the wind, the moaning in the rain (the weather was still foul after this killer typhoon, and exceptionally so for this period of the year), words being hurled about and exploding like hand grenades:

"Why?"

"What did you fight for?"

"What did we die for?"

"Haven't you learned the lesson?"

"Can't, once and for all, you break out of the vicious circle of ignorance-contempt-hate-war which caused us to fight, and caused us to die?"

"Do we have to rise again and – this time – fight against you living ones, you invaders, you polluters, you who are now killers, and suicide candidates?"

"Wake up! Open your eyes! Be more human! Be more human. We paid so dearly for you to find the Way ..."

The Milky Way – Closer to Bloomsday

Which way? – The *hinayana*, the 'lesser action or vehicle,' the Way of Wisdom through which individuals can defeat *maya*, the world of illusions? The *mahayana*, 'the great vehicle,' or liberation through compassion? The *vajrayana*, the Way of the Diamond, and ascension through metaphysical visions? The way of dialogue with the divine, the Christian way of exaltation of the person, or the Oriental way of communion and harmony? The Pascalian Way of the Reed (i.e., the head), or the African and Asian Way of the Tom-tom (i.e., of the heart, stomach, fingers and feet? To think or to dance? Is not dancing to be? – as says Leopold Senghor ("Danser, c'est être")? To be (indeed we must) – but how to be?

And what about the Rainbow Way? ... What is it really? How to invent it, and reinvent it unceasingly? And from the Rainbow, through the Rainbow, to where? Surely, through this Rainbow Bridge, there must be a way to ... the Milky Way, which itself should take us closer to Bloomsday – and further away from doomsday.

"How can man become human? This is the problem that has confronted me every-day in my practical work." Those words, written by C.G. Jung (in a letter to Philip Wylie, dated 27.06.47), could very well have been written by you, Laurens, and by all those who care for our survival, and who know that the answer is *in ourselves*, that Man should first try to save, create and recreate Man, before begging for outside help ... For that, we have to heal, to be made whole again, as Jung strove to do, by the Shamanist Way, and the Alchemical Way.

Nevertheless, today, in Saipan and elsewhere, the problem seems to be not so much to become more human, as how to stop being inhuman. How? How to heal, to make whole again, to calm the angry spirits, the angry winds, the angry ocean of Saipan, and let the music – here the lullaby, there the rhapsody – flow again?

First, one could perhaps try to remember ... *La recherche du temps perdu, c'est aussi la recherche du bonheur perdu.* One could remember, for instance, that, once upon a time, an island was born in this blue sky, this pacific blue sky of the ocean, born to be happy and to make happy. To remember – not sunburns, not napalm burns – but sunset burns, or moonburns ... romance, in a word. In the beginning, was it not Romance – before the Word?

À la Recherche du Bonheur Perdu

Do you remember, Isoko? That was only fourteen years ago: Saipan was then almost inaccessible. There was no daily direct flight from Tokyo, as there is today. You had to take a little Friendship plane from Guam and try to squeeze yourself in between a Chamorro girl carrying stems of bananas and another one carrying bags of rice. Then, it was Russian roulette with the hazards of island-hopping: from Guam to Rota (what a good laugh we had when the little fire-tender there crashed into our airplane, even though the airfield was deserted and there was plenty of room to maneuver), from Rota to Tinian (our hearts twinged when we touched down on the airfield that had been used for take-off by the two B-29's which had inflicted the nuclear holocaust on Hiroshima: having both been blessed by an Army chaplain, *Enola Gay*, with its Little Boy bomb, and *Great Artist*, with its Fat Man bomb), and finally, from Tinian to Saipan. That was quite an adventure.

And do you remember the Saipanese Tetsuo, the dark-skinned Chamorro who was speaking Japanese fluently? Under his guidance, we used to dive into a rhapsody in blue (and gold), searching with our submarine torches for lobsters, which, just as rabbits love to do, were prancing about under the moon? During those years, it was still possible to hear the Saipanese and Chamorros singing and joking and laughing, and getting moon-burned. Today, they are busier trying to make money, and most of them tend to be bitter. And they are poor (by American standards) – so much so that food tickets are allocated to them. Instead of taking to the sea or toiling the rich volcanic soil, they find it easier to drag themselves to the nearest supermarket and buy some frozen tuna from California, lettuce from Nagoya, or deep-frozen fruit bats from Hawaii. ...

Can Little Sparks of Music Light Big Fires?

Is there any hope to stop the delirium, the engorgement, this sleep-walking towards the cliff?

The evening after I had seen 'my' Christmas rainbow through my clouded mask, we had supper by the sea. A pianist (we knew by then that he was Italian) was playing the piano, and in a surprisingly professional manner in such a remote place – from Bach to Mozart, Rachmaninoff, Gershwin to "*La Vie en Rose*" or "I Left My Heart in San Francisco"... He then asked each of us to select a piece. Isoko chose a Chopin Waltz; to deal with my cold and my malaise, I asked for something more vitamin-packed: Gershwin's "Rhapsody in Blue" – which he then kindly played, dedicating each piece to us. For Claire-Yumi he personally chose to play and sing an old Venetian folk song, a lullaby, "*Falla nana bambin,*" which was composed especially to send off in the sweetest way a '*bambin*' to his or her travel in life, from the Milky Way to the swamp, as I believe. He finished by singing a traditional Chamorro lullaby, which he had learned from the island-ers, and had transcribed and harmonized.

While talking with this new acquaintance, we came to learn that he had actually studied piano and composition at the Venice Conserva-tory, had traveled all around the world and then, via Guam, twelve years ago, had finally arrived in Saipan, where he decided to settle for good, teaching music and judo (he had obtained the first dan in that sport) at the local college. Two other passions of his, besides music and judo, were Esperanto and orchids. After three years of hard labour, he had just finished building his own house, when Kim, the typhoon killer, demolished all his work, wiping out his garden and most of his beloved orchids. Then I committed a blunder. … I knew, of course, that orchid lovers are a very special tribe, but I naively asked if orchids were not parasites, and whether their charm and beauty were not in fact derived from vampirism. … *Mama mia*! I got it right back in the neck. How could I say so foolish a thing?! Didn't everybody know that orchids are self-sufficient, and are, in reality, quite human-like; i.e., pirates (?).

"Orchids feed on the wind, on moisture, are all lips, all smile; they metamorphose themselves like rabbits inside silk hats; they have moods and whims … Orchids, you see, are women – I mean, some are ladies, and some others are real … you can guess what," he said to me with a wink.

Then this Italian judoka pianist orchid-lover told me how his orchids committed suicide when the typhoon struck …

"You see, it was my fault. I took inside the house the varieties which seemed to be the most vulnerable, and left the most robust ones, the country girls, if you like, outside, under protection, of course. And, do you know what happened? They survived the typhoon. But afterwards, what a tragedy: they let themselves die. It was a suicide, and I'll tell you why. Because they were vexed, they were jealous, they wanted to take revenge, you see … *Ça, à tous les coups, c'était du dépit amoureux*!" he concluded in French.

(Oh! Romance, romance! … Could romance still exist on Saipan?)

"Perhaps, one day, you could produce orchids on a big scale, and transform this island into a garden?", I suggested.

"It's a possibility. But for the present time, I'm engaged in cross-breeding local varieties, which are too weak and too pale in colour, with other ones from different countries …"

We parted with a promise to exchange recorded tapes of folk music: he would send me the Chamorro lullaby and the Venetian song he had sung for Claire-Yumi, and I would send him various pieces I had collected during my travels, in particular a Siberian song and some Dogri folk tunes from India played on santoor and guitar; he wanted to use those materials for his teaching. "They're so poor here," he said with his contagious smile. "They're so hungry for things different from the stuffy punk-rock-pop diet that is inflicted on them."

(O music, music! Could little sparks of music, like orchids in the hearts of men, light big fires in Saipan again?)

"Truth is (not only) a Tempest"

Two days after our supper by the sea with this interesting and active Italian, on the first day of 1987, the Year of the Rabbit, my family and I flew back to Tokyo, and there it was, waiting for me on my desk, Daimon's letter inviting me – among others – to contribute to the commemoration of your birthday, dear Laurens, by dealing with the theme of the "Rock Rabbit and the Rainbow"... Frankly speaking, I was quite at a loss. Of course, the French have a lot of rabbit or hare stories to tell, but, alas! – they often end with a click of the tongue, and are not as poetic and meaningful as the Bushmen stories. As for rainbows ... yes, what a coincidence (or was it?). I had just seen one in Saipan. But what kind of story went with it? Well, I told myself, just try. Try to remember, try to understand ... and I started writing, as if I were sending a note in the form of a holiday postcard, Laurens.

Now that my postcard is almost filled up, what should I say? How to conclude, how to interpret the whole message of this rainbow over the heart of Saipan, that seems to have been seen by nobody except me? Is there any significance behind that symbol? What is it? – I don't know. Don't find a clue.

But, today, I read an article in *The Japan Times* of the 8th of January of this new Year of the Rabbit, entitled: 'Soldier's Book Reveals Military Confusion of 1939 Border War.'

Akira Nishida, 71, one of the very few survivors of the battles which raged in 1939 along the border between Northwestern Manchuria and Outer Mongolia, had just published a book based on secret military documents. The bloody episode is known under the name of the 'Nomonhan' or the 'Khalkin Gol Incident,' during which the Japanese Kwangtung Army was defeated by superior Russian forces. Seventy per cent of the 36,000 soldiers and officers of the 23rd Division in charge of keeping watch over the border were wiped out. For the very first time in the modern era, Japan had been defeated, which explains why the whole truth was censored and the records kept secret. But it so happened that Nishida, who was one of only three men from his unit to survive the battle and ultimately recover from his serious injuries, had been assigned to the staff office, where he came to have access to the most sensitive documents. His conclusion: "The Kwangtung army's line of command was in confusion, and military operations were carried out haphazardly."... "Operation Staff Officers were too concerned about saving face to think rationally."...

And then, Akira Nishida tries to tell in his book about his passage through hell, the suffering; how he tried to help console his dying friends, dying uselessly; and then how he tried to survive amongst decomposing bodies. To us, for whom wars, terrorist attacks, genocide, hunger, desertion, the menace of a nuclear winter, or the disappearance of the precious ozone layers, are part of the everyday diet, there is nothing really new in Nishida's testimony. Nothing particularly moving, either.

However, Nishida is angry, and his book vibrates with his anger, like the wind and the rain and the ocean in Saipan. In his preface, Nishida shouts to the Japanese and to all of us who tend to forget, and become less and less human: "Even today, many people are dying from environmental pollution. The same thing that happened during the past war is being repeated. Nomonhan is still with us 47 years after the war."

Of course, everyone knows that cry from the heart; it has become a cliché to say that Dachau, Buchenwald, Pearl Harbour, Hiroshima, Nagasaki, Minamata, the Inquisition, witch-hunting, re-education camps, prisons and gulags of all kinds, are very much part of our times. ... Is it built in? Is it in our genes? Can we never escape the vicious circle?

Truth – alas! – often begins with the experience of fear, anger, out of a tempest. In fact, "truth is (not only) a tempest," as Solzhenitsyn wrote: truth is also a scandal. "God's death is believable, since it is senseless; His Resurrection is bound to happen, since it is impossible," has said Tertullian, who was fond of this verse from Isaiah: "If you do not believe, you shall not understand."

Do we have to understand, and accept, that evil shall always be with us, even if we shoot towards the stars, as if ... it were a guarantee of our freedom, of our humanity, as well as the necessary condition – along with the good and the divine – of our progress, of our happiness, and, ultimately, of our redemption. Was Hitler, then, necessary for us to live better, to feel better? Hell, no, – of course not! But this monster, one of the cohorts of monsters and Lucifer's horde, accident or not, should help us to remember ... to forgive, if possible ... and to get closer to the side where there is Light – yet, where darkness is seemingly still used to produce more Light. Yes, what a tempest, to recognize that hard fact of life and death, here and over there. What a scandal!

Their Rainbow ... Your Rainbow ... My Rainbow ...

What, then? What happened exactly in Saipan? Was it nothing more than a holiday which turned out to be spoiled by a typhoon and a bad cold, and the blues? Was there no message behind that Rainbow Bridge I saw? Perhaps there was, and is, but why should you interfere?, – I told myself. Listen to Nishida instead. Listen to Solzhenitsyn or Elie Wiesel. Listen to the real actors, the real survivors and witnesses of black holes of cosmic proportions, those who paid the price for being angry and shouting at us. Come on, don't you see that in Saipan you were just a disappointed holidaymaker? Don't try to be a troublemaker now.... After all, you are not Saipanese, not a resident of Saipan, not an American, mind your own business ...

All right, I get the message high and clear: this rainbow over Saipan was not 'my' rainbow. It was, and so it should remain, just a gift, just Christmas under the tropical sun. Perhaps it was even part of a package deal, like the sunset and the nuptial benediction for the others. ... Yes, indeed. I quite agree; this rainbow belongs to Saipan and to the Saipanese. It's *their* rainbow. So it should be their responsibility to find – if they wish to, if they are in the mood, and there really is one – a meaning for it.

Now what about *your* rainbow, dear Laurens?

The Spinning '8' of Love

For those who are close to you, known and unknown friends, we know that, from the very first moment we accepted to follow you in the red sands and under the starry sky of the Kalahari, or accepted the invitation to contemplate the moon through snowy cherry blossoms in Japan, or through the barbed wires of your prisoner-of-war camp in Java, nothing really strange can happen – yet everything can happen. What is strange amidst all is when nothing happens, and all stands still – contrary to the intuitive, Dyonisian, zigzag race of the rabbit/hare, or the magic materialization of a rainbow between the visible and the invisible, as well as the hunting for greater meaning and the ceaseless weaving of rainbow colours amidst the storm we are made to witness throughout your books.

For what purpose is this rainbow-weaving, this hunting, this building of bridges of yours, this exploring further and further on? Of course, it is for yourself first; I suspect that you are only comfortable, like the Bushman, or Chateaubriand's René, in the midst of the tempest. You pursue your dreams, and make us dream – as does the fisherman in the famous Noh play, Hagoromo, when he found on a bush somewhere along the pine-dotted Mito beach, at the foot of the old lion, Mt. Fuji, the rainbow dress of a heavenly fairy. …

For all those reasons, the celebration of your anniversary, dear Laurens, cannot be a rupture, a stop in your hunting, but rather a collective rejoicing and dance, in the eye of the typhoon, for, if '8' is not your lucky number (that, as we know, is '13'), '8' is nevertheless the symbol of love and infinity, of joy spinning and rebounding ever and ever.

Could we then throw some '8's in your cauldron, and see what happens with their spinning round, and round, and round, all around the Earth, which itself becomes an '8' when moored to the Sun, or the Moon.

Rhapsody – O So Blue, O So Peaceful…

You certainly know of the old custom on Volendam Island, in the Zuider Zee. I have been told by an old man selling smoked eels – as black and stiff as vanilla husk – in the streets of Moleckendam that, when a young man was seeking somebody's hand in marriage, he had to have a special pair of clogs made, adorned with various symbols, including three intertwined '8's. Then, with the pair of clogs under his arm, he had to present himself on the doorstep of the house of his beloved. Without a word, the mother would take the present and shut the door. The young man could then do nothing else but go out to sea, fishing. If, on his return, his beloved was wearing his clogs, then he knew that he was accepted as her husband; if she was carrying them under her arm, however, he had better look for another girl, or else marry with the sea for life – like Captain Mori, one of your best friends in Japan, did in a way.

Eleven years after I learnt of this old Dutch custom, I heard of another custom very similar to it, this time at the antipodes and in another context, on the Japanese Island of Hachijojima.

This tiny island, quite some distance from Tokyo, was once the place to which opponents of the Shogun were exiled. Little by little, they turned this place into a garden; males were scarce, although there were plenty of women. By contrast, on the neighbouring island of Aogashima, there was a majority of men. So, once a year, during the hot August nights, the young men of Aogashima would dash into the phosphorescent sea and paddle frantically towards Hachijojima and her beauties, who would be waiting on the black sand, dressed in the *yukata* they had woven with their own hands, with moire-like dragonflies, sitting with their *zori*, their straw sandals, with red thongs by their side. Once the young men, with phosphorescent moonbeams and wave-spray on their shoulders, landed, helped by the southern wind, they would look for the signal ... the signal of the red-thonged *zori* sandals. As soon as they seized the zori, they were snatched, enfolded in arms, entangled in a forest perfumed with camelias. The rest of the night was spent in merrymaking and dancing to the sound of giant drums – drums unknown on the Asian continent, drums which certainly came all the way to Hachijojima on rafts, centuries ago, from Java and Sumatra, and perhaps from Africa. ...

Those were the coded signals of love – in times when eyes could still see, ears could still hear, dreams could still be dreamt – and not be dreamt for us. ...

***

By way of conclusion, dear Laurens, let me formulate a wish, would you? I wish that this message from the antipodes, from a country for which you have a particular feeling, Japan, this message which is being sent to you, as part of a friendly conspiration, will some day be received, and possibly read, by our new Italian friend in Saipan, and that, to exorcise the somber and negative things which I have written about his Saipan, he will follow the custom of the Japanese, who, when they want a prayer to be fulfilled or evil to be exorcised, write their prayer down on thin paper, fold it, and then tie it to the branch of a tree. ... If this could be so, let the prayer be tied to a branch of one of the flame trees on San Antonio Beach – close to the rainbow I saw, and which is no more mine, but his and theirs, the Saipanese, when I brought back a blue star to our mermaid, Claire-Yumi – in the hope that these somber and negative words, not to mention these blues of mine, may be scattered to the winds; to dissolve – and be absolved – in and by the rain, in and by the sun, then to fuse with the sapmilk of Mother Earth, or with the rhapsody – o so blue, o so peaceful – of the Ocean.

Laurens van der Post on the day before final departure from Java, 1948

A Royal *Bouillabaisse*

Laurens van der Post

A Writer in Prison

Perhaps my strangest writing experience – among an immense variety and density of experiences by now – was writing in the circumstances of the kind of captivity we endured under the Japanese. I was, on the whole, far too busy in prison to write, but nonetheless, there were occasions when the writer in me insisted on writing. It is because of the reassurance I found in this strange insistence to return to writing, no matter how long my separation from writing had been, that I think it belongs in this volume. It goes back, after all, to the beginning of the beginning of the human spirit.

The Japanese starved us of food, and after three-and-a-half years, had starved us close to death. But there was one substance of which they always gave us an over-abundance, and that was lavatory paper. It was by far the greatest service – short of giving us more food – they could have done us. We never used it for the purposes for which it was intended: those who were smokers used it to smoke, because there was always a supply of Javanese tobacco, but by us as a camp, it was used as the basis for the educational service we built up, and, in the good periods when the Japanese overlooked it, printing our own newspaper, *Mark Time*. Occasionally, there was even a magazine issue of the daily news-sheets, and I sometimes found myself writing for *Mark Time* features, something of my own, which somehow lifted the vision we had of life in camp to something which shone like a little candle in the dark behind us.

One of these pieces was called "A Royal *Bouillabaisse*." The introduction to the story was designed to convey atmosphere rather than literal truth, but once I came to the part where the fishermen were sheltering in the cave against the storm, the story is true in every detail and as accurate as a memory which has been rather good allowed it to be.

And so here it is, accompanied also by an example of what we did in our lighter moments to make us laugh or smile at ourselves. Our "Director of Education," Gunnar Penry Rees, an inspired teacher and profoundly cultured person, wrote weekly in *Mark Time* a feature called *Pity Ditty*. This is how one of his "Pity Ditties" pictured me:

A Pity Ditty
    Pity poor Colonel van der Post
    who has more jobs to do than most
    He never chides
    He never disagrees
    but sometimes smiles in high Chinese.

***

The following story is true and, because it is true and may also make a difference to people's understanding of a great personality, I must tell it before it is lost. It was a favourite story that I used to be asked to tell over and over again to my troops in the war when we were in a Japanese prison in Java.

The story was first told to me by an old fisherman called Galthier when, as far back as 1929, I was sailing my boat round the islands near Porquerolles in the Mediterranean. The Mediterranean world is, of course, so old that you almost want to hold your breath when you think of it. I myself have never gone back to it without realising anew how old it is. Nowhere else, it seems, has both earth and sun and the life of man been interwoven in so frank, continuous and rich an association for so long. Elsewhere, time may indeed be *the winged chariot hurrying near,* but here in the Mediterranean, it is more like an ancient black ship beating up slowly, way back, over the blue and gold horizons, its purple sails filled with the winds of fate. Oh, those Mediterranean winds! They have in them the quintessential of all the winds that have ever blown, something of the first wind that man ever heard and something of the last wind that will bring time up to our side. They seem indeed to come and blow through a man with the breath of the ancient gods.

No wonder old Jean, who used to help me sail my little boat, always called on the sacred blood of the wood when he had occasion to mention the mistral. And on this particular morning of which I am speaking, in the Mediterranean far back in 1929, I heard him muttering as he groped below very early to come and call me. "Good blood of the wood, sacred name of names, dirty and most pestilential of ladders! Up my captain, up, because before long it is going to make as fine a mistral for us as we have ever seen."

Mistral! What a royal Mediterranean name for a good Mediterranean wind! High up in the frozen, crackling air over the peaks of Mont Blanc and the Matterhorn, where these winds are bred, they may be just like any other wind to the shivering mountaineers, but here on the sunny shores of the Mediterranean, it is typical of the high social and intimate standing nature has in the mind of man, that they all become personalities and have all had personal names given to them. Mistral, I like to think, is the oldest name of the lot. I cannot imagine a better name for this great grey creature of air which comes hurtling down the flanks of Mont Blanc, and am not surprised that, on the Camargue, where the cavalry wind breaks out of the long twisting Rhône Valley into the straight for its final charge down to the sea, that the people there have given the name Mistral to their greatest poet. I cannot imagine anything more appropriate than that the Mistral should be linked with poetry and song, for even in the moments of its greatest importunity the mistral knows how to make music out of its own violence. Often at sea, or in the depths of the antique forests of the Dom, I have heard it pluck a cataclysmic note out of the sky above it and throw it on the tumult of the storm like the reverberation of a giant harp string.

It interested me this particular morning when I came on deck, to see again how well the heavens knew what was coming. There seemed not one unnecessary speck of dust in the air, no more vapour than was absolutely essential left in the sky. As a result, a pointed brilliance clattered down on us from above, and even that grey pointed peak far behind La Crau stood sharp and clear-cut in the moonlight. Then, suddenly, I saw a long wisp of manilla cloud hurl itself unexpectedly, like a lassoo round the peak. It missed the top, clutched at the sides, held on for another moment, then slid down the slide again and in a second came streaking toward us. At the same time, I heard a low, desperate wail put off from the distant land, like the cry of a hungry wolf pack on the far side of the Siberian steppe.

"Jean," I said curtly, "we shall never be able to sail round Black Cape today."

"*Entendu*," he replied.

"We had better run for the shelter of the near islands, quick," I added, going forward.

"*Allons*," he replied and immediately went aft.

Five hours later, we brought the little ship trembling and dripping with spray right between the needle points of the Cape of the Two Brothers into the ample shelter of one of the bigger of the Islands of Gold. We dropped anchor near an ancient cave, called *Le Souterrain des Pirates*. The Galthiers, the fishing island dwellers and descendants of the pirates who gave the cave its name, and who had already watched our arrival through the storm, were there to meet us. They greeted us in the hospitable manner of their antique calling and for forty-eight hours, landlocked by the storm, we all sat there together in the cave burning large fires of driftwood and making one interminable *bouillabaisse* after another; drinking honest red wine and watching the gulls shoot past like arrows from the cliffs overhead, and waiting for the wind to abate. At night when the mistral sang like a chorus of Greek furies overhead, we drew deeper into the cave and there over the fire swapped tales as we sipped steaming hot coffee and rum out of our glasses.

On our last night there, Le Père Galthier, the patriarch of the island community, stood up dramatically and spoke directly to me. He was a tall man and very thin. He had a long straggling white beard and a curious interest and talent for painting. He painted endless monotonous pictures of the sea on very large canvasses and sold these paintings by the square metre to tourists who came to the island. He always wore a large black hat, even when he went out fishing to sea, and both inbreeding and what he called his artistic temperament had inflicted him with quite an un-Mediterranean nervousness. As he stood straight up there in the cave with his black hat firmly on and his long beard flickering uneasily in the back-eddies of the stormy air, he made a macabre impression on me, as if he were an Old Testament prophet about to deliver a message.

"My captain," he said, "is it true what Jean tells us, that you are indeed an English captain?"

I nodded.

"Well then, my captain, I want to tell you a true story. Do not doubt for a moment that what I am going to tell you is the sacred truth. I saw it happen with my own eyes just about here where we are sitting now. So if you will fill up your glasses, my children, and you too, my captain, and come a bit nearer, I will tell you what the story is."

We gathered around this macabre old man and he went on.

"I was a boy when it happened," he said, "and there by the entrance of the cave, there was still a bit more beach than there is now. In fact, there, not far from the mouth of the cave, grew as fine a tamarisk tree as you have ever seen in these islands … That tree has died, for it was so long ago. But I remember what happened as if it were only yesterday. We were sitting round the tree making one of the finest *bouillabaisses* which has ever been made in these waters."

"The day was calm. The sun was shining. Our catch had been good and as a result, my father was very generous to the grail. Lobster, crayfish, crab, shrimps, some nice long grey wolves of the sea, some first-rate mullet, a long, fat, juicy eel, onions, garlic, potatoes, salt, black pepper, bread, saffron (the best yellow saffron from Marseille) all went, one after the other at their appointed moment, into that steaming pot."

"Then suddenly, what should we see but a beautiful white boat come sailing round the headland. It was spick and span, shining like a mirror in the sun, and this brand new shining boat sailed straight for the mouth of this ancient dark old cave. Oh, my captain, that boat still sails like a thing of wonder in my dreams! We all stood there gaping at this miraculous shining white ship coming straight for us and my father stood up like a man in a dream to go down to the water to meet it. As it touched the shore, some sailors leaped out and, in a moment, were helping out the most wonderful old lady you could imagine."

"She had a large bonnet made out of some very purple material on her head. It was so large that it almost hid her face, yet in the blue of the shadow it made round her face and features, we could see the most commanding and the bluest of her blue eyes. Blue, my captain, like the blue of the Madonna's own robe. Only mark you, my captain, they were sad eyes of a sort of sadness that you could not forget afterwards. We saw her say a few words to my father, who, to our amazement, suddenly bowed low before her like a Prince of Provence in a manner which we had never seen him bow before. She then came over with him towards us and I saw that she was rather a short old lady. Her shoulders were rather square and firm for a woman. Her black and purple velvet skirt budged all round her, and made her face look like a white something coming out of a kind of fountain of shining velvet. But heavens above, my captain, how white her skin was! You almost had a shiver looking at it. In these islands, we had never seen, and I have not seen since, a skin as white as that old lady's. Straight to the pot she came, sniffed daintily and, there and then, for all that, she was a very wonderful gracious old lady like someone out of an old story, and she sat down in a seat which my father offered her beside the pot and ate this wonderful *bouillabaisse* with us. Before she went, she counted five bright yellow coins into my hand and then she sailed away over the sea again in that boat, like a white swan with a purple bonnet on. It made the day suddenly empty."

He broke off. Then looking slyly at me, the old patriarch said again, apparently irrelevantly, "You English are strange. When you are cold and tired of yourselves and your misery, you come here to France to rest and be refreshed … Not only just a fine military gentleman like you, but even your greater ones; they, too, come."

"But who was she? Who was this greater one?" Jean asked excitedly. "Tell us!"

"She was tired of her ministers," old father Galthier went on. "She came to that place Hyères over there on the mainland, to rest, and once, when I was a boy, she came to eat a *bouillabaisse* with us here on this very same spot … except that the tamarisk is longer here."

"*Zut alors!*" old Jean exclaimed, getting impatient. "Who?"

Old father Galthier held his tumbler, full now of the reddest of red wine, to the light. He turned his head to the shadows, as if from the other side of the world he heard her footsteps approaching and said quietly, and yet so clearly that the cosmic voice of the mistral outside could not dim his words: "*La Reine Victoria!*" And raising his glass high, he drank it down in one draught.

Crying on the Wind

Jane Taylor

A week before we set out on our final trip for the filming of *Testament to the Bushmen* with Laurens van der Post in September 1982, and just before Laurens himself joined us, a bright green praying mantis suddenly appeared in the drawing room of my Johannesburg home. Filled as I then was with the old tales of Mantis, as recounted early this century by some of the now extinct /Xam Bushmen of the Cape to Wilhelm Bleek and Lucy Lloyd, I saw this visitation as an omen holding both a caveat and a benison.

For those old Bushmen, this curious insect had symbolized all that was most creative, profound, paradoxical and divine in their lives; and both insect and divinity, the 'Master of all things,' shared the name Mantis. "I shall have wings," explained Mantis in one of the stories. "I shall fly when I am green, I shall be a little green thing." The Mantis of these stories was creator, hero and fool, as multi-faceted in his character as he was protean in the physical shapes he assumed; and this very protean faculty also gave him the role of trickster. He acted with passion, and often with compassion; with uncommon, rather than common, sense – therefore, he was frequently misunderstood, even by members of his own family. He encountered many dangers and difficulties and did not always emerge unscathed.

I am ill-equipped to expound the mythology of the Bushmen, already illuminated by Laurens van der Post's vision; what I have said is simply to explain the complex benediction that my mantis visitor seemed to confer. Kolben, an 18th century traveler, wrote that, for the Bushmen, "the arrival of this Insect in a *Kraal* brings Grace and Prosperity to all the inhabitants"; as producer of the films, I deemed my kraal to be inhabited by all of us involved in making *Testament to the Bushmen*. For two days, the mantis remained in motionless prayer on my window; then, as suddenly as it had come, it vanished. The

Jane Taylor and Sir Laurens at the van der Post Panel during filming of Testament to the Bushman

following day, Laurens arrived, and two days later, we set off for the Kalahari Desert, to the Tsodilo Hills in the northwestern corner of Botswana.

The location had been carefully chosen, for we wanted to take Laurens back to this numinous spot which had played so momentous a role in his filming trip twenty-eight years before. In all the vast expanse of the Kalahari Desert, these are the only hills, ramparts of rock rising clear and commanding above the flat surrounding bush, designed, it seemed, by Nature herself, for something special. For millennia, they had been known to the Bushmen alone; later, to the Black peoples who came to inhabit this area of Africa; and in 1954, Laurens was the first white man known to have set eyes on the Tsodilo Hills – the Slippery Hills – to the !Kung Bushmen of the area, the home of very old and very potent spirits.

At one end stands the inhospitable cone of the 'male' hill, the tallest of the three – just a little over one thousand feet, but seeming higher from its very sheerness; straggling away from it is the 'female' hill – more a cluster of hills whose gentle undulations are dotted with craggy protuberances. At the far end stands the third and smallest hill, somewhat apart from the others. As with all things of great significance to them, the !Kung here have many stories about the origin of the hills, with variations in detail that are very characteristic of all Bushmen for whom no one person's story, or perception of the supernatural, is regarded as inferior to another's – each tells its own truth and can illumine some aspect of the divine.

One thing is universal in the !Kung stories and beliefs about the Tsodilo Hills – that they are a place of strong *n/um*, or supernatural power. They say that the Great God made the hills and lived here himself; here, too, he created and kept cattle, sheep and goats, as well as all manner of wild animals. They say this must be so, for their hoofprints can be seen in the rocks – and there are indeed strange marks which look like the prints of some fiery creatures impressed deeply into what was then the molten rock. Even the paintings on the rock faces here – the only Bushman art in the Kalahari – are said by many Bushmen to be the work of the Great God Himself, whose presence fills the hills with special magic. No one should complain here of hunger or thirst, or of being plagued by wind, thorns, flies or the incessant bees. We had cause to remind ourselves of this stricture.

In 1954, as he recounted in *The Lost World of the Kalahari*, Laurens was brought here by a remarkable grey-headed African called Samutchoso whose name, he said, meant 'he who was left after the reaping.' Samutchoso was a prophet and healer among his people, and he believed that the inside of the hills was divided into many compartments, in each of which lived the master spirit of every animal, bird, insect and plant that had ever been created. In a part of the central hill, he said, lived the greatest spirit of all, beside a spring of everlasting water and a tree bearing the fruit of knowledge. Not far away was a rock on which we may still see the marks where this great spirit knelt on the day he created the world and all that is in it.

Today a small airstrip has been made beside the Tsodilo Hills, to which we flew daily from our luxurious camp on the Okavango River, feeling uncomfortably like voyeurs from another world. The airstrip is the only modern invasion as yet, and those primordial hills still made a powerful impression on us, thrusting up from the flatness surrounding them as if they had indeed been propelled by an irrepressible leap of divine imagination. As we landed on that first day, there gathered about us almost immediately a handful of people, alerted by the sight and sound of our little plane. Gradually, one by one, the handful grew to a small group who watched in fascination as we set about filming. But there was not a Bushman to be seen. We asked our local guide if there was a Bushman group nearby, and he said gravely that there was and that they would be brought to us. It was very clear that the Bushmen were at the beck and call of the local black Africans.

For the first few days, the weather was dispiriting: overcast, but sunny at the same time, the air hot and heavy, and we were attended constantly by our chattering corona of spectators. First we filmed the Bushman paintings, executed as we had been told by the Great God Himself in a lovely monochrome red ochre. Elands in particular throng the rock faces, the Great God's most beloved animals, just as they had been for Mantis in the south. Surrounding them are other antelopes, giraffes, zebras, white and black rhinos – a painted procession of some of the Great God's creations. Amongst the animals are also some primitive, sticklike human figures of great vitality, and here and there are some human hand-prints, where the artist had covered his tiny hands in red ochre and pressed them against the rock as a signature to his work. As usual, several stories are associated with these hand-prints: we had been told earlier that they had been made long ago by a man who was hunting giraffe. As he crept silently along, he occasionally put his hands on the rock at the places where we now

Sir Laurens stands beneath a frieze of eland in Eland Cave
during the filming of Testament to the Bushman *in 1982*
(Photo Jane Taylor)

see the prints. The last hand-print, immediately beside the painting of a giraffe, marks the spot where, we were told, he finally shot his poisoned arrow at the giraffe he was stalking. While we were filming the main gallery of paintings, a tall gangling, and very black African approached me. 'Vampo,' he said, beaming excitedly and pointing in the general direction of the camera and Laurens. 'Vampo?' I queried, utterly mystified. 'Vampo. Vampo,' he repeated, clearly hoping by much repetition to awaken my flagging imagination. 'Bottle. Letter,' he added, almost bursting with urgency and frustration. Suddenly it dawned on me. In this spot twenty-eight years before, Laurens van der Post (Vampo) had written a letter to the spirits of the hills, put it inside an empty gin bottle, and buried it in the sand in a cleft of the hills near the paintings that we were filming at that moment. The reason for this was that Samutchoso had told Laurens that he and his companions must not come to the hills with blood on their hands; in the press of problems, Laurens had forgotten to pass on the message and one of his group had killed an animal for food. The old man had been deeply disturbed at this sacrilege, albeit unwittingly committed; and indeed, from that moment everything had begun to go badly awry – they were attacked by bees, the tape recorder ceased to function and the film camera broke. In an attempt to reverse the cycle of ill fortune, Laurens had written a letter begging forgiveness for having broken one of the fundamental laws of the spirits of this holy place. It was this incident that this man was reminding me of in a burst of joyous recognition from twenty-eight years before.

The recognition was haunting enough in itself, but the confession that followed was even more so. This man had been a child at the time of Laurens' previous visit, but he had recognized him at once, for he had known he would come back. 'My name is Samutchau,' he told me, now with the help of our interpreter. 'Samutchoso was my uncle.' He added that the bottle was no longer there, but had been taken away, complete with letter, to the Museum in Gaborone, the capital of Botswana.

Needless to say, Laurens was deeply moved by the encounter, and by yet another example of the precision of the apparently fortuitous in life. Whenever we broke from filming he would draw Samutchau into conversation and seek his opinion as he had done with his uncle of old. Samutchoso had been so at one with the mysteries of life, a slight, ascetic man whose perceptions seemed more of the heart and the spirit than of the physical senses; his nephew was out of a quite different mould – a genial giant, filled with a wealth of unreflective good nature. For the rest of our visit, Samutchau was never far from us, keeping close to Laurens as if to reassure himself that this was not the dream that it seemed, but tangible reality.

With Samutchau and our other friends, we climbed the 'female' hill. At first, the path was bordered by a procession of animals painted on the rocks, creating a special kind of sacred way. The higher we climbed, the further apart the paintings became, until they ceased altogether and we were on our own with the bare rocks and the brown and waterless plants. At a narrow point on the path, not far from the top, Laurens found two hollows in the surface of a rock where, he had been told, the Great God had knelt to pray that all would be well for all the living things of His creation. As Laurens now fitted his knees into the hollows, and looked across at the aridity around us, some of us became aware of his profound unease.

By the time we had reached the top of the hill, the unease had deepened – where, twenty-eight years before, he had found a brimming pool, and beside it a tree laden with what Samutchoso had called the fruit of knowledge, now there was a dried-up hole, parched and cracked, and all the vegetation around was dead. Certainly there had been a long and hard period of drought, but the unease was not just because of the vanished water – it seemed, as Laurens articulated for us all, that "the spirit that presided over these hills had vanished too ... the water has gone, the tree has gone, the legends and the stories have gone."

It was two days later that the Bushmen arrived, a sorry, bedraggled group from whom – as by now we were expecting – the spirit appeared to have vanished. They simply allowed themselves to be ordered about by their more forceful black neighbours, who acted as their agents. With a profound sadness, we watched them build a couple of rough and ready huts, obediently setting up a spurious campsite for our benefit.

That night, we set up camp by the hills so that we could film the Bushmen as the sun went down and the full moon rose into the clear Kalahari night. Earlier in the evening, Laurens had danced and played with the children, gradually overcoming their shyness, his own merriment bringing out theirs. Later, under the moon and the stars, the Bushman women started to chant quietly; then the clapping began. Gradually, the rhythm became more insistent, and some of the men, unable to resist the call of the music, leaped into the firelight and began to dance – short, rhythmic steps, sometimes with both feet together, sometimes with one foot performing a complicated counterpoint to the main theme executed by the other foot. At first, they seemed lethargic, as if it were too great an effort to go through the age-old routine. But gradually, they warmed to the chanting, to the complex rhythm of the clapping, the stamping of their feet, the eerie swish of the dance-rattles around their ankles, and for a short moment, the present was drowned in the timelessness of the dance.

It did not last long. The chanting and the clapping became more desultory, and then stopped, and the men again sat around the fire. One thing they had not lost, and it seemed to us the one hopeful thing about this group – they still preserved the universal chattiness of the Bushmen. Wherever we had gone in the Kalahari, we had found them to be the most delightfully voluble of people, discovering in the everyday events of their lives a rich source of interest and amusement, to be shared and picked over like a good marrow bone till the last morsel of value and fun had been extracted. On this night of the full moon at the Tsodilo Hills, as Laurens in that magnetic voice of his, re-told an old Bushman story about the moon, these sad Bushmen of today kept up a gentle buzz of chatter in the background.

The story that Laurens told was of the creation by Mantis of his beloved eland, and of the eland's death at the hands of Mantis' own family. "So," he recounted, "Mantis had a moment of great bitterness, which is symbolically represented by an argument that he has with the gall of the eland. In the end, he pierces the gall to try and get rid of it, but the gall explodes and covers him over with blackness so that he cannot see. Not knowing what to do, blinded by bitterness, he writhes about until he finds a feather; and this feather is most important because it is the feather of the ostrich, the bird which gave Mantis fire, which is consciousness. He wipes the bitterness from his eyes with this consciousness enlarged through suffering. Then he throws the feather up into the sky and he says to it, 'Henceforth, you shall be the moon. You shall shine at night in the sky so that the men who have gone out hunting and got lost by day, shall have a light to show them the way home in the darkness to come.'"

The story summed up for me everything that my mantis visitor in Johannesburg had seemed to presage – difficulties and bitterness indeed, but the hope of light and of renewal, just as the moon itself is renewed. As I looked at the faces around the fire, men, women and children, many of them ravaged by sickness and suffering, those last words seemed painfully apt: the Bushmen of today desperately need a light to show them the way home in the darkness that for them has already come – something to help them find a new way of life that will enable them to survive with dignity, and on equal terms with their more assertive neighbours. We, too, need an illumination of mind and heart to recognize the value of a people who, in their gentleness, gaiety and creativity of spirit, are so different from ourselves.

That night as we lay in our sleeping bags under the spreading branches of an acacia tree, the wind began to stir. Quickly it grew in intensity, blowing sand into our hair, eyes, noses, mouths, and into every inch of our sleeping bags. It whined and sighed through the trees, and howled through the gullies and caves of the hills. By dawn, every one of us, and all our equipment and food, had become covered with a layer of Kalahari sand, and it was with the greatest resolution that we reminded ourselves that the wind of the Slippery Hills was one of the things we were enjoined not to complain about. At least we had not been set upon by bees, though we had seen plenty and they had seemed quite capable of an attack; and even if our food and drink were crunchy with sand, we would not go hungry or thirsty. As for Laurens, he had seen all this before, and was the least complaining of us all, though with the most cause. Despite a still painful back after some broken vertebrae a few months before, he had for several days put up with the vibrations of a light aircraft, the jarring of jeeps in sand, climbing among the hills, and now a night not merely on the sand, but covered with it.

When the wind is fierce and howls, the !Kung of this area give it the same name that they give to a spirit of the dead – *gauwa*; and for the extinct /Xam of the south, too, the wind was often associated with grief and death. "The wind does thus when we die," one of Bleek's and Lloyd's informants told them, "the wind makes dust, because it intends to blow, taking away our footsteps, with which we had walked about." Another said, "When the wind sounds as if it cries, it is sending its crying on the wind."

The footsteps of the Bushmen of old, with their traditional hunter-gatherer way of life, have indeed been taken away by a fierce and howling wind of change. Today, little seems left to them except the crying on the wind; yet, with their painful awareness of their own inferior status and the injustices heaped upon them, few have the energy or the optimism to cry out. There are some exceptions. An old !Kung Bushman told an American anthropologist, "People should cry out for themselves. People should protest. Black people cry for themselves, and they are alive. The Afrikaaners cried for themselves, and they are alive. These people over there went about crying and crying, and they were lifted up. We who are Zhu/twãsi (!Kung), let us cry out, so that we will be lifted up. Unless we do, we are just going to ruin."

A Last Look at a First Encounter

Aniela Jaffé

It is a great pleasure for me to contribute a few words of remembrance and gratitude to the *Festschrift* for Laurens van der Post. He and I first met nearly fifty years ago, when I was secretary of the C.G. Jung Institute in Zürich.

One morning as I worked in my office, the door opened and an unknown man entered. He introduced himself as Laurens van der Post and a lively dialogue ensued, during which I learned of the stranger's origins in the far-off land of South Africa. I listened in fascination as he told his tale and found myself gripped, not only by the content, but even more by the mighty *dimensions* being spread out in my tiny office.

It was, of course, an expression of his far-ranging personality, and I feel it to this very day each time I meet Laurens van der Post. It soon dawned on me that this man and C.G. Jung simply had to be brought together, for in an inner way, they had so much in common; indeed, to me, they seemed comrades. As 'fate' would have it, a formal dinner was being planned by the Jung Institute for the very next day. Laurens van der Post was quickly added to the guest list, and 'a benevolent spirit' arranged for him to be seated to the left of C.G. Jung. What a joy it was to see that my intuition had been right on the mark! For immediately, the two men fell into deep conversation, and before the meal was over, they had left the hall to continue their talk in the privacy of Jung's home, where it lasted until well into the night.

C.G. Jung's deep friendship with Laurens van der Post began that evening and continued without interruption until his death in 1961. His journey in the twenties to Kenya and Uganda had always been of great importance to him, and in Laurens van der Post, he indeed had encountered a friend capable of understanding the significance of his stories, for he had gone through similar inner and outer experiences of his own. Jung read his books with passion, and, as his correspondence attests, there were few men he so fully trusted as Laurens van der Post.

At the same time, perhaps no one had ever understood Jung so deeply as Laurens van der Post, as borne witness by his biography, *Jung and the Story of Our Time*. This beautiful book not only presents so aptly the significance of Jung's scientific work, but also succeeds in portraying that great expanse of his unique personality: a highly differentiated cultural understanding in harmony with an almost magical kinship with Nature.

Laurens van der Post is a preciously rare man for whom the intimate lives on even in the remote, and yet he is capable of creating distance without so much as a word or gesture when the occasion calls for it. At the root of his most genuine, while also disciplined, benevolence is a thorough knowledge of human nature. His far-ranging writings, for which we are so grateful, are not our subject here, but they cannot remain unmentioned, for they share with us the stories of a fairytale-land-that-was: Africa, with its deserts, its animals and its endearing inhabitants, the Bushmen, providing a never-ending treasure for us all.

(translation from the German, R.H.)

C.G. Jung and Aniela Jaffé at Eranos in the 1940's

Sir Laurens and Frances Baruch, London, Summer 1996

Jung and the Stone

Frances Baruch

The invitation to do a talk for "Grass Roots" came at an interesting time for me. A whole group of astonishing coincidences had occurred just when I was feeling that there was no connection between the area of my work (which is doing sculpture) and the one of my involvement with analytical psychology. The ideas for this talk popped up quite suddenly and immediately on the day the invitation arrived and seemed to suggest a kind of answer to the feelings of disconnection. As a consequence, I delivered what follows as a lecture at the Analytical Psychology Club in London.

I had first thought of focusing on Jung as a sculptor and artist – but this narrowed things down too much, as his 'flirtation' with his artistic anima was short-lived, while his relationship to the stone was life-long. However, it was just this experience (hearing the comments of this artistic 'lady') who first spoke through the voice of an actual patient of Jung that first introduced Jung to his anima and, having resisted her tempting urges to look on his painted and written images from the unconscious as art, he was able to maintain a creative dialogue with 'the lady' for many years to come.

Jung first encountered the stone very early in his life – he was only seven or eight years old when he experienced the curious interaction between himself and the rock he used to sit on in the garden of his home in Klein Huningen. He called it "my stone" and said, "Often when I was alone I sat down on this stone and then began an imaginary game that went something like this: I am sitting on top of this stone and it is underneath."[1] But the stone could also say "I" and

[1] Unless otherwise noted, quotes from C.G. Jung throughout this work are from *Memories, Dreams, Reflections by C.G. Jung*, recorded and edited by Aniela Jaffé, Pantheon, New York, 1962.

think, "I am lying here on this slope and he is sitting on top of me." The question then arose, "Am I the one who is sitting on the stone, or am I the stone on which he is sitting?" This puzzle gave Jung, as he says, a feeling of curious and fascinating darkness, but he adds: "There was no doubt whatsoever that this stone stood in some secret relationship to me..."

This experience, embedded in the eternal world of childhood, resonated with multi-toned echoes down the years in what seemed at times an alien place. Jung says, "The pull of that other world [the childhood one] was so strong that I had to tear myself violently from the spot [where he sat on the stone] in order not to lose hold of my future."

About a year or so later (maybe two), Jung carved a little man out of the top of a ruler, formally dressed in top hat, frock coat and shining boots – he even gave him a little woolen top coat. This figure took up residence in a pencil case and was given as a sort of companion a smooth oblong pebble from the Rhine which Jung had painted, to divide it into an upper and lower half, and which he had carried about with him for a long time. This stone then belonged to the carved figure and the two of them in their pencil box home were carefully hidden away in an attic, and kept as a great and important secret. The possession of this secret – the second in Jung's life (the first was the amazing dream of the underground phallus) – was somehow a great comfort to the boy, and healed, for the moment, what he calls the tormenting sense of being at odds with himself. He also says, "This possession of a secret had a very powerful influence on my character. I consider it the essential factor of my boyhood." The carving of the mannequin was the first attempt to give shape to the secret, and its emergence gave rise to the awareness of a great mystery, the answer to which Jung began to sense and search for in the world of nature. "At that time my interest in plants, animals and stones grew, I was constantly on the lookout for something mysterious." He also says, "It does seem to me, however, that I had a vague sense of relationship between the 'soul-stone' and the stone which was also myself."

At this point, we might just look at some of the ways in which stones have always fascinated mankind, starting with the connection that Jung himself found, many years afterwards, of the stone belonging to the mannequin with the 'soul stone' or 'churinga.' The churingas were magic objects, either stone or wood, which were kept by

Australian aborigines and handed on from one generation to the next and not only endowed with magic power put into them when they were made, but they also acquired some kind of virtue from every individual to whom they had belonged. They contain the spirit of the tribe and its continuity and represent the eternal and enduring. Stones piled on graves by many different peoples symbolize what survives after death – stability, durability, immortality, imperishability – the eternal cohesion, the in-destructibility of the Supreme Reality – these are all qualities of stone. The caches of stones kept by Stone-Age men in secret places were felt as repositories of their strength. Stones are the bones of the earth, the first solid form of creation. In primitive symbolism, stones can give birth to people and gods (like Mithra, who was born from a rock), and have a life-giving potency; conversely, people can be turned into sacred or other stones. Tall, upright rocks, columns or pillars are an *axis-mundi* and represent the supreme support of all things in the universe. They are also an *omphalos*, navel or fixed point or center, where man can regain Paradise or find enlightenment. In the Bible, the stone on which Jacob slept when he dreamed his dream of the angels on the ladder, and which he later anointed and set up as a sacred altar called Beth El – House of God – was a meeting place of heaven and earth and of communication between them. The foundation stone of the Temple was said to be the center of the earth, and supported the world. Moses brought the law from Sinai on tablets of stone. Stones are also connected with the cults of many Greek gods, especially Apollo – notably the *omphalos* or navel of the world at Delphi – regarded as the durable, reliable and indestructible center from which all the cosmos radiates and to which it refers back for stability and movement.

The stone, as the goal of the alchemical process, the 'lapis,' is something we must return to later. When Jung was about twelve, he started to have problems with school. One of the difficulties, which seems strange to me in view of the skillfulness of his later paintings, was with drawing classes, from which he was exempted on grounds of "utter incapacity!" Of course, he could only draw what stirred his imagination and not copies of prints of Greek gods or goat-heads! A spell of fainting fits made him able to avoid school for more than six months and he had a wonderful time drawing pictures of violent battles or besieged and burning castles, and exploring the woods and water. "Above all," he says,

I was able to plunge into the world of the mysterious. To that realm belonged trees, a pool, the swamp, stones and animals and my father's library. ...What had led me astray during the crisis [the six months away from school] was my passion for being alone, my delight in solitude. Nature seemed to me full of wonders, and I wanted to steep myself in them. Every stone, every plant, every single thing seemed alive and indescribably marvelous. I immersed myself in nature, crawled, as it were, into the very essence of nature and away from the whole human world.

At this same time, however, Jung's ego really began to appear consciously. "I had the overwhelming impression of having just emerged from a dense cloud. I knew all at once: now I am myself..."

Then came the fateful vision of Basel cathedral and the ensuing torment and at last the great and courageous leap to confronting the complete picture of the vast turd that smashed the roof of the Cathedral. After the initial immense relief, followed the beginning of the awful awareness that God could also be something terrible. The experience of such a profound paradox made the young boy deeply thoughtful and often, according to his mother, depressed, though Jung says he was really brooding on the secret (this was the third and perhaps greatest secret), and one which induced in him an almost unendurable loneliness. "At such times," he says,

it was strangely reassuring and calming to sit on my stone. Somehow it would free me of all my doubts. Whenever I thought that I was the stone, the conflict ceased. ...The stone has no uncertainties, no urge to communicate, and is eternally the same for thousands of years, while I am a passing phenomenon which bursts into all kinds of emotions, like a flame that flares up quickly and then goes out. ... I was but the sum of my emotions, and the 'other' in me was the timeless, imperishable stone.

The feeling Jung had of being and having always been two persons grew stronger. The number two personality, "The Other," was remote from the world of men but close to nature, the earth, the sun, the moon, the weather, all living creatures and, above all, close to the night, to dreams and to whatever 'God' worked directly in him.

Between twelve and sixteen, this feeling for nature contrasted with the unreliable world of people was again expressed. "In fact, it seemed to me that the high mountains, the rivers, lakes, trees, flowers and animals far better exemplified the essence of God than men with their ridiculous clothes, their meanness, vanity, mendacity and abhorrent egotism – all qualities with which I was only too familiar from myself, that is from personality number one, the schoolboy of 1890." Besides this world, there existed another realm, like a temple in which anyone who entered was transformed and suddenly overpowered by a vision of the whole cosmos, so that he could "only marvel and admire, forgetful of [himself]."

And later, he writes,

Trees in particular were mysterious and seemed to me direct embodiments of the incomprehensible meaning of life. For that reason, the woods were the place where I felt closest to its deepest meaning and to its awe-inspiring workings. …

This impression was reinforced when I became acquainted with Gothic cathedrals. But there the infinity of the cosmos, the chaos of meaning and meaninglessness, of impersonal purpose and mechanical law, were wrapped in stone. This contained and at the same time was the bottomless mystery of being, the embodiment of spirit. What I had dimly felt to be my kinship with the stone was the divine nature in both, in the dead and the living matter.

As Jung grew up, his number one personality gradually took the upper hand, though there was always conflict. But an increasing interest in science led him further into the practical world and a meeting with a young chemist excited him very much. "… A chemist who had attained that pinnacle of glory – the doctorate. This chemist was a fascinating novelty to me: here was a scientist, perhaps one of those who understood the secrets of stones…" In fact, the young man only taught Jung how to play croquet and imparted to him none of his "presumably vast learning…" Nevertheless, Jung says, "I revered him as the first person I had ever met in the flesh who was initiated into the secrets of nature, or some of them at least…"

During his later school years, and born out of the clash of opposites embodied in personalities one and two conflicting with each other, Jung had, as he says, his first systematic fantasy. He imagined the Rhine becoming a vast lake with boats and a large port in Basel. A kind of medieval city on a rock surrounded by canals and connected by a causeway to the mainland grew in his imagination and in the city was a fortified castle with a watch tower. This was Jung's house. There were many details of the town and castle and how it was governed, with Jung as chief adviser and arbitrator. The keep contained an immensely complicated machinery-cum-tree of copper – and there was a laboratory where he could make gold. These processes remained vague, but it is a fantastic image. The goings-on in this city and castle and on the ships on the lake provided Jung with wonderful fantasies as he walked to and from school and lasted several months. But at last it paled, and he began instead to bring it down to earth by actually building the castle and fortifications and houses out of small stones and mud. Models were constructed of various types of fortifications, taken from real existing plans. For more than two years, this filled Jung's leisure hours, while, as he says, "my leanings towards nature study and concrete things steadily increased, at the cost of Number Two [personality]."

Apart from the towers he used to build with toy bricks when he was a young child, this is the first emerging of the profound image that would later solidify still further and attain durable earthly existence in the building of his tower at Bollingen.

Many years later, after his break with Freud, when he was in a state of great inner confusion and, as he says, felt suspended in mid-air, Jung had a series of vivid dreams which left him feeling under constant inner pressure. Conscious looking back to the events and memories of his childhood did nothing to help to relieve it. So he said, "Since I know nothing at all, I shall simply do whatever occurs to me." What occurred to him was the memory of a time when he was about ten or eleven and had spent a lot of time building little houses and castles with building blocks and stones and bits of whatever came to hand. This memory had quite an emotional quality to it. Eventually, overcoming a lot of inner resistance to what seemed a terribly humiliating and childish activity for a grown-up psychiatrist, Jung began to collect stones from the lakeshore and the water and then to build – houses or castles – a whole village. The church remained incomplete for lack of an altar until Jung found a red pyramid-shaped stone which he placed in the center of the church under the dome. At once, he recalled the childhood dream of the underground phallus, which pleased him very much. He continued to play this building game whenever he had a spare moment, and, during these sessions, was able to clarify fantasies that, until then, had remained only a vague presence. These released fantasies were later written down in what Jung called the Black Book and afterwards, in good alchemical progression, in the Red Book, which he illustrated like medieval manuscripts with amazingly intricate, skillful and beautiful paintings. The wealth of fantasy and the extraordinary ability to give it form in writing, shape and color, not surprisingly, stirred the unknown woman in Jung's depths to voice her admiration and encouragement and to state firmly that these creations were indeed art. She tempted him to see himself as an artist, preferably a misunderstood one, and to devote himself entirely to his muse (herself?). But Jung was more concerned with where the images would lead him and what they meant, than with their existence as objects of purely aesthetic interest and pleasure. He valued his anima for communicating these images to him, but managed to avoid her more dangerous seductions. From this time on, whenever Jung got stuck, he painted a picture or carved a stone. He says,

> *Each such experience proved to be a* rite d'entrée *for the ideas and works that followed hard upon it. … Everything I have written this year, 1957, and last year:* The Undiscovered Self; Flying Saucers A Modern Myth; A Psychological View of Conscience, *has grown out of the stone sculptures I did after my wife's death. The close of life, the end, and what it made me realize, wrenched me violently out of myself. It cost me a great deal to regain my footing, and contact with stone helped me.*

According to von Franz[1], Jung once said, "Sometimes I know so little about what the unconscious demands that I simply leave it to my hands, so that afterwards I can think about what I have shaped."

These years (between about 1914 and 1920) when, with immense courage, for it was dark and dangerous territory and he was absolutely alone in his descent, Jung pursued his inner images which were, as he says, the most important in his life, "in them everything essential was decided … It was the *prima materia* for a lifetime's work."

With the building of the tower in Bollingen, which Jung began in 1923, two months after the death of his mother, he came to grips with stone in a new way; and yet, though on a vastly enlarged scale, it was not entirely new, only a fulfillment of an earlier blueprint in his imagination. As he says, "Words and paper did not seem real enough to me; something more was needed. I had to achieve a kind of

---

[1] von Franz, *C.G. Jung, His Myth in our Time*, C.G. Jung Foundation and G.P. Putnam's Sons, New York, 1975.

representation in stone of my innermost thoughts and of the knowledge I had acquired. Or to put it another way, I had to make a
confession of faith in stone..."

Now the model castles and fortifications took on a human-sized
reality as Jung began to build around himself, like some immensely
inventive deep-sea creature, a shell of stone into which he would
grow. It protected, as it also grew around him, the still vulnerable core
of his personality (his Number Two personality), but also the emerging totality of himself being forged between the world outside and the
larger landscape of the inner world. He says,

> *From the beginning I felt the tower as in some way a place of matu-*
> *ration – a maternal womb or a maternal figure in which I could be-*
> *come what I was, what I am and will be. It gave me a feeling as if I*
> *were being reborn in stone ... I built the house in sections, always fol-*
> *lowing the concrete needs of the moment. It might also be said that I*
> *built in a kind of dream. Only afterwards did I see how all the parts*
> *fitted together and that a meaningful form had resulted: a symbol of*
> *psychic wholeness.*

Originally conceived as a sort of round African hut, representing,
as Jung said, the maternal hearth, the first part of Bollingen grew into
a circular tower instead. The place expanded with new parts being
built at four-year intervals, until four sections had been constructed.
But it was not quite completed until twenty years later, after the death
of Emma Jung, when an upper story was added to the central section,
which Jung saw as representing his ego personality, or an extension
of consciousness achieved in old age.

Jung did the initial construction himself, at least of the first tower,
with the help of two Italian masons. In a letter of 1934, he says, "I
learned to split stones in the Bollingen quarries, and the masons also
taught me a lot and I learned their art relatively quickly..." Later, in
the same letter, he adds, "One of the motives [for the building work]
was the workableness of matter to compensate for the airiness of
psychology."

Many years later, von Franz[1] tells how the son of a local stone-
mason from the Bollingen area said to her one day, "These days,
masons don't know how to work with natural stone any more. But old

[1] von Franz, ibid.

Jung, down there by the lake, he knew all right. He knew the right way to take a stone in your hand!"

At Bollingen, Jung lived consciously linked to the past. His own outer personal ancestors, as well as those of his wife, were honored in the stone plaques in which he carved their coats-of-arms. He also did this for his inner ancestors, and indeed those of the Bollingen ground itself. He says,

> *My ancestors' souls are sustained by the atmosphere of the house, since I answer for them the questions that their lives once left behind. I carve out rough answers as best I can. I have even drawn them on the walls. It is as if a silent, greater family, stretching down the centuries were peopling the house. There I live in my second personality and see life in the round, as something forever coming into being and passing on.*

The spirit of Philemon, the wise old man and essence of Jung's Number Two personality, reigned over Bollingen, where Jung was most deeply himself, "there everything has its history and mine; here is space for the spaceless kingdom of the world's and the psyche's hinterland."

In 1944, Jung had a severe heart attack after breaking his foot. During his illness, he had a vision which began with the appearance of a huge monolithic meteorite or granite boulder floating in space. It contained a temple, hollowed out of the rock as Jung had seen stone temples in India. Inside sat a dark yogi, meditating and, Jung felt, waiting for him. All the elements of his earthly existence seemed to fall away from him and he seemed to be about to meet his eternal self. But he was called back to life by a vision of his doctor (in the ennobled form of a prince of Kos): apparently it was too soon to learn the answers held in the rock temple.

Shortly after his recovery, Jung had a dream in which the yogi, sitting in the lotus position, appeared again, this time meditating in a little country chapel by the wayside in the hills. Now Jung looked at him more closely and realized with great fear that the Yogi had his own (Jung's) face. He awoke with the thought: "Aha, so he is the one who is meditating me. He has a dream and I am it … I knew that when he awakened, I would no longer be." This dream echoed strongly Jung's childhood feelings as he sat on his stone and wondered who – he or the stone – was 'I.'

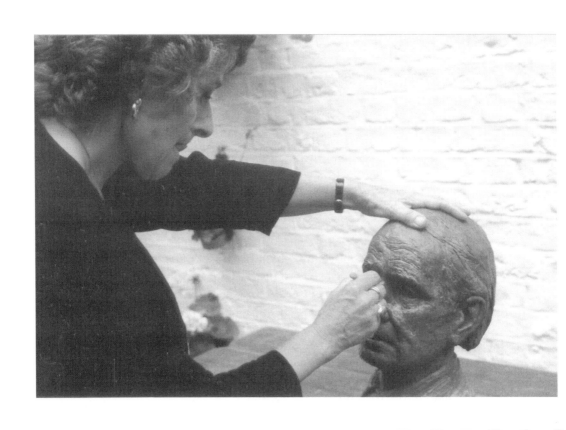

Frances Baruch and her sculpted head of Sir Laurens, 1996

Sir Laurens and sculpted head by Frances Baruch, 1996

With Jung's research into the world of alchemy, the stone took on its final and complete dimension. Now, from its secret and primitive beginning as a companion to the pencil box figure, it revealed itself as it truly was, always had been, always would be. All the threads were brought together – the soul stone, the denizen of the world of nature, the raw material for construction and creation and the 'lapis', the once and future stone of alchemy – all of these achieved their final expression in the square stone which began its career as a mistake!

A triangular stone had been ordered as a cornerstone for a wall for Bollingen but a square one was sent instead, in spite of careful measurements having been given to the quarry owner. A perfect cube arrived, much larger than ordered, and caused fury in the mason who was about to send it straight back. It arrived by water on a barge with the rest of the stones for the wall, as if the lake itself were presenting Jung with a mysterious gift. "When I saw the stone," he says, "I said, 'No, that is my stone. I must have it!' For I had seen at once that it suited me perfectly and that I wanted to do something with it. Only I did not yet know what."

So the rejected cornerstone became the solid space in which Jung could draw the opposites together – could join spirit to matter – the word to the earth's foundation. Although the Bollingen stone is neither really a work of art, nor a monument to a specific event or person (in fact, I see it almost as Jung's totem, connecting him with his spiritual ancestors), in a way, I still want to digress a bit about the actual business of chipping stone! Considering that he was already seventy-five years old when he started his carving, it is quite amazing that he had enough strength to do it, because, whatever else is needed to carve, brute force is high on the list! Although he was mainly carving letters, and the figures and ornamentation were done in low relief (as were his other carvings on the wall stones, the woman drinking from the mare and the bear with the ball), it is nevertheless very hard and dusty work to make any kind of marks on stone with a chisel. The Bollingen stone is made of blue-green sandstone, which is not one of the harder stones to cut, but the quality and design of the lettering is amazingly professional. It may be rather fanciful to bring Michelangelo into this – although he is the most archetypal of sculptors –, but a few lines from one of his madrigals and sonnets seem to suggest a fleeting analogy.

… There for the taking, Lady, deep within
The hard unyielding marble,
A figure lives,
Growing as the stone is cut away:
Like some good deeds,
Hid from the shivering soul
Buried in superfluity of flesh
Beneath a rough, hard uncouth crust…

The sonnet says,

The best of artists hath no thought to show
Which the rough stone in its superfluous shell
Doth not include: to break the marble spell
Is all the hand that serves the brain can do…

These lines express the conviction that the form already lies dormant within the stone, waiting to be revealed by the removal of the excess material. I found a little technical description of how Michelangelo used wax models for his carvings very intriguing. Vasari (the Italian historian who wrote biographies of many artists of the Renaissance) relates that Michelangelo would take a finished wax model and immerse it in water. The figure was then gradually raised so that one saw exactly which points were revealed first, and thus corresponded with the outside of the stone, and then the next highest parts where one worked down to next, and so on, until one could tell where the deepest cuts should be made.

It always surprises me to hear, when one talks about Michelangelo, how many people say that they prefer the unfinished figures – such as the three slaves or prisoners (in the Academia of Florence). These were actually abandoned in their present state and differ from the works in which an 'unfinished' or rough treatment of certain parts of a figure are used deliberately to heighten effect. Is there a parallel here with our greater involvement with the process of becoming, rather than the ideal and perhaps ultimately unattainable goal of achieved creation? We are more concerned with the journey than the arrival. Possibly the journey *is* the arrival. My fantasy consisted in the analogy between Michelangelo chipping away to reveal the figure waiting in the stone and Jung seeking to reveal the 'true' personality in the analytic process, dissolving the hardened layers of neurotic petrification in the magic solution of the analytic relationship or indeed chipping away the 'excess' material to allow the 'original' form to emerge.

It is immensely satisfying when you are pounding away at a tirelessly resistant lump of stone to know that, in the end, what you manage to wrest from it or impose upon it will be there forever. In a letter to his daughter Marianne, Jung says, actually about the stone he carved in memory of his wife, "The stone I am working on... gives me stability with its hardness and its meaning governs my thoughts."

In another letter, this time to the American ethnologist, Maud Oakes, Jung writes, "When I hewed the stone, I did not think, however, I just brought into shape what I saw on its face..." He managed to express in it not only everything that the tower itself meant to him, but, as he says in another letter to Maud Oakes, "All the volumes I have written are contained in it *in nuce*. The mandala itself is just a sort of hieroglyph, hinting at and trying to express a vast background in a most abbreviated form." In the center of this circle, the natural structure of the stone suggested another smaller circle, and inside this, Jung carved a little figure in a hooded cloak, carrying a lantern. This was a Kabir. These dwarf gods of antiquity can symbolize creative impulses and, in the form of Telesphoros, lead to a goal of some sort. The little pencil box mannequin, carved by Jung as a child, represented a first meeting with this member of the Pantheon. In one of Jung's early fantasies during his inner voyage of discovery, a figure called 'Ka' came to the surface. Jung says of him, "In ancient Egypt the 'king ka' was his earthly form, the embodied soul. In my fantasy, the ka-soul came from below, out of the earth, as if out of a deep shaft. I did a painting of him, showing him in his earth-bound form, as a heron with base of stone and upper part of bronze... " Incidentally, *De Vries' Dictionary of Symbols* says, "Some derive the name of the god Hermes from 'herma' which means stone or rock; and point out the stones as the origin of the Hermes cult. Ka represented a kind of earth demon or metal demon. Philemon was the spiritual aspect or 'meaning.' Ka, on the other hand was a spirit of Nature, like the Anthroparion of Greek Alchemy ..." To this, Aniela Jaffé adds, "The Anthroparion is a tiny man, a kind of homunculus... To the group – which includes the Anthroparion – belong the gnomes, the Dactyls of classical antiquity and the homunculi of the alchemists. As the spirit of quicksilver, the alchemical Mercurius was also an Anthroparion." Kabirs are also connected with the dwarves of Northern mythologies, who mined the earth and were skilled metal workers and craftsmen. The Telesphoros of Asklepios (Telesphoros means 'he who brings completeness.'), carved on the Bollingen stone, is such a Kabir, a phallic figure or earth spirit in a hooded cloak, who carries a lantern and points the way in the dark to "the gates of the sun and to the land of dreams…"

Von Franz[1] mentions two other such figures. In the garden in Küsnacht, Jung erected a statue (done by a mason after two wooden carvings made by Jung many years earlier) "to the phallic God" in his first dream. It was another form of Kabir, which he names *Atma victu* (Breath of Life), and in Bollingen, he carved an ivy wreath around a phallic cornerstone which stands near the edge of the lake, with the inscription "Attei to Kallisto" (to the most beautiful Attis). The stone stands alone among wild anemones, the flower of Attis, a god who symbolized the eternal spring-like glory of life. The Telesphoros, however, was the second thing that Jung carved and thereupon, the first thing that occurred to him was a Latin verse by the 14th century alchemist Arnaldus de Villanova. In English, it reads:

> Here stands the mean, uncomely stone,
> 'Tis very cheap in price!
> The more it is despised by fools,
> The more loved by the wise.

This, then, is the lapis, the philosophers' stone, both the beginning and the goal of the alchemical process. In its 'mean and uncomely' guise, it represents the *prima materia,* chaos, the base matter, the common earth beneath our feet – seen, but ignored – used, but unrecognized. The stone-like the Self – which it can symbolize –and which is also at the beginning and at the end of the process –has, in its primal and chaotic aspect, no boundaries and contains all things. In her paper, "The Search in Alchemy," Molly Tuby[2] quotes from the Hermetic Museum, which says, "Our Matter has as many names as there are things in the world; that is why the foolish know it not." But this base stone is both transformer and transformed. It is the "stone sent by God" which can turn any metal into gold and which, says von Franz, "according to some authors is hidden in the human body and can be extracted from it." It is God's mystery in matter and is even described as "the stone that hath a spirit," a spirit which must be extracted from it. One remembers Jung's words describing his early

---

[1] von Franz, ibid.
[2] Guild of Pastoral Psychology, London, pamphlet no. 17.

experiences of stone, in which he said that the stone "contained and at the same time was the bottomless mystery of being, the embodiment of spirit." His kinship with it he described as "the divine nature in both the dead and the living matter." In far Eastern alchemy, the diamond body corresponds to this stone. The alchemist creates this body through his meditative exercises, thereby attaining immortality in his lifetime. In the West, the stone later became identified with Christ who is taken as the rejected cornerstone and becomes the Redeemer, but, as Aniela Jaffé writes in her book, *From the Life and Work of C.G. Jung,* the lapis was also a *deus terrenus* – an earth god, the begetter not only of light, but of darkness.

Carving his stone at the age of seventy-five, after a lifetime of inner exploration, it is almost as if Jung recognized it for the first time – hearing its language at last, and giving enduring form to its words.

He says, in fact, "On the third face, the one facing the lake, I let the stone itself speak, as it were, in a Latin inscription." These sayings are more or less quotations from Alchemy:

> *I am an orphan, alone; nevertheless I am found everywhere. I am one, but opposed to myself. I am youth and old man at one and the same time. I have known neither father nor mother because I have had to be fetched out of the deep like a fish, or fell like a white stone from heaven. In woods and mountains I roam, but I am hidden in the innermost soul of man. I am mortal for everyone. Yet I am not touched by the cycle of eons.*

Under this, Jung carved, again in Latin, "In remembrance of his seventy-fifth birthday, C.G. Jung made and placed this here as a thanks offering, in the year 1950." Standing outside the Tower and, as Jung says, like an explanation of it, the Bollingen stone represents Jung's totality in its immutable dynamic.

The fourth face of the stone is left blank. It is the unseen face, the always unknown, perhaps the eternal future. Jung had wanted to carve on it the 'cry of Merlin,' but never did so. Merlin the Celtic bard, sage and magician, brought about the Brotherhood of the Knights of the Holy Grail – the round table of legend. The grail, in the version of the Parsifal story by Wolfram von Eschenbach, was itself a stone fallen from heaven – not a vessel. It was called the *Lapis exilis* – the term used by the alchemists for 'their' stone. Merlin was himself known, in various French versions of the story, as the 'real secret of the Grail.' At the end of his life, it is said, he retired into the forest, very old and with immense but lonely-making knowledge. He was surrounded by many pupils who had learned about the things of the spirit from him, but, says von Franz, "he bids farewell to all this and withdraws into eternal silence." He vanished into his forest house or into a rock tomb and, with the passage of time, men speak only of "Merlin's stone" – *perron de Merlin,* where time and again, heroes meet together to set out upon some brave adventure. According to other versions, he becomes entangled in love with the fairy Viviane and disappears with her into the beyond, and now only his distant cry is heard – the famous *cri de Merlin.* Jung says:

> ... *for what the stone expressed reminded me of Merlin's life in the forest after he had vanished from the world. Men still hear his cries, so the legend runs, but they cannot understand or interpret them ... His story is not yet finished and he still walks abroad. It might be said that the secret of Merlin was carried on by alchemy primarily in the figure of Mercurius. Then Merlin was taken up again in my psychology of the unconscious and remains uncomprehended to this day!*

In some strange way, this lack of comprehension is illustrated by some letters Jung wrote to Maud Oakes, the American ethnologist we mentioned earlier. She had written a treatise on the Bollingen stone and had understood it as (says Jung) "a statement about a more or less limitless world of thought images..." Jung agreed with this up to a point, but objected to his text and symbols being seen as a sort of confession or belief. He says,

> *They are just no gnosis, no metaphysical assertion. They are partly even futile or dubious attempts at pronouncing the ineffable. Their number therefore is infinite and the validity of each is to be doubted. They are nothing but humble attempts to formulate, to define, to shape the inexpressible... It is not a doctrine but a mere expression of and reaction to the experience of an ineffable mystery.*
> *There is one point more I want to mention: the stone is not a product only of thought-images, but just as much of feeling and local atmosphere, i.e., of the specific* ambiente *of the place. The stone belongs to its secluded place between lake and hill, where it expresses the* bea-ta solitudo *and the* genius loci, *the spell of the chosen and walled-in spot. It could be nowhere else and cannot be thought of or properly understood without the secret web of threads that relate it to its surroundings. Only there in its solitude can it say* orphanus sum, *and*

only there it makes sense. It is there for its own sake and only seen by a few. Under such conditions only the stone will whisper its misty love of ancient roots and ancestral lives..." (February 1956)

In another letter to Maud Oaks, he stresses these views still more:

Since you want to hear my opinion about your essay on the stone, I should say that I find it a bit too intellectual, as it considers the thought-images only... If you want to do justice to the stone you have to pay particular attention to the way in which it is embedded in its surroundings: the water, the hills, the view, the particular atmosphere of the buildings, the nights and days, the seasons, sun, wind and rain, and man living close to the earth and yet remaining conscious in daily meditation of everything being just so. The air round the stone is filled with harmonies and disharmonies, with memories of times long ago, of vistas into the dim future with reverberations of a faraway, yet so-called real world into which the stone has fallen out of nowhere... (October 1957)

This is such a wonderful description – it reminds me of the Zen stone gardens or the Chinese feeling that certain rocks are a distillation of the essence of landscape as an expression of Tao.

The stone, which had been a companion and inspiration in Jung's youth, steadfastly accompanied him into the beyond. His last recorded dream was of a great round block of stone sitting on a high plateau, a barren square. At its foot were engraved the words, "And this shall be a sign unto you of Wholeness and Oneness." There was also a quadrangle of trees whose roots reached around the earth and enveloped him and among the roots golden threads were glittering. I think a sentence from the end of Marie-Louise von Franz's book, *C.G. Jung – His Myth in our Time*, sums up this dream beautifully. She writes, "When the Tao, the meaning of the world and eternal life are attained, the Chinese say: 'Long life flowers with the essence of the stone and the brightness of gold.'"

A Sort of Freedom

Ray Parkin

Apologia

Real knowledge is action, not words, and its safe repository is in True Instinct. This is exemplified by the whole of the Natural World. Only Man trims his sails to windy wordiness.

> Not by words does God get answers:
> He calls them not and all things come.
> [Tao 73]

Thus,

> So the Wise Man will do
> What his belly dictates
> And never the sight of his eyes.
> Thus he will choose this but not that.
> [Tao 12]

On such questions, even the greatest may only speculate. I can say no more than experience prompts. I know that any words I use may well change their meaning in mid-air, between writer and reader. St. Paul said, "The Letter killeth; but the Spirit giveth life." Unstable words may be held firm only by understanding. Without this, all such castles as one builds fancifully along the shores of thought are most vulnerable to the recurring winds and tides of change, which are human opinions.

The proper function of the Intellect (the word-processor) should only be, I believe, to act as an index to our Ignorance.

And it is with such a realization, that the following words are offered.

Original cover design of The Night of the New Moon *(L. van der Post)*
by Ray Parkin

A Sort of Freedom

(A Personal Rumination)

More than fifty years ago, I sat on the ground in central Java, painting a tree.

This was not my normal habitat: that had been the Sea. But political expedience in the middle of a war had found us confronted one midnight by an overwhelming enemy force at the northern end of Sunda Straits. After an hour's violent action, the intrusion of four torpedoes into our ship had literally blown me from that world to this.

Now I knew [know] nothing of 'Art.' Any form of pictorial expression I made was, for me, an exploration of the subject. I strove for a close visual representation but seeking, also, to clothe it with that subtle reality I could only call 'atmosphere' to suggest the inner and all-pervading spirit of the thing and place.

I was in a prison camp in Bandoeng. There was a high barbed wire fence between me and my subject. As I worked, thus concentrating, I became aware of another presence. I looked up and saw, just behind me and looking benignly down, a khaki figure foreshortened against the bright cerulean of the tropical Java sky. I saw at once by the uniform that we were from opposite sides of the world. Yet, the first few words (whatever they were) somehow convinced me that my inner thoughts would find no embarrassment here. It was an immediate intuitive one which indeed proved correct: despite the fact that I was untutored, ill-informed and, no doubt, rather brash, for my own opinions were rather stronger in me then than those of others. The Colonel was obviously quite different, shaming my brashness. There was a wide gap in rank, of situation and, as it turned out, of our immediate destiny. Our contact was to be only of a few months before diverging orbits drew us apart again. But not before I had received much wise counsel and understanding. I was given the courage to think my own thoughts, and to adventure in my own dimension – however idiosyncratic that may seem to others.

I had only recently come to Bandoeng from Tjilatjap, on the south coast of Java, near where we had been captured. Capture had made a complete change in our life-style. This had been drastically simplified down to one word: Survival. In it, I saw three elements: food, health and mental stability. For the first, we should have to rely upon what our captors would give us; for the second, it would be largely upon what our ancestors had given us; and the third, I suppose, would have to be what we could dig up for ourselves.

This present situation had been brought about abruptly. The violent end of our ship had some quite dramatic overtones. In one light cruiser, in just one hour, we had two-thirds of our ship's company killed, which was more by sixteen than the total number killed in the whole British fleet at Trafalgar; and while we had lost two-thirds of our shipmates, Anson, in his four-year circumnavigation of 1740-1744, had lost only one half. But I mention this only to show that it is not unduly dramatic for us to have felt that we had had a wondrous escape, and that this had added a distinct appreciation of the quality for any life remaining. With all this, then, if one's thought-processes have not been quickened, I think that they may be considered moribund.

In outdoor painting or sketching, there is an old trick: stand with your feet wide apart, bend forward, look back between your legs and you will see your subject upside-down. This novelty will allow you to see with a fresh perception that which habitual rightway-up seeing had dulled. Now, fortuitous Circumstance had taken me and thrust my head between my legs, showing me the world anew.

At Tjilatjap, I had befriended an Indian who had continually thereafter shown his gratitude in various practical ways: a boiled egg left on my bedplace; a Quaker-oat tin of bamboo shoots in a delicious white sauce; but, most significant of all, that same tin full of strong, sweet Java coffee. I had drunk it at sundown. At 10 p.m., I was still unable to get to sleep because of the unaccustomed stimulant, and was listening to the sounds of other men still awake gradually being changed into the spasmodic noises of the machinery of sleep.

Outside, the sweet, shrill chirping of the Java bush at midnight suggested an absolute purity of atmosphere. The dry, rasping rachet-winding-up of the toc-ta lizards, followed by their flat call of deflation: toc-ta, toc-ta, toc-ta … was followed by a clear ringing silence in which one seemed to sense even the imperceptible radar of a million distant pinpoints of starlight. The deep black of the sky between seemed eternity itself, across which the slow-turning stars passed their zenith and set beyond, immeasurably beyond, that death-still frieze of frozen ink-black palm-fronds. One was feeling the slow endless turning of the Universal Loom, weaving us all into the perfect incomprehensible fabric of All-being.

Despite the racing sleepless thoughts within me, my body lay still and unobtrusive – I had simply become a voyaging mind, sailing out and around those stars and deep into the black nebulae of the unknowable, with a serene and unimpeded unity with all things. Or, so it seemed to me then. I was as wide awake as ever I have been. Never had my mind felt so clear, so sure, and with such a completely absorbed ego. As if being counselled by the universal Id, I seemed to see clear across and through all things with no confusion, and with a crystal-clear simplicity. Confusion, I felt then, was only in the ego-minds of men obfuscated by immediate desires and wishes in a myopic search for comfort, salvation, power and profit. So confident had I become, that I calmly posed myself the question: *I, myself, what am I?* In this state of never-doubting, I mustered my evidence, stated my postulates and ran through my thesis. It was almost dawn when I finally fell asleep.

In the morning, only an hour later, the Dutch bugle woke me, and I joined the other milling prisoners at the Japanese count-parade. Immediately afterwards, I gulped down my red rice breakfast, but, all the while completely preoccupied, so that I had hardly spoken a word to anybody. For, unlike most dream states or nocturnal revelations which fade or become illogical with daylight, this was persisting with me *verbatim*. And I was compelled to write it down:

I, myself, what am I?
I am that coincidence through which thought flows, that fantasy of Being: the meeting place of ideas in the conscious; the point in the path of the abstract transmuted to the sensual in me – sensing and being sensed. I am the imperfect reflector of those ideas.

Though incalculable masses pass through this point of 'me,' my knowledge is only of that number within the range of my senses. My physical and mental spectra probably fall roughly into parallel, if not upset by ego. To these, add my 'psychic' spectrum which I believe can only exist in the unconscious, but able to intuitively communicate with Intelligence if absolutely free of ego-intellect.

All things pass me in space (or time); or, I them; or, we each other. All is movement in space. The difference of speed and velocity and direction is the apparent difference of things by perception or coincidence with the senses. Thus mortality is but the limited perception of mortal senses: yet, this limited perception is quite adequate for mortal existence under natural necessity. However, intellectual ambition,

from the limits of the senses and, further, by the inadequacy of lan-
guage to fully explain, must find itself always without the fullness of
that deep knowledge whereby all things exist.

Perhaps all the I-myselfs find the urge for expression out of the in-
stinct for harmony, but I find Intellect no adequate tool. Perhaps I-
myself is the harmonic of a wave-crest cohesive in motion and time,
with the ability to know and travel with other forms in harmony,
each having varying receptivity and sensibility. I-myself suspects that
what we loosely call 'love' is a strength of cohesion, inherent and
emergent; and that which we call 'hate' is a force of disruption by dis-
harmony.

What will the death of I-myself be? Can it suffer annihilation? Will
there be a further mingling of harmonic waves which is beyond hu-
man sensibility? Will the deterioration of I-myself-now be the disrup-
tion and dissipation into something we know not, or know not that
we know, be the 'death' absolute?

The present faith of I-myself is in the greater mingling through har-
mony to a greater 'perfection' as perceived by me now. Yet, I am in-
clined to believe that there is already an unperceived perfection in the
order of things as they are now.

But, when I think of home, I feel that I-myself is not alone, but that
I have already encountered a wave-crest with which to merge and
travel through time.

[My wife and two children were vivid to me then.]

Having written this down, I went along to a fellow prisoner, a
Cambridge Don (though the remnants of his uniform proclaimed him
only a R.A.F. 'Irk'), who was sitting on his pack on the dirt floor
reading some of his favorites in Greek. We talked about what I had
written. I said I would see how it worked out as we unrolled the
Oriental Scroll of this present experience. And he said: "Look, what
thy soul holds dear, imagine it to lie the way thou goest – not whence
thou comest."

Not all such detached thoughts came by night. Sitting one day with
my own animal body warm in the dust in the high hills of Bandoeng,
I was watching the beautiful blue-and-white cirrus-streaked sky and
feeling the exquisite tingle of the arrow-shafts of sunlight shot into me
from the blue vastness above. I fell into a perfectly transcendental
state, wrapped around with the warm companionate glow of panthe-
ism.

The clouds draw smoky trails
  Across the sky;
Or paint, with coloured daubs,
  A theme on high.
Light plays with dappled shades
  Upon the leaves,
And luminosity
  Beneath the eaves.

The warmth of sunlight warm
  Upon the ground
Impels all growing things
  Within our bound.

Gold of Day-departing,
  Blue of Noon,
Rose of early morning,
  Silver Moon:
Sing the simple joys of Pan
To this heart of prisoned Man.

These and many things Laurens and I talked over during those short months until we parted in November, 1942. We did not see each other again until 1976. But the foundation had been laid and, about a year after the war, we made contact again and have continued in this vein to this day. It was Laurens who encouraged me to finish my first book, *Out of the Smoke*, of which he had read the first chapters written in Bandoeng. Finished, I sent it to him, and he delivered it into the hands of Leonard Woolf, C. Day Lewis and Norah Smallwood, to whom I now owe so much.

After this parting, I was taken to the hinterland of Siam to help build a railway from Thanbyuzayat in Burma to Bampong in Siam, linking two existing rail systems. Our taskmasters were the Southern Railway Army Corps under Field Marshall Terauchi. We, the slaves, totalled 330,000 of which 61,000 were prisoners-of-war and the rest, Chinese, Tamils and other native peoples. We had now achieved proper slave-status – with all the rights of those who had built the Pyramids. Along the 263 miles of track we laid, we left one man dead for every seventeen feet, six inches of the track.

LIFE....? BUTTERFLY
ON THE SWAYING GRASS, THAT'S ALL!
BUT EXQUISITE!
(SOIN 1604-92)

Ray Parkin
1966.

CHANTING AT THE ALTAR
OF THE INNER
SANCTUARY . . . .
. . . A CRICKET PRIEST.!
(1564)

R. Rankin
1965.

The mind could become numbed by the sheer monotony of endless toil with little to look forward to but the horrific prospect of tomorrow, and tomorrow, and tomorrow ... until many simply ran out of their tomorrows. In the struggle to escape this captivity of the mind, I soon found that the ego-centric and the anthropocentric views of life were like additional jailers. The only avenue of escape was with a 'wider' view. This allows one to stand outside oneself and to view our sorry lot even with some touch of a wry humour which could save one from the deadly scourge of self-pity which I saw many take. I don't think that my mind has ever ranged so far, even while my weary so-constricted body dragged itself about. Years later, I came across Basho in his *Narrow Road to the Deep North:* "What is important is to keep our mind high in the world of true understanding, and returning to the world of our daily existence, to seek therein the truth of beauty. No matter what we may be doing at any given moment, we must not forget that it has a bearing on our everlasting self." And I think I now know what he was talking about. I have a copy of this on a kitchen cupboard to remind me.

Gradually, I began to realize with the Sufi that, "When the heart mourns for what it has lost, the spirit rejoices for what it has found."

We worked in a mountain jungle 3,000-4,000 feet high, cutting a path in the mountainside along the valley of the Kwai Noi River. The jungle was a world of its own and, in our misery, seemed quite inimical to man. It was only slowly that I began to see that this was an inverted truth: it was man that was inimical to *it*. If one could, to some extent, begin to ignore the inconveniences of bare feet on sharp rocks; or the foot-eating slushed-up mud of the Wet Season beneath which so often lay the razor-blades of split bamboo; or the enervating heat of the Dry Season's days and the chill of its nights (for we wore only G-strings or sad remnants of erstwhile clothes – while some had no more than rice sacks for blankets); or the perpetual hunger of starvation; or the belly-draining pains of dysentery and dysentery-like afflictions; or the caricaturing of the body by famine oedema; or the malaise of malaria, which seldom left us; or the other inconveniences endemic to our situation and the close attention our overseers constantly gave us – *then* the existence of this other world could be realized. Such a realization could take one from the miseries within to the wonders without.

With a realization of how incidental man was to all This, came oddly comforting thoughts that could shrink personal suffering to a truer size from the enormity it had been within one's own mind. There was then room for redeeming thoughts which were literally Salvation. It would seem that one of the curses of the intellectual mind is its passionate ego-centricity, not only as individuals but as a species with its 'God-chosen' fetishism. Once this realization had begun, it was as if I had an unseen hand in mine leading me to greener pastures. At first, the outer eye began to perceive colour and form and pattern more vividly again in this liberation from self. The senses came to life again as my prime informers. And, with this, the inner eye became unclouded. It was as if those nagging inconveniences now stood at a distance, not daring to intrude.

This 'hand-in-mine' was like an all-pervading Presence enveloping one. There was a kind of cathederal atmosphere now within the vastness of the jungle which seemed to create a similar vastness to be explored within one's own 'being,' too. Yet, there were no churches, parliaments, universities, art galleries nor institutions of *any* kind. *Here* the Presence gave to *each* and *every* individual *everything* it would ever need, and more than any Institution could ever offer, with a scrupulous impartiality. "God does not proclaim himself," the Katha-Upanishad says, "He is *everybody's* secret." And Pagan Plotinus: "God is not external to anyone, but is present in all things ... the Principle of all things is always present." And the Mundaka-Upanishad tells us simply: "My son! There is nothing in this world that is not God. Find Him in the cavern; gnaw the knot of ignorance."

I got the ridiculous feeling that, as if at Chuang Chou's behest, I had 'identified myself with the Infinite to wander freely in the Unfathomable.' But, without humbug, I felt freer then than I had ever felt before. It was not just a silly euphoria, for it gave me, at the same time, the sharpest contrast between the civilized intellectuality of Man and the intrinsic Way of Nature.

With some wryness, which became a habit of the time, I observed with pleasure this implied slap in the face Nature gave to self-congratulating intellectual Man. It was being clearly shown to me that for some 4 000 000 000 years (Man's own estimate), this world had been able to come to such a wondrous state completely without him. And it was being made equally clear that, in the last few moments since his arrival – with the comparison of this pristine forest before me, and my experience of the civilized world behind me – and from the most disinterested of clinical observations, Man must be symptomized as more cancroid than benign. There are detailed reasons for this conclusion, for which there is no space here.

My general conclusion, however, was that all human problems are self-inflicted, arising from a frustration of unreal expectations reacting within the species. Hence Rabelais' 'commotions so continual' in his Prophetical Riddle. And it is in these commotions that friend and enemy alike are, with one mind, destroying the very fabric upon which all depends for life. If man were able to pursue his vanity to the bitter end, then all reality would be consumed on the altar of his Synthesis – but in the consummation, he himself would be inevitably consumed: who, then, would remain to worship at the Shrine?

Who, but such an aspirant, would give to *himself* the name of Homo...... *sapiens*?! But there are evidently those among us who can see its irony, for the dictionary (Oxford) tells us under *sapient:* "Wise (now rare); would-be wise, of fancied sagacity, aping wisdom." But who reads a dictionary?

Now it happened in this sorry state of slavery in which we were, that, at times, men became so overwhelmed by a sense of absolute impotence in the face of its humiliation, that tempers flared, to be taken out on one another. So it happened in my hut one night. A violent commotion arose between entrenched Believers and equally entrenched Sceptics over the question of Original Sin, which, of course, centred around Sex. Angry and bitter things were hurled from one side to the other until enough heat had been generated and expended as to achieve some measure of catharsis; finally, it died down. And each went out the same door as in he came.

But my curiosity was aroused: what *was* the Original Sin? I borrowed a Bible from a Believer and found myself absorbed in chapters two and three of Genesis, which I have since come to consider as probably the two most significant in the whole Bible. But then, perhaps, I am too overweening in this regard. I find myself skimming from these to the Tower of Babel (exemplary of one of the admonitions given to Adam), then to Ecclesiastes (for more of the same), then to 'consider the lilies' and 'blessed are the meek' on the side of Eden. This was possibly because I was so under the direct influence of the Jungle then. A Japanese poet of the 8th Century had also been so affected. Isonokami no Yakastugu had written:

> *These things the small man spurns*
> *The wise shall nourish.*

The Great Creator, in the variety of his works,
Blesses as well the lowly and the small.
When all philosophy I resolve in this one act,
I may stride the leviathan seas and they will not hold me!
Into the dark heart of all being I shall ride
And dwell in the spacious halls of the ant.

So, from chapters two and three, I proceeded to draw my own conclusions, home-spun though they are. It is said that these were written later than Jeremiah, Isiah, Amos, Judges, Samuel and Kings and yet, to me, they seem older than all of them – perhaps older than the Bible itself. They seemed to set as time-worn stones stuck in a later alluvial deposit. And I could not shake the impression that they had come from a much older tradition and were here used as a pre-history for the essentially Tribal History to follow. Nevertheless, I felt enough of the original thought had been retained, unknowingly, perhaps, as to make them still compelling and fundamental. I say 'unknowingly, perhaps' because of the controversions and interpretations that have been made of it since in support of the Religion it preambles. I came to the personal conclusion that these two chapters and the *Tao Te Ching* are blood brothers.

However, to the Fundamentalist, they are carved in stone by his own God. To the Theologian, they become his keystone, while the Sceptic probably balks at the personified God therein. Thus, each in his own way will miss the point, I feel. Britannica says (with apparent authority) "... it is impossible to regard them any longer as genuine history or as subjects for an allegorical interpretation." Not an allegory?? What, then, can be left? Of this, we are reminded in another place:

For the excellent masters of old,
Subtle, mysterious, mystic, acute,
Were much too subtle for their times.   [Tao 15][1]

Perhaps my point of view was influenced by being in Eden at the time; and of realizing that while *in* it, we sons of Adam were not *of* it.

---

[1] Note: [Tao] thus indicates the *Tao Te Ching*. Translations are from R.B. Blakkney's *The Way of Life, Lao Tzu*. Excepting [Tao 14] which is Legge. *Tao* or the *Way* used elsewhere refers to the forever indefinable *Tao* or *Ultimate Principle*, synonymous with my general use of *God* or *Nature*.

I had seen that the language of men and their conduct had visited accusations upon the innocent of sins which were, in fact, specifically their own, so that they may (if one scratched a little under the surface) stand in apparently unsullied priestly-white before their own created God.

Yet, I had seen the fungus[1], silent and still, in colours making Solomon drab, and sometimes glowing in the dark, obedient to its nature: taking the dead and, by transubstantiation, returning it to the living. If the fungus had the vanity and the voice of man, it might, with greater justification, proclaim, "*I* am the Resurrection!" I had seen the worm and its kind, too, about their business and found it, on short reflection, to be of more service to Creation than all the arts, sciences and industry of mankind. But this we denigrate that we may be inflated. When we don't approve of the table manners of Nature, we too readily cry, 'base instincts' and 'bestial behaviour.' But, when a little old lady sits down nicely to a lamb chop, where are the cries for her and her hired assassins of, 'Slaughter!'?

I had thought mordantly upon this proposition then, and the mordant had etched deep, especially when the cholera 'season' came. I watched emaciated fellow-slaves, in death, being carted by other emaciated fellow-slaves and placed, with a 'rice-sack' shroud at best, upon their funeral pyres, when it was almost impossible to get the wood to burn in that exceptionally wet Wet Season of 1943: when the blue smoke swirled, but the flames were most reluctant; when, even in death, the slave was cheated of his dignity and his final dissolution was only partial – for all we could do was to assure the death of the cholera germ that we bore there with him. And this smoke of lost dignity went up within the dripping green walls of Eden, and *its* population retained full dignity and freedom under its rule.

I thought how history would write of our 'bestial' treatment. And a bitterness arose from the rank hypocrisy of it: the treatment we were getting was *civilized* and *only* civilized, and never such as could be found among the beasts. If ever the essential significance of the Innocence of Eden, and of the Original Sin of Man could be more starkly illustrated, I have yet to encounter it.

A cynicism had entered my mood. I thought of the funerals of the 'great' of Church and State, paraded with cozened comfort and endless eulogy of how their achievements had left the world a better (?)

[1] Saprophytic.

place. Their acts, as I saw them now, had been but to bolster the Civilized Way of the Great Artifice – otherwise, there would be no eulogy. And the 'greatness' of *that* Way had been built upon such things as these present inadequate funeral pyres around me.

> *The victory after a conflict*
> *Is the theme for a funeral rite.* [Tao 31]

> *The mighty Way declined among the folk*
> *And then came kindness and morality*[1]
> *When wisdom and the intellect appeared,*
> *They brought with them great hypocrisy.* [Tao 18]

And this, to me, is the whole nub of The Fall.

I see two aspects to this story. The first is the general one with 'Adam' being *mankind:* in the Hebrew, 'son of man' was used for the individual, I have read. In the general account, mankind has lost its faith in Eden and decided to 'hoe its own row.'

Genesis Chapter Two brings us to a point at the end of some 4 000 000 000 years of Creation, being the seventh day of God's calendar, at a point, say, 1 000 000 years ago. This is nicely summarized as:

> *Creatures came with order's birth,*
> *And once they had appeared,*
> *Came also knowledge of repose,*
> And with that was security.[2] [Tao 32]

This verse indicates, I think, an insight into the prime and then healthy function of Instinct being able, through Intuition, to communicate to Intelligence: its executor of *right action* in the conscious. Perhaps it is in the last two lines of this verse that is encapsulated the whole wistful dream of psychiatry. It is important to differentiate between Intelligence and Intellect.

In the beginning, Intellect probably emerged naturally as an adjunct to Intelligence; however, this is only my own guess. But Intellect would seem to have since assumed its own supererogatory role. In this chapter at verse 19, there is a most significant sentence

---

[1] i.e., value–judgment.
[2] emphasis added.

"INSECT ON MY PALM",
MY YOUNG GRAND CHILD SAID TO ME,
"MAKES MY WHOLE HAND LAUGH!"

Ray Parkin
1984.

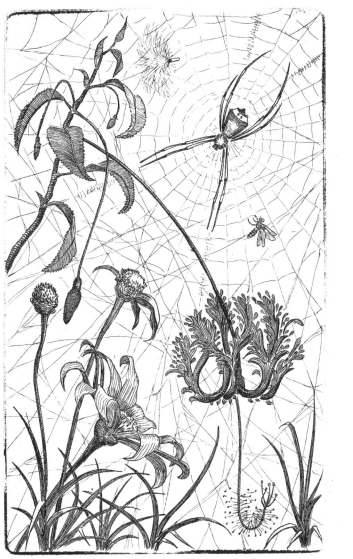

WINDY - WEB SPIDER
WHAT IS YOUR SILENT SPEAKING...
YOUR UNSUNG SONG?
        BASHO (1644-94)

Ray Parkin
1980.

which brings us to a precise (relatively) point of evolution and to the climacteric of the human mind:

> *... and God brought them [animals] unto Adam to see what he would call them: and whatsoever Adam called every living creature, that was the name thereof.*

Thus, we have the birth of language established, which must imply the emergence of a concomitant Intellect: i.e., the juggling of abstract concepts. With the tools of Reason and Imagination (the *imaging* of abstract concepts for which language is essential), Intellect makes comparisons from which it forms judgements. These may sometimes be based in Intelligence, but, with a growing frequency, now more upon its own imaginative synthesis offering the promise of 'better things to come.'

This I see as no less than a presumed 'knowledge of Good and Evil,' as the product of its comparisons: value-judgement. Such 'knowledge,' I feel, becomes more pretended than real when divorced from the ancient triumvirate of Instinct, Intuition and Intelligence. But the promise of what this new Intellect appeared to offer beyond his present state, proved too much for Adam. Imagination gave him visions of seemingly limitless possibilities. It was a direct challenge to Eden and all its principles which, he had decided, were not good enough for him and did not measure up to the Promised Land envisaged by Intellect.

In short, from his comparisons, the erstwhile perfection of Eden was found wanting, for he had envisaged even to a point of his own apotheosis! This is no anachronistic imposition of my own. It is there in the story as plain as day. Its revelation comes with superb irony:

> *Behold, the man is become as one of us [the gods] to know Good and evil: and now, lest he put forth his hand, and take also the Tree of Life, and eat and live for ever: therefore the Lord God sent him forth from the garden of Eden to till the ground from whence he was taken.*

Which was God's way of saying, "Have it your own way, *now* let's see just how good you *really* are with this new toy."

I began to see that this was intended to indicate how the *hubris* of Intellect was developing the illusion that it could take all-that-had-been and change it into the world-as-one-would; that it could, step by step, create its own synthesis and become itself the Creator and effect its own apotheosis.

One can now see, perhaps, how Intellect has taken these successive steps towards this end. This *urge* may be variously stated: as Intellectual *ambition;* as the *inner drive* of the Ego; or as the *destiny* of the Soul. I see them only as different as Tweedledee is from Tweedledum. But the *Intellect* seems more recognizable as the faculty which manipulates and conceptualizes; the *Ego* as the end to be served; and the *Soul* (made sacrosanct from a conceived 'divine origin') as the bastion of Authority. Thus, I find 'Intellect' as the most embracing term for all this. However, I would make a distinction with what I think of as *the pristine intellect* naturally emergent in man and with a trusting hand still in those of the old Triumvirate. It is with the capital 'I' that I distinguish what I see as Intellect-unrestrained, Intellect-rabid, Intellect rejecting all reality but its own. As in a community where all are 'mad,' such becomes the norm and goes unnoticed, and so it seems with Intellect today.

Man is ever-prone to conceive himself as 'different' from all other, and indeed I think he *is*. It is not from that 'divine spark' which he thinks is in him. As usual, in his own defence, he inverts the truth. It is because that divine spark which was once *within* him has been rejected. He has turned his back on Eden, he denies Tao, both of which the rest of the natural world embraces. He *alone* is *different*, but in a negative and not a positive way. And, in his vanity, would not, will not, have it any other way. I sense that it is the Flaming Sword of two-edged Intellect which keeps him out of Eden and from the Tao. The whole thrust of the *Tao Te Ching,* those remnants of the ancient Tao, is in negation of this meddling and self-destructive Intellect.

> *For those who would take the whole world*
> *To tinker it as they see fit,*
> *I observe that they never succeed:*
> *For the world is a sacred vessel*
> *Not made to be altered by Man.*
> *The tinker will spoil it;*
> *Usurpers will lose it.*   [Tao 29]

These are the conclusions I have privately drawn from Genesis chapters two and three, from thoughts begun in the Siamese jungle in 1943-44. This has dealt with the general destiny of mankind as a result of its self-willed actions. But there is more to the story than just that. There is, as I began to see it, the strongest implication, not just of the dichotomy occurring then between Man and Nature, but of a mind-splitting dichotomy also within the Individual (*son* of man).

It is a drama with only four performers on the stage. I have characterized them thus: *The Man:* active Intelligence *cum* Intellect; *The Woman:* Instinct and Intuition; *God:* the voice of Tao; *the Serpent:* the figure for Intellectual self-justification through Reason. We already know that the time is that of full evolutionary development, and the emergence of Intellect in Man.

The excuse put forward by Adam when asked why he had eaten of the fruit of the Tree of the Knowledge of Good and Evil, was, "*She* made me do it." This is, perhaps, the first recorded 'victory' of the *Ego* (Intellect) over the *Id* (Instinct): Ego placed an 'apron of leaves' over the Id in conscious denial of it, and this is plain evidence, to me, that the Innocence of Eden had been displaced by a Morality which would constantly use Nature (Instinct) as its whipping-boy by denial from thence forth. It was a well-calculated defence mechanism.

Although we have been led, so far, to imagine this Creation to have been a Man's world (remember that this story in *this* context was being addressed to a man-dominated culture), for the Woman was only Adam's Rib. But this, in fact, was not at all the case.

In the pristine world of Eden, the Female was dominant, and the role of the Male was brief: for, when Nature went beyond bisexual organisms, the Male was at the beck and call of the Female – a Galant, as it were, like a cocked gun only to be fired at Female behest. And, though in animals the Male was charged with the necessity of dominance, it was only as a means of security for HER.

Now, when God questioned Adam, it was as if the maleness of Intellect wished to compensate for this 'humiliation' of second place. And its overcompensation is evident today. The Woman (Female) is blamed and intellectually covered with shame, as the Temptress, etc. This has brought about a dichotomy, not only between the sexes, but within the personality: which is itself a necessary blend of maleness and femaleness and perhaps an inheritance from bisexual times.

The primacy of the Female, the Mother, the Valley Spirit, had been well-established in human thought by the time this drama was written, so that there is no wise-after-the-event anachronism in the introduction of this element.

> *It began with a matrix:*
> *The world had a mother ...*   [Tao 52]

The great land is a place to which the streams descend;
It is the concourse and
The female of the world:
Quiescent, underneath,
It overcomes the male.   [Tao 62]

Be aware of your masculine nature;
But by keeping the feminine way,
You shall be to the world like a canyon,
Where the Virtue eternal abides,[1]
And go back and become as a child.   [Tao 28]

The valley spirit is not dead:
They say it is the mystic female.
Her gateway is, they further say,
The base of heaven and earth.

Constantly, and so forever,
Use her without labour.   [Tao 6]

I must admit to the possibility of a bias on my part here for I received this vital Clue to Tao from One who gave it to me unconsciously by being none other than herself. Some fourteen years ago, a thing called 'death' came along to intervene. It did its worst, yet it has not touched this thing. Ten years before I had written:

From this Only-One
Have I deeply known this age –
Old, old All-wisdom.

When, dead, my wormwood
Shall drift ashore: this foredoomed
Time is not the end:

The million shells dead
On the beaches – long, long dead –
Silently sing Life.

---

[1] This is in sharp contrast to Eve as the Temptress.

Now the Woman was indeed instinctual, and had quite realized what had happened to her 'other half.' With a subtle symbolism, transcending Adam's slow Intellect, she simply said to God that the Serpent was the cause of all this trouble in Paradise. And God understood: for the Serpent has no limbs; it is long, writhing and insinuating as its only method of progression; and its only defence is a mouthful of poison. Now this was not so unlike a long string of self-justifying words with a damning judgement to offer. Thus, both God and the woman *knew.*

> *And the Lord God said unto the Serpent:*
> *Because thou hast done this, thou art cursed above all cattle, and above every beast of the field; upon thy belly thou shalt go, and dust shalt thou eat all the days of thy life: and I will put enmity between thee and the woman, and between thy seed and her seed; it shall bruise thy head, and thou shalt bruise his heel.*

Cursed above all cattle ... The Serpent Reason will lose the instinctual *nous* which the cattle had ('and, with that was knowledge of repose').

Upon thy belly thou shalt go ... Instead of the swift intuitive perception of necessity, the slow crawling serpent of words with the halting gait of a striven-for certitude.

And dust shalt thou eat ... Compare du Noüy's theme in *Human Destiny*: "Man is capable of creating an unreal world by drawing the elements from within himself. ..." *This* is the 'dust' of synthesis upon which it will feed.

I will put enmity between thee and the woman ... This will be the inner clash between the incompatible Intellectual and Instinctual with the conflict of demand and defence between Intellectual compulsion and Instinctual necessity.

> *And unto the woman he said, I will greatly multiply thy sorrow and conception; in sorrow shalt thou bring forth children; and thy desire shall be to thy husband, and he shall rule over thee.*

The man, Intellect, would dominate and there was no escape from this unhappy union, and sorrows would flow from it.

> *And unto Adam he said:*
> *Cursed is the ground for thy sake: in sorrow shalt thou eat of it all the days of thy life. Thorns and also thistles shall it bring forth to thee; in*

the sweat of thy face shalt thou eat bread, till thou return to the
ground, for out of it thou was taken: for dust thou art, and unto dust
thou shalt return.

The implications of this are too obviously being demonstrated;
with Intellect having brought humanity to the brink of self-destruc-
tion, and with the natural world passively submitting to an extinction
at the hand of Man. And the blunt reminder, cutting Man down to size
amid all his dreams of grandeur: *For dust thou art, and unto dust thou*
shalt return.

The sober warnings were out thousands of years ago, and man took
no heed. Man chose to abandon Eden in favour of his own Pandora's
Box which, the dictionary tells us, 'By its rash opening all objects of
desire were dispersed to play havoc among mankind.' And still he
pays no heed.

Thus, ever since the abandonment of Eden and the beginning of the
Great Artifice, the life of Man has become a restless sea of confused
and conflicting ideas in which he must swim or drown. Each individual is marooned upon an island of primal self, continually washed
over by demanding and conflicting waves. It is as the old Arabian said
in *1001 Nights:* "You are caught in the web of the world, and the
Spider Nothing waits behind it."

How then to breast the Waves??

Then, in the jungle, this became my all-consuming thought. And,
what was begun then has become a habit since. But it was begun in
what I think may be fairly called 'an extraordinary state of mind.' I
don't know if it was the continuing starvation, or the recurrent fevers,
but I seemed to have developed a strange detachment as if there were
no distinction of Past, Present or Future, for now I seemed to see
them all as one. It was as if I were 'Above' on some lofty perch
witnessing the judgement of some Greater Power; as if my mind had
been freed from the trammels of its limitations and some new
discovery were imminent; as if by sitting quite still in this special
place all ideas would, in their nakedness, parade before me. It was by
no means a feeling of cleverness, for what I was most conscious of
was my profound ignorance. It was rather the suspenseful expecta-
tion, upon what grounds I did not know, of being *informed.* It was as
if I was about to come face to face with the Simple Truth.

It seemed to me then that I was not *thinking* thoughts at all, but
that thoughts of their own volition came to me, and I was merely an

amanuensis to record them. It gave me a peculiar feeling. When I stopped to think, I realized that I didn't *know* anything at all – things just 'came.' And I wondered, who the hell was 'I'? Whence come the words 'I' write?? I got the uneasy feeling that the 'I' that writes is just a 'front' whose vanity somewhat outdoes itself in performance. I wondered: is our outward 'knowledge' no more than some pretentious script we write for ourselves, that we may so outwardly perform our little dramas, while the real Management conducts all important business far beneath our verbose veneer?

I wondered: What is this 'I' that has been taken for granted yet never really known? 'I' only know that 'I' have taken up residence somewhere 'up here' on the top floor, as it were, of a commonwealth of cells which, with astounding ingenuity, manage to carry around with them in a skin enough of the Archean Sea in which to continue swimming. How they do it, I can truly say, 'Only God knows.' This, I suppose, is the real 'ME' and it is lucky for this 'I' that they know what they are doing. All 'I' have to do is to sit up here to keep a lookout so that 'we' don't bump into trees or fall over precipices or otherwise come to grief from various casual causes. But 'I' must admit that a growing preoccupation with my own fond thoughts makes me negligent and inattentive to my simple job. Yearning constantly for grander things, I tend to become more incompetent with what is necessary and keep a bad lookout.

I am afraid that this 'I' of Intellect is paying less and less attention to the essential 'I's of Instinct and Intuition and Intelligence, and we are bumping into more trees and falling over more precipices. And with such inattention, I am afraid that there is worse to come. Consider what Intellect has been saying lately: [Le Compte du Noüy, *Human Destiny*]

> *Henceforth, contrary to all others, in order to evolve he must no longer obey nature. Man is capable of creating an unreal world by drawing the elements from within himself and no longer from his surroundings or his experience. It is not a question of utilitarian adaption, but of an absolutely new intellectual construction in which material reality is only a pretext … Behind his discernible universe, man invents another conceptual universe, which becomes indispensable to enable him to think, to interpret his experience, and eventually dominate the first.*

These are the sober thoughts of Intellect. And, as if of them, the Japanese poet Shiki wrote with a perceptive evocation:

As I light the lamp
Behold! ... To every single doll,
Its own real *shadow!*

As I said, the caution was there thousands of years ago. Compare these:

And so there is a proverb:
"When the going looks like coming back,
The clearest road is mighty dark."
Today, the Way that's plain looks rough,
And lofty Virtue like a chasm;
The purest Innocence like shame,
The broadest Power not enough,
Established Goodness knavery,
Substantial worth like shifting sands.   [Tao 41]

And Shakespeare's *66th Sonnet:*

Tired with all these, for restful death I cry, –
As, to behold Desert a beggar born,
And needy Nothing trimm'd in jollity,
And gilded Honour shamefully misplaced,
And maiden Virtue rudely strumpeted,
And right Perfection wrongfully disgraced,
And Strength by limping Sway disabled,
And Art made tongue-tied by Authority,
And Folly, doctor-like, controlling Skill,
And simple Truth miscall'd Simplicity,
And captive Good attending captain Ill,
    Tired with all these, from these I would be gone,
    Save that, to die, I leave my love alone.

So, what is the nature of this Intellectual Idea that has spread like some fanatic faith? And, how can one assess it?

By 'one,' I mean the average person for, to him, the Experts are not readily available, especially in the jungle. Nor are they consistent, but often in a direct conflict. I was once deferring to an Expert for whose integrity I had great respect. I readily granted him a point, 'as an expert' was the phrase I used. This he deprecated, asking me if I knew what an expert was. I waited for his answer. And he told me, "An expert is someone who has not been found out yet." So, perforce, the average person must become an expert on Experts, if he is to get anywhere.

And it was while working for the Imperial Japanese Army, cutting a scar through Eden, that I managed to devise for myself a home-made key to unlock the Idea. Could there be something common to all, I first wondered: some common anatomy to dissect and then to examine the bits? And I thought that I had found just this.

The first question was: "Why have an idea in the first place?" The simple answer seemed to be: "To satisfy one's mind." Then the question arose: "How?" The answer came: "By telling it something which will make it comfortable." Was this a cynicism or a simple fact?

Well, it seemed to be a fact because, in surveying all the 'truths' I could think of, I saw that only those had survived which had *kept* the mind comfortable. Many 'truths' had come and gone because they had rendered only transient comfort. This was, it seemed to me, a constant for all truths, from superstition to science. Therefore, I called this prime-mover of the Idea, *The Wish.*

Throughout all animate nature, there is a Deep Wish, which is instinctual. Spinoza expresses it thus: "Individual things are modes by which the attributes of God are expressed in a certain determinate manner ... It is opposed to everything which could negate its exist-ence." This is in close conformity to Natural Necessity (my term). And this I called *The Pristine Wish.*

Now, the Idea is an intellectual and not an instinctual product. Its *Wish* may be seen as the *'will'* of Schopenhauer; or the *'desire'* which the buddhas strove to subdue. It may be seen to arise as an intellec-tual compulsion; therefore, I called it *The Intellectual Wish.* This Intellectual Wish, from its very nature, will produce ideas which will argue towards a preconceived end, and, in this sense, tend to be self-defeating, for:

> *The secret waits for insight*
> *Of eyes unclouded by longing;*
> *Those who are bound by desire*
> *See only the outward container.*   [Tao 1]

So the Wish will conceive its own *prime assumption,* upon which all ideas are founded. Thus, the conclusion may only be *As-If* that prime assumption were true. Yet the mathematician Kurt Gödel has given us rigorous proof of the fact that every logical system *must* contain a premise which it cannot define without contradicting itself. Therefore, I called this part of the Idea its *As-If.*

Thus, for the understanding of any idea, I see the identification of its *Wish* and *As-If* as essential. It gives a much simpler picture to deal with; as, when you know a person's motive, it is easier to understand his actions. The whole Idea I call an *As-If Tale.*

As Francis Bacon wrote in his *Novum Organum* under *Idols of the Tribe:* "The human understanding is no dry light, but receives an infusion from the will and affections, whence proceed sciences which may be called 'sciences as one would'. ... For what man had rather were true, he more readily believes."

I observed, too, that ideas were *rejected* from the same *Wish* as that by which, in the same subject, others had been *accepted.*

In that the idea becomes the justification of The Wish, so it follows, I think, that Man may be distinguished from all other animals, not as one who laughs, nor one who uses tools, but as a *self-justifying* animal. And it is passing strange to me that he who considers himself at the apex of all evolution, top of the heap, should be so continually so self-justifying. His language is full of it, and his argument vociferous. No other animal bothers. Has he, with all his 'victories' over Nature, still a sense of insecurity? Will he ever find peace?

> *All things bear the shade on their backs*
> *And the sun in their arms:*
> *By the blending of the breath*
> *From the sun and the shade,*
> *Equilibrium comes to the world.*   [Tao 42]

But, having run down *The Wish* and the *As-If,* how then is it possible to *assess* the worth or validity of an idea? My solution was: just as Intellectual judgement is made on comparison, so I would compare *it* with *Natural Necessity.* This is a term of convenience I coined for myself, something I suppose I gleaned subconsciously from my old friend, Spinoza. "... [that] which we call God or Nature, acts by the same *necessity* as that whereby it exists." And "The more things the mind knows, the better it understands its own powers and the order of Nature. The better it understands its own powers, so much the more easily can it direct itself and propose rules to itself. The better, also, it understands the order of Nature, the more easily can it *restrain itself from what is useless* [my italics]."

In simple terms: all thoughts were to be suspect until ground small in the Mills of God, i.e., *Natural Necessity*. They were to be examined to see if they were a 'needy Nothing trimmed in jollity' and if, in fact, they may be wearing 'the King's New Clothes' only. Each idea was to be stood on its head and shaken to see if there were anything in its pockets. Ideas based in Reason and Logic could be found very barren, I was thinking. For some reason, perverse, perhaps, an upside-down thought came to me: what about the myths of the primitives?

These, I thought, with all their apparent illogicalities, seemed to recognize their limitations by the fertile variety of their As-If's. They made of each only one small candle to illumine a single facet. They spoke with simple, but subtle, evocation which was more readily apprehended by minds not yet divorced from Instinct and Intuition; nor yet shackled to reason and logic which, Judas-like, deny the Parent which does not bow to Intellect's new gods. The quality of life of the myth-makers cannot be looked for among the trash of technology, nor among the conveniences and comforts of civilization. For it was, perhaps, in the ancient marriage with Instinct that the myth-maker possibly came closer to significant knowledge than science is today. The oral literature of the myth was not literal, was not bound to reason and logic with its halting gait of an assumed certitude, but was able to transcend these with swift intuitive insights to evoke, from within, in a thousand illogical ways, ineffable verities which have flowed through all Creation since the Beginning: As-If from a Universal Umbilical. The very multiplicity of these As-If's of the myth's wild illogicalities only added to and strengthened the evocation of a Truth not chained to any *one* point of view, and which made of it a night with a thousand eyes: as in the vast variety of ways Nature solves one central problem. Perhaps there may have been something of Jung's *Collective Unconscious* in this; but where it has remained faithful to the Pristine Wish born in Natural Necessity, it has been, I feel, Pure Art.

If only Man could see that all his ideas are but his As-If Tales, his somewhat stilted myths, perhaps there would be more life-saving tolerance in the world. No organism in Nature needs, generally speaking, *anything* outside its skin to be able to get a living or fulfil its nature. Compare this with the profligate demands of Man upon the World – and he puts back nothing, save his world-wilting waste.

For Man, haughty now, and presuming himself above the Law, stands greedy before the altar of the Golden Calf, oblivious, it seems, that he himself must be its sacrifice: for he has turned his back upon that vital clue to Tao, given to him long ago and which, if heeded, might have saved him. For it was written in Genesis chapter 9, verse l: *"Be fruitful, and multiply, AND REPLENISH THE EARTH."*

But, Verse 2 is a strange and awful prophecy, as if realizing the nature of Desire in Man, its captive:

"And the fear of you and the dread of you shall be upon every beast of the earth, and upon every fowl of the air, and upon all that moveth upon the earth, and upon all the fishes of the sea; into your hands they are delivered."

> *No sin can exceed*
> *Incitement to envy;*
> *No calamity's worse*
> *Than to be discontented;*
> *Nor is there an omen*
> *More dreadful than coverting.*
> *But once be contented,*
> *And truly you'll always be so.*   [Tao 46]

We call ourselves human BEINGS, yet, perhaps, we are the only species who has lost the Art.

I came out from that jungle, and from captivity itself, at last; and I brought with me some measure of that which Spinoza so aptly calls the 'acquiescence of spirit' which makes life simpler and sweeter.

This gave me the personal realization that:

The first rule of Life is	– TO ACCEPT IT.
The greatest thing is	– TO BE.
The greatest wisdom is	– HOW TO BE.
The greatest problem is	– To escape the Net of Intellect.
That: The cycle of Life is	– TO BE BEGOT. TO BEGET. TO BEGONE.

That: From the grain of sand to
    the greatest star, the
    whole rhythm of Existence
    is, simply,   COMING and GOING.

That: if understood properly, this will not give rise to a cynical despair, nor to the abyss of Nihilism: for what fleshes-out these bare bones is all the wonder of Creation.

That: There is no new wisdom under the sun, *except* it would be new if the old were heeded.

But the Way, when declared,
Seems so thin and flavourless!
It is nothing to look at,
And nothing to hear;
But used, it will prove
Inexhaustible.   [Tao 35]

It seems odd that, out of a closely confined *Captivity* came a sort of *Freedom* to venture in the Infinite; that, from *Intimidation* came a kind of courage – the *Temerity* to till fields for which I had not the slightest of qualifications!

Addendum

I was asked, after coming out of three-and-a-half years of captivity, what I had learned from my experience. It was apparently thought that I *must* have gained some oracular insight. So I said, aphoristically, "Life is just Gossip and Sitting-in-the-Sun."

I am afraid that this was taken as a cynicism or a hedonistic surrender. I found it hard to make clear that *Gossip* was my summation of all human intellectual activity as against some greater Totality; or that *Sitting-in-the-Sun* was simply our Being experiencing the warmth of the Sun-of-our-Origin through the simple virtue of Passivity. For I had come to the view that, for a true acquiescence of Spirit, one must be the Instrument and never the Player.

A Pattern of Meeting

Robert Schwartz

The gifts that Laurens van der Post received from God were bountiful in scope and poetic in nature. The gifts he returns not only pay homage to the Creator, they add wings to the spirit of those on the earthly human journey here below.

Some twenty years ago, I first met Laurens at a small dinner at the on-campus home of Charles de Carlo, the then-president of Sarah Lawrence College. I was at the dinner because a week earlier I had asked de Carlo if he had ever had a guest speaker at Sarah Lawrence who appealed deeply to both the students and faculty. After a pause, he replied, "In the eight years I've been here, only one such speaker has appeared – the English writer, Laurens van der Post. Normally speakers appeal to either students or faculty, but everyone here of every age is enthralled by van der Post. I've invited him back and he'll be here for dinner next week: do come."

"What seems so special about him?" I asked.

"We refer to him as a writer, but he's more than that; some of us here think of him as a philosopher, but he's more than that; my personal feeling is that Laurens van der Post is some kind of saint."

Laurens and I had such a delightful time at dinner that the next day, I invited him to come and see my business venture, The Tarrytown Conference Center overlooking the Hudson at nearby Tarrytown, New York. As we arrived in Tarrytown and turned into the main local road, Laurens interrupted my ramblings about business and said firmly but gently, "Shh, Bob, – we must be still and hear the legends that are all about us. I've never been here before, but I can sense that much of American history and many American myths were created in this valley; these surrounding hills cry out with legends that demand to be heard. Am I right? Is this true?"

It was true, of course – everything from the Sleepy Hollow legends to battle lore of the Revolutionary War was lodged in those hills – but it was equally true that I seldom let this enter my consciousness.

Thus the pattern began on our first meeting and thus it continues today: every meeting with Laurens van der Post has widened and deepened my awareness of the world around me.

I'm not sure I agree that Laurens is actually a saint: my theory is that he's a Boddishattva. These are people in the Hindu tradition so enlightened, so Buddha-like, that their role on earth is not to proceed directly to heaven, but to share their awareness with the rest of us so that our days on earth may be more enlightened and our journey to heaven more pleasantly traveled.

Biblical sculptures by Frances Baruch on the Sir Laurens van der Post Wall of the Cathedral of St. John the Divine in New York City

The Turning of Tides

Pamela Uschuk

for Laurens

I

Through Blue Spruce overshadowing our house,
the cries of coyotes recede
then scream forward
        intuiting blood sacrifice
inevitable as stars.

At this altitude, sky is wide
as the Veldt that dreamed your fortune
in the shift of the seasons' regular tides.

Outflanking Biblical tales, Bushman
myths were your first history –
how Mantis brought fire, why Eland
laughed, and the apocalypse
of the All-Devourer who would one day
consume the known world.

Divining the quick of each wanderer's heart,
a full moon reveals the autumn valley.
        Below us, water circles stones
defining the creek's path.

I listen to a solitary vireo flute through
brambles and think of you,
early this century
        at the Cape of Good Hope,
a junior reporter who signed on the whaling ship
and watched slaughter bruise the sea.
        Lone scout in the crow's nest,
you rocked, imagining
the formation of the nascent world
etched on the horizon's far skull.

Back on land, with Plomer and Campbell
you began Vorslag –
        the crack of the whip –
South Africa's first anti-apartheid gazette.

In Nature there are no straight lines
nor coincidence. In the all-White restaurant,
you intervened for dark strangers,
never dreaming these men
were Japanese ambassadors
who'd invite you on a cruise
to the exotic curl of their islands.

Journeying East, you learned the subtle
brushstroke of each character,
ritual politeness, the warrior code
of the Samurai, his absolute
devotion to the flowering moon.
You were so young, even Geishas laughed
when you dove drunk into a scalding bath.
Still you regretted going home.

I imagine you now, returning
to Africa, leaning against
stormstruck swells
that smashed your vessel
as you passed Borneo and Java
then through the Bay of Bengal.
And beyond longing, a hairline fracture

of fear, remembered from Conrad,
the dark heart of the All-Devourer to come.

II

Laurens, you love the sea and its depths
reassuring as the moon's long hands
that pull wrinkles from scored tide,
the way everything returns.

When the world war broke, was it
the brilliant constancy of waves
that held your faith, after you were captured
and tortured in a Japanese prison camp?

Four years, barb-wired
in squat bamboo cages, you survived
each hour defined by brutality,
by unnamed fevers that claimed your friends
under the decaying sweat of Java's sky.
Above gorgeous palm trees, madness
swelled with each full moon, increasing
murders with its ripe tug.

Even in hell there are miracles –
like the time the ancient voice
sang from your throat at the precise moment
it erupted from fellow soldiers,
a synchronous hymn no command could stop,
despite the executioner guards
who prepared their swords.
The entire body of prisoners you led
would not be silenced
        even when the three men who began the chorus
were beheaded in front of you.

How does the soul survive? Grace
was the other voice come back when, blood
crazed, the Commandant ordered all prisoners be beaten

one by one for no reason.
Alphabetically, each prisoner stepped forth
until the bamboo canes slid
red in the Korean guards´ hands.

During your beating, it came to you
exactly what to do.
   The next man was called
and you stood in his place, stood
again and again and were caned until
the Commandant lost face.
No one died; the guards stopped –
like fire on fire, the spell was broken.

III

Tonight the shadows of mountains surround us.
   Rising whole, over houses
that would insulate us, the moon
is weighty as the shaved head of a sentry
assessing the world turned liquid in its path.
   It shrinks to a new coin
unpolluted by the torturer's hand.

   Light is the invention of forgiveness,
moon the instructor of the heart.

Laurens, who else but you
would Mandela and LeClerc trust
for advice to reconstruct South Africa's bones?
After centuries charred by apartheid's terror, it is
the same voice that rises as thousands
sing, black and white, demanding
equality, an end to hate's reign.

I can't forget the stories of your caged days and nights
or that when you were released
to command your captors, you asked no revenge

but with Mountbatten remained
and arranged for Javanese independence.

Between the night branches of Spruce and Pines, we listen
        to what survives, the cries of coyotes
as they hunt, canny under the Milky Way's far arc.

Perhaps, this is the cure, knowing
        what breaks renews, a chorus
striking the dark for meaning,
refined and passionate as the turning of tides.

Sir Laurens at Maun in the Kalahari, 1986

To the Memory of Thomas Chalmers Robertson[1]

Laurens van der Post

Between Robertson, or to give him the name by which he was known and loved among all races in South Africa, "T.C.," and myself, the story was always known as the story of *The Secret River*. We knew that at other places it was known by other names and connotations. As part of the great spoken literature of Africa, on which the writer of stories today is perched like a dwarf on the shoulders of a giant, it had, of course no specific author and no fixed 'Bureau of Standards' to go by. It lived and was alive in the cultures of the great African nations and dependent for its life and vitality on the impact it made on the lips of living men from generation to generation, and dependent on its survival entirely in the welcome it found there.

There is in the story's regard, as far as I know, only one written version and that was by a lover of African peoples called Dudley Kidd, who, in the last decades of the nineteenth century, traveled among the Bantu peoples from the Cape Province into the heart of Central Africa and across to Broken Hill and the great Suthu kingdom in Barotseland. In his version, the heroine had a name, and her name was given to his version of the story. As far as we could judge, it was our only clue to the origin of his version. There must, of course, be on record somewhere an exact indication of where and from whom he obtained the story, but as boys in love with the prehistory and natural world of Africa, we were no scholars and could guess at its origin only by the fact that the name suggested a Suthu or Barotse beginning.

---

[1] This is an adapted version of an introduction Laurens van der Post recently wrote for a book entitled, *The Secret River*, published by Barefoot Press, U.K., 1996. The story being referred to is told by Frances Baruch on page 39 of this volume.

In due course, I myself came across other versions of the story; the most important, perhaps, of all I obtained on a visit to Shembe, when a rumor of his stature as a prophet first penetrated to where I was starting out in life in Port Natal. With my upbringing, the news that a great new prophet had arisen among a great African people like the Zulus was an event of supreme importance. My own imagination was formed as a child by intimate contact with the lives of the indigenous peoples of Africa and their world, where prophets and storytellers and interpreters of dreams were still far more important than district commissioners, tax collectors and missionaries.

I was so interested in this phenomenon that I persuaded a remarkable Zulu pioneer of education among his people called Champion to leave the school which he had founded near Durban for a few days and accompany me into the country around the Sacred Hills of Inanda, where Shembe had built his kraals and collected a remarkable little community, mostly of women, around him.

There one night I heard the story which T.C. and I had already heard in other ways during our excursions on our ponies into the Eastern Transvaal in search of new rock paintings and contacts with what remains of primitive life in that part of Africa.

Today, of course, Shembe is a great and deeply honored name. He was the founder of what is perhaps the largest religious sect in Zululand, with a following even far beyond its frontiers, and it is unique in the sense that it is a blend of the New Testament and all the intuitive and instinctive aspirations of the spirit of the Zulu people for a life and meaning beyond the inadequate here and now. His followers today are to be numbered in the millions, and through them and the quality of his own purity of spirit and the profundity of his instinctive perceptions, the Zulu people are perhaps the only indigenous people in Africa to realize the necessity of going into the modern world with a fully contemporary interpretation of the timeless values so movingly expressed in their traditions and, for me, their spoken literature.

At that moment of which I am talking, I remember clearly how, in the early winter sky, the hill of Inanda stood clear-cut, almost as a cardboard silhouette, under the Milky Way, and how deeply moved I was about what Shembe had told me of what he had seen and heard and discussed with a Voice that always called him, often alone at midnight, to the summit of that hill. I remember, above all, that, when he had asked me in the first place why I had wanted to see him and I told him it was because I had hoped he would tell me more of the first great spirit of the Zulus, 'Mkulukulu, he had shaken his head sadly and said that people talked less and less of 'Mkulukulu and more and more only about things that could be useful to them.

Yet, in the three days and nights that followed, after the women had come in from the fields which they cultivated and we had eaten and we talked, we did not talk at all about the material things that are so useful to modern man, but about the history and all the things in life that had brought the Zulus as a people intact out of the past to where they were then.

In that setting, my requests for stories were always met, and this story of the Secret River was the one, no doubt because it was already part of my own imagination, that impressed me most and stayed with me and was very often the subject of conversation between T.C. and myself, partly because, I think, both T.C. and I had remarkable mothers. T.C. felt very keenly, though he would never have said it to anybody except me, that his father, who, incidentally, was a remarkable and heroic person in the male sense of the word, did not appreciate or realize sufficiently what a wonderful woman he had married, and somehow deeply resented the fact.

As a result, the story, which we both felt was unique among African stories, because it was a story that was almost an allegory of the way the predominantly male cultures of the world had come out of the past with a profound and stubborn unawareness of the caring and feminine values of life and to the evolution of societies and establishments which led to the personification of all those values of woman in flesh and blood in their own societies. And it was most notable, as the years went on, that, whenever we discussed more consciously these matters of the great and timeless feminine and masculine values in life, the more we found in the story.

I have, at other times and places where I told the story, because of my knowledge of African life and history, decoded the meanings which I think are implicit in the imagery and the symbolism of the story. I think they are of immense importance, particularly to the time in which we live, and particularly important to the evolution of the modern psychology in depth. But in this version of the story, I do not propose to subject it to any interpretation or analysis of mine beyond this general remark that it is a profound expression of the hurt feminine soul in man and woman and full of hints about how these two dynamic factors in life have been the source of such conflicts and loss of meaning in the great collectivities of humankind.

I will only allow myself one exception to this rule I have tried to obey in introducing this version of the story, and that is to say that the great symbolic meanings implicit in the story were first recognized in the world outside Africa by an interpreter of the abiding values of the human spirit, Helen Luke.

Her recognition of the significance of this particular story, therefore, was an event of great importance to us both, because it was such a confirmation of our belief that through these stories of Africa (more, perhaps, than in the spoken literature of any other part of the world), the "great memory" – as I call it –, which invests the child already at birth, feeds the human imagination with a wisdom derived not only from generations of man to man, but rooted in the experience of creation itself and creation's sense of the ultimate meaning and direction of life in the universe.

I feel that the story has a wider and deeper role in the evolution of the human spirit and a need to be heard for the first time in its own right. By itself, it is far more creative than any conscious elucidation and advocacy, however important, can make it, and wherever I can, I prefer to release these great stories from our far, far beginnings into the imaginations of an age so deprived of its sense of continuity with the primordial past, and let its robust and eloquent imagery and symbolism speak directly to each soul as it encounters it. One's own help in the matter, I believe, is rather like that of releasing a spirited young horse which has been kept in stables too long, for duty under the saddle and in the harness of the rational spirit of our time, and to let it recover uninhibited the freedom of pace and rhythm which was its own at birth.

To know it in its more dutiful role in our imaginations is, of course, of the greatest significance, but it is a role nonetheless which has been subjected to sophisticated human choices and has already been confined, in a sense, in partialities of mind and judgment. I am certain from my own experience that, no matter how good the mind and judgment, they are only provisional and a preparation for enabling the story to convey, on the next occasion when it is told, qualities and nuances that were not perceived before.

To come to the story for the first time in this way is to allow the story to introduce itself undefeated in the larger purpose, which preconditioning would deny it, and for the storyteller to remember the impact which his spirit registered, and will retain forever, of the moment when on his newborn senses there fell, for the first time, as the call on a bugle of reveille falls on the senses of sleeping soldiers before battle, the summons conveyed by his nurse or mother in the opening statement: "Once upon a time…" and he heard his first story and, though he knew it not consciously at the time, was changed for good by it.

I myself have found that the original impact of the stories I heard from primitive people was not diminished but enhanced by the fact that I have never written them down and, although the one written version of The Secret River to which I referred made a great impression on me when I first came across it among my father's papers more than seventy years ago, these things have all been left in the keeping of my memory.

One of the many elements which made the spoken literature of the world so dynamic was that it observed the rule of positive forgetting. There is an immense danger to the human spirit in trying to remember everything that has happened to a person on his way through life. So much of what is poured into the human mind and spirit must be forgotten as soon as it has served the purpose for which it appeared in the immediate awareness of the human being.

Stories may be an essential part of the baggage that the human spirit needs on its journey through life, not as messages of meaning so much as containers of meaning; containers, moreover, which become outworn and out of date and have to be discarded at the changing of situations and direction at the next marshalling yard on our journey through life. This is Nature's way of keeping what is abiding and forever in the story immediate and contemporary and discarding that which would retard and, to change the metaphor, make indigestible the nourishment which the story is there to provide.

I have a hunch that, in the timeless view of creation, all cultures and civilizations, even the most deeply rooted and apparently permanent of them, are manifestations of the great paradoxes that life is compelled always to be absolutely provisional and that not only the term of service of flesh and blood, but all manifestations of creation in the here and now are rather like tents raised at nightfall, but struck again at dawn so that the caravan can be on its way again.

There is, however, one clarification which I owe my 'listening readers' and that is a word or two about the title T.C and I instinctively gave the story: The Secret River. The story itself, of course, shows in a sense why it is a secret river and how it is the home of secrets of great importance to the people who live in the natural world by rivers. This sense of the secret powers of rivers, and what they conceal and nourish, is reflected in many stories of Africa, and of course other cultures as well, but here, principally because of the introduction of Tokoloshe.

We, as children in Africa, were afraid of Tokoloshe. The stories about him and his great powers told by our African playmates, nurses and other companions, were almost without number. Tokoloshe was a natural African spirit, known by this name from the great Fish River in the Cape to the frontiers of what was called Central Africa and so on to Broken Hill, the great Suthu kingdom of the Barotse. He was said to be a small and extremely powerful male person and also a kind of Bantu Priapus, who, in some of the stories, was pictured as a man endowed with overwhelming sexual powers and a phallus so great that he wore it coiled around his neck. In this role, he was depicted particularly as preying on young, innocent girls, and the fear of him was so great that young girls and women would not go near a river, even to fetch much-needed water, at nightfall. It would explain, therefore, why he appears naturally in this story and why preserving the connection of the story with the secret of a secret river made us remember it in this fashion.

Finally, a word about my dedication to T.C.: I have dedicated other things to him because he was a friend as no other friend and made friendship an experience for me, I believe, which other friendships could have equalled, but not surpassed. But there is another compelling reason which I think is of interest and perhaps, in a way that one does not adequately understand, part of the Wonder and the Mystery on which the storyteller always draws.

What Would Smuts Have Done?

T.C. Robertson

Laurens, my old mate, you have really given this old trek-ox a very heavy load to pull through the road and its shifting sands. But never mind. I will do my damnedest to sum up in this letter the mind and spirit of Jan Smuts, statesman, philosopher and scientist. On Smuts' 80th birthday, I wrote a double-page feature on the same subject in the Sunday Times, and the old mater (*oubaas*) said to me, faintly sarcastically: "Well, old T.C., you seem to be learning, but very slowly." However, without further ado, I will take up the yoke and write to you in the language of the red stranger.

I think that you have the key to a synoptic view of the thinking of Smuts in what you wrote to me in *Jung and the Story of Our Times*. You speak of my endeavour "to make the earth of our native Africa whole again," while that of Jung is "to be whole within." W.K. Hancock's biography gives an adequate outline of the intellectual and emotional process by which Smuts, from his boyhood, shaped his guiding philosophy. His explanation of the unitary character of time, space and matter also brought in mind and personality. (See Hancock, Vol. 2, p. 176-77).

But the "whole" of Holism embraced more than all the material of the universe in an arithmetical sense (Hancock, Vol. 1, p. 294-96). It includes the concept, which, like the Kingdom of God, is within you, the personality – the ultimate product of the evolutionary process. (I observe the influence of having a copy of Kant and a Greek New Testament in his saddle bags while on commando in the Boer War!) This sketchy outline of Holism gives you the guideline I used during the years that I had to translate Smuts' ideas into practical propaganda procedures. It may help you if I give you one or two examples to show you how this worked in practice – and, I believe, can still be applied to the situation in which we find ourselves today.

The Africa Idea

To the selection of speeches by Smuts which I compiled shortly after the outbreak of the war in 1939, I gave the title, "Greater South Africa – Plans for a Better World." We were busy formulating our war aims and Pan Africanism had come back into fashion. Smuts liked the title and especially the phrase, "Better World," which could be used in opposition to the Nazi "New Order." (This actually happened and soon all the allied leaders were speaking of the "Better World.") But the snag was that, in all Smuts' speeches – including Ouma's roomful of *plakboeke*, carefully preserving Oom Jannie's Press cuttings – I could nowhere find one devoted to his ideas on Pan Africanism. He proceeded to make such a speech when he opened the Rand Show in April, 1940. (Indeed, he even wrote it out, which was a rare thing for him to do.) His conclusion was that "The African idea should become a practical force in the shaping of the destiny of this continent"; in other words, a Holistic concept of Africa. In spite of his wartime duties, he set about in trade and commerce and especially science to establish the contacts which made the "whole" physical. I served on two of these bodies and it made me sad when the tide of Black nationalism flooded over even these bodies. The climate now seems more opportune for the application of the practical policies and Holistic outlook which Smuts adumbrated in 1940. I think your analysis will gain much in news value if you could show how many of the ideas of Smuts can be of value to us in the present situation.

Drought and our Destiny

Robert Broom believed that the evolutionary process was not the outcome of haphazard chance mutations. He believed that its ultimate outcome, the "Purpose" (a dubious philosophical concept) was the production of higher spiritual types of man. As the theologians put it: he brought God back to science. (See his Presidential Address to the Barberton meeting of the S.A.A.A.S.) Broom used the enlargement of a photo I published of him looking at the fossilised skull of Mrs. Plea (Pleasianthropus) and sent it to his friends with the inscription: "To remind you of me when I'm examining the origin of man at headquarters." (Broom shared your views about survival!) Smuts smiled at his old friend's joke, but had many doubts about its validity. He contemplated with equanimity the possible disappearance of all life in another ice age. But the optimist in him reasserted itself with the thought that, in the past, this calamity had always been followed by the emergence of a higher type of homo sapiens. Then, too, he was impressed by man's growing technical ability to modify his environment. (See the introduction he wrote for Prof. Bew's book on human ecology.) This made him take a lead in the conservation movement, as you can see by his interest in the work of Eugene Marais and the load he took in starting a movement like the National Veld Trust. Notwithstanding the determinism of his Calvinistic youth and background, he did not believe that the environment alone shaped the conduct and destiny of man. But he did not believe that political planning alone would do so, either. Today the politicians are obsessed with constitutions and endless dialogues, forgetting that South Africa is in the midst of the greater food crisis in its history. You cannot reason with empty stomachs. But there is no Smuts in parliament to tell them that our problem is essentially biological. It's Pap more than Pax which the exploding millions of Africa are crying for.

Smuts the Afrikaner

There are two reasons why Smuts would not qualify for membership (if he had ever wanted it) of the Afrikaner Broederbond: He could not take an oath to work with all his heart, body and soul for the everlasting continuance (*voortbestaan*) of the Afrikaner, his *volk*, his religion and his language. Smuts, with his deep insight into the evolutionary process, did not believe that anything could be everlasting (*ewigdurend*). In the second place, he was not a Utopian. These people had built their Afrikaner heaven and were pursuing it regardless of changes of culture and fact in the environment around them. Like one of Ibsen's characters, this nation had become a victim of the tyranny of an unattainable ideal. I summarised and collated the enormous mass of material which came into our hands as a result of wartime security measures and often discussed it with Smuts. When Louis Esselen, my immediate chief, wanted to prosecute them for high treason, I disagreed and Smuts backed me. "They're not evil – just tragically foolish." Piet Meiring, whose background and outlook is so different to my own, discussed *Smuts – the Afrikaner* with me at length before he published his book with that title. If Smuts were alive today, he would be delighted with the young Afrikaners of 1984, especially many of the journalists on papers like *Rapport*. I can almost hear him say: *"My mense kom reg. Hulle trek nou in die nuwe wereld in. Mooi so."* (Strangely, unless we were discussing technical matters, he always talked to me in Afrikaans. *Net soos jy en ek.*)

Now I put it to you: Have you been able to research, and give your lecture's preparation the time to discuss "what Smuts would say of Afrikanerdom today." I wish you had all my books and papers on Smuts at your disposal and that you and I could have spent a month together. I would even have gone on the water cart for that joy.

Race Relations

What would Smuts say if he came back and stood at the deathbed of Apartheid, or segregation, as he called it when he saw the approach of the end? If you look at his speeches and the Rhodes Memorial Lectures, you find only one example of him attempting to put forward ideas about a future solution. I refer to his plan (backed by Amery) of a white state down the highlands of the east side of Africa – a superior White civilisation guiding the Blacks of the bush. For the rest, he sticks to the processlogic that later made him such a good ecologist. Recently, I read the Hansard report of the debate in February and March, 1925, on the Mines and Works Amendment Bill, in which Hertzog made the industrial colour bar a fundamental South African principle. Hancock gives a very good summary (Vol. 2, p. 208ff.). Some of the basic concepts that Smuts adhered to emerge in this debate, and I have always regarded them as the guidelines he would follow today. They are:

One of his main political efforts had been to establish and render safe in this country a white civilisation.

He regarded that civilisation as superior to the Black and it would require the lapse of evolutionary time to achieve equality. Hence his proposed test of "standard of civilisation as well as education in granting of voting rights," in spite of the fact that the younger generation of scientists were already talking about "punctuated equilibrium" in evolution, and that he himself had considered the consequences of the great climatic disasters, the lawyer-politician in him wanted an orderly transition – none of your Communist "revolutionary transitions" for him.

But there were wrong and right ways of maintaining white civilisation and against the colour bar, he warned: "… if we want to entrench our position merely as a white oligarchy by getting round us a ring fence of hate from all the other communities in South Africa, we shall have a very hard and difficult row to hoe in future." (Hancock, Vol. 2, p. 209).

So I think that his biggest job today would be to assist in breaking down that "ring fence of hate" and in narrowing the cultural and civilisation gap. If I had to deliver a memorial lecture, my thesis would be: "Had Smuts been alive today, the depth and range of his intellect and knowledge is such that he would have been able to make the greatest contribution to interpreting and guiding the process of change in Africa – to an extent that is quite beyond the grasp of the small minds, both White and Black, that are at the helm today."

Laurens, as I read through this letter again, I feel that I have failed dismally in my promise to give you that "synoptic vision" which my old professor of logic, Alfred Hoernle, would have approved of. But I might have given you a few ideas to ponder and to argue about if we do meet when you come out here. Please forgive the dreadful typing, but my fingers are swollen with arthritis and the diabetes is attacking me from under. I have great difficulty in walking these days. There are some young engineers and soil scientists working on a job near Scottburgh and they often drag me out on a pub crawl. It gives me much satisfaction that I can still drink them under the table and lie most convincingly to their wives when we come home.

One more story about Smuts: "Last summer I went to Rus der Winter, where so much conservation history has been written, and also visited Rooikop, where his grandson, J.C. Smuts III, applies new ideas to this Bushveld. He asked me what achievement I thought his grandfather was most proud of. I replied without hesitation: "The fact that he discovered a new species of grass, which has been named after him, *Digitaria smutsili*." That name, as well as the concept of Holism, will live as long as science. The political struggles and ideas are transient – things of a generation or two.

Until we meet again, you old writer of books that will live much longer than the readers!

World Without as World Within

Bipolar Nature of the Archetype

M. Vera Bührmann

I would like to explore the two poles of archetypes, the spiritual and the instinctual, and to demonstrate how these opposites are combined in a Xhosa ritual where the Self is constellated.

The critical dictionary of Jungian analysis defines archetype as 'an inherent part of the psyche; a structuring of psychological performance linked to instinct – archetypes are recognisable in outer behaviour, especially those that centre round basic universal experiences of life.'

The ritual for consideration, *inthlombe* and *xhentsa*, has already been described in detail[1]. Briefly, it is a round dance in a round hut. It consists of four concentric circles. The outer circle is the wall of the round hut, the second circle consists of the clappers and singers, sitting tightly packed against the wall. Within this circle, separating the men and women, is the drummer sitting at the *entla*, the place where the Ancestors congregate, positioned opposite the only door in the hut. The third circle consists of the dancers. Their composition varies a lot, depending on the type and circumstances of the *inthlombe*. The fourth and inner circle of this mandala-like structure is the traditional fireplace, a small circular rimmed space.

The aim of this paper is to look at the basic instinctual structure of the psyche, to follow the transformation into the spiritual, and to look at the final result, the union of the opposites and the constellation of the self in terms of this ritual.

As the observance of participation in such a ritual is experiential, some of the essence will be lost in writing about it, as an *igqira*

---

[1] Bührmann, M.V. "Living in Two Worlds," *Journal of Analytical Psychology,* 1981, 26, 178-201

(healer, diviner) said to me when we discussed a ceremony: "There are things one cannot put into words, only feel them in one's body."

I think this is what Jung had in mind when he wrote: "The symbols of the self arise in the depth of the body and they express its materiality every bit as much as the structure of the perceiving consciousness – the more archaic and deeper, that is, the more physiological the symbol is the more collective and universal, the more material it is."[1]

The Western world is losing contact with this 'archaic physiological' part of the psyche on account of the increasing split between psyche and soma, the spiritual and instinctive and the undisputed rule of the rational. These are aspects of civilisation and culture which are leading to a loss of the totality of being and hence to the increasing sense of the meaninglessness of life. The rural Black people I worked with never questioned the meaning of life. There can be many reasons for this, but an important one is their relationship to their ancestors, which is strengthened by frequent ceremonies and rituals and the value they attach to dreams, which are regarded as communications from the ancestors. In their ritual acting out of their beliefs, they can share and communicate some 'soul substance' because they activate and embody archetypes.

The ritual I want to look at, the *inthlombe* and *xhentsa*, I have described previously as the 'Healing Dance' or 'Mandala in Motion.' The rhythmic stamping dance is performed whenever circumstances permit. It lasts for many hours and has marked transformative effects. For a description of the structure, contents and functions, the previously mentioned publication can be consulted.

To start with, the outer environment is unstructured. It consists of an undifferentiated group of people trying to organise themselves sufficiently to start an *inthlombe*. They have to drop their external ego-oriented objective activities to join a group and enter into an inner-oriented subjective psychic world. They are usually aware that their outer-oriented interests have to become inner-directed and in the service of the ancestors. They know that each of them will have a special function to perform in the ritual. It is usually those that feel compelled to dance who are most active in assembling and organising others, especially the singers and clappers. There are usually several gifted drummers who can be enticed to participate.

---

[1] Jung, C.G., *Collected Works*, 9i, p. 173

There are several varieties of *inthlombes* with minor differences, but I will concentrate on one, the one where the Self was most clearly demonstrated.

The point I want to make is that mostly the participants are driven by an inner instinctual urge to perform an *inthlombe*. In certain situations, the assembled visitors, members of the family (clan) and the outside community know that an *inthlombe* is being organised as part of a more comprehensive ceremony and they come because they want to participate, knowing that they will benefit in some way or other, even if it is only to enjoy the beer which is an integral part of the ceremony!

To me, to start with, the *inthlombe* is instinctual and physiological. The Black people say they do the *inthlombe* to perspire profusely, to get rid of all the dirt (evil) in their blood and thus 'freshen' it and to 'wake-up the *umbelini*,' which is a rather complex concept. It is briefly described as being in the lower half of the body. 'Nothing lives without it.' The clapping, singing and drumming awaken the *umbelini*. From the lower parts, it gradually rises to the head, enabling one to see things clearly and enabling one to say the right things at the *inthlombe*. If it goes up the wrong way and gets on top of one, 'one may go mad,' i.e., become over-excited, manic. It sounds very much like *kundalini*.

This is to me the first indication of the sensual instinctive pole of the archetype which is to be transformed into its spiritual pole. This process is not without its dangers, because it can lead to inflation and inflation is not part of the Self – and it can lead to a fully developed manic state.

In the early stages of the ritual, one becomes aware of the conscious (ego) and unconscious opposites. In their singing, the ancestors (complexes of the personal and collective unconscious) are invited to be present and their help is invoked in the particular ceremony and with their illness and problems in general. There are many other opposites: for example, in the seating arrangements, with the men on the right, the conscious side, and the women opposite them on the unconscious left hand side. The regalia of the fully qualified *amagqira* (healers) symbolise spiritual qualities by the upper part of their bodies being clothed in white and a profusion of white beads, and the instinctual qualities being symbolised by their skirts made of pelts of wild animals.

In the early *hotting-up* part of the ritual, the performing *igqira* and his colleagues are not present. They seem to arrive to join the dancing circle when a certain amount of structure and cohesiveness had been established, as though the group ego must be firmly established before it can cope with the power and numinosity of the archetypes which are to be constellated by the healers. This arrangement also intensifies the anticipation and tension and heightens the dramatic effect of their entry. With their arrival, the atmosphere changes markedly. An urgency and vibrancy become palpable and the singing, clapping and drumming rise to a pitch. On one occasion, a participant in the dancing group (he was a trainee), ran out wildly, unable to stand the tension.

When the performing healer (in this case, it was my chief mentor) was ready emotionally, instinctually and spiritually to *vumisa*, he called for his special song, *Vumisa*, the literal translation of which is to concur, to accede, but it is the term generally used for the performing of the divining function, of getting in touch with and interpreting the wishes and wisdom of the ancestor spirits.

His song is:

> *Here comes* Vumani /*I divine by him?*
> *My horse of news* /*I will die calling* /
> *It is coming* / *Ho! my horse of news* / *is coming* /
> Vumani

When the urge is very strong he calls for another song:

> *The doves are roaming around*

Both songs are frequently repeated and the latter one seems to settle his excitement; it seems to prevent his *umbelini* from 'getting on top of him.' He then starts talking rapidly in a prereflective but coherent way that is the *vumisa*.

He becomes the mouthpiece of the ancestors. The meaning of the messages from the ancestors is clarified in discussions between him and the senior male clan members. This part is orderly and structured, but riveting in its intensity. Everyone's attention is focussed on the drama of the interaction and the presence of the ancestors. All libido is withdrawn from the outside world and there is intensive introversion. The unconscious powers are clearly dominant.

In this atmosphere, a suprapersonal, a transcendent power, is present and a *coniunctio* takes place. The real meaning of the *coniunctio* is that it brings together something that is one and united – the pictures of the *coniunctio* are to be understood in this sense. Union on the biological level is a symbol of the *unio oppositorum* at its highest level.[1] This was well-illustrated at a particularly gripping *inthlombe* where two *amagqira*, a husband and wife, joined hands and performed a lovely courtship dance at the termination of the ceremony while leading the assembled people to the outside. There, a free and spontaneous atmosphere developed with the ritual drinking of beer from a canister which was passed around. There was much discussion of the *inthlombe* and how it affected each of them.

During the *vumisa*, many things are discussed, clarified and brought to consciousness. A *vumisa* is always done when people are troubled in some way. It can be an apparent physical illness, for example, asthma, infertility, discord in the family, bad luck of some kind, accidents, failure in business or disturbing dreams. By consulting the ancestors, they hope to derive help, solutions and comfort from their superior wisdom – that is, introverting and getting in touch with the complexes of the unconscious.

The content of the consultation almost invariably indicates a disequilibrium between the troubled ones and their ancestors in some way or other. The living kin could have failed to pay homage to their ancestors by neglecting to perform the required customs, or they offended by not doing their duty towards their family or clan members, or they have been leading dissolute lives or offended their ancestors in other ways, such as having committed some crime, often unconfessed.

To restore their health, good fortune and peace of mind, they are advised to perform some custom or other, i.e., they must communicate with the ancestors in a proper and correct way.

Psychologically, I see the whole *vumisa* as an effort to heal the split between the ego and the unconscious.

It is the spiritual, even moral, pole of the archetype which strives towards wholeness and constellation of the Self. From my experience, by participation, I have no doubt that they, the people, are deeply involved with unconscious and archetypal material – they embody the archetypes. The symbolic language used during a *vumisa* is reminiscent of that used by the alchemists – 'a cat defecated in your house,'

---

[1] Jung, C.G., *Collected Works*, 16, par 458 and 460

'a dog and bitch copulated,' 'there is a wild animal in your cattle pen,' 'monkeys play in the trees and you can't catch them.'

The atmosphere and feelings after a successful *inthlombe* and *vumisa* is that of excitement, but mainly one of peace and tranquillity. It was said to a healer: "You are a great *igqira* and reducer of anxiety.'

The songs sung during the terminal phases of the *inthlombe* are of thanks towards the ancestors and their mediator, the *igqira*, for the light which had been brought and for the darkness and chaos which had departed. I see that as the organising function of the Self, which combined several opposites, for the purpose of this article, especially the instinctual and spiritual parts which have been united to give a sense of wholeness.

"The body/mind split should be healed but not become a permanent static union. The goal is to restore a creative tension and a working partnership between the spiritual and animal portions of the soul."[1]

In the African culture, this is clear where the unifying *inthlombe* is performed weekly, and during training of prospective healers, more often. The healing of the split is not a one-off event.

This healing effect was demonstrated by the history of a gifted healer who stopped attending and performing *inthlombes* because she was too busy in her shopkeeping business. She became obese, developed severe asthma and other physical and psychological complaints and depression. Eventually her dreams and events at her home forced her to arrange an *inthlombe* at her home. During this ceremony, she became united with her kin and her ancestors. She returned to her practice as a healer and her health and family life improved dramatically.

After a successful *inthlombe*, as in her case, the participants all confess to feeling much revived. In some cases, severe depressed feelings and symptoms disappeared, anxiety was reduced and physical symptoms such as pains and tiredness and headaches vanished. There were observable changes in facial expression and body movement and speech became animated.

Such transformation can only be attributed to major shifts in psychic complexes and largely to the constellation of the Self and the experience of numinosity. The Self had the effect of organising the internal and external world.

[1] Stein, Robert, *Incest & Human Love*, Third Press, New York, 1973, p. 27

Experienced healers, when they feel their powers of divination and healing are becoming impaired, can arrange for a ceremony to be done, a sacrificial ceremony including an *inthlombe*. They claim that it makes a big difference to their practice. The ceremony I attended was the sixth one for an ageing healer during his thirty-five to forty years of practice.

In conclusion, it must be said that not all healers are equally gifted. I have attended dull ceremonies where one was not touched by anything suprapersonal or numinous. People went through the motions, but there was no transformation.

Transformation only occurs when both poles of the archetypes, the instinctual and the spiritual, are constellated and unified. In the ceremonies by the Black healers, both poles are embodied and they act out what we talk about and sometimes experience in-depth psychotherapy or analysis.

The Lark Ascending

Robin Page

I used to think that in conservation we want to train leaders; but it has gradually dawned on me that this concept is out of date. It is no good waiting for leaders, we have to lead ourselves. By forming the Countryside Restoration Trust, you have led yourselves. You are now leading by what you do, and I find this example of immense importance, not only local but national.

Laurens van der Post, 1994

I first met Laurens van der Post in the Fifties during my early teens. Well, to be honest, I did not actually meet him, I felt that I had met him, on our small black-and-white television set. I still remember the vivid images that came from *The Lost World of the Kalahari*, and it helped to cement an interest in Africa that is still with me. But, in the long term, it did far more: it helped to focus on a process that is continuing today, a process by which Man is losing his World; he is losing his links with nature, the land, with reality – with the real world.

Within a few years of watching the Bushmen lose their world, it became apparent that I was losing mine. I was born on the farm in East Anglia where I still live and work. It is the farm where I want to die, and, as I write, the field where I will be buried is a place of autumnal fruitfulness where butterflies still fly and the foxes have turned their attention to the ripening blackberries.

My childhood was fortunate; it allowed me to see the last of pastoral England. We still had heavy horses working the land, there were otters in the brook and every evening at dusk, barn owls quartered the water meadows. Each farm in the parish had its herd of dairy cattle and free range hens scrapped in the yards. There were small meadows surrounded by hedgerows and the elm dominated the landscape in hedge, spinney, wood and even in glorious isolation. During the summer, swallows nested in almost every building and from every direction, high in the sky, larks sang. I was born with the music of the lark all around me:

> *He rises and begins to round,*
> *He drops the silver chain of sound,*
> *Of many links without a break,*
> *In chirrup, whistle, slur and shake,*
> *All intervolved and spreading wide,*
> *Like water dimples down a tide,*
> *Where ripple ripple overcurls,*
> *And eddy into eddy whirls ...*

But now we are losing the skylark, too. It is incredible, almost unbelievable, that in half a lifetime, I have seen my own world lost.

Of course, people say that I am locked into the nostalgia of childhood; the countryside was not full of birdsong and the driftways never were awash with cornflowers and field scabious. They are wrong – and how do I know? Because a group of friends, with the full support and encouragement of Laurens, are bringing the birds and flowers back; we are trying to restore what has been lost, and already the richness that has been ploughed, drained and sprayed away is returning.

During the Second World War, there were real food shortages in Britain and even after hostilities ended, I remember ration books continuing for chocolate. They existed for meat and cheese, too, but for me, it was chocolate that was most important. The politicians said, quite rightly, that food shortages must never occur again, but already a majority of those who ruled us were urban with city minds. They saw 'self-sufficiency' in food simply as a matter of cultivating more land; bringing more land into production. They paid subsidies for grassland and water meadows to be ploughed and drained. More money went on the removal of hedges and the felling of woodland. They did not realise that, with advances in technology, chemistry, biology and botany, food production would increase anyway, without the destruction.

So, as land was brought into arable production, the new methods also guaranteed future overproduction. Chemical fertilizers, pesticides and herbicides were thrown around like new toys – farming was ceasing to be a way of life, with man working in harmony with nature; it became an industrial process, often conflicting directly with nature.

My countryside and my world were devastated. Throughout the Fifties and Sixties, the wildlife that had shared the land for centuries disappeared. What the plough left, DDT sprays poisoned. The barn owl, otter, sparrowhawk and even the green woodpecker disappeared. Common cowslips, quaking grass and bee orchids became rarities.

In 1971, another disaster struck. Our little brook was 'cleaned out.' Its bed was lowered by an absurd five feet; marsh marigolds, flowering rush and arrowhead were gouged out as weeds and pike starved to death for lack of prey. The official reason was to make the brook 'a more efficient drainage channel,' as if nature did not know how to handle surplus water. In nature, a flood plain was an area for flood water to flood slowly and harmlessly; to the drainage engineer, the 'flood plain' was a fertile area to be cultivated for quick profit, while at the same time, allowing the fertilisers and chemicals to wash into our river systems. The fate of our little brook was similar to that of countless other rivers and streams throughout lowland Britain. It was madness on a grand scale, a policy of destruction and over-production taking the 'culture' out of agriculture. At the time, I said it was a policy guaranteeing food surpluses – but what did I know, I was a country boy living on the farm where I was born.

Nearly all the water meadows went; but my father refused to go with the flow. Most of his grassland remained; his cattle stayed in the fields; he was unimpressed. Still, the process of intensification went on; every last wild corner was tidied, mown, drained or cultivated. What could be done, and did anybody else care?

At about this time, I met two men who both cared. At last, I met Laurens face to face, not through a television tube; he could see the damage being done and was shocked. Behind his beloved Aldeburgh, wetland was being turned into wheatland, and for the first time in England, he was seeing the summer sky filled with both smoke and dust. He could see a diverse and productive countryside being turned into an industrialised monoculture. Farm was being turned into factory and farmers were becoming 'land managers.'

The other man who cared was painter Gordon Beningfield, who, like me, was from almost peasant stock and was in a state of revolt at the damage being done. Like me, he was seeing the countryside of his childhood ruined. 'Efficiency' was being put before 'responsibility' and 'productivity' before 'sustainability'; Gordon was both horrified and outraged.

In 1980, Gordon and I went to see the then-Director of The Royal Society for the Protection of Birds. We pleaded with him to become involved with the general countryside: farmland, wetland, hedgerows, etc. We argued that wildlife should be where it had always been, 'over the hedge' and 'in the next field,' in every parish. He was not impressed; he argued the case for special areas – island conservation, and we were shown the door. Fortunately, the attitude of the RSPB has changed quite considerably since then. But what could we do and where could we go?

At about that time, too, I managed to persuade the National Rivers Authority (now the Environment Agency) to leave the banks of our brook alone, and gradually vegetation and scrub returned. But still, the relentless process went on – larger fields, tidier hedges, larger equipment, more chemicals. At the same time, too, with fewer people working on the land and a steady process of urbanisation, people were losing their links with the land. Children could no longer tell the difference between wheat and barley; a woman visited the farm who did not know the difference between a cow and a donkey; a whole generation was growing up cut-off from its natural and historical roots.

It was then that I began to think about 'restoration.' Would it be possible to restore our ravaged countryside beyond the brook banks and would it be possible to restore our own spiritual and physical links with the land? The banks of the brook were gradually restoring themselves and I reintroduced yellow irises that quickly became re-established. As an experiment, we then planted a small seven-acre field with a wildflower and grass seed mixture developed by Miriam Rothschild. Soon that, too, showed that the countryside could be restored if given the chance – that nature could heal itself very quickly when offered a helping hand.

Restoration seemed to be the conservation of the future and the Countryside Restoration Trust seemed to be the way forward, so the CRT was born. Laurens agreed to be a Trustee, and later our Patron, and Gordon Beningfield, too, joined the Trustees.

After much deliberation, we chose the skylark as our emblem. Somehow, its song sums up the British countryside and it is a sound that is in rapid decline. Over the last twenty years, Britain has lost over half its skylarks – 3 million birds. It is a sad indictment.

Almost immediately, the CRT was formed and forty acres of monoculture became available by the brook. It was land that had been turned from wetland into wheatland. Then something remarkable happened: otters returned to the brook, after an absence of over thirty years. Along the restored length of bank, there were clear signs of otters, and they spread along the banks of the forty acres, too. So, with no members and no money, we publicly launched the CRT in 1993. The aim was simple: to buy the forty acres of land and improve the adjoining habitat for the otters. We wanted to show that profitable farming, abundant wildlife and attractive landscapes can co-exist – we wanted to start putting the culture back into agriculture.

A financial advisor advised that, if we went public, we would raise only £ 2,000 and the venture would fail. With Laurens' encouragement, we ignored his advice and launched the Trust and an appeal. Money and letters poured in. Three years later, we have over 3,000 members and have raised £ 300,000. The forty acres have been transformed. The brook's flood plain has been given back to the flood and planted with more of Miriam Rothschild's hay meadow mixture. In June, cars stop and tears come to the eyes of old ladies as they remember the flower-filled meadows of yesterday – we have already shown that they can still exist today.

Our tenant farmer has a grass margin around the reduced area of cereals and the edge of his crop is unsprayed to allow poppies to flower and insects to breed. We have brought back the cornflower and it will soon be joined by the corncockle. The otters are still visiting and we have reintroduced marsh marigolds, flowering rush and purple loose strife to the brook. People are visiting, seeing and getting back their links with the land. But what about the lark?

Each winter, we have planted trees using volunteers from as far afield as Yorkshire and London. We have planted hedges almost half a mile in length, as well as a spinney, and we have used up to twenty species and 5,000 saplings. It was a cold day in February when we finished our main planting. It had rained and the level of the brook was rising as we started our work. The spinney was planted and we moved on to finish our main hedgerow, left unfinished from the year before. It was a long hard day and at last light, we completed our task. A few of us decided to walk back to the spinney to take in our day's work; the brook had spilled over, giving the flood back to its flood plain and the sun was setting in wild, wet beauty. As we stood there taking in the scene, and our achievement, a skylark flew up from the grass meadow opposite. If I had not seen it myself, I would not have believed it: on fluttering wings, it flew over the brook and began singing; it passed directly over us still in song before falling back to earth behind us. We stood there in silence; it was a moving, precious experience, almost like a blessing.

Now we are still going forward and our next aim is simple. We want to buy a complete farm, a wrecked farm and we want to restore it. We want to produce good food; we want to keep animals humanely; we want people to visit, learn and renew their links with the land; we want to create beautiful landscapes and we want skylarks singing over every field. Then, after the first farm, we want another, until we have a network throughout Britain. There can be only one name for our first farm: we hope to call it "Lark Rise Farm."

Our Mother Earth[1]

Laurens van der Post

In lieu of making a public appearance himself at the Earth Day celebration of 1990 in New York City, due to a scheduling conflict, Sir Laurens van der Post met with Robert Hinshaw and Peter Ammann and their recording equipment on December 16, 1989, in his Chelsea home in London to share his thoughts and feelings about how consciousness must re-establish a living relationship with the depths of the unconscious if we are to truly 'conserve' the wholeness of ourselves and of the earth we live on.

Laurens van der Post: When I was a boy, I was already passionately interested in conservation. When I was age six, I was horrified to hear that there were only nine white rhinos alive in the world. So what I have to say begins with the rhinoceros, begins with an animal that goes back to prehistoric times, the nearest flesh-and-blood creation that we have in the world today of which the unicorn was a symbol, this animal that is so much involved in the imagery of our search for individuation and wholeness. What I felt then as an apprehension about the white rhino has grown into a certainty that, unless we succeed in arresting the assault and violation of the natural world, we ourselves will not survive.

The battle of conservation on earth is an indelible part of all Jung's ideas and comes through in all his work. His concern is with the 'nature' within us as it is very closely linked to the nature outside of us, in the world. It seems to me that the battle started, or the threat started, long, long before the rhino was threatened, perhaps long before the rhino existed, long before I was born. But what amazes me

---

[1] A slightly different version of this transcript was previously published in *Quadrant: The Journal of Contemporary Jungian Thought*, XXIII:2, 1990.

today is that in the Europe where I live, in the Britain where I live, people have this fantastic concern for the destruction of the forests of the Amazon, the great rain forests of Brazil. Quite rightly, they feel outraged and angry about it, but they seem to think there's a special kind of villainous, thoughtless, uncaring society in Brazil that is perpetrating this destructive business we all deplore. They don't seem to ask themselves, 'Where did it start?' They seem to think it all started in Brazil, as I thought it all started in Zululand, in Africa, with the threat to the white rhino.

It seems to me that the most important thing we have to grasp is how old this battle is. For example: Where did the Sahara come from? We know that the Sahara was the granary of Rome. All the wheat came from there. What happened? What was a great extension of the Nile delta has disappeared; the waters have receded. The forests and the savannahs are gone. The animals are gone and there is this great desert left. The same with the Syrian and the great Assyrian deserts right through Asia to the Gobi desert. Where did all that come from? All man-made in the past behind us. The Mediterranean today, the Europe that I know, is for me, really, when I think of what it was in classical times, a scorched earth. Where have all the European animals gone? The last bear in Switzerland was shot at the beginning of this century. There are perhaps a few bears left in the Pyrenees. Where are the wolves? Where are the mammals? They've all gone. This devastation, this spoilation of nature has gone on for centuries, and unless we realize how old, how stubborn, how devastating is this thing in us that exploits nature this way, we will not tackle the problem properly.

And where does this strange urge to go on destroying come from? I can go back in my own mind and say that when I ultimately come to where the record vanishes, to where my vision of the world vanishes, there is a myth. There is a Greek myth that says to us very clearly where it began. It began with the Promethean gift of fire. When Prometheus stole fire from the gods and gave it to human beings, the trouble began. What Prometheus did was, in a way, Christ-like – he gave divine power into the hands of flesh and blood. He gave us fire. He made us conscious. The gods suddenly allowed a particular animal species on earth to become conscious. And in the history of life on earth, of course, consciousness is a young phenomenon. It's young, it's new, and it's vulnerable. And it's conferred on us great power over what is unconscious. But this great power of consciousness has gradually corrupted us. Our spoilation of the earth is part of the spirit of the corruption of consciousness itself, unless it's used in keeping with the greater value. In other words, the Promethean gift is the gift of divine power, and in order to use it, we ourselves must become divine and take over a sense of responsibility for creation. And the whole trouble comes down, in a simple sentence, to the fact that we have never developed a sufficient sense of responsibility to what we know and toward the power that we have over nature and over ourselves.

So here, for me, is the conclusion that we're not going to win this battle unless we win the battle for greater awareness. In this task that Jung called individuation, we must learn that we are in an awesome partnership with what we call God. Unless partnership is also restored with this great Mother Earth, so that what the earth gives to us in such great abundance and with such willingness, unless we accept that love and use it with love, we are doomed. Because the time is going to come when the earth itself will turn bitter, when nature will turn bitter, as it's increasingly turned bitter, when the air we breathe will turn bitter and no longer give life, when everything on earth will turn against us and we'll vanish.

But I do believe that if the hubris, which is an expression of the abuse of power, this hubris of power, this hubris of consciousness that we suffer from, if it includes also the Eros element, which transcends consciousness, the Eros that has in its keeping all the emotions and the energies of metamorphosis, it will transform matter in such a way, at such a pace, that something not there before will enter in and a new act of creation will happen. We need to pull our conscious power together with the spirit of metamorphosis, the Eros, if we are to become whole again. Otherwise we are not going to win the battle for conservation.

Any other course is going to be concerned with symptoms, and not the problem proper. So I would suggest to you to think about the gift of fire, the process of divine power being handed over to human beings so that the whole calling of people on earth was altered. If we have a meaning, if we have a right to continue to exist, it's only insofar as we respond to the charge: as keepers of the trust of creation and the continuing task of creation. Just as the gods, or what we call God, sought to become human, humans must seek to become more worthy of what is divine. These are joined, and only in that can we win the battle.

The van der Post Panel in Botswana's Tsodilo Hills,
named in honor of their discoverer

For me, personally, the Promethan myth is the greatest of the classical myths. It's a great point of departure not only in human life on earth, but in what one feels is the whole pattern of creation in the universe. It's this sense that what is godlike suddenly became part of humanity. But more than that, in making us conscious, a lopsidedness occurred, which the unconscious abhors. You can't talk about consciousness unless you think of the unconscious, because consciousness is a product of the unconscious. So there is the extraordinary process that even the gods themselves couldn't visualize, this yearning, this longing of the unconscious to become totally aware. That's why the Eros aspect of the myth is so frightfully important, the mystery of love that one must accept in silence: the idea that the gods suffer with us for our awareness.

It is the mystery of love that motivated Prometheus to sacrifice himself; he was a Christ-like figure. He is the first, one of the first clear announcements of the pattern of the Christ in the human spirit. We may not think of him as the Christian Church would, but, in essence, he is of a Christ-like pattern, and he's punished very severely by the gods. He becomes a suffering god. He's bound to a cliff in the Caucasus where an eagle comes and feeds on his liver by day. And he suffers agonies, and then the liver is healed by night. And the process continues by day. It's healed in sleep; it's healed in the world of dreams. But then the next day, he has to give himself again to the eagle, which is a great bird of awareness. The eagle represents the inspired awareness, inspired consciousness that comes winging out of the blue. He has to feed his eagle that ravages him day after day out of his own suffering. There is the message: there is a god suffering with us in our suffering. It gives a meaning to suffering on earth, which nothing else does, so it is a very important myth, because it's as much of a crossroad for what we call God as it is for us and it puts both humanity and God really firmly on the same path.

The battle for the earth without is a battle for the soul, for the Self within. The Self also demands. In one of my stories, I have an old hunter at the end of his life who encounters a thunderstorm, and he smells this wonderful rain coming toward him. A wonderful fragrance comes out of the earth. It's the end of a great drought. He gets off his horse, and he wants to say thank you, he wants to say a prayer. The only prayer that comes to his mind is, "Our Father which art in heaven." And he feels this is not enough. It seems arrogant; it seems presumptuous. He feels he's got to add to it; not to improve it, but to say what he feels, and he says, "Our Mother which art in earth." He says, "Our Father which art in heaven, and our Mother which art in earth, may your love, O Mother, be fulfilled, and Father, may your will be done. May love and will be one." And that is the message that comes through if you follow the Promethean myth and all the religious quests in primitive cultures.

Question: Some of us have been accused of being too poetic and too idyllic about our thoughts and our goals for the wilderness and for the environment. What would be your advice on a more concrete level? What can the individual do today?

LvdP: I'm a little bit worried by your using the word 'concrete,' because I think what I've been saying is concrete. Of course, I know what you mean, I know the importance of what you're asking. The battle for rehabilitation is so great that we've got to meet it on all levels of awareness where it presents itself to the individual. I'm not saying that dealing with the symptoms, for instance, is unimportant. I'm just saying that doing something about the white rhino is to deal with the consequence and not the cause of the problem. I realize that it's important to do that, too. So I think that all the conventional ideas, like having laws forbidding the cutting down of trees, are necessary. There's no question about it, I think we have to respond in this way.

And don't forget that there are, all over the earth today, the people who preserved the white rhino to this point, the people who founded the Wilderness Foundation, for instance. They are already expressing what is of this divine thing in themselves. And on every level, however humble, even if it's only establishing window boxes for flowers in the cities, these responses are frightfully important. I don't want to say that one thing is more important than another.

What I'm trying to say is that these things we are seeing are hints of the collective unconscious coming to our aid. To me, there's a great shift going on the collective unconscious. The answer does not come from us, it comes from something beyond us, and this is where I have my trust. What I'm saying right now comes out of a stirring of my own collective unconscious. I know that all over the world an increasing number of people, from politicians to taxi drivers to scientists, are thinking now, are already moving in this direction. This is vitally important. But the other level is also vitally important. I'm not inventing it in a spirit of idealism. It's been thrust upon me in my experience of conservation. And in the moment when I realize where it comes from, I feel strangely emancipated.

A lot of fear left me because Prometheus was not abandoned to suffer indefinitely. Prometheus was rescued. He was rescued from his chains, and a substitute put in his place. That was Chiron, the centaur, the great healer and trainer of heroes in Greek mythology. He was made to suffer in his place. In other words, whatever there is in the Promethean myth, there is also that which heals as represented by Chiron. So there is a remedy, if you will. There is the shadow that consciousness casts in the unconscious realm, and the means of dealing with the shadow. We have the ability to transform the suffering. It is there. I can put it only in mythological language at the moment. It means there is a power in the collective unconscious to unchain a suffering conscious, to heal it.

Q: Do you see some way of accomplishing a more general awareness of this mythological truth, this mythological development that you feel coming?

LvdP: It'll start, as always, with individuals. The world is already full of individuals who are pledged to this, the most unlikely people. It's already there, and I think of the pace that has been gathering. I speak as somebody who, all my life, has been working, wherever I've encountered this problem. As a young man, I wrote for newspapers in which I advocated doing the sorts of things in Africa that have been done in the United States, the idea of conserving certain areas that are very important. And then I joined up, in my part of the world, in South Africa, with a friend of mine, Ian Player, who started the Wilderness Foundation, which understands that conserving nature is part of the conservation of the human spirit. And for the first time, we've had, for instance, in Great Britain, a prime minister who has spoken out about ecology and the importance of ecology. This has never happened in Europe before. People say that she's talking rubbish and she doesn't really hear, but she has. And laws are being changed all over Europe. There are people from all over the world meeting politically. It's become a political issue. The thing is on the march and I think it will accelerate. It's going to be the most important political issue within our time, within a generation. It's going to be far more urgent than economics, and it's far more urgent than the search for markets and profits, because it really is a battle for survival. This urgency is increasingly coming to us from the collective unconscious. The collective unconscious never brings anything to human attention without also bringing the energies to deal with the changes.

Q: Is there still time?

LvdP: There always is time. I believe in death-bed repentances. They're very effective. Much more effective than the vows taken in childhood. I think that the moment a person sees necessity, there's time to rehabilitate the earth. There's no time to lose, of course. But I really don't believe that human life was created to destroy life on earth. That's just a hunch, an intuitive perception; I can't prove it. This is the point again of consciousness. People always say, "Oh, yes, I know, but there's no time," and they cop out of the burden put on us by our fine consciousness, obedience to our greater awareness. That is where the destruction of nature started. Because we were never obedient to the greater awareness. We were obedient only to the immediate awareness. And so that's why I think it's so important, this enlargement of human consciousness. Something is stirring. And there is a great community of new awareness. I think it always starts with one person, you know, and for me, Jung is a great turning point in history, not Jung, but what was expressed through Jung. Lots of people contributed to it, but he became singularly aware of it and made it his life's task to communicate it, and look what's coming out of it. And that's all you can do. We may not be asked more than what we can do.

Q: What about the role of legislation? You've been talking about how it begins with the individual, so where do you see laws and agreements and this kind of thing coming in?

LvdP: I'm saying the battle must be fought on every level. It's got to be fought in Parliament. Parliament is now beginning to tackle the question of pollution, for instance. This won't save us, but it will give us more time. What life there is left on earth should be conserved. We need to worry not only about the pollution of the earth, but the pollution of the sea. All these things are becoming desperately important. All the chemical pollution. Do we need all this bloody chemistry that we're getting? You see, it's no accident that we have this drug problem on our hands. Our own society is drugged. We use drugs in the earth, we are looking for shortcuts all the time, and the irony of it is that chemistry is no longer ours. You see its benefits in the works of the alchemists who are using it as a way to the ultimate wisdom, which is the mystical marriage of heaven and earth. We've forgotten this side of chemistry. We've got to bring the 'al' back to chemistry.

Q: Where would you see the danger or the possibility of shadow in the movement toward more concern for the environment, the Green movement, political activity in this direction, and so forth? That worries us profoundly.

LvdP: It worries me profoundly, too. I think the Green movement doesn't really know what conservation is about because it looks upon it as purely an external process and thinks that something is being achieved by a political approach to it, and usually a very one-sided and slanted political approach. The movement is being consumed as far as I can see by its own collective shadow. The moment they got two million votes here in England in the last European election, the whole scene was transformed. People said, 'Ha, now we've got them.' In the Green movement, they said, 'Now that the politicians have to do what we tell them to, what shall we do?' They very wisely decided not to become a political power. Although real conservation must have political expression. It should have consequences in all phases of life.

Q: Could you talk some more of the places where you see things happening today, either on the diplomatic level, or perhaps in Great Britain or South Africa, areas you're familiar with.

LvdP: Well, I can only tell you there's a lot not been done that can be done on this safe level. For instance, we've now had the Second World Wilderness Conference in Cairns, in Queensland, Australia. As a result of their conference, Malcolm Frazer, the prime minister of Australia, declared the Great Barrier Reef a world heritage forever, an area on which exploitation of any kind would be prohibited forever. It would be there as a blueprint of what its creation was like in the beginning. There was the battle to prevent Tasmania from becoming one huge dam and destroying one of the most precious, ancient forests in that country. That battle was won. So there are a few examples of these things that are being done, you see, and I think you can think yourselves of battles that we've had and won. When I was last in the United States, I was talking with your environmental people in Washington, and I was terribly excited that they had succeeded in preserving one river from its source to its emerge into the ocean. And they told me about the plans they had for preserving parts of the original prairie grass areas. There is, I think, an immense urgency for population control because people are really, in an indirect sense, cannibalistic. We're consuming ourselves indirectly; I mean, this is going to be the end of us if we go on like this. The threat of number to nature is colossal. All these things come into it.

It all starts with what used to be called our relationship with God, and you have to decide: What is that relationship in a contemporary way? What is the Self that we are pursuing? What is this journey toward the moment when the 'I' gets down into this area of the Self and the 'I' and love can meet and become one? This is what it involves. It's not some ultimate Nirvana of the mind. It is how we have performed this dreary little journey in the here and now.

Q: You mention at times taking people on treks in Africa even today, and the hunger, the yearning that people have for this. Could you talk a little bit about the wilderness within and without and the importance of what these kinds of safaris can mean to people? What is the idea behind this kind of trek?

LvdP: I think the whole idea is for the person who has never been in contact with nature: if he comes in contact with nature, nature speaks to him. It speaks to him. You needn't say any more and the less you say the better. He can have his own experience with nature. The experience becomes his and he changes. It changes him and it confirms something in him. Somehow, hunger is satisfied in him and that's a fact. That's all we do and that's what distinguishes the Wilderness Foundation from other conservation organizations; this seems to us the most important thing to encourage in a person. Once a person recovers reverence in contact with nature, he becomes a conservationist. You see, a lot of people feel like the Wildlife Society: they do admirable work, but they're concerned with particular forms of life that they think are in peril. We are trying to conserve the spirit of the conservationist in people. We think that unless this spirit is increased, people won't do the other things that are so necessary. If you keep the earth as close to the initial blueprint of creation as you can, and you bring a person into contact with it, a person who is not whole, from a lopsided society, poof, that person changes. I've never known it to fail. Problem children, all sorts of people who have lost their way in life, once they've had this experience, they're different.

So that is why I personally have gone with the Wilderness Foundation. It's amazing that we thought it was purely a thing we'd started in Africa, but if you read a poet like Gerard Manley Hopkins, you find it already. He is a religious poet, perhaps the greatest religious poet we've had in the English language, a Jesuit who said that the whole world is charged with the grandeur of God. These ideas are already here, all around us.

Q: I think in a certain way the word 'conservation' suggests maintaining something that is already behind us, but all the things you've said point to the future as well. So the word, 'conservation,' may not be expressing exactly and entirely what you're aiming at.

LvdP: Yes, of course, that's a valid point, but I've been trying to deal with it by saying that conservation is essential for what is most important, which is metamorphosis. That's what Prometheus was about, metamorphosis, or what the Greek call *metanoia*, which is the awareness that transforms. So conservation is from one end of metamorphosis, of continuing, as I said, the task of creation. One of the great fantasies of religious fundamentalism is a feeling that creation is something that happened behind us, that it's all been done and we are just contained in the now. But the task of creation is ongoing, and we've just got to discover and continue to realize it.

The message that creation has barely begun is to read the Promethean message right. We are given powers not for our own use, but to continue the task of creation, to continue it consciously. Consciousness properly used is an instrument of creation, and if it's properly used, there is a moment when the spirit of creation enters and something is added to life that was not there before. This is metamorphosis, because the whole of mythology, as Ovid discovered, is metamorphosis. This is renewal, and in the process you are adding something to life that was not there before. This is evolution. Even the zoologists have discovered that in evolution, you can say, "Well, this and this brings this other thing about," and suddenly there is this extraordinary thing they call mutation. For no reason that anyone can fathom, life takes a leap into the dark and into a shape that wasn't there before. This is metamorphosis. Everything is metamorphosis. Conservation is an essential prelude to metamorphosis. And you'll find that, in conserving life, you are equipped with the power to create life, because survival is legitimate. If you use survival properly, it becomes not only a form of procreation, but the re-creation of the species.

The Dreamer that Remains

Laurens van der Post

The wind blows low on the mountains; the image of decay.

I-Ching on the symbol of *Ku* or the need
to work on what has been spoilt

Over the years since his death, Jung and his work seem to have loomed even larger and the man himself to have come nearer. That remains for me one of the most significant consequences of this experience with which I continue to be concerned. Death does not seem to have removed Jung further, nor to have diminished, strange as it may seem, the physical presence of the man. By the year he draws closer and by now stands so clear-cut beside one that one would seem unreal to miss and mourn him.

Placed beside this new clarity and nearness of Jung, one's own slight remaining measure, however human, of wanting to hear him and sit with him in his garden of Küsnacht or in the sunlit shelter of the yellow stone of his own choosing at Bollingen to look out at the wind-darkened water of the lake and hear him talk in a way that invested the most insignificant of things with significance, shrinks into a weightless triviality. And I can only take it all as signs of how man and work were hewn into such an imperishable oneness as few lives have been in recorded history; how the greatest necessity of our time called and continues to call for just such a person with such a being and a vision, and how swiftly this need is ascending towards a fateful climax.

Something of this, I am certain, compelled me, against the trend of the necessities of my own work, to make a film, reinforcing an instinct that there was no time to lose in rendering both the man and his work more accessible to the ordinary non-specialist and apparently normal, educated men and women; above all, to the young people of my day. The young, in particular, could not go on following the illusion that they had no option but to turn to other cultures, Oriental religions, Whirling Dervishes and alien esoteric practices and formulae to answer their deepest needs, as they are in multiples of thousands. Neither they nor we can afford to lose their exertion in any other area of action in life than the field of battle into which they were born. Not only are there no answers for them or us at the end of the road from Kew to Katmandu, Minneapolis to Ajunta or other highways and byways to Middle and Far East, but only a great and dangerous evasion of their first obligation to fulfil themselves in their own context and place in time. Through Jung, they have one key at hand for all the answers they need, not for magical transformation and abolition of the problems imposed on them by life, but for a way of living them out without sacrifice of the values they have inherited.

In Jung, these values are converted into a contemporary currency and interpreted in such a way that their history is forged into a living instrument of reality, capable of renewing both themselves, their decaying societies and the sick spirit of their day. What negatively observed appears as decay and danger, interpreted this way can become seed of modern growth and opportunity for far greater increase than life has yet known.

That the hunger for this new meaning in an idiom of our own is there was proved for me by the reception of even this inadequate film of Jung. It is still in constant demand and, in America in particular, continues to be shown to crowded university halls, lecture rooms and churches. The increased demand that follows the film for Jung's books, particularly *Memories, Dreams, Reflections*, and also the *I-Ching*, wherever it continues to be shown, added more substance to the proof of how he expresses and fulfils the necessities of our day. And yet, as time went by and this sense of his nearness increased, I felt I had not done all I had to do.

In the first place, the film showed only a narrow section consisting of an hour and a half of material which took thirteen hours to film and which we thought was the minimum necessary for conveying the essence of Jung. The Foundation which acquired the rest of the film on the understanding that it would make a longer film of the story of Jung from it, inexplicably reneged on its undertaking. So what was, to me, even as a full film, still an inadequate representation of Jung, was reduced for public consumption to this fragment so much in demand.

Somehow, this fact, added to the other that, even in the full film, I had not attempted to describe the whole of Jung as I had experienced the man and his work, would not leave me at peace. I could not and, of course, never attempted to describe the whole of Jung. Even Jung could not do that, great as his achievement was. Until the end, he, too, was more than he could express in words and work. But I could at least try to define the whole of my experience of him and his work. In addition, there is this growing acceleration of deterioration and proliferation of decay, as I see it all around me, to add to my sense of this inner duty only partially done.

Men by the day have become more bigoted, sloganeered, abstracted from their natural selves, and caught up in shallow collective power groups, at a rate I would not have thought possible even three years ago. The individual man made specific in a self capable of holding out against collective and totalitarian pressures, which is such a unique creation of the West, is in greater danger than he has been for centuries. As his danger increases, so does the peril to the cultures and free societies which once contained him and provided him with his communal foundation for growth.

As the mental asylums become increasingly overcrowded; as the churches empty; as one dictatorship of man and tyranny of state after the other take over new and larger segments of the international scene, it would seem as if the world itself had gone insane. All the signs of an international schizophrenic seizure are multiplying. The feeling values, considerations of love and emotion, not only are fast vanishing, but people appear increasingly incapable not just of experiencing them, but even recognising and honouring their reality in others; all symptoms of schizophrenic man.

Moreover, there is a strange incapacity abroad for experiencing real grief or allowing ourselves the tragic awareness commensurate with our general and particular plight, an I-could-not-care-less attitude to the suffering of others. The great cathartic role of tragedy in life and in art, and the reclamation of human suffering in the discovery of its position in the progression of universal meaning, seems for the moment to have been abolished.

Insofar as it is acknowledged in art, anyway, it is more and more as a kind of sick joke played by life on man, if not a meaningless farce. It is as if the human spirit is increasingly in the grip of an age of ice and cold, impersonal indifference in command of its values. The free exercise of fantasy, which is the imagination unsevered from its instinctive roots at play, has gone from literature and art. Characters no longer bubble up fountain-wise in the art of fiction, but have been replaced by men and women who have been 'researched,' as novelists proudly assert, and so are not individual conceptions any more, but statistical abstracts of humanity that live only as a form of dead accountancy. The visual arts more and more have withdrawn from the objective without, severed links with its counterpart within and see and portray in this dark averted dimension the symptoms of anger, rebellion and dissociation caused by the stubborn neglect of our natural spirit. D'Annunzio's resounding objection to the science of his day, because it presupposed a corpse, could be applied to the immense, laborious exercise of dissection which occupies so much of the spirit of our time and prevents it from a renewal and re-integration of its wounded, fragmented self.

Moreover, the world watches, as a matter of course, displays of violence and the taking of human life on television screens or reads about them in newspapers with a comparative absence of feeling that would have been unthinkable at the end of the last war. Less and less do we seem to be aware, as we review the daily casualty list of this new disordered spirit, that each one on that roll-call of the dead was a miracle of life extinguished without sound reason or meaning. The natural reverence for life which the first man took for granted in himself is vanishing from all but a few. All the symptoms, of which these are the more obvious examples, are of an invasion of consciousness that we call disturbance, delinquency or madness.

"Insanity," Jung said already in the 'thirties,' "is a state of mind possessed by an unconscious content which, as such, is not assimilated to consciousness, nor can it be assimilated, since consciousness itself has denied the existence of these contents. Religiously expressed, the attitude is equivalent to saying that we no longer have any fear of God and believe that everything is to measured in terms of human standards. This hubris, that is, the narrowness of consciousness, is always the shortest way to the insane asylum."

All the evidence of such a narrowing of consciousness in modern man is here for those who can still be aware. Already in a country like Britain, which we love, and which one might have thought more immune to this disorder of spirit and depletion of values, politics are increasingly politics of power and less and less a free institution designed to serve the greatest values and highest aspirations of an uniquely intuitive people. If there were one nation, one unique complex of races and cultures alive to the truth that politics worked for the human good, if only in service of a truth greater than itself, which by definition, therefore, could neither be political nor one directed merely to a political end, it was the British. Yet, on the British scene, not only in Parliament, but in churches and universities, splintered into increasingly specialised and compartmentalised faculties, incapable of relation of communication with one another, there is a growing tendency to make their highest value political as well. And all this is happening despite mounting social evidence of how discredited and bankrupt a development it is.

I deliberately use Britain as an example because it is one that I know well, but it would be dangerously misleading to think it is exceptional. I travel the world more than most and can testify that I found no race, culture or nation in the modern world which is not suffering in its own way from a similar profound affliction, and in one significant dimension shares the same common symptoms. In all countries, there is the same wide gulf between young and old and, as a result, two archaic polarisations of two opposites in the forces of the collective unconscious in man. In the young, there is a tendency towards a total submission to the Dionysian elements of the spirit and a rejection of the validity of the 'ego' without which no individual awareness, let alone existence, is possible, hence the outbreak of tribalism and an upsurge to hunt in packs, which one sees among young people from the Isle of Man to the Californian coast, and Leningrad to Tokyo; among the older, there is a compulsion to stand fast in an over-egotistical law-and-order stance, ignoring the profound shift of focus in the collective unconscious and the clamour for change from underneath. The greater the clamour, the wider and closer the grouping to compensate for the sense of insecurity caused by the struggle for a change of ground below.

Even the world economic scene bears striking evidence of the failure of such an approach to administer to the real necessities of our day. One would have thought by now that the grave labour unrest everywhere could have testified irrefutably to the fact that its causes are not to be found in what are called inadequate living standards and social insecurity, because this unrest and a new, subtler and more lethal kind of feeling of insecurity has grown with geometric progression as living standards have risen and social security increased. I would have thought it obvious by now that what makes not only labour, but societies, churches, doctors, historians and even the least specialised or ordinary human hearts alone with themselves in the silence of night full of a fearful unease, is the fact that there is no discernible meaning for man in what he is asked to do, and no overall and honourable value in the evolution of the society or culture to which he belongs to compensate him for the meaninglessness which affects him in his personal work and condition of being.

The crisis, I believe, is plainly one caused by an almost total loss of meaning, both individually and collectively. The human heart, as history proves, I believe, can endure anything except a state of meaninglessness. Without meaning, it dies like a fish without water on the sands of a wasteland beach.

Maynard Keynes, in my youth in London, once said to me that ultimately economics made no sense except in a supreme human context and failed if its own material instrumentally was not related to ultimate and classical humanistic preconsiderations. He had not long before written a book that made his reputation, *The Economic Consequence of the Treaty of Versailles*. I wish he were here today to write on the economic consequences of, say, the inferiority complex, or, for that matter, on the totality of complexes which represents the loss of meaning men find in themselves, their institutions and societies. The loss of output on the factory floor, the loss of attendances in church, all I am certain are directly proportionate to the decline in the input of meaning from the life of our time.

For the highest price men have always paid and still pay for all they acquire, whether of matter or spirit, is a psychological one. Human cultures at their most creative best have tried to ensure that whatever was bought or earned or sought after was also psychologically or spiritually or, at the very least, aesthetically worth it, and of some abiding value, unconnected with any functional significance of the moment. But all these considerations have tended to vanish from contemporary value, and man is increasingly regarded as output or export fodder, and the reward he earns in the process more and more exclusively calculated in materialistic terms. Behind all this, there seems to me to be a betrayal of the most reprehensible kind, subversion of a kind not spun by some subtle Russian with snow on his boots in some unheated basement of the Kremlin, but by the institutions and the vocations which Western man has evolved precisely in order to protect himself against this sort of treason. It is, of course, in a more obvious social dimension, the treason so aptly described by the French, who are experts in the matter, as *trahison des clercs*, but this treason in itself is more mongrel offspring of a master betrayal, as it were, in the fourth-dimension betrayal of man by the guardians of his spirit, the churches, priests, doctors and teachers of his day.

I lump them together because they are uniquely charged by life with the task of keeping man and his societies whole. Perhaps at the beginning of this century still, they could have pleaded justification for their failure because of ignorance of its causes. But they can do so no longer because, since Jung, his rediscovery of the collective unconscious and his empiric demonstration of its imperative role in the life of man, they cannot excuse themselves by a claim of ignorance of the causes of failure they continue to promote instead of arresting and correcting.

The priest, the doctor, the psychiatrist living seventy years after Jung first cured a schizophrenic, taking only one extreme of his endeavour from his split and sick soul and demonstrated how the pattern of God in man was a scientific fact and a mighty activity, bear a crushing moral responsibility for the sickness of men and their societies, because they have today the means for healing at their disposal, but refuse to apply it. It is a scandal of a moral kind so great and general that no-one will proclaim it as it ought to be from the housetops. Yet, wherever men are, they have only to listen and look and see it as some dry-rot in the basements of their surroundings or hear it at work as some death-watch beetle in the hollow wainscots of their spirit. Unless the keepers of the spirit of man at this hour, so much later than they think, will reassess their vocation in its ancient as well as its most contemporary of terms, life, as always in these arrested moments, will be compelled to call in the most terrible of all healers to do their work for them, the disaster cataclysmically proportionate to the centuries of neglect of their calling and failure to follow on the Pentecostal light into the darkness of unknowing ahead of which they have been guilty.

This cataclysm could be so great that they and their societies may well vanish forever. And yet, one does not believe this because there is an answer to all this by following the way Jung pioneered in his own life and work. Sooner or later, he will be seen by all for what he is, one of the great turning points in history, as he is already being recognised by growing numbers in Old and New Worlds, West and East and even in my own native Africa.

One day soon now, man will come to reappraise the whole of recorded history in order to uncover, as archaeologists uncover the ruined cities of the crumbled civilisations buried in the dust behind us, the decisive role the collective unconscious has played in it. They will see the decline and fall of civilisations at last in their true light as partial expressions of the human spirit which, valid as they were for brief moments of time, perished because, in their own specialised establishment, they became increasingly separated from the natural forces of the collective unconscious that initially raised them so high until the support of this primordial world of infinite energies was totally alienated and withdrawn, and they had to fall. History, no matter how remote, re-examined in terms of this great hypothesis, will show precisely how not the uncertainties of physical environment and external disaster, but the inadequacy of men's conscious relationships with their collective unconscious and their failure constantly to renew, deepen and widen them were the real causes of decline and fall.

Once this point is reached, the road to a more meaningful future will be clear again because history for the first time will not only be as precise and honest as the best of historians have always tried to make it, but it will also be whole. Without a history that is as whole as it is precise and honest, aware of all the forces that have gone into its making, our future cannot possess the sanity which is wholeness. Since Jung, no true historian any longer has either excuse or lack of means for doing the whole of his vital task for the first time on record, and our future be brighter than ever before. But the hour is late.

And indeed, it is because there is no time to be lost in this as in so many other fields for Jung to be the beginning of our unique contemporary way, I have found it imperative to express the meaning he has for me and the extent to which his example confirmed my own natural endeavour in life and added meaning to what I have tried to do.

Indeed, so much did I want my book about him to be a record of my own experiences of both the man and our own day, that I did practically no academic research in writing it. I consulted none of the numbers of my friends who knew and worked with Jung. I read no books about him in this period and only turned to his own work as I remembered what was significant to me in it and wished to confirm it.

My account, therefore, is as fallible as I am myself, but nonetheless it is the greatest truth of which I am capable. Anything else from me would have been pretence and would have failed, because the time has come when men can only truly communicate with one another out of what they themselves have experienced and suffered. For they can no longer speak to one another out of pure knowledge alone. The knowledge which is peddled in so great abundance in so ready a market today, seeing that it is bartered without human commitment, historical evaluation or moral obligation, is no longer a vehicle of legitimate exchange, because it only communicates the facts and statistics of itself and nothing of the person who passes it on, nor anything of the one who receives it, let alone trails along with it a curl of the cloud of the aboriginal meaning which somewhere below the horizon of our time once inspired it and which alone can feed the great hunger we feel.

In any case, I could not do more. Even in the process of doing the little I have done, the immensity of my subject has shown up my own inadequacies, so that at times I could hardly continue. Yet, strangely enough, out of this archetypal pattern of meaning which is the proper dimension of my subject, it is striking how often the relevant coincidences have come to encourage me. Only last night, for instance, above the reddening snow on the highest peak, its marble head bland and broad over the valley among the mountains of Switzerland which Jung loved and among which I am writing, I saw the planets Venus and Jupiter close to each other as they have not been since 1859, so that some starry images of the greatest masculine god of all, Zeus, as I prefer to call him in his aboriginal Greek, and the goddess of the feminine, Aphrodite, who has the principles of love, the Eros, in her keeping, and once rose out of the mist and spray of a wine-dark sea of morning at our European beginning, shone there close and reconciled, bright and trembling with their nearness, as if set deliberately there to remind me how they are forever united in the self Jung rediscovered for his time.

Then, on a day of particular despondence, when I had just finished the account of the meaning of *The Odyssey* for me and come to the patters of the wise old man in Jung, the owner of this hotel, who is an old friend, appeared with a large magnified copy, faithful even in colour to the original, of a detail from a Greek vase some 3,500 years old. It was an illustration of an old Greek shepherd leaning on his staff by a classical fluted marble column, as the old shepherd in

Ithaca might have done when patient, resolved, and uncomplaining, he stared out to sea for signs of his master's safe return. He was looking out of infinitely experienced eyes as if from the other side of the world there were stirring into movement towards him something of overwhelming import. I had only to look up from my writing table to see that wise old face and feel that between him and me some thread of meaning was intact and, though unrecorded, and names and faces in-between unknown, I had appropriate and great company in what I was trying to do. Indeed, no personification of a great archetype could have been more accurate or vivid, nor so timely.

But most of all, though perhaps least in itself, something happened high up on the side of a great white mountain when I was on my way to meet a guide to take me to the top one afternoon. I found two little Swiss boys full of life and mischief, waiting by the track across a steep slope for their own teacher. Tired of teasing one another and some rather pompous, over-fleshed adults going inexpertly by on their skis, one turned to the other and asked in his Graubünden dialect: "What is the difference between theology and psychology?"

"You're showing off!" the other exclaimed, taken aback. "I bet you don't know yourself."

"I do," his friend replied, suddenly solemn and rather shy, "Theology is the knowledge and study of God; psychology is the knowledge and study of the soul."

My immediate reaction was that this could only have happened in Switzerland, but coming down the mountain on skis at sunset to a darkening valley, with a vortex of crows tormented in the calm of evening over its deep centre, tossed like crumpled sheets of black, burnt-out paper in a current of heat rising from the ashes of a dying fire, the incident struck me another way. If these questions and the differences implied could be of concern to so young a boy, late as the hour was, there was both time and material to work on the decay of our day and restore it. I felt instantly that we all owed life itself all we could do to prevent the child of the future from being educated out of the natural spirit that had prompted question and answer, as indeed so many children are being educated out of it today.

For it seems to me that it is precisely out of these questions with their deep roots in our remote origins in the search for their truthful answer that the human spirit has always derived its clearest inspiration and found its greatest meaning, and will continue to do so until the end of time, despite all impediments of confusion and partialities of unawareness thrown in its way by no matter how disorientated, determined and powerful men and societies. And I could not say this with such certainty were it not for Carl Gustav Jung, through whom the universe dreamt a dream, giving him capacity and the courage to live it, and our desperate time the vision that could save it from itself.

Sir Laurens and Lady Ingaret van der Post, about to embark on a Kalahari journey with the Land Rover known as 'Kalahari Kate.'

A Pattern of Synchronicities

Laurens van der Post

There has always seemed to be, ever since I can remember, a vast area of what passed as reality for me that seemed to be neither dark nor clear, but transformed into a vast transference in which phenomena seemed to be beyond cause and effect and make vast distinctions between mind and matter and real. None of these seem to me more meaningful than the phenomenon which Jung described as synchronicity. Anyone who wishes to understand how little we know about this phenomenon and yet how meaningful it can be, should read the correspondence which Jung and Pauli had with each other,[1] which also transformed itself into a dialogue which Pauli continued to conduct between his scientific work and his dreams. I, for my part, noticed that it seemed to be there already when I first met Jung, and the more I knew him, the more frequent it became, and when he died, did not cease, but in any areas concerned with him, they were, if anything, on the increase. At the beginning came for me what was, perhaps, the greatest and most significant synchronicity of all, when I turned up as rather a lost sort of soldier from the last war, and Aniela Jaffé, who had a feeling that Jung and I should meet, arranged one of the first dinner parties which Jung annually had for many years with what were called the first students at the Jung Institute in Zürich.[2] We had no sooner sat to begin our meal when quite a distinguished scholar, I think, although it doesn't matter what he was, who sat at the right side of Jung, started a discussion about fire. He was obviously a deeply committed rationalist of some kind, because he maintained that there was nothing really very remarkable about fire,

---

[1] *Wolfgang Pauli und C.G. Jung: Ein Briefwechsel 1932-1958*, Hrsg. C.A. Meier, Springer-Verlag, Heidelberg, 1992.
[2] For Aniela Jaffé's recollection of this encounter, see her contribution on page 217.

except that it was one of those many striking manifestations of energy. And I remember Jung said to him, in a voice which went deeper when he was about to express something that was important to him, "Of course, it is a form of energy, too, but before it becomes energy, it is many other things in the life and spirit of the human being. First of all, it's light in the dark when there is no other light. It is warmth against the cold, and it is the source of many, many things before we start regarding it as a pure manifestation of energy." I cannot vow that these are the exact words, but it was to this effect and started what became quite a heated argument. And when there was a sort of moment when I said to them both, I wonder if they realized that, in the beginning, man not only made fire by rubbing sticks together, as the world seems to be continuingly assuming; there was another way which seemed to me far more remarkable. At that, they asked, "What was it?" Because neither of them seemed to know, I told the men of an experience I had had in the jungles of southeast Asia, where it rained very often for days and nights at a time, and there was hardly ever anything dry to be obtained. And there, because rubbing wet sticks together might not prove very profitable, the indigenous inhabitants of these forests had another method. Each man had a little thorn around his waist and from this thorn there dangled a long square box-like something, which we would discover had a cylinder drilled into the center of it all the way down, and obviously tapered somewhat. And I saw that the lid of this box-like contraption had a long tapered rod which fit very neatly and tightly into the hole which I have described. And when this man wanted to make fire, he took out the little rod tied to the same thorn, and some very dry moss, and put it in a place sheltered from the rain. At the bottom of the rod, there was a deep niche carved through the middle of it. The man would then take some of the moss, put it into the niche and put the rod with the moss tightly in place at the mouth of the hole. He then knocked the two ends together, pulled out the rod and the moss was on fire. And I said that, when I saw this for the first time, startled at the sophistication of this, one of my officers, who was an engineer in ordinary life, exclaimed utterly astonished: "Good God, Colonel, the Diesel engine!" And there it was! These most primitive of people knew, had access to, used the Diesel engine principle for making fire. The laugh of satisfaction and joy that broke out of Jung was wonderful to hear. And I think, as a result of that, we instantly sort of became friends, and I went home with him that evening and we sat and talked until early in the morning. And all the time we talked, I felt as if I was

talking to one of the first spirits of life at the moment when he had
first discovered fire. I could really think of no greater synchronicity,
and to me it was wonderful to find this truly great spirit, even more
at home in a world into which I had been born.

As time went on, the number of synchronicities increased. I can
only concentrate on a few of the more important ones to show how
full of unexplained meaning these synchronicities were, and they
became even more so in the last years of his life. Perhaps greatest of
all were the synchronicities which accompanied his end. He died
rather like a great ship going down into the sea and drawing after it
all sorts of synchronicities that reached into the lives of people who
knew and loved him, as his ship drew flotsam and jetsam from all
around itself out of the life and circumstance to mark the place where
he vanished. Even the universe seemed to join in this event: while he
was dying, a great thunderstorm broke over Lake Zürich, and one of
its greatest flashes of lightning was into his garden and abolished his
favorite tree. I mention this because whatever produced this event
was still part of reality. A decade after he died, I was making, with
friends of mine, with great difficulty, a simple film version of his life
and thought for broadcasting for television and, on the last day, we
went to his home at Küsnacht to film, where we had already filmed a
great deal before. Surprising and very valuable help came from his
son, Franz Jung, who, in the beginning, had tended to be against the
idea of a film being made about the life of his father. And all the
morning of this last day, we thought we would go and film the end of
Jung's life at Küsnacht, which had been his home all those years in
Zürich. We were very anxious to do it at sundown because I remembered something Ruth Bailey, who looked after Jung in the bleak
years after Mrs. Jung's death, had told me about his end. Tired one
afternoon, she asked Franz Jung to sit with his father while she went
out for an airing. The moment she left the room, Jung had called his
son and asked him to be quick and help him out of the bed while Mrs.
Bailey was out, because, he said, if she came back and saw him, she
would insist on his going back to bed and he wanted very much to
watch the sun going down over the Alps. When Ruth Bailey told me
this, I was very moved, because I remembered one of the earliest
memories of Jung – a memory, I think, which is recorded almost in
the first paragraph, if not the first page, of *Memories, Dreams,
Reflections* – of how, on a summer evening, he heard a voice, I think
the voice of an aunt, saying from somewhere behind him at sunset,

"Now look over there – the mountains are all red." It was to me as if he were back near the beginning of his life. He was back at what might be called finding his beginning in the end and recognizing it for the first time. Franz Jung helped him to the window and kept him supported until the sun had gone down behind the mountains across the lake. Jung then, strangely at peace, went back to bed. As far as I recollect, he did not speak again and died two or three days later. And we thought we wanted to include, to relate this part of his life, the sun from his house going down behind the hills. All day long, going about working on the last scenes, it was most noticeable how the film crew and I, who had been so close in our work to the man, all had the feeling as if he appeared there: he would became almost a presence around us. The cameraman in particular, on several occasions, said with enormous disbelief, in a half-joking, half-serious voice, "I really feel that the old man is directing my camera." However, a very warm summer's day had – towards evening, when we were about to move into position at Küsnacht with our cameras for the final scenes – suddenly changed characters. Clouds seemed to gather by magic over the lake and, when the time came, when I had to speak, to describe the dying, the death of Jung itself taking place in a great thunderstorm, and the moment came when I described how that lightning hit his favourite tree, there was another flash of lightning which hit the place where the tree had been. It was so startling, so close and so loud that anybody watching the film to this day can see how I once had to struggle to compose myself and carry on to the end of the scene in spite of the obvious violence of the storm.

In a strange way, I was not surprised, because, among those synchronicities which I describe, which I compare to things marking the place where Jung went when his life went down like a great ship at sea, I myself was at sea. I had left South Africa extremely depressed and strangely, it was at the time when all the security forces in South Africa were looking for a terrorist whom the government called 'Mandela.' And only a few weeks before his arrest, which led to his trial and his twenty-seven-year-long imprisonment, I was deeply depressed about what was going on in my native country. For the first day or two at sea, I couldn't sleep. And then one night, when I was really very tired and rather desperate for want of sleep, I suddenly had a vision of myself walking in a deep valley in Switzerland, and at a time when the whole country was experiencing a devastating series of avalanches. This valley itself was so threatened by avalanches that I

Sir Laurens rests near C.G. Jung's carved stone depicting Telesphoros at his Bollingen tower while filming for the BBC in 1971

knew I had to walk quietly and not shout or raise my voice, because it might precipitate one. And then, high on a ridge towards the end of the valley against the sinking sun, Jung suddenly appeared and he waved his hand at me in this vision, half-dream, whatever it was, as he used to wave his hand when he said good-bye to me. He would often walk with me to the gate of his garden and stare at the gate and, as I went away, he would wave his hand at me, and in that funny sort of schoolboy English which he often used, would call after me, "I'll be seeing you." There he was, looking so happy and so confident and the voice came to me so clear and reassuringly that I instantly went to sleep. And early in the morning I awoke, and instead of waiting for my steward to bring my tea before getting up, I felt impelled to get up myself, threw open all the curtains over my porthole and looked out to the sea. There, just coming slowly alongside the ship and looking closely at the ship, came an albatross. And coming opposite my porthole, it looked at me in a very very strange way, as if it was there to tell me something. I went back to my bed rather horrorstricken and laid back thinking and feeling that it could mean something, but I didn't know what. Then my steward came in with my tea, as he always did, and a plate of grapes and the ship's news. I opened the ship's news, which had been recorded at night on the ship's radio, radio news. And the first thing I saw, at the top of the news, was that C.G. Jung, the great Swiss scientist and psychologist, had died at his home in Küsnacht during the night. I knew then what both, the vision of the evening and the albatross, had meant. Comparing the difference in latitude and therefore in time, my vision of the night before had occurred precisely at the moment when Jung died.

Then, some ten years after the filming, I was doing a series of talks at the C.G. Jung Institute in Küsnacht, and we were driving towards the lake and Jung's old home. I told my companion at the time about an evening just like the sunset moment in which we were driving along the lake on the last day of the filming, up to the event of the great albatross. And when I came to the albatross scene, I said something about the almost supernatural impact albatrosses had in the minds of sailors, and indeed to an extent on poets and even a person like myself, who had so often had their company for three or four days after sailing away from the Cape of Good Hope. I expanded somewhat on the role that birds had played as messengers from the world beyond in the stories and lives of the primitive people of Africa about whom I was going to be speaking that night. And I told him a story about the evening after the death of Bleek, the German scholar who devoted so much of his life to study the language of the persecuted Bushmen of South Africa, and who had, for the purposes of his studies, obtained permission to have Bushmen living on the grounds of his home at the Cape of Good Hope. I told him how depressed the Bleek children all were and how all of the Bushmen had come to sit with them in the kitchen to drink some tea, and have the comfort of the warm kitchen fire while night fell outside. It was a moment of great depression and outer silence, and it grew completely dark. Suddenly, there was a loud flutter at the high kitchen windows, and there was an owl on the window ledge. It seemed as if it was trying to look in and attract the attention of everyone in the kitchen. The Bleek children were terrified and started to cry, but all the Bushmen there jumped up and started dancing and clapping their hands, and calling out: "He's arrived, he's arrived!" They meant that Bleek had arrived where departed souls arrive.

I had hardly finished the story, and the sun had gone after an intense and very beautiful twilight, when an owl started to hoot. And that evening, through much of my talk, we could clearly hear at intervals the owl continuing to hoot.

I was not the only one to experience these synchronicities. I think of one that influenced Aniela Jaffé greatly. When the BBC, some ten years or so after Jung's death, asked me if I would make a television program about Jung, I said "No" very firmly and rather angrily, because for many, many years while Jung was alive, I had wanted to make a program and they had refused me, saying that Jung was too controversial a figure, and I was too friendly with him and would not do it properly. Fortunately, John Freeman, who had a very prestigious program of his own called *Face to Face,* and the right to decide exactly whom he wanted to interview on that program, had sufficient sense of the importance of Jung to the time in which we lived and he made a splendid interview with Jung. (It is all the more impressive because I know from my acquaintance with Freeman that he was at heart no great friend of Jung. The program therefore speaks infinitely more of Freeman's professional integrity that he could do it so well, and for the indefinite future that interview will continue to be of immense importance and meaning.)

At this moment when the BBC approached me and I had declined, I began to feel strangely uneasy and almost felt as if I had let Jung down and should have said "Yes." I telephoned Aniela Jaffé, told her what had happened and said, perhaps I would have answered the BBC differently if she would have agreed to join me in making the film. She responded almost angrily that I should do nothing of the sort, and put the telephone down. Half an hour later, the telephone rang and it was Aniela. She said: "Laurens, I've just been to my kitchen to prepare my lunch, and as usual turned on the radio for the lunchtime news. At that moment, they were playing the piece of music which is the signature tune of John Freeman's programme, *Face to Face*. I can't ignore that. If you still want to do the film, I will agree to it."

And so, we made the film.

But perhaps of all the many synchronicities connected with Jung, the greatest was the one that accompanied the ending of my book, *Jung and the Story of Our Time*.

I had been writing every afternoon in a room of our skiing hotel, high up in the Swiss mountains, a room lent to me by the proprietor, who was an old friend. I looked out over the valley leading down to Lenzerheid, at the opening of the pass into Italy along which the Christian legions had invaded Switzerland. For a fortnight or more, I had been watching how the twilight seeped into the valley, and how the planets of Venus and Jupiter were closing in on each other. It seemed to me that their approach to a meeting was somehow connected to what I was writing.

On the last day, as I was writing the final passage, I looked up and to my amazement, they seemed due to meet: the planet of love and the planet of ultimate cosmic power and authority. I was writing: "And I could not say this with such certainty were it not for Carl Gustav Jung, through whom the universe dreamt a dream, giving him the capacity and the courage to live it, and our desperate time the vision that could save it from itself."

As I finished the word "itself" and put a full stop to what had been a long and, for me, fruitful examination of my experience of the man and his work, I looked up: the love and the will of creation were one. It was so awesome that I wrote immediately to Patrick Moore, the astronomer, whom I knew, and asked him how often that occurred. He answered (I quote from memory and may be out by a decade or more): "Every 169 years." Somehow, ever since, it's been to me a sort of confirmation of all that I felt about Jung and his work.

A Confession of Faith[1]

Laurens van der Post

"What is faith?" I asked myself one time in the heart of an unexplored desert in Africa, and this is what followed immediately after the question: It is the not-yet in the now; it is the taste of the fruit which does not yet exist, hanging as the blossom on the bough.

There is, I believe, hardly a contemporary notion of progress which is not in desperate need of reappraisal. In this regard, as an Elizabethan sundial in a secluded English country garden one nostalgic autumn afternoon informed me: "It's always later than you think."

For, in the vast proliferating empire of progress, in the technological field of human endeavor and applied science and its consequences, in the conduct and spirit of man and his societies, it is not just the matter of increase it so plausibly purports to be, but also a mortal danger to almost all forms of natural life and even the earth itself. This profound ambivalence at the heart of progress is all the more awesome because it has been a dark potential since our conscious beginnings and implicit in the evolution of man from the moment the Promethean gift of fire came into his hands.

One of the earliest, and, for me, most striking images of its paradoxical role, is the story of the struggle between Jacob and Esau in their mother's womb. From then on, the Jacob in man, with a fearsome increase of power, has been joined in conflict with the Esau, with all that is natural in man and represented by the hunter who is close to his instincts, dependent on nature, and obedient to its urging and the wonder and reference it evoked in his spirit, until we arrive at a moment when the triumph of Jacob in man, and the nations and cities it fathered, seems final and complete.

On the horizons, the great empires, the Ninevehs, the Tyres,

---

[1] Another version of this essay was previously published as the Foreword to a book entitled, *Progress without Loss of Soul*, by Theodor Abt, Chiron Publications, Wilmette, 1989.

Thebeses and Babylons, have gone down into the dust and rubble which is all that is left of themselves and the abundant world of nature which nourished them, and there is a terrifying statement of its danger to man, beast, and flower. There were, for instance, the great forests of Central Asia which stretched from Istfahan eastwards to the Himalayas and the Hindu Kush, and north to the seas of the Caspian, and west to the wine-dark ocean of the Mediterranean. They have all gone. Humble woodcutters and charcoal burners feeding the needs and greeds of cities have left hardly a tree between Tehran and the Caspian. Where is the grass that Nebuchadrezzar ate? And where are the hanging gardens of Babylon? And what would not have been done sooner with the bulldozers and mechanical saws of today? North Africa from Nile to Atlas Mountains and the Pillars of Hercules, which was the granary of Europe, today is an impoverished fringe of earth on a man-made desert of the Sahara. The European shore of the Mediterranean, in spite of the vision of wealth and luxury it still holds for the weary industrial man, is a ghost of what it was in its Athenian day. Then, there was not a valley, a mountain, or a stream where men did not walk and commune with their gods and dream in the company of satyrs, centaurs, nymphs, fauns, and the titanic forces of a world charged with magic and wonder. No one who has read his Homer, Thucydides and Vergil can be anything but terrified by what is left and, in comparison, looks like a scorched earth today.

At the same time as this devastation of the earth and plunder of its natural resources gained force, it was accompanied by an equal and opposite kind of radioactive fall-out in the soul of man. Pericles, in the course of one of his great orations during the Peloponnesian Wars, warned the Athenians how much of the desperation in which they found themselves was caused by the way they had allowed their city-state to fall into the hands of men who had developed a slanted, soured and revengeful environment. He urged the Athenians, there-fore, to go back to their ancient rule of choosing men who lived on and off the land and were reluctant to spend their lives in towns, and prepared to serve them purely out of sense of public duty, and not like their present rulers, who did so uniquely for personal power and advancement. He was already demarcating in his own context of time the danger of a growing imbalance between the Jacob and Esau minds, between the separation of the spirit of man from its natural roots within and without, and a consequent loss for the reverence of the feminine values, our great mother earth and all her instinctive and caring heart that made life once so rich and productive. It is extraordinary how contemporary Pericles still sounds.

Euripides, having just failed in the great debate with Aeschylus in the Kingdom of Pluto to gain the right to return to life and speak for the true spirit of Greece, penned perhaps the most fearful warning of all in *The Bacchae*: the horrendous story of how Bacchus and his followers subverted and brought to ruin one of the greatest empires the world had ever seen, and how all the long-rejected, powerful energies in the soul of man rebelled and overthrew the law and order and power which had so long tyrannised them. Significantly, in *The Bacchae*, the harbinger of the great catastrophe to come is "a city slicker with a smooth tongue," and all the stories and legends of the coming of Bacchus read almost like a report of the World Narcotics Bureau on the rising drug traffic of today, and the cry everywhere, the same old Theban call, for more police and for more and more law and order, without any inkling of how societies and their unlived selves are accessories before the act.

In the thousands of years between the moment when the King of Thebes was pulled limb from limb by his own wife and daughters, this great divide has continued to deepen faster. What we call 'civilisation' has tended to become, with geometric progression, also a form of technological barbarism, invading not only what is left of rain, forest, savannah and virgin water, but every aspect of human endeavour, and even the genes of the human body. It is not for nothing that this difference between what I've called a city mind and a country mind was one of the first things that struck Jung when he went to school and university at Basel. Jung once told me how this town mind was to him daily more unreal and nightmarish, and how the longing for a return to the natural or the country mind became greater and more urgent. Already as a young boy, he said, as he became more familiar with life in the town, the stronger became his conviction that what he was getting to know as reality was not reality at all, but belonged to a totally different order, a dis-proportioned abnormality of man which passed itself off as the total reality. He longed for the view of reality which it seemed he lacked or had lost. He came to write:

I longed for the vision of the world as a country among rivers and woods, among men and animals, and small villages bathed in sunlight with the rims of the clouds moving over them encompassed by clear dark nights – a world in which happily uncertain and unpre-

*dictable things can still happen and the surrounding world of nature
would be the world of the country which is no mere locality on the
map, but is God's world so ordered by Him that it would be filled with
secret meaning ...*

(Memories, Dreams, Reflections)

And he went on to write how trees for him were not just trees, but
rather represented the thoughts of Our Creator. He told how he
walked through a forest as if we were looking at the act of creation
itself and could feel the voice of creation speaking over his shoulder.
This view, this vision, accompanied him to the end of his days and
made him one of the greatest healers that life has ever known: a
healer in the ancient religious sense of a person who unites that
which has been divided and rejected, that which is hurt and wounded,
and brings them together so that they achieve a wholeness which is
greater than the sum of the parts.

This totality, this wholeness, it is important to remember, has the
same origin, the same root in our language, as the Saxon word for
holy. Holiness and wholeness implied the same condition of mind
and instinct, feeling and intellect, intuition and the transfigurative
indefinable mysterious something which dreamt through human
beings and ultimately maintained a vision beyond themselves and
their societies.

What would be needed is on the trail of this indescribable dreaming element in life and time, which will restore man's wholeness and
unify him, centered in the self where he is at last invulnerable and
inviolate against the slanted and corrupting pressures which the life
of our time would inflict on us. There is no dimension of contemporary life which is not threatened with fragmentation and so, incomplete, and it must not be thought that all I have been discussing is a
universally orchestrated form of Greenpeace and conservation of the
earth and its wildlife. I have chosen them only as examples because
they are the most striking and represent the physical dimension in
which the slanted man in his cities began to abuse the power
conferred on him by science and its many technologies in the world
without and, as in the world without, so above, so below and so
within. This corruption of power and this abuse of power over nature
has indeed gone so far that, not surprisingly, everywhere there is the
temptation to despair and feel all now is always too late. Moreover, in
our centuries and the pursuit of reason and the indulgence of a hubris

William Plomer, Roy Campbell and Laurens van der Post on the coast of Zululand in 1926, at the time they published the first literary magazine in South Africa, Voorslag. This was one month before van der Post and William Plomer set sail for Japan.

of a tyrannic rationalism, we have lost touch with this dreaming element which still, night and day, seeks to re-direct us to a destination where beginning and origin are one and whole. The deserts and vast stretches of plundered earth which I have described as evidence of our devastation of nature therefore warn us also of the profound crisis of meaning which is bearing down on our spirit and producing what might be called a loss of soul. Or a state of 'unbeing,' as called by Thomas Berry, the remarkable historian of religion, who, from his base in the Passionist monastery in Riverdale, has so profound an insight into the crisis of soul of which progress is so disturbingly symptomatic. For Berry, all the negations of progress were symbolised in the nuclear cloud concentrated once over Hiroshima. Dispersed, no longer easily discerned, for him the same cloud "shrouds in death the living earth." What he calls the comfortable disease of progress "leads on in a more generous time scale, to the same dead earth that the nuclear bombs produced in a moment." The result is always the same: only the efficiency changes. What the bomb does quickly, surgically, he says, progress will achieve more slowly if men continue to un-selve themselves and remain lulled in their cushioned unbeing.

Human beings, I believe, can endure anything except a state of meaninglessness, and ultimately our concern must be the bringing back of meaning, and the sense of totality it confirms on all life. Anyone who knows his history knows how, in the beginning, on the very rim of the first horizon, man found a dreamer and a dream, and how from then on, this dreaming process was active at every unforgiving second of life, reminding the being chasing after his favourite partiality to pause and allow his shadow, lengthening behind him, to come up and join his bright and impatient other with the sun at last on his side. As he stands there with a horizon, which still seems to hem him in, wondering how to go beyond, the dreamer abolishes it only to renew it endlessly ahead.

Africa's greatest poet has put it far better than I can, in a poem about the terrapin which, according to one of the oldest of old myths, supported the feet of the great elephant on whose back stood the pillars that hold the earth in position. This terrapin, in the poet's wild and volcanic epic, is the saving element that rises above the sea and flood to help the ark of Noah and its precious cargo of living things to survive. All done, the terrapin, the redeemer, sinks back into a dark, unfathomed ocean, we might say back into the dreaming unconscious, leaving all living things on earth safe and free to scatter like jewels over emerald grass, or move like flame through the forests and savannahs, still glistening and wet, and man reprieved and able once more to listen to the 'silent chanting of his soul,' proclaims:

> *Though times shall change and stormy ages roll,*
> *I am that ancient hunted of the plains*
> *That raked the shaggy flitches of the Bison:*
> *Pass, world: I am the dreamer that remains,*
> *The Man, clear-cut against the last horizon.*

Roy Campbell, *The Flaming Terrapin* (1926)

Laudatio for Sir Laurens van der Post

On the occasion of the presentation of the prize of the Research
and Training Centre for Depth Psychology according to C.G.
Jung and Marie-Louise von Franz Sunday, 24. November, 1996,
Guildhouse *zum Rüden*, Zürich, Switzerland

Theodor Abt

Sir Laurens van der Post, we are honoured to have the opportunity
to express to you in person our gratitude for what you have contributed to human culture by your life and your work as writer, soldier-
statesman and researcher. Ever since you wrote your first story at the
age of eight, you have stood up for the redemption of the existence of
an inner world with its images – images that can serve as a compass
to guide us through life. You called this inner other in us the
Bushman, that otherness in us that Jung liked to call the 'two-million-
year-old human.' Your life in close companionship and friendship
with your inner, great, old Bushman shines forth today like a beacon
in this nebulous period of transition we are going through. Your life
has become a convincing paradigm of what Jung succeeded in
communicating in the framework of science, namely, that the unique
value and meaning of an individual can become manifest if we simply
try to live in companionship with the inner, great, old human, who
speaks to us in dreams. In this way, modern man can connect with
the most ancient elements within himself and regain a feeling of
belonging and being known, which is how you characterized the
essence of the value of a Bushman's life.

Your research has come to us in the form of meaningful and
healing stories, stories that tell about your own life experience and

stories that testify about the outer and inner life of the Bushmen of the Kalahari. These stories were also a feature of the early days of your friendship with Carl Gustav Jung, which began 47 years ago, here in this Guildhouse *zum Rüden*. Like yourself, Jung loved stories. So what could be more fitting on this occasion than a little story?

The story of your *laudatio* started two months ago in Upper Egypt, on the banks of the river Nile in Luxor-Thebes, when I wanted to write down this text in the way I thought it should be done. In spite of being on African soil, I realized that the words just didn't flow, and I could gather only bits and pieces from the immense richness of your life and work. I started to regret once more my typology as an extraverted intuitive, who optimistically just accepts new challenges only to get into trouble later. At one point, I just brushed aside all my papers and, leaning back, wondered what is really the one message of your life and work? SERVICE was the word that sprang to mind. Truly, your life is one of service to that great spirit that leads man to a meaningful future, as your own life-story testifies. You served this spirit as a journalist, in the army and as a statesman, fighting the tyranny and arrogance of a one-sided conscious attitude. Later you served this spirit by defending the rights and the values of the life of the Bushmen in the Kalahari. All your life, you served this spirit by communicating your insights into the reality of the human soul, the vessel that enables us to experience this very spirit.

At that moment, sounds of wonder and surprise reached my ears from nearby and I saw a group of people looking up at the top of the pole of a large straw sunshade. As the scene continued, I went over and looked up at the same spot as everybody else. And there, at the highest point, I saw a large insect. It was a green Mantis. Never before, during my more than thirty journeys to Upper Egypt, had I seen a Mantis. Knowing what Mantis means to the Bushman and in your life, Sir Laurens van der Post, I was just stunned by the coincidence. When a man started to tease the Mantis with a long stick, I decided to climb up and let the little insect walk over onto my right hand. Down on the ground again, I answered people's questions about Mantis. And as the interest of the people around grew, I told them more about the Mantis, how it was the God of the Bushman. During all this time, the Mantis stayed on my thumb and first finger, while in the background, on the other side of the Nile, the red-glowing sun went down, lighting up from behind the Mantis and the palmy skyline of the auspicious West Bank of Luxor-Thebes. When I had finished, the Mantis just turned its head and looked at me. Then it crept over to a branch of a nearby pagoda tree.

At that moment, I knew that I just had to follow the Mantis, the bringer of the fire to the Bushman; Mantis, who might have had a redeeming dream, as the Bushman would have said. I felt relief and pleasure that your *laudatio* could be brought by Mantis, and I sensed that I might just have to wait and trust this working of the spirit, just as your life has shown how this trust is not misplaced.

Back in Zurich again, while reading your book, *A Mantis Carol*, I read: "Mantis in particular could only have been chosen [by the Bushman] as the image of their greatest value because no other would have served as well. I had a feeling that all together, these creations of Bushman imagination constituted an ancient HIERO-GLYPHIC CODE of great primary import and if only I could find the key to the cypher used in the encoding, I would uncover a most immediate message of vital significance."[1] Well, Sir Laurens, you have definitely found the key to help modern man to understand better the symbol of Mantis.

Yet, I still wondered what the significance could be of Mantis appearing in Luxor-Thebes, while I was working on your *laudatio*. Your mentioning the HIEROGLYPHIC CODE provided the key. There actually exists, among the over 5,000 known Hieroglyphics, one hieroglyph of a Mantis. Yet, oddly enough, it appears in just one place in the huge, over-3,000-year-old pharaonic literature, namely, in the text of the ritual of the Opening-of-the-Mouth, as I learned some years ago from my respected teacher in Egyptology, Professor Erik Hornung. In this ritual, the so called Sem-priest brings to life a statue that represents the deceased person. In so doing, he helps with the resurrection of the dead.

On one of my recent journeys to Egypt together with Erik Hornung, we came to a newly-opened tomb of a nobleman called Thutmes. There we saw different paintings from the ritual of the Opening-of-the-Mouth. In the key scene (Nr. 8), when, according to the text, the Sem-priest is searching for the soul of the deceased person, in order unite it with the statue, the Sem-priest is painted sleeping; in all the other known representations of this scene, however, the Sem is shown standing.

---

[1] Laurens van der Post, *A Mantis Carol*, London, Chatto & Windus, 1975, p. 16

The sleeping Sem painted without head, Tomb of the Nobleman Thutmes,
Luxor, West Bank, Khokha Nr. 295

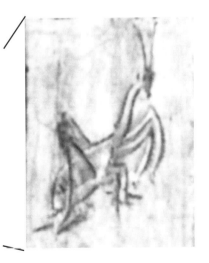

Previous page:
A representation of the kneeling Sem-priest with the
statue of the deceased King Seti I in front of him. Below,
the hieroglyphic text to the 8.-10. Scene of the ritual of
the Opening-of-the-Mouth. The picture is taken from the
book of Erik Hornung, The Tomb of Pharaoh Seti I,
Zurich 1991.

Left: The enlargement of the Mantis hieroglyph.

The text explains what is taking place while the Sem is sleeping: in his dream, a Mantis is catching and bringing back the soul of the deceased. And that is the only place in the known pharaonic literature where the hieroglyph of the Mantis appears. The picture of the sleeping Sem (see pictures on previous page) gives us the confirmation that the text really has to be understood in this way.

The Mantis, which, according to Bushman belief, is the great dreamer, is also in pharaonic literature the one who is able to bring back the soul of the deceased father, that living light, which guarantees the continuity of culture and which alone is able to guide us to our future. Whether there is a direct cultural bridge between the Bushman story of the dreaming Mantis and this scene of the ritual of the Opening-of-the-Mouth, or whether this image came up as an archetypal image independently, can probably never be answered. In both ways, it is a remarkable 'coming together,' showing the relationship of the beginning of our western culture with the original man.

It is assumed by today's Egyptologists that originally, the ritual of the Opening-of the-Mouth was performed by the eldest son of the deceased father-king, in order to bring back the soul of his father to a statue representing him. The ritual of Opening-of-the-Mouth-and-the-Eyes is the final act, when the statue comes alive and thus the old king is resurrected and the kingdom will continue without loss of soul. With that ritual, the son of the old king can become the new king, for he was able to bring back and thus renew the essential value of the father world, and hence guarantee the continuity of culture. The son who performs this ritual was later represented by a priest, called the Sem.

Sir Laurens van der Post, this pharaonic myth really is a story that characterizes your life. From your early days, you allowed the dreaming Mantis to guide you. For example, at one point in life you spontaneously interrupted the writing of your book, *The Heart of the Hunter,* and went to the United States of America. Why? Because of some enigmatic dreams about the Mantis, together with an invitation to lecture – an invitation sent to you by a lady from New York called Martha Jaeger. Thanks to that decision, you brought back from your journey to America an incredible story that you named, *A Mantis Carol,* a story that you wrote in honour of Hans Taaibosch, a Bushman who, by a strange twist of fate, also happened to be in New York, the very opposite surroundings to the desert of the Kalahari, where he had been born and had his home. Your story connected us to this great Bushman, Hans Taaibosch, and hence, finally, to the essence of our dreaming spirit. Indeed, you could be called the Sem-priest for Hans Taaibosch, letting Mantis dream in order to bring back his soul and thus bringing alive the statue of this one Bushman. You were able to open his mouth, enabling the great old man, our forefather who lives in all of us, to speak to us again. In this way, we might once again become able to be guided by the living dream spirit.

Looking at the outer events that mirror your inner work as a Sem-priest, we see that you made a major contribution in bringing the soul back to your nation in South Africa, where it is known that your influence in the background with political leaders has been building a bridge between the white and the black people so that they can share a common future in South Africa. But also earlier in your life, you acted again and again like a Sem-priest, for instance in the Japanese prisoner-of-war camp or after World War Two in service of the British Army in Indonesia, when it was crucial to prevent the imminent outbreak of civil war. Your main contribution was always to bring back the uniting soul that transmits meaning, 'making the dreams become flesh,' as you once named it.

But you also brought the soul of the father back in a much larger sense, as you brought to life the father of all the Bushmen. You opened the mouth of the Bushman within us, so that we might hear what he has to say. This has become important for countless people from all over the world, for your books about the Bushmen have been translated into all the main languages, except Chinese. What you brought back is the evidence that renewal comes from letting Mantis dream, that means trusting in the images of the night, the feminine principle that gives birth to the renewed sunlight each day and each year. And by your life, you showed one of the most important prerequisites for that renewal: we need a completely receptive atti-tude, one that is able to listen to and understand properly the tiny little hints that come to us from the insect-level of our soul, the voice of the dream and fantasy world, the little synchronicities that happen around us and thus allow things to happen.

To round off the story, just a week after the encounter with the Mantis, I was with some friends, sailing down from Aswan to Luxor-Thebes on a Nile-boat. There, just after three o'clock in the morning, we witnessed on the upper deck the eclipse of the full moon over the West Bank, while at that very moment Saturn entered into a conjunc-tion with the moon. This event took place at the spring-equinox, which is now at the end of the zodiacal sign of Pisces. After the union, both the full moon and Saturn became invisible. About three hours later, the new morning sun was rising on the east side of the Nile. This remarkable constellation or synchronicity seemed to be somehow connected with the unexpected appearance of Mantis. For whenever time is out of joint, as ours certainly is, the story of the Bushman says that Mantis has a dream. It was as if the dream of Mantis had become visible on the night sky, a dream representing an image of the hope that, in the background of our troubled times at the end of the Aion of the fishes, the old sun, or our worn-out collective attitude, represented by Saturn, can unite with the moon, the light of the night, and thus be reborn as a new sun in the east again. After Saturn's-Day (Saturday) comes Sun-Day: the beginning of a new era with a new general attitude, which is again in accordance with the cosmic constellation in the night sky of the collective unconscious.

It is precisely this myth of renewal that you, Sir Laurens van der Post, have been serving all your life with all you have done. In different places you wrote about the new moon and the renewal of the sun and compared it with the urgent need for a change in our general attitude towards nature, starting with the redemption of due respect for our own inner nature. This myth of renewal of the old sun, with the aid of the light and the regenerative power of the motherly night, has been your vision. And you were, in a unique way, able to communicate this myth to other human beings from all over the world and from all walks of life. This makes you a messenger of a future spirit and a new collective consciousness.

Sir Laurens van der Post, from your earliest days, you have been inspired by the Mantis, the great redeemer, and you have really served this spirit all your life. Rest assured that we will do our utmost to honour, keep alive and hopefully pass on to the next generation this attitude, which you have been able to communicate in poetic language through your books and which corresponds to the psychological insights of Jung. Your work and research have shown that the foundations of Jung's psychology are to be found not only in Alchemy, which has its main roots in the pharaonic books of the underworld, but that the continuation of culture goes back far beyond that to the Bushman, to original man. What C.G. Jung and Marie-Louise von Franz did in the field of science, you did as a soldier, field researcher and writer. Your life and most valuable creative work, and your humble attitude in the service of the Self are a *Vorbild* for us at our Research and Training Centre for Depth Psychology. We would like to express our deep respect and gratitude by awarding the very first prize from our Centre to you, Sir Laurens van der Post.

Postscript

Memorial Service Address for Laurens van der Post

London, December 20, 1996

Lawrence Hughes

I am truly honored to have been asked to say a few words this morning about Sir Laurens van der Post. For the last 37 years, I have had the extraordinary privilege and great pleasure of being Sir Laurens' American book publisher. But even before I came to William Morrow, the publishing house with which I am still associated, it had brought out *Venture to the Interior*, the first book Laurens wrote after the War and the first to be made available in America. Thus, his affiliation with Morrow has spanned a period of 46 years and a catalog of 25 books. That must be some sort of modern record of author loyalty, at least in my country.

My colleagues have asked me to extend to all of Laurens' family, those here and those absent, their loving sympathy and to thank him again for the trust he placed in us. It is a trust that we must continue to honor, because, although Laurens van der Post is no longer among us, his books, his words, his ideas will endure.

I won't talk this morning about Sir Laurens' life. We all know the extraordinary facts, facts that, if they were put into fiction, would not be believed. I could never do justice to a review of his philosophy or his deeply-held beliefs. They live on in his books and films, and I know there are many of his friends who can write and speak more eloquently about them than I.

What I do want to talk about is Laurens van der Post, the human being as I knew him.

I remember that the first time I met Laurens, and I believe it was in 1960, a group of us had planned a luncheon party in his honor. Just before he arrived, Miss Frances Phillips, his American editor, said to me, "Larry, you are going to meet a very extraordinary person. Laurens van der Post has the command presence of a Colonel of the Regiment and the spiritual presence of a saint." I don't truly recall the details of that luncheon, except that Colonel van der Post wore a monocle, which was not your everyday eyewear in Manhattan in those days, and that he told us some wonderful stories about Africa and that he didn't seem very saintly to me.

But what I do remember vividly was his next visit to New York. It was a summer evening, and I was accompanying Laurens to a supper party. When we entered the large lobby of the building in which our host had an apartment, we saw three or four people excitedly running around trying to catch a pigeon which had flown in through the front door but couldn't find its way out. Immediately, but in a very quiet way, Laurens took charge. He directed that someone open a back door which led out to a garden and that all of us stand absolutely still. Within minutes, the pigeon flew down to the lobby floor and, from about ten feet away, stood inspecting Colonel van der Post with that side-to-side movement that pigeons employ when sizing up a situation. Then the pigeon took one last look at this smartly-dressed stranger, turned and flew out the open back door into the garden. Am I imagining that Laurens spoke to this bird? No, I believe he did, because I remember thinking, "Miss Philips was right. Here we have Montgomery of Alamein and Francis of Assisi rolled into one."

Later, as I came to read and learn more about Laurens van der Post, I realized that communication with animals was a very natural part of his life. Can we forget his persuasive chat with that stubborn camel or his meeting with that tiger on a jungle trail or his marvelous portrayal of Blady, the horse, or of Mantis or of Hintza, the African ridge-back? As the hunter in *The Hunter and the Whale* explained: "One of the reasons why Nature, and animals in particular, were so important to us today was because they are a reminder that we could live life not according to our own will but to God's."

So that was my first vivid memory of Laurens who, as the years progressed, did me much honor by calling me not only publisher, but friend.

The last time I saw Laurens was this past September in America in Boulder, Colorado, at the Laurens van der Post Festival. For four consecutive days, Sir Laurens showed films, gave talks, answered questions and entered into discussions with his audience on subjects ranging from his association with Carl Jung to his journeys into the Kalahari to his memories of the Bloomsbury set in the prewar London of his youth.

In Boulder, I was staying with some very old friends. I urged them to accompany me to the festival, and so my hostess asked me to tell her something about him. "Even if we had all day," I said, "I wouldn't be able to tell you half of what I should. But maybe I can put it all into one sentence. 'Sir Laurens van der Post is the most wonderful human being I have ever met.'"

And, of course, that is what touched us all about Laurens. The marvelous humanity of the man. The gift he had to connect at once with people of all races, all colors, all conditions, all stations of life and all ages. I took the measure of this American audience in Boulder and it was young. Moreover, the sessions were being held in a very large former movie theater, and there for all to see was the name, "Laurens van der Post" in letters two feet high emblazoned in lights on the theater's marquee. I felt this could just as well have been a gathering of rock concert fans with Sir Laurens as their pop star. The enthusiasm, the energy, yes, even the adulation, were infectious. After each session, his listeners rose as one, and the applause of appreciation only stopped when the moderator suggested that it would be nice if we let Sir Laurens get some rest.

I think these young people sensed that here was that rare being – all too rare, in their experience – a man of complete honesty, of forthright beliefs, of genuine modesty, without pomposity and definitely with a lovely sense of humor. Here was someone whose counsel had been sought by monarchs and world leaders, but whose life had also touched and influenced the most primitive human beings still on our planet. Yet, the members of his Colorado audience felt instinctively that at *that* moment he was entirely interested in *them*. Speaking to them was a man of four score years and ten who wasn't living in the past; he was living vibrantly in the present and deeply concerned about their future.

He was giving his all. And indeed, that's what Laurens van der Post always did, whether to his comrades-in-arms, his fellow prisoners of war, his friends, his family, his country. Even to those who had tortured and beaten him – when they asked – he gave. He never held back. He gave us his all. So, after the evening was over, my hostess turned to me and said, "Now I understand."

I remarked that someone had suggested that Laurens had the spiritual presence of a saint. I myself came to feel that his spiritual gift was more that of a prophet. Indeed, the title of his first major book, *Venture to the Interior*, was prophetic. That book was the story of his mission to what was then Nyasaland, and, as his life progressed, his writings became concerned more and more with ventures to the interior – the interior of the human psyche.

As Laurens explained, and I quote from *Yet Being Someone Other*, "In the Western world to which I belonged, all the stress was on the 'doing' without awareness of the importance to it of the 'being.' Because of a lack of such 'being' we were constantly in danger of becoming too busy to live."

And Laurens wrote that if we are to rid life of villains, we must rid ourselves first of the villain within.

I myself take these as prophecies, and I believe that if we ignore his warnings, we do so at our great peril.

I'd like to now mention something that *was* to be, but won't happen. It had become a tradition for Laurens to give a sermon on the last Sunday of Advent at the Cathedral of St. John the Divine in New York City. This year that Sunday falls on December 22, which is the day after tomorrow. And this year, we in America were particularly looking forward to it, because we had also planned a very small but festive birthday celebration for Sir Laurens. That is not to be, but on this coming Sunday, he will, in a sense, still be there. As some of you know, just as there is a poet's corner in that great New York cathedral, there is also a corner dedicated specifically to Laurens van der Post. In it are mounted the beautiful Laurens van der Post Biblical reliefs by Frances Baruch.

Before I flew over here, I called Laurens' good friend, Jim Morton, Dean of the Cathedral. Jim said to me, "Laurens often reminded us that the Bushmen of the Kalahari believed there is a dream dreaming us. I believe that we are, perhaps, a part of his dreaming today. We know his dreams are in our hearts and our souls. May they always be." Dean Morton also told me that, this coming spring, the Cathedral will hold a reading from Laurens' work. So in this and many other ways, his intellect and spirit will live on.

As I said to my hostess in Boulder, "Even if we had all day, I wouldn't be able to tell you half of what I should about Laurens van der Post." So how can I now bring to a close these few personal thoughts about one of the most remarkable human beings of our century?

When I was a young editor, an older and wiser colleague advised me, "Always let the author have the last word."

Thus may I end by reading two sentences. The first is from *Yet Being Someone Other*, in which Laurens says, "Death has always seemed to me one of the greatest moments of truth, when all that is false and imprecise in life is erased."

And in conclusion, from his book *About Blady*, "Ultimately all endings are happy endings. The human comedy finally is divine."

Laurens van der Post, Willerzell, Switzerland, 1992

Last Words

Mangosuthu Buthalezi

The news of the death of Sir Laurens van der Post has saddened me beyond expression. A few days ago, being unaware of Sir Laurens' state of health, I sent to him a message of congratulations on his ninetieth birthday. For me, his unexpected departure renders this world of ours just a little more uncomfortable and lonely place to be. I know that he will be sadly missed by many, but for me, this loss bears a special sorrow. The whole world, which basked in his great wisdom for so many decades, is left poorer by his passing away. He leaves a void which no one can fill which will remind us of his great personality for many years to come. We were enriched by his contributions.

Even though separated by distance, I have always maintained a dialogue with Sir Laurens which expressed itself not only in the correspondence we exchanged for many years, but most of all in the silent but intense dialogue of our respective innermost discourses. In my own reflections, I have often pondered the advice I received over the years from Sir Laurens, and I knew that he, even from a distance, could understand the deep reasons and significance of my actions, though no words needed to be uttered between us. It is a consolation in sorrow to think that, for me, this dialogue will survive the separation of death. Because in such circumstances, my first thought goes to his family. I hope that they will also find comfort in the realisation that the spirit and humanity of a man of the magnitude of Sir Laurens continues to exist within us, if we treasure and dialogue with them as living memories.

For me, Sir Laurens will always remain the ever-present memory of a man who in all his actions carried the uneasy realisation that the book of life contains numerous truths which are open for everyone to read, and yet, for only a few to understand. He understood truths confronting all of us which few were courageous enough to recognise. He spoke for and defended the culture of the Bushmen because he saw the treasures, compassion, and quintessential human values encapsulated in their traditions and way of life. For him, the defence of the Bushmen was not dictated by fashionable political correctness following a trend of his own world's culture, but rather, it expressed his capability of immersing himself through empathy and compassion into a world other than his own.

Sir Laurens leaves the world the legacy of an outlook on life in which the boundaries of philosophy, intense religious perception, and the awareness of the human race's complex richness are merged in a unity, the texture of which is reflected in Sir Laurens' own life. His writings, ideas, and advice remain multifaceted expressions of a true and unified value lying beyond them, which words can often not fully express.

Sir Laurens can be described, in one sense, as someone who lived ahead of his time. His involvement many decades ago as one of the founder members of the Capricorn Society was an indication of his rejection of racism and colonialism, and of the apartheid ideology which did so much damage to the image of his country of origin. Because he was also an Afrikaner, he felt the pain of the unacceptable things that were the lot of the victims of the apartheid system. He made this very clear over many decades to his fellow South Africans, and to Afrikanerdom in particular.

He perfectly understood that South African society, being such a diverse society, needed policies which recognised that diversity, while rejecting apartheid at the same time. He felt that South Africa was enriched by its diversity and that such diversity was a plus and not a tragedy, as some would think. It was for this reason that I received such great inspiration from his great wisdom as I advocated policies which accommodated the cultural diversity of our great South African Nation. He felt just as I do that we will have lasting peace in South Africa through the distribution of power to the Provinces, a trend which is happening in many parts of the world. It was his vast knowledge of the world and of the species *Homo sapiens* which broadened his view that not many blessings have been brought to many countries which follow the route of over-centralisation.

He was so abundantly equipped to deal with all these human questions by the fact that he was a conservationist *par excellence* who was recognised as such throughout the world.

We have lost a giant amongst men. We should, however, thank God for so much that he has bequeathed to the human race through his prolific writings, which have not only enriched those of us who are living today, but which will enrich many generations to come, long after all of us have joined him in his sleep.

His experience of violence during the war in which he was a participant made him an apostle of peace and enabled him to appreciate the futility of war. The likes of Sir Laurens come once in a generation. Although we are all poor mortals, and he was one of us in that sense, his contribution to world knowledge makes him immortal in another sense.

I was one of those privileged people who maintained a long-lasting dialogue with him, which enabled me to benefit from his advice and share with him the crucible of my own life experience during the many stages of our fight for freedom. Throughout this dialogue, I was surprised by the fact that he understood what was simple and evident and yet escaped the understanding of many. His understanding was based on immediate empathy and intuition, and, as such, it could not be corrupted by the violence of propaganda and trends of political correctness. He was one of the few highly self-educated intellectuals in the whole world who gave me the impression of having truly understood the most intimate nature of black African culture in general, and that of the Zulu Nation in particular. His European culture and heritage did not limit, but indeed, enriched him because he had the daring and simplicity to go beyond them. He was one of the greatest South Africans of our times and one of the greatest human beings who ever trod on the planet earth, and it is now essential that, from our shared sorrow, we begin treasuring and fully exploring the teaching of his life experience.

Laurens van der Post upon being commissioned as a Senior Lieutenant,
March 1940

Last Words

Nelson Mandela

I was most saddened to learn of the passing away of Laurens van der Post.

Laurens van der Post could, by virtue of his birth, have embraced a life of privilege in our divided country and with it the dehumanising view of most South Africans, which blunted the conscience of the ruling minority. Instead, he was driven by a larger vision to affirm the common humanity of all who share our land and our continent as their home. Through his life's work, he used his talent and his passion to help break through the veil of self-imposed ignorance.

Such spirits, treading a lonely path ahead of their time, helped lay the foundations of our Rainbow Nation.

Portraits of the Contributors[1]

By way of introducing the contributors to the readers and, not least of all, to one another:

Abt, Theodor

Professor Theodor Abt, born in Zürich, Switzerland, is a graduate of the Swiss Federal Institute of Technology (ETH), Division of Agriculture. From 1973-1979, he was project leader of a regional development plan, first for the Canton of Uri in central Switzerland, and then for the highlands of the Canton of Zürich. He received his diploma from the C.G. Jung Institute of Zürich in 1975, and since then has maintained a private practice as an analytical psychologist in Zürich. In 1977, he received his Ph.D. from the ETH in regional economics and rural sociology. From 1977-1995, he was a lecturer at the C.G. Jung Institute of Zürich, specializing in the topics of picture and dream interpretation, as well as alchemy and the Egyptian books of the underworld. Since 1979, he has lectured regularly at the ETH on the topics of rural sociology, social change, complex systems and environmental archetypal dreams, and he was a training and control analyst at the C.G. Jung Institute. His professorial thesis was entitled: *Progress without Loss of Soul* (published in English by Chiron Publications, Wilmette, 1989). From 1983-1989, he was a member of the Curatorium of the C.G. Jung Institute and in 1990 he became a

---

[1] At the time of his death, Sir Laurens was in the midst of preparing subjective portraits of each of the contributors to this volume, all of whom were personal acquaintances. The resulting incompleteness presented a difficult editorial dilemma: because it would be impossible to construct further portraits in the way he had so beautifully begun, it was decided to retain much of what had been prepared, while adding others that unfortunately are of necessity rather more 'factual' and perfunctory. A certain unevenness is the result, but this solution was considered preferable to the alternative of greatly reducing – for the sake of 'equality' – the work that Sir Laurens had so feelingly begun.

professor at the ETH. In 1994, he became a co-founder of the Research and Training Center for Depth Psychology according to C.G. Jung and Marie-Louise von Franz in Zürich. Since then, he has been a member of the board and regular lecturer at this Center. He shared a deep concern for earth and soul with Sir Laurens and was instrumental in founding the Laurens van der Post Foundation in Zürich.

Akiyama, Satoko

Satoko Akiyama wrote seven books addressing the role of woman in Japan, and the necessity of Japanese women taking themselves seriously. She was the daughter of a famous Daisetz Zen Master, whose temple still stands in Kyoto. She first met Laurens van der Post in Zürich, where she was one of Prof. C. A. Meier's outstanding trainees. She and Sir Laurens subsequently met upon numerous occasions in Japan. Although she died far too young of a stroke, the brevity of her life was compensated by the meaning their encounters had for them both, and resulted in the book she came to write about their friendship in her native Japanese.

Ammann, Peter

Peter Ammann works as a Jungian analyst in Geneva and Zurich. As a young man, he did his analysis and analytical training in Zürich and wrote a thesis reflecting the interest he had had in music since childhood. Thereafter, he spent many years working in the world of film, in part with Fellini in Italy and when this period ended, he moved to Geneva, where he played cello in a Geneva orchestra and established a practice as a Jungian analyst and worked as an independent filmmaker for Télevision de la Suisse Romande, while continuing to look for ways of combining Jungian psychology and the making of films. Two of his better-known films from this period were *Braccia si, uomini no* and *Le train rouge*. In the late Eighties, he was invited by the newly-founded Center for Jungian Studies in Capetown to lecture there, and this led over time to the making of a film about inner and outer wilderness: *Hlonipa – Journey into the Wilderness*. At this moment, he is again addressing Africa, as he works on a film about the first painters of South Africa, the Bushmen cave-painters of primordial art: when the first Europeans landed, rocks and their requisite surfaces gleamed like old canvases in the shadows of Africa and turned the whole country into a kind of prehistoric Louvre.

Baruch, Frances

Frances Baruch is a sculptor of great distinction, a fellow of the Royal Society of British Sculptors and one of the finest British portrait sculptors of her generation. But her work is by no means confined to portraits alone. She has followed a highly individuated evolution as an artist and explored great classical themes in her work, through Greek mythology and the Bible, which has led recently to eight of her Biblical sculptures finding a permanent home in the great Cathedral of St. John the Divine in New York City. Her work is varied with significant excursions into abstract patterns and a long journey of fantasy delighting in the world of the harlequin, and other forms of joy in a playful imagination which became a spirited and witty transformation of modern waste material into works of art. Some of her friends call this 'waste in transfiguration,' while she herself refers to it as polystyrene sculpture. Drawing from the nature of the material, she titled a recent exhibition, 'Package Deal.' She shared much with Sir Laurens and was a source of great strength to him.

Baumann, Dieter

Dieter Baumann, of all of the grandchildren of C.G. Jung, is perhaps the one who was closest to him. His voice, his manner of speaking and his sense of humor are very reminiscent of his grandfather. This was due not only to the fact that he seems to have been born in every way in the dimension which his grandfather explored so profoundly and uniquely throughout his life, but also to the fact that in his most impressionable years as a boy, particularly during the early days of the war, he lived in the close company of his grandfather.

Knowing that Jung was on the Nazi blacklist and that he would be one of the first to be eliminated by the Germans should they invade Switzerland, he was evacuated to Saanen in the western and more defensible part of Switzerland. Baumann has a vivid description of how, when they arrived at Saanen, a great storm was beginning to blow up over the valley, and as they stood – grandfather and grandson – at a window watching it, there was a flash of lightning and the lone church was struck and set alight. This synchronicity, along with Jung's vision of God and the cathedral at Basel, made a very deep impression on him, no doubt contributing to his lifelong sense of faith in his grandfather's vocation and his own total commitment to do what he could to enlarge human awareness of all it implied for the future of the human spirit.

At this moment, he is still working as hard as ever, not only as a Jungian analyst in Zürich, but particularly in spreading knowledge and understanding of Jung's work outside of Switzerland, most notably in Italy and in Spain.

His first meeting with Laurens van der Post was typical of how the element of chance, the great and enigmatic instrument of providence that conditions even the fall of a sparrow, was always as pronounced in his life as it was in his grandfather's. Van der Post describes how, after an evening in Basel spent with Professor Reichstein (to whom the Nobel Prize was awarded for his pioneering work in chemistry, and who died only recently), he boarded the Amsterdam-Zürich Express and went straight to the dining car for his breakfast. At his table was a young couple, conversing with great spirit over their coffee and croissants. Since the train was coming from Amsterdam, he was not surprised to hear them talking in Dutch. He himself, of course, understood and spoke Dutch, and therefore felt he ought to inform them of this fact, in case they wanted to talk about anything confidential. They were amazed to meet somebody who looked rather un-Dutch speaking to them so fluently in that language, and asked how he came to speak it. He said he had been born in Africa when Dutch was the official language of his country. "In that case", the young man said, "I wonder if you have not run into a great friend of my grandfather's who was born in that part of Africa, Laurens van der Post."

From that moment, they were friends, and one of the many things that they have in common is a feeling that in a mature democracy, one has to share fully in all the national obligations imposed on individuals. In the case of the Swiss Army – which so closely resembled the South African Army, in which Laurens van der Post was commissioned many years before the last war –, they exchanged ideas on the critical referendum and its future (see Baumann's article on page 99). This made Sir Laurens follow particularly closely the debate preceding the referendum, which he considered to be of immense importance, not only to Switzerland, but to all the democracies in Europe.

Bellinger, Paul

Since his school days, Paul Bellinger seems to have had only one overwhelming passion, and that was making films. Accordingly, he has made films not only in Africa, but in Europe, England and America. He served his apprenticeships as an inspired cameraman himself, and most of his reputation as a highly independent maker of television films is based on this expertise. However, in a number of his films, he has taken on the roles of director and producer as well. He first attracted the attention of the outside world in his work with Stephen Cross, and together they made several television films of distinction, most notably one on the life of T.S. Eliot. Stephen Cross then chose Bellinger as his cameraman for a film with Laurens van der Post which has been shown repeatedly on the BBC and in the rest of the outside world: *A Region of Shadow*. With Jonathan Stedall and again with Laurens van der Post, he produced a film called, *All Africa Within Us*, in which he had to be his own cameraman and he also became Jonathan Stedall's sound recorder, as well as one of the bush cooks and bottle washers, because all three of them knew that to make a film of real intimacy on the life in the bush, everything would have to be kept small. As director of films, producer and cameraman, he and Jane Taylor produced a notable television series for the BBC, *Testament to the Bushman*. In establishing himself in Britain, he also had to work as a film reporter on most of the major events in the world of the past thirty years and, in between, do independently what his searching spirit demanded of him.

Jonathan Stedall has said that, of all the many truly gifted camera-men he has worked with through his long and varied career, he has never known one who films as Paul Bellinger does with both eyes open. Laurens van der Post believes that this also explains why the visual impact of Paul Bellinger's films is so satisfying: it not only conveys the subject superbly, but also its context. The view of the camera, as it were, matches with what the eye sees from without and thus gives Paul Bellinger's work an atmosphere that is unique.

Brooks, Vernon

Vernon Brooks was born and raised in West Virginia. He served in the U.S. Navy as a communications officer in the South Pacific from 1943 to 1946, and attended Columbia University from 1946 to 1948 and the University of Zürich from 1975 to 1980. He worked as a freelance editor in New York from 1948 to 1952, was co-host of "The World in Books" on Station WEVD, New York, from 1955 to 1959, and served as a reporter for the American-Scandinavian Foundation in Sweden, Norway and Denmark in 1959. He was associated with the C.G. Jung Foundation in New York, as Managing Editor of the Publications Department from 1960 to 1965 and as Director from 1965 to 1972, then moved to Zürich for analytic training and eventually graduated from the C.G. Jung Institute there in 1988. Since his return to the U.S., he served as Associate Director of the Centerpoint Foundation in Nashua, New Hampshire, as Editor of *In Touch* for the Centerpoint Foundation and as President of the Training Board of the C.G. Jung Institute in Boston. He maintains a private analytic practice in Nashua and has published papers in such journals as *Quadrant* and *The Journal of Analytical Psychology.*

Bührmann, M. Vera

Vera Bührmann's story is deeply rooted in that of European engagement in South Africa. She grew up in the former Northern Transvaal and can trace her family back to the first European settlers in the Cape Colony in the Eighteenth Century. She graduated from Cape Town University Medical School in 1935.

After a few years of general practice, she devoted herself to maternal and child welfare services, where she became a pioneer in South Africa in promoting structures that specifically addressed mother-child relationship issues. This led her to London in the 1950's, where she trained both as a child psychotherapist in the Public Health Services and as a Jungian analyst with Michael Fordham's group. On her return, she served as a consultant and later established the first Child Psychiatric Clinic in Cape Town.

In the mid-Sixties, she was instrumental in founding the first school for autistic children in Cape Town, which was named the Vera School for Autistic Children in her honor, and she also served on various government committees of enquiry into mental health and care for children.

She initiated a reading group in Jungian psychology, which eventually led to the founding of the Cape of Good Hope Centre for Jungian Studies in 1987. She was greatly supported in realizing her dream of a Jungian training center by Sir Laurens van der Post, who also dreamed of adding a Jungian element to the ongoing transformations in South Africa. Their common dream led to the founding of the Southern African Association of Jungian Analysts in 1992, which was granted training group status by the IAAP in 1995.

Her immersion in the complexities of South African culture led her to undertake extensive transcultural research in the traditional Xhosa homelands in the Eastern Cape in the Seventies and Eighties, which resulted in more than twenty publications and her book, *Living in Two Worlds*, published in 1984 (Human and Rousseau, Cape Town).

In 1990, the University of Cape Town awarded Vera Bührmann an honorary doctorate on the same day they bestowed one on Nelson Mandela. She received it for her contributions to child psychiatry, the care of autistic children and the founding of the Cape of Good Hope Centre for Jungian Studies, a fitting tribute to what has been a career of selfless devotion to critical aspects of soul in South Africa. Dr. Bührmann is now retired and lives in Somerset West, just outside of Cape Town.

Buthalezi, Mangosuthu Gatsha

Mangosuthu Gatsha Buthalezi is a member to the Royal Zulu Household: he is a Prince of the Buthalezi clan and an uncle to the Zulu King, King Goodwill. As the Chief Minister of the Zulu homeland territory in Natal, he leads the largest ethnic grouping in South Africa. In this role, he actively opposed the apartheid system in South Africa, while initially remaining a member of the African National Congress. In the mid-Seventies, however, he was instrumental in forming the Inkatha Movement, and by the time of the first general election in the new South Africa on April 27, 1994, Inkatha had become ideologically estranged from the ANC in its development from a primarily cultural movement to the political party of which he is President. He worked throughout Nelson Mandela's years in prison to try and secure his release. He was named Minister of Home Affairs in the first Government of National Unity in the new South Africa.

Laurens van der Post came to know him over the years, particularly through the various struggles fought within the country against apartheid. They held one another in high regard, and their friendship spanned the years.

Charlton, John

From the time he first joined the Hogarth Press many years ago, John Charlton, with Nora Smallwood, was, until he retired recently, Laurens van der Post's publisher.

In the last years of the great Nora Smallwood's tenure, John Charlton was increasingly occupied with Laurens van der Post, who said that, in the sixty years of his connection with the Hogarth Press, no one among the successors of Leonard Wolff and Ian Parsons and Nora Smallwood, did more for him and his writing than John Charlton. The moment he appeared as a director in the premise of William the 4th Street, he increasingly took charge of Laurens van der Post's affairs and, after Nora Smallwood's departure, he was singularly responsible.

Sixty years ago, the world of publishing had been undergoing a process of profound change, and was in its most difficult period. The war then compelled publishing, as it was, to close the ranks, as with the amalgamation of the Hogarth Press with Chatto and Windus. This process now was grossly accelerated and publishing increasingly becoming a matter of forming larger and larger units, until it was changed out of recognition by the hubris of the takeover-world. Both the identity and the independence of publishers were attacked and slowly eroded and individual relationships which the Hogarth Press had had from the time of Leonard and Virginia Wolff were threatened with total collapse. Thanks to John Charlton's love of the world of literature and books, Laurens van der Post felt totally blessed with the continuity and freedom to be just a writer, and to leave the rest to his publishers, a state which continued until John Charlton's retirement a few years ago. Of all the people in a period of sixty years with one and only one publisher, no one gave him more. No one except, perhaps, Leonard and Virginia Wolff, he says, had such a feeling for writing, wrote so well himself, and was such a superb editor of manuscripts. It is not surprising that, even in retirement, Laurens van der Post often consulted John Charlton and of course they remained firm friends.

Douglas-Home, Jessica

Jessica Douglas-Home (née Gwynne), a long-time friend of Sir Laurens together with her late husband, was born in London and began an artistic career at Cranborne Chase, later studying at Chelsea School of Art and then the Slade, where she learned etching, studied theater and won an Arts Council scholarship to work in provincial theaters. She also made stage designs for productions at the National Theatre and in the West End. A figurative artist, she has at times used dreams and subconscious images as starting points for her works. She has exhibited throughout Europe and in the United States and illustrated two books of poetry.

Also a writer, she has recently published a well-received biography of her great-aunt, Violet Gordon Woodhouse, and over the years, she has contributed articles to *The Guardian, The Times, The Telegraph, The Spectator* and *The Wall Street Journal*. She lives and works in London and Gloucestershire.

Dunlop, Sir Edward 'Weary'

Laurens van der Post felt that Weary Dunlop was one of the truly great figures who emerged from the war in the Pacific. The two men first met in a demoralized prison on Bandu in Java and for some months were closely linked in a shared command. A Canadian obituarist said of this incident that not only Weary and the Japanese turned in that moment, but the whole of the cosmos as well. Dunlop left Java to rise to his full heroic stature as a doctor-healer and creative leader of men driven by unbelievable suffering, almost to the end of sanity. His published war diaries have become classics, and his services to all the nations of Southeast Asia, not excluding the Japanese, as well as his native country, are of an epic nature. It is to the credit of Australia that the nation went into mourning when he died, gave him a national funeral, and remembers him to this day by printing his likeness on coins and on postage stamps.

But, in the last analysis, nothing illustrates the essential quality of Weary's doing and being so much as an incident described in his war diary. One of the most brutal of the many brutal Japanese encounters in the Second World War, of which he encountered one of the worst on the Burma Road, arose there and time and again, and he nearly lost his own life in his utter commitment to heal the sick, the starving, the wounded, and all those in peril of their lives. When, at the end of the War, Weary had to face a line of Japanese candidates for trial and judgment before a war criminal court in Southeast Asia, he crossed the line without picking anyone until he came to where he faced one of the most brutal of his captors. He paused and looked at the man for quite awhile in his eyes, and then turned and walked away. Laurens van der Post, who himself refused to take any part whatsoever in the postwar trials, has written that Weary Dunlop, in turning away at that moment, gave the whole of creation a nudge.

Fay, Carolyn Grant

Carolyn Grant Fay earned a B.A. in music from Vassar and an M.A. in counseling/dance therapy from Goddard. She co-founded the C.G. Jung Educational Center of Houston, today a well-respected center of Jungian thought, and served as its president for 30 years. She also founded its School of Expressive Arts, where she still teaches and maintains a private practice. In her work, Carolyn Grant Fay uses Jung's concepts experienced through authentic movement, music, painting, clay, writing, and sand play. She and her husband were friends of Laurens van der Post for many many years, and he first went to their home not long after the war. Today, she continues to teach, to write and to produce video films of her pioneering dance work. Her dance therapy is based on C.G. Jung's active imagination and is an example of the natural healing power of the arts.

Carolyn Grant Fay, through her work in the field of movement therapy and her study, practice, and support of analytical psychology, has been a pioneer in the integration of Jungian psychology and expressive arts therapies. The impetus was Jung's recommendation that his patients use the expressive arts (writing, painting, building, dancing, sculpting, and working in sand) to more deeply experience themselves and connect to his concepts.

In a recently completed film of her work, *At the Threshold*, Carolyn Grant Fay talks about how the union of analytical psychology and movement therapy has enriched her life as well as the lives she has touched. She refers to Jung's development of the concept of active imagination at a critical juncture in his life. He described it as the dialogue between the conscious and unconscious mind, in order to contact unknown aspects of one's self and to integrate them into one's conscious life.

Carolyn Grant Fay has been a member of the American Dance Therapy Association since 1972, was mentored by Mary Whitehouse, and trained in depth with Joan Chodorow, both pioneers of dance therapy. She developed her work to encompass not only the principles and methods of analytical psychology and movement therapy, but all the expressive arts – music, visual arts, story telling, sand play and writing.

Henderson, Joseph

Joseph Henderson, for his 90th birthday, came to Europe and celebrated it in such a youthful manner that all of his friends were as overjoyed as they were astonished. They took it all as typical of Joe Henderson: never against the stream of his own nature, but as the nature of the current.

He was one of the founders with the Wheelwrights of what is today the flourishing Jungian Institute in San Francisco, and through his writing as well as work, he continues to make an invaluable contribution to the world of his vocation. His wife was the daughter of Frances Cornford, the poet, and a granddaughter of Darwin, and she kept her husband close company until her recent death.

Joseph Lewis Henderson, who can rightfully be seen as the dean of North American Jungian analysts, was born in 1903 in Elko, Nevada. Trained medically in London, and with travels to Zürich for work with C.G. Jung, he eventually returned to the U.S., closer to the American Indians, who have remained a deep interest throughout his life. Of all the many things he has done in and for the C.G. Jung Institute of San Francisco over the years, one of the most significant is his advocacy and chairmanship of the Archive for Research in Archetypal Symbolism (ARAS). Among his many publications are *Thresholds of Initiation* (Wesleyan, Middletown, 1967), "Ancient Myths and Modern Man" in *Man and His Symbols* (C.G. Jung, Ed., Doubleday, New York, 1964) and "The Four Eagle Feathers" in *A Testament to the Wilderness* (Daimon, Zürich, and Lapis, Santa Monica, 1985). He is Lecturer Emeritus of Neuropsychiatry at Stanford University and continues to maintain an analytic practice in San Francisco.

Hinshaw, Robert

Born in the United States and living his adult years in Switzerland, Robert Hinshaw shared a love of diverse cultures with Sir Laurens, as well as a life that includes the worlds of Jungian psychology, publishing, film and wilderness. Reflecting this, they worked together on numerous projects of various kinds, including *The Rock Rabbit and the Rainbow*. "Our Mother Earth" (see p. 301) is one example of an abiding dialogue, collaboration and friendship that continued over the years: Laurens van der Post had originally been invited to speak to the C.G. Jung Foundation in New York on the occasion of Earth Day in 1989, but was unable to attend and could only deliver his message in the form of this conversation, which was recorded.

Robert Hinshaw is the publisher of Daimon Verlag, home of many Jungian-related works in English and German, including *A Testament to the Wilderness*, a *Festschrift* compiled for the 80th birthday of C. A. Meier in 1985, with essays by Sir Laurens and several of the other contributors to the present volume. In addition to his publishing work in Einsiedeln, he maintains a Jungian analytic practice in Zürich and is on the faculty of the C.G. Jung Institute there, where he also serves on the Curatorium, or Board of Directors, as Vice-President. He is currently Honorary Secretary of the International Association for Analytical Psychology (IAAP) and, when time allows, continues to pursue projects involving intercultural phenomena.

Hughes, Larry

Larry Hughes has been, through William Morrow & Co., a publisher for almost the whole of his post-war career. The first book by Laurens van der Post after the war, *Venture into the Interior*, was first published by William Morrow & Co., just before Larry Hughes, who himself, although he never talks about it, had a grim war of his own to go through. He joined the firm, and very soon thereafter, its founder, Thayer Hobson, had, because of damage done by poison gas to his lungs in the First World War, to retire to the cleanest possible air in Arizona. No one has meant more in the world of publishing to Laurens van der Post as a writer and a human being than Larry Hughes.

Besides what he feels about the man's many qualities and generosities, his own written work has benefited tremendously from his association with Larry Hughes. Larry Hughes is as great a publisher as he is a great and natural gentleman, with qualities which are hard to earn recognition for in the confused and ungrateful modern world.

In the increasingly desperate battle for the living word, to which the writer, no matter how good, could not do his part without a publisher to match, Larry Hughes has performed, totally committed with courage and unusual integrity, in such a way that, in the other scene of warfare, as in the Second World War, he would have long since been awarded what is the greatest honor an officer in the British Army can receive, that is the private soldier's comment, "both an officer and a gentleman."

Jaffé, Aniela

Of all the many human spirits who were originally drawn to Jung because they felt that he alone could help, and then remained to settle and work, not necessarily for him, but in the vicinity and special atmosphere which life created around him, the life of Aniela Jaffé achieved the purest objectivity: her own self was never hypnotized or diminished. She was, to the end of her days, her given self: grateful to Jung for all he gave to direct it to its own natural evolution, and in this way able to serve him and to serve the vast vision of new meaning which his work evoked, without in any way losing herself in the process. Her writing about Jung and his work therefore has an astonishing clarity and a precision of expression and lack of exaggeration which is truly inspiring. No one else could have performed, says Laurens van der Post, the task of helping Jung to write through her his *Memories, Dreams, Reflections*. This book was, of course, published after Jung's death, but was so complete that, just before he died, he authorized her to do whatever she felt was appropriate with the new material which had emerged in all the recollection and research done for that remarkable 'autobiography.'

She also had a gift for laughing at herself, as she did when she first met Jung. In the early days of her relationship with Laurens van der Post, which lasted nearly fifty years, she explained to him that she came to Zurich "because, I thought, of a skiing accident, but now I know better," and there followed an endearing laugh at the figure she made of herself.

Aniela Jaffé had come to Jung already as an accomplished writer on her own account. This fact contributed a great deal to the objective concern for the totality of Jung's achievement and it is good to remember that her greatest service in that dimension was not only helping Jung to write his own biography just before he died, and later the editing of his letters for publication, but also the writing of her own contributions, among which the book, *The Myth of Meaning*, was one of the most significant works to come out of what was known as Jung's circle. She was a very private person and her work was all the better for that, and to use, for once, the much abused Victorian adjective, the purer. They all made contributions in part, she as a whole.

Janson, Charles

Those who best know Charles Janson often wonder where his gift for music would have taken him if his musical studies in Paris had not been interrupted by the outbreak of the war, at which point he immediately and characteristically volunteered. He was battled as an officer in the Welsh Guards. But in 1940, his platoon, covering the historic retreat of the British army to Dunkirk, was overwhelmed by the immensely superior German forces brought against them and he was then a prisoner until the end of the war. It was there that he discovered another gift. ...

He emerged from prison having utilized his time to pursue his gift for languages and friendships. Speaking fluent Polish and Russian, he returned to Paris, where he performed notable service as a newspaper correspondent.

Charles Janson is such a singularly gifted and many-sided person that it is impossible to compress his diversity and abundance of talents even in paragraphs, let alone a few sentences. He lives to this day with his wife, Elisabeth Sutherland, mainly in Scotland and in London, but paradoxically, it seems only so as to live also the life of his time in a rounded and whole way. He could easily have been a concert pianist, as well as a good and brave soldier and a first-class correspondent in Paris. He was one of the first people to join David Stirling and Laurens van der Post to form the Capricorn Society in Africa. He, with a few friends, indeed formed Africa Confidential, which became perhaps the most successful and politically influential newspaper of its time and continues to this day with undiminished vitality.

Perhaps his greatest gift of all is that of friendship: he has countless friends among a great variety of people among races and cultures of all kinds. His knowledge of Russian has enabled him to translate works of the most difficult kind, for example, writings of the outstanding Zinoviev, and he keeps all this abundance of relationships alive with what amounts to genius for writing letters full of real insights and perceptions of events of his day: witty, funny and wise. If all of his letters were gathered together, it would be an unrivalled and incomplete history of our enigmatic and tumultuous time. What is more, through these letters and these friendships, the private way they are lived does not prevent them from being of great public and objective consequence.

Lehmann, Rosamond

Rosamond Lehmann has made a notable contribution to English literature and, with Elizabeth Bowen, she is ranked as one of the two outstanding woman writers of their generation. Her books are still being published as an abiding memorial of what she achieved, from the day of the publication of her first book while still a student at Cambridge. She was born in 1901 and educated at Girton College and Cambridge, of which she later became an Honorary Fellow. Her many publications include: *Dusty Answer* (1927); *A Note in Music* (1930); *The Weather in the Streets* (1936); *The Gypsy's Baby* (1946); *The Swan in the Evening* (1967); *A Sea-Grape Tree* (1976); *The Awakening Letters (1978). She died in 1990.*

Mandela, Nelson

Rolihlaha Nelson Mandela was elected President of South Africa in the first proper General Election held in the new South Africa on April 27, 1994. He had been released from prison four years earlier, in February, 1990, after serving a sentence of 27 years, mostly on Robben Island, with fellow political prisoners. They were, like him, predominantly members of the African National Congress (ANC), accused of treason for trying to undermine the policies and ideology of the apartheid system implemented by the white Nationalist Party government of the day. He is a Xhosa, being a member of the Thembu clan from the Transkei region of South Africa. He trained as a lawyer and, with his friend and equally well-known ANC anti-apartheid activist, Oliver Tambo (who went into exile abroad with other ANC members), had opened the first black law practice in Johannesburg in 1952. His recently published memoir, *Long Walk to Freedom*, has become an international best seller.

McGlashan, Alan

Alan McGlashan's life spans almost the whole of one of the most eventful centuries in the recorded history of the world. Still in his teens, he was participating in the First World War as a fighter pilot. He discovered in himself a natural love for flying and, from all accounts, did his part in that totally unexplored dimension far beyond the call of duty. It included, among his many sorties against the enemy, two encounters with the legendary Baron von Richthofen and on each occasion, they departed with all of their ammunition spent and parted with a knightly salute to one another.

Fresh from the war, like his brother, he returned to become a physician, for which he qualified at Cambridge. However, characteristically, he did not go to an established practice at once, but rather went to sea as a ship's doctor, and then was active for a spell in London as a dramatic critic before he became a totally committed general medical practitioner.

The practice soon was both a success and highly esteemed, but somehow never seemed to be quite the whole answer there was for Alan McGlashan; as a born healer, something to him seemed absent in an orthodox medical approach to his profession.

His unusual intuitive nature soon drew him to the emerging dimension of psychology in depth and, as a result, he left his practice and for some years took to training himself as an analytical psychologist with a fellow Scot, the famous Eddie Bennet, who had already become a firm friend of C.G. Jung and, to the end of his days, a pioneer extending the roots of Jungian Psychology in Great Britain. From that time onward, Alan McGlashan said to his friends, he felt that he could now come near to doing the whole of what the challenge of healing demanded of doctors.

A highly-differentiated individual, as his own nature demanded, a person who discharged his debt to the community and life of his time, he never identified himself with a group or person, and continued to see life steadily and to see it whole. Wholeness was as important to him as it was to Jung, and to make modern man whole from what St. Paul called the principality, he tried to make all the hundreds of alienated and disturbed people of all sorts of conditions whole, as he himself strove to be whole.

However his consulting room may have been the principle field in his strivings for wholeness, he was also a born writer. He was convinced that only by increasing the awareness of modern individuals could this perhaps ultimately be done.

He naturally continued what took him into the world of the theater so early on, and began to write. And through countless reviews of modern literature and some notable broadcasts on the BBC and articles in the sadly irreplaceable magazine, *Listener*, helped to make the BBC for many years one of the best instruments of the best of modern culture to the world. Two of his books are already regarded as classics and will become better and better known as time goes on. The first, *The Savage and Beautiful Country*, of course describes the country of the spirit and the soul of man, and in the other, *Gravity and Levity*, he makes special sense of fun and humor, which only a resolved spirit and imagination at its most profound can produce. As he approached his own blessed century with time, he continued his daily analytical work in his practice and was much sought after as an analyst until his death in May, 1997.

Meier., C. A. 'Fredy'

> *… whose urgent heart of music often demanded instant notes instead of deliberate chords …*

The collaboration of Fredy Meier with C.G. Jung was longer than that of any of the others who worked with him. He was drawn to Jung while still a young boy in Schaffhausen and irresistibly felt that the diverse and thorough disciplines of medicine, surgery and biological research he had developed along the way were to make this experience 'training,' as it were, to be a profoundly committed collaborator of Jung. His work, unfortunately, is not well enough known in the English-speaking world, because the books that he wrote on Jungian psychology in German were not originally translated, except for his outstanding book on incubation, *Healing Dream and Ritual* (Daimon Verlag, Einsiedeln, 1985), which has had a wide demand from the time it was issued. His last book, *Personality* (Daimon Verlag, Einsiedeln, 1995), on synchronicity and the personality of type, is a masterpiece of condensation without loss of complexity or sacrifice of depth.

To the Jungian community of Zurich, he was an enigmatic and often controversial person. But to his students in the department which Jung founded at the Federal University of Zurich, and to the many people who came to him for analysis, he was much loved and gratefully remembered, and he was consulted to the end of his days by people from all over the world. His appreciation in private was, perhaps, all the more fastidious and real for never 'going public' and, in a sense, life recognized his fundamentally creative spirit by enabling him to live a full life to his 91st year. When he knew he only had a few months left to live, he lived them as if they were to be lived forever, using them almost until the last reading, for example, Goethe's correspondence with Schiller, as he confided to his old friend, Laurens van der Post, who made repeated trips to Zurich to see him in his final weeks (see photograph on page 158).

Monley, Eva

Eva Monley has had a long, remarkable and outstanding role in the post-war world of making films. Raised as she was there, it is not surprising that her first work in films had to do with Africa, and she worked in somewhat junior capacities on one of the many revivals of *King Solomon's Mines* and in a more distinguished way in the production of *The African Queen*. From then on, her role was progressively more important and embraced films based in the wider world. There, perhaps one of her most remarkable contributions was as a producer in the making of David Lean's *Lawrence of Arabia*, where she demonstrated her inventiveness and her initiative capacity for seeing difficult things through to their true end.

She has worked with several of the most famous directors of the last decades, many of them no longer alive, but whose names still live (among them, John Huston and David Lean). Her latest film has been Walt Disney's *A Story Like the Wind*, based on Laurens van der Post's two books, *A Story Like the Wind* and *A Far-off Place*. She worked with him on various film and television projects for some fifteen years.

Her partnership with Africa perhaps remains the most important of all her relationships and she continues to serve it as an influence and source of continued inspiration.

Mori, Katsue

As Sir Laurens van der Post has described in his writings, Captain Katsue Mori came into his life when Laurens was barely 19, at a time when he himself had just become the youngest but most promising commander in the Japanese mercantile marine. Although separated by time and distance and the horrendous war in the Pacific, they remained friends to the end of Mori's one hundred years.

"I ... saw much of Mori and came to know him well. The more I knew him the more I liked him and appreciated the elements of greatness in him. He was by far the greatest sea captain I was to meet. For him, sailing the seas was not just a physical and technical venture, but the fulfillment of a mission to which he felt himself born by life itself. ... Love of his country and people, love of duty and, above all, love of a life of meaning and a search for greater being were all united. ..."

From *Yet Being Someone Other*, Chapter 6

Oshima, Nagisa

One of the younger of the most distinguished creators of films in a nation of great filmmakers, Japan, one of his films, *The Empire of the Senses*, won the highest award at Cannes. He is known for his great and original gifts, as well as his courage in venturing beyond the frontiers of convention, and even established tradition. He has written a great deal, and in his trial on a charge of immorality in the highest of Japanese courts, he conducted his own defense, which was not only successful, but a work of great literary art. Outside of Japan, he is particularly well-known in France, where his written work has also been published. In the English-speaking world, the work by which he is best known is his film version of Laurens van der Post's *The Seed and the Sower*, called *Merry Christmas, Mr. Lawrence*.

Osler, Richard

Richard Ridout Osler lives with his family on Bowen Island off the west coast of Canada. He lives his life primarily in two areas: business and the arts. He began his career as a journalist and then developed into an investment and finance professional in the oil and gas industry, where he now runs his own business. For over ten years, Richard Osler was a business commentator on a national Canadian radio show. He became interested in the writings of Sir Laurens van der Post in the early 1970's and met Sir Laurens for the first time in the early 1990's. From the time of their meeting, he and Sir Laurens had a deepening friendship, which led him to co-produce a documentary film about Sir Laurens' life and work: *Hasten Slowly – The Journey of Sir Laurens van der Post* premiered in Canada in June, 1996. Richard Osler's published works include a chapter called "Richard's Diary" in *The Latest Morningside Papers* by Peter Gzowski (McClelland & Stewart, 1989).

Page, Robin

A little more than halfway through his expected life span, Robin Page finds himself one of the most authoritative voices to speak up not only for the conservation of the natural world, but also for its total rehabilitation. His love of the land and the earth come from a childhood spent on a farm where he still lives. Bird's Farm, on a rather old college in Cambridge, has been the compass of his remarkable voyage on that troubled and dangerous sea. The many books he has written from the history of a village in the country are all successful. His writing appears regularly in the best newspapers in Great Britain and his is a very special voice on BBC channels. He practices all that he preaches on his family's farm and has created around it a public trust for the rehabilitation of the land, of which Laurens van der Post is a patron. No conservationist in Great Britain has worked harder in so many different channels, not excluding the public and political dimension, and the pragmatic success and the way he practices all the way what he preaches have made him, if not the best known, the most effective conservationist in Great Britain.

Parkin, Ray

Ray Parkin's love of the sea took him at an early age into the Australian navy. When the war in the Pacific broke out, he was quartermaster of a light cruiser, Perth. Although Perth was mauled and spent a lot of its ammunition in the Battle of the Java Sea, it managed to disengage when the naval task force under Admiral Durman was sunk along with almost the whole of the rest of his fleet. Perth, after a hurried refueling and taking in of ammunition at Batavia, was ordered to set sail immediately and head for Australia through the Sunda Strait before the overwhelming Japanese forces could encircle and destroy them as well. However, the three ships encountered the advance units of a Japanese task force as they were about to enter the Sunda Strait and in the night ultimately engaged the entire Japanese fleet. The story of the battle was told by Parkin himself in his book, *Out of the Smoke*, published after the war with an introduction by Laurens van der Post, who compares the battle to that of "Grenville's Revenge" in the war against Spain.

As the quartermaster, Parkin had steered Perth throughout the battle and finally it was sinking fast and the surviving crew had abandoned ship. Parkin himself was also ordered by the captain to abandon ship, but he refused to leave. Finally, the captain ordered him from where he was then alone on the bridge, "Now get the hell off the ship, Parkin. This is an order!" Parkin felt he could not disobey and left the ship to go down, captain and all, and ultimately drifted ashore to the coast of Java in a life-jacket and soon to imprisonment. There, some months later, Laurens van der Post also was incarcerated and found among those who made a special impression Ray Parkin, sitting as a painter painting calmly and what appeared to be happily under a large rain tree, indifferent to the flying lizards that from time to time flew around him. His book, *Out of the Smoke*, was followed by *Into the Smother* and another about his imprisonment in Java and his life thereafter.

In later years, he conducted research into the life of Captain Cook and the historic voyage which brought him to Australia. A close friend, too, of Weary Dunlop, he is still alive and writing and adds to the life of his noble publications with his paintings and etchings, for which he has a special genius (see pages of his contribution to this volume for examples thereof).

Player, Ian

Ian Player is known world-wide for all that he has done for conservation. When, after a harsh war with the South African forces in Italy in the Mediterranean world, he was discharged, still hardly more than a boy, and in casting around for what do for a living in the so-called world of peace, he turned to service in the Parks Board of Natal in South Africa. In one of the remotest parts of Zululand at that moment, the battle for the survival of one of the most endangered species of the day, the white rhino, was far from being won. His training took place in the bush and in Zululand and a unique friendship evolved with the Zulu Chief attached to him. Their friendship was a most remarkable and fair exchange from two totally different cultures of the sort that was not encouraged, and even condemned by most South Africans as impossible. But the result of it all was that Ian Player gained through his experience an extraordinary aptitude for the world of the bush and when they put him in charge of operations to ensure the survival of the white rhino, he did it so well that it is today the unequaled success of a major project of conservation. The story of how this was done is told in his book, *The White Rhino Saga* (Stein and Day, New York, 1973), and is widely known to such an extent that he has received the highest environmental awards in the United States and other parts of the world.

Ian Player was deeply impressed at how much the wilderness experience gave to people and how rich their spirits became, almost as if a profound healing was started in the soul of modern people when exposed to nature and wilderness, no matter how out of touch with it they might have been. He felt that, unless we recognized how, in our separation from wilderness, our spirit was increasingly alienated, that in their spirit modern humans would be perhaps the most endangered species on earth. More and more, it seemed to him that the last parts of Zululand and Africa, as he had come to know them, were the last real churches left on earth, if only they could be preserved and made accessible.

Eventually, he left the park service to create the Wilderness Leadership Movement and, over the years, has taken even the youngest of people and the most extreme of delinquents on trails into the bush and let them live there for a few days in the company of people like his Zulu guides. They almost inevitably become completely changed and their lives set on course for pursuing the kind of wholeness which derives its meaning from what was the task of all keepers of the soul.

Typically, he did not leave it at that and his intuition took him to the work of C.G. Jung and Jungian psychology. For him, the world without and world within should always be sought and served as one and, as a result, he became a founder with other pioneers of Jungian

Psychology in South Africa, Vera Bührmann, Laurens van der Post, and Graham Saayman, of a center for Jungian studies in the Cape of Good Hope. It is the first institute of its kind in South Africa and in its founding, put down roots and has a goal of working at training other people psychologically for the future.

Pottiez, Jean-Marc

Jean-Marc Pottiez is perhaps best known in the English-speaking world as a partner with Laurens van der Post in their bestseller, *A Walk with a White Bushman*. Like Laurens van der Post, Jean-Marc Pottiez was born in Africa and this explains as nothing else can why, from the moment of their first meeting, the two of them have been friends. Although born in Africa, he left in his youth to be raised in France.

After many years of a career, which first took him as a young soldier in an airborne unit to Algeria, he went out as a journalist to China and Korea and Japan, where he was for a considerable time a principal correspondent for his newspapers and for French Television. The distinction he earned in that world led to a professorship at the United Nations University in Tokyo. While in Japan, he married a beautiful and gifted Japanese woman and would no doubt still be in Japan if his department at the University had not been closed down. At the moment, he is engaged in writing a book about Japan.

In the course of his life that followed, he says he overlooked that he, too, was born in Africa, but left it as a youth and his life subsequently took a course which seemed to be totally unrelated to its beginnings. As he says at the end of his introduction to their book: "... through this walk with Laurens, I confirmed what I knew from the beginning but had tried to forget: that homes, orchards and gardens cannot offer shelter to those who have been born with tom-toms in their hands." This perhaps explains as nothing else can why he and Laurens van der Post did so much together and felt so bonded.

Raine, Kathleen

Kathleen Raine is a poet, a friend of Yeats and a lover of Blake, of whom she has written and lectured with ultimate illumination.

Her poetry for many years has been a source of great joy and enrichment to her own generation and what there is left of men and women who still find satisfaction in poetry which does not sever its umbilical cord from the totality of the great English poetic tradition, but is truly rounded and contemporary. In addition, in her eighties, she has founded an academy for the discovery of the gnostic sources of sacred knowledge, the sources from which she has never been estranged, but served with total commitment, and still does. The name of her academy flies like a banner over all she has done during all of her life. The pacific name by which she has baptized her academy, *Temenos*, of course was the magic protective circle which inspired the concept of the saint with the halo and also the metal or ivory ring which is worn among the truly wise of Zulu sages and prophets.

Rees, P. Henry

Laurens van der Post always referred to Henry Rees as his Director of Education, because he was in command of all the educational activities while in prison. He said that he wished that Rees after the war had been put in charge of education in all of Great Britain, because he was so good at it in a Japanese prison.

Rees wrote an extended series of *Pity Ditties* which were printed in each edition of the prison weekly, written or typed on lavatory paper and called, *Mark Time*. It was an unfailing cause of a moment of amusement, sometimes even on the grimmest of days, and as such, was an invaluable element in sustaining prison morale. It was an example of how one and all, according to their gifts, never failed to contribute to the spirit of the community.

Robertson, T.C.

Thomas Chalmers Robertson was born on the 15th of September, 1907, on the Transvaal highveld and first studied law at the University of the Witwatersrand. He switched to journalism and travelled extensively in Southern Africa. During World War II, General Smuts, then prime minister, put him in charge of nation-wide propaganda campaigns. Postwar reconstruction plans began a forty-year career in a similar capacity in the fields of soil, water and nature conservation. For this work, he was awarded the Golden Sable of the Wild Life Protection Society, the Golden Protea of the Land Service Movement and an honorary doctorate from his alma mater. The government awarded him the Decoration for Meritous Service, South Africa's highest civilian decoration.

T.C. Robertson died not long after he wrote his contributions to this collection. He was one of Laurens van der Post's oldest friends, they having met when they were both journalists in the 1920's, and he became one of South Africa's most original and distinguished sons. During the war, he was first a member of the intelligence forces and then belonged to General Smuts' small circle of intimate advisors and, after the war, he refused to enter the world of politics as Smuts wanted him to do, but turned all of his great energies to what was left of the natural world in Africa. He was appointed head of the Veldtrust, which had been created to look after conservation in the entire country, and he is today fondly remembered in a large area devoted to the protection of birds along the great Umkommas River along the coast of South Africa, since it was established as a memorial to his services for conservation. Already two thousand species of birds have been identified there.

T.C. Robertson had a penchant for being irreverent to almost everyone – and at the same time, a wonderful charm, so that those he met almost always came to love him. This was a great gift during the time of apartheid, when he had friends on all sides and could help to keep the dialogue going.

Few men of his generation in Southern Africa are thought of so fondly and joyfully as is he to this day. (See also Laurens van der Post's memory of his old friend on page 277 of this volume.)

Root, William Pitt

William Pitt Root joined our circle of friends first through his poetry. He is a born and abundant poet and, though not well-known outside of America, thrives in a country where provincial poets enrich the literary climate of the greater national scene. *Trace Elements from a Recurring Kingdom* (Confluence, 1994) recollects his first five books of poems.

He was raised near the Everglades and now lives with his wife, Pamela Uschuk, also a contributor to this volume, in Tucson, Arizona, where they first met Laurens van der Post in 1982, and he commutes weekly to teach at Hunter College in Manhattan. After he told Sir Laurens a story by way of thanks for the many stories he had shared while lecturing with nary a note for eight hours over two magical days, he was invited by Sir Laurens to one of the most important international conferences of the World Wilderness Foundation, held at Inverness more than a decade ago, where he gave an excellent paper, as well as reading his own poetry. After the opening address of Professor C. A. Meier, it was perhaps the outstanding intellectual event.

William Pitt Root and Pamela Uschuk are both known leaders in poetry at outstanding universities, but in addition to the planes of their poetry, they have other things they shared with Sir Laurens and with all of us and that is consciousness of the planet. Both have a particular love of the natural world.

Schwartz, Robert L.

Robert L. Schwartz has had two professional careers: as a journalist, he was New York Bureau Chief for *Time,* Assistant to the Publisher at *Life,* on the editorial board at *Harper's* and on the Board of Directors at *New York* magazine. As an entrepreneur, Schwartz created the Japanese-designed Motel on the Mountain in New York, and, twenty-four years ago, converted the former Mary Duke Biddle Estate into the Tarrytown Conference Center, the first commercial facility of its kind.

Schwartz was founder and chairman of the Tarrytown Conference Center for twenty-four years; he founded the Tarrytown Group with anthropologist Margaret Mead before her death in 1978 in an effort to expand the conference center's role into the arena of ideas. Evidence of the Group's expansion was the *Tarrytown Letter* (published monthly), the School of Entrepreneurs and frequent weekend events held at the Tarrytown Conference Center. In support of the facility's role in educating and preparing the business executive to be a better leader in a changing world, Schwartz formed the Tarrytown One Hundred in 1983, a membership organization of innovative business executives who, both individually and collectively, work toward identifying the role of the business executive in creating a new type of workplace.

In addition to frequent platform appearances in the United States, Schwartz speaks around the world on the subject of social change, primarily exploring the importance of personal achievement as a central goal in both personal life and the workplace. A friend of Sir Laurens for many years, he has been instrumental in helping to building bridges of communication between disparate groups and in arranging speaking engagements to his end.

Stedall, Jonathan

Jonathan Stedall hardly needs any introduction to the English-speaking world because he is one of the outstanding and most gifted filmmakers. He met Laurens van der Post some twenty-five years ago when he proposed that the two of them should join and make a television film on the life of C.G. Jung. The result, entitled, *The Story of Carl Gustav Jung* (1971), was much acclaimed and shown repeatedly all over the English-speaking world. As a result, both he and Sir Laurens found that they had so much in common that they made more films together, one most conspicuously perhaps, being the highly original and beautiful film, *All Africa Within Us* (1973/74). However, his great service to television started many years before the two of them met and continues to this day. No one in this world has for so long and so abundantly served their vocation better than he has. On December 28, 1997, his final tribute to Sir Laurens, a 50-minute retrospective entitled, *Voice from the Bundu*, was broadcast on the BBC.

Taylor, Jane

Jane Taylor was born in Malaysia. She and her mother left just in time to escape from its total occupation by the Japanese. She took a degree in history at St. Andrews University in Scotland and has followed her love of history in various ways directly as well as in her writing.

Straightforward history she did so well in her book, *Testament to the Bushman*. Significantly, this book is illustrated with her own camera work and shows how this is an abiding part of her interest in life. Laurens van der Post first met her when she joined the staff of the Hogarth Press under the indomitable Nora Smallwood. She then went to work in Constantinople, where she did valuable research both with Julian Norridge, the son of Diana Cooper and Stephen Runsow, whose books on Byzantine history and the crusades are histories of true class proportions and will indefinitely endure. She also subsequently went to Africa and ultimately returned to the Middle East and particularly Jordan, where she pursues writing with her camera and a sense of history in her own way, as, for example, in her remarkable book on Petrarch. After *Testament to the Bushman*, she had contemplated making a major feature film in the Kalahari, but in the end, settled in Istanbul and found herself drawn to the Middle East, which resulted in her settling in Jordan to compile her impressive work of photos and the history of Petrarch.

She is presently in the process of preparing the story of a most unusual and privileged excursion to what is almost forbidden territory to women.

Uschuk, Pamela

Pamela Uschuk is a highly-regarded American poet, living in Tucson, Arizona with her poet-husband, William Pitt Root, who also is a contributor to this volume. She holds degrees from Central Michigan University and the University of Montana and she writes, publishes and teaches widely. Her poems have appeared internationally in all matter of anthologies and periodicals, and there have been three collections of her work published: *Without Birds, Without Flowers, Without Trees* (Flume Press); *Loving the Outlaw* (Mesilla Press); and *Light from Dead Stars* (Full Count Press). She has been awarded numerous writing prizes, including the Ronald H. Bayes Poetry Prize in 1996.

Besides academics and writing, she is an avid birdwatcher and lover of the natural world, and she enjoys hiking among the animals in nature and working for environmental protection causes.

Wheelwright, Joseph

Joseph (Jo) Wheelwright, whose ancestors traveled to North America on the Mayflower, was himself a pioneer of Jungian psychology in the United States and, along with Joe Henderson and others, a co-founder of the C.G. Jung Institute and the Analytical Psychology Club of San Francisco. He and his wife, Jane, also a Jungian analyst, first traveled to Zürich and C.G. Jung in 1931, and then went on to study medicine in London before moving to California, where he had a long and illustrious career as an analyst and teacher. He was a professor at the University of California and edited an important work on sex and the college student in 1967, was coeditor of the widely-used Gray-Wheelwright typology test and was president of the professional international Jungian organization known as the IAAP. He has written numerous psychology papers, on subjects such as psychological types, marriage and the second half of life. Known for his wit, extroversion, humor and his gift of storytelling, which was an inherent aspect of his relationship with Sir Laurens, Jo Wheelwright now lives in the solitude of retirement on a ranch in Southern California with his lifelong companion and wife, Jane.

Wilmer, Harry

Harry Wilmer is one of the outstanding analytical psychiatrists of our time. For many years, he held a professorship of psychiatry at the University of Texas in San Antonio and while there, did most remarkable research and remarkable work with schizophrenics. But he will always be remembered with gratitude for the brave, courageous and ultimately successful battle he fought for the rehabilitation of the veterans from Vietnam, who were treated as outcasts and human untouchables by their fellow countrymen. Today he has retired from academic work and devotes himself entirely to his Foundation for Humanities in Salado, Texas. He has published many outstanding books in the field of psychology, two of the better-known titles being *Practical Jung* and *Understandable Jung – The Personal Side of Jungian Psychology*.

Wood, Lady Sue

A friend of Sir Laurens for many many years, Lady Sue Wood was born to a distinguished family of missionaries in the Congo at the beginning of this century. Although raised and educated in England, the impact of those first years in Africa brought her and her husband back to Kenya, where she made a unique contribution in her own right to the people of Africa. She and her husband, Michael, the founder of the Flying Doctor Service in Africa, were founding members of the Capricorn African Society. Her life, one way or another, has been devoted to Africa in many diverse ways, but more and more recently in the expression of her great love of literature and her gifts as a poet and general writer of distinction, as evidenced in her autobiographical recollection of a great adventure with her husband and Laurens van der Post by air in Central Africa, *A Fly in Amber*. She also designs ceramic jewelry and heads an enterprise with 200

Kikugu women, with shops in London, New York and Sydney. The late Sir Michael Wood was knighted for his great services to medicine and healing in Africa.

List of Illustrations

Bibliography

This is a listing of the English language editions of the major works of Laurens van der Post, along with some of his introductions to other works, and a selection of his essays and lectures.

Works by Laurens van der Post

Race Prejudice as Self Rejection: An Inquiry into the Psychological and Spiritual Aspects of Group Conflicts. New York: The Workshop for Cultural Democracy, 1957.

In a Province, London, The Hogarth Press, 1934; Penguin Books, 1984. New York, William Morrow, 1965.

Venture to the Interior, London, The Hogarth Press, 1952; Penguin Books, 1957. New York, William Morrow 1951; Harcourt Brace 1980.

The Face Beside the Fire, London, The Hogarth Press, 1953. New York, William Morrow, 1953.

A Bar of Shadow, London, The Hogarth Press, 1954.

Flamingo Feather, London, The Hogarth Press, 1955; Penguin Books, 1965. New York, William Morrow, 1955.

The Dark Eye in Africa, London, The Hogarth Press, 1955. Braamfontein, South Africa, Lowry Publishers. New York, William Morrow, 1955.

The Lost World of the Kalahari, London, The Hogarth Press, 1958; Penguin Books, 1962. New York, William Morrow, 1958; Harcourt Brace, 1979.

The Heart of the Hunter, London, The Hogarth Press, 1961; Penguin Books, 1965. New York, William Morrow, 1961; Harcourt Brace, 1980.

The Seed and the Sower, London, The Hogarth Press, 1963; Penguin Books, 1966. New York, William Morrow, 1963.

Journey into Russia, London, The Hogarth Press, 1964; Penguin Books, 1965. New York [entitled *A View of All the Russias*], William Morrow, 1964.

The Hunter and the Whale, London, The Hogarth Press, 1967; Penguin Books, 1970. New York, William Morrow, 1967.

The Night of the New Moon, London, The Hogarth Press, 1970; Penguin Books, 1977. New York [entitled *The Prisoner and the Bomb],* William Morrow, 1970.

A Story Like the Wind, London, The Hogarth Press, 1972; Penguin Books, 1974. New York, William Morrow, 1972; Harcourt Brace, 1978.

A Far-Off Place, London, The Hogarth Press, 1974; Penguin Books, 1976. New York, William Morrow, 1974; Harcourt Brace, 1978.

A Mantis Carol, London, The Hogarth Press, 1975; Penguin Books, 1989. New York, William Morrow, 1976; Covelo, Island Press, 1983.

Jung and the Story of Our Time, London, The Hogarth Press, 1976; Penguin Books, 1978. New York, Pantheon Books, 1975; Vintage Books, 1976.

First Catch Your Eland, London, The Hogarth Press, 1977. New York, William Morrow, 1978.

Yet Being Someone Other, London, The Hogarth Press, 1982; Penguin Books, 1984. New York, William Morrow, 1983.

A Walk with a White Bushman (in conversation with Jean-Marc Pottiez), London, Chatto & Windus, 1986; Penguin Books, 1988. New York, William Morrow, 1987.

The Lost World of the Kalahari, illustrated edition with photographs by David Coulson and a new Epilogue by the author, London, Chatto & Windus, 1988. New York, William Morrow, 1988.

About Blady: A Pattern out of Time, London, Chatto & Windus, 1991; Penguin Books, 1993. New York, William Morrow, 1992; Harcourt Brace, 1993.

The Voice of the Thunder, London, Chatto & Windus, 1993. New York, William Morrow, 1994.

Feather Fall, An Anthology edited by Jean-Marc Pottiez; London, Chatto & Windus, 1994; Penguin Books, 1995. New York, William Morrow, 1994.

The Admiral's Baby, London, John Murray, 1996; New York, William Morrow, 1997.

A Selection of other Writings by Laurens van der Post

Introduction to *Turbott Wolfe* by William Plomer, London, The Hogarth Press, 1965.

Introduction to *Collected Poems* by Ian Horobin; London, The Jameson Press, 1973.

Introduction *The Secret River,* published by Barefoot Press, U.K., 1996.

Foreword to *A Candle on the Hill,* ed. Cornelius Pietzner; Edinburgh, Floris Books, 1990.

'Wilderness – The Way Ahead,' essay, Scotland, The Findhorn Press and Wisconsin, The Lorian Press, 1984.

'Wilderness – A Way of Truth' and 'Wilderness – Appointment with a Rhinoceros,' essays, Scotland, The Findhorn Press, and in *A Testament to the Wilderness, Festschrift* for Prof. C. A. Meier, edited by Robert Hinshaw, Zürich, Daimon Verlag, and Santa Monica, Lapis, 1985.

'Our Mother Which Art in Earth,' address, with interview by Robert Hinshaw and Peter Ammann in New York, *Quadrant*, The Journal of Contemporary Jungian Thought XXIII: 2, 1990 and in this volume under the title, 'Our Mother Earth.'

'The Creative Pattern in Primitive Africa,' Eranos Lectures, The Eranos Foundation, Ascona, Switzerland, 1956.

A Selective List of Films by and with Laurens van der Post

A Region of Shadow, for BBC program *A Pair of Eyes*, 1951,

The Lost World of the Kalahari, BBC Series, 1956.

All Africa Within Us, BBC, 1975.

The Story of Carl Gustav Jung, BBC.

The Tempest, BBC, 1976, for *Shakespeare in Perspective* series.

Zulu Wilderness: Black Umfolozi Rediscovered, BBC, 1979.

Laurens van der Post at 80, BBC, 1986 (Jonathan Stedall).

The Heart of the Matter (film by George Wagner).

Merry Christmas, Mr. Lawrence (based on *The Seed and the Sower*), by Nagisa Oshima, 1982

A Far-Off Place, by Mikael Salomen, 1993

A Story Like the Wind (based on *A Story Like the Wind* and *A Far-Off Place*), 1993

Hasten Slowly by Mickey Lemle, biographical documentary film on the life of Laurens van der Post, New York, Lemle Pictures, 1996

Voice from the Bundu, a last film in tribute to Laurens van der Post for the BBC by Jonathan Stedall, December, 1997.

Numerous other radio and television documentaries and interviews.

Hamba ga'hla

SELECTED TITLES FROM **DAIMON**:

A Testament to the Wilderness
Essays on an Address by C.A. Meier
edited by Robert Hinshaw

Swiss Jungian psychiatrist C.A. Meier delivered a fascinating paper at the 3rd World Wilderness Congress in Inverness, Scotland: "Wilderness and the Search for the Soul of Modern Man" addressed not only the tragedy of our vanishing natural wilderness and the need to preserve it, but also the necessity of preserving man's 'inner wilderness.' *A Testament to the Wilderness* consists of Meier's original address and thoughtful and provocative responses by eight concerned writers from around the world, including Laurens van der Post, Joseph Henderson, Ian Player.
(142 pages, paper and cloth, Co-published with the Lapis Press)

Talking with Angels – Budaliget 1943
A document transcribed by Gitta Mallasz
Budaliget 1943: A small village on the edge of Budapest. Three young women and a man, artists and close friends are gathered together in the uneasy days before Hitler's armies would destroy the world as they knew it. Seeking spiritual knowledge, and anticipating the horrors of Nazi-occupied Hungary, they met regularly to discuss how to find their own inner paths to enlightenment.
For 17 months, with the world locked in a deadly struggle for survival, the four friends meet every week with the spiritual beings they come to call their 'angels'; Gitta Mallasz takes notes, the protocols which form this book, along with her commentary. The angels' message of personal responsibility is as meaningful and as urgent today as it was for its initial recipients half a century ago. (474 pages, third edition)

Aniela Jaffé
From the Life and Work of C.G. Jung
with an *Epilogue* by Sir Laurens van der Post
Aniela Jaffé was given permission to quote from Jung's highly personal "Red Book," and she does so in her essay on Jung's creative phases. Shortly before her death, the author also updated and expanded her long-famous article addressing the National Socialism accusations leveled against Jung. Sir Laurens van der Post provides a sharp echo in his *Epilogue*, written especially for this edition. (200 pages)

Miguel Serrano
C. G. Jung and Hermann Hesse
A Record of Two Friendships

The author, a Chilean diplomat and writer who has travelled widely in India studying Yoga, had a close friendship with Jung and Hermann Hesse at the end of their lives. This book is the outcome of his meetings and correspondence with them. Many letters are reproduced including a document of great importance written to the author by Jung shortly before his death, explaining his ideas about the nature of the world and of his work. (110 pages, second edition)

Alan McGlashan
Gravity and Levity
The Philosophy of Paradox

This book heralds a breakthrough in human imagination, not a breakthrough that may take place in the future, far or near, but one that has already occurred – only we may not have noticed it. Life, as the author shows, is open-ended and full of paradoxes. Its principles cannot be understood by logic and causal reasoning. We can only come to terms with life if we accept that there is no final answer to it and that adjusting to life's natural rhythm is the key to finding release from the horrors and problems around us.
(162 pages, second edition)

The Savage and Beautiful Country
Alan McGlashan presents a sensitive view of the modern world and of time, of our memories and forgetfulness, joys and sorrows. He takes the reader on a safari into regions that are strange and yet familiar – into the savage and beautiful country of the mind. No 'cures' are offered, but we are provoked to reflect on our roles and attitudes in the contemporary world jungle.
(228 pages, second edition)

Alan McGlashan conveys a poetic vision which has more to do with life as it can be lived than all the experiments of the laboratory psychologist or the dialectic of the professional philosopher.
– The Times Literary Supplement

C.A. Meier
Healing Dream and Ritual
Ancient Incubation and Modern Psychotherapy
C.A. Meier calls for modern psychotherapy to honor the role that the dream has played in the healing process, from ancient times to the present.
"Healing Dream and Ritual is one of the most significant and lasting witnesses of how far beyond immediate psychology the implications of Jung's work stretches. This book is, in my feeling, as important for today's healers as was the early work of Paracelsus to the redirection of medicine in the Renaissance." – Sir Laurens van der Post
(168 pages, with illustrations and indexes, second edition)

Personality
The Individuation Process in the Light of C.G. Jung's Typology
Carl Gustav Jung never produced a systematic treatment of his own work – he was always moving forward. His assistant-of-many-decades, Carl Alfred Meier, made it his life-task to gather and present in detail the various aspects of Jung's far-reaching discoveries. This final volume of Meier's work addresses the human personality in its encounters between consciousness and the unconscious, a process referred to as *individuation*. In describing such encounters, the author extensively explains the notion of Jung's *psychological types*.
(192 pages, first edition)

Susan Bach
Life Paints its own Span
On the Significance of Spontaneous Paintings
by Severely Ill Children

The pioneering work, *Life Paints Its Own Span,* with over 200 color reproductions, is a comprehensive exposition of Susan Bach's original approach to the physical and psychospiritual evaluation of spontaneous paintings and drawings by severely ill patients. At the same time, this work is a moving record of Susan Bach's own journey of discovery. (208 pages text, 56 pages pictures, first edition)

ENGLISH PUBLICATIONS BY DAIMON

Susan Bach – *Life Paints its Own Span*
E.A. Bennet – *Meetings with Jung*
George Czuczka – *Imprints of the Future*
Heinrich Karl Fierz – *Jungian Psychiatry*
von Franz / Frey-Rohn / Jaffé – *What is Death?*
Liliane Frey-Rohn – *Friedrich Nietzsche*
Yael Haft – *Hands: Archetypal Chirology*
Siegmund Hurwitz – *Lilith, the first Eve*
Aniela Jaffé – *The Myth of Meaning*
      – *Was C.G. Jung a Mystic?*
      – *From the Life und Work of C.G. Jung*
      – *Death Dreams and Ghosts*
Verena Kast – *A Time to Mourn*
      – *Sisyphus*
Hayao Kawai – *Dreams, Myths and Fairy Tales in Japan*
James Kirsch – *The Reluctant Prophet*
Mary Lynn Kittelson – *Sounding the Soul*
Rivkah Schärf Kluger– *The Gilgamesh Epic*
Paul Kugler – *Jungian Perspectives on Clinical Supervision*
Rafael López-Pedraza– *Hermes and his Children*
      – *Cultural Anxiety*
Alan McGlashan – *The Savage and Beautiful Country*
      – *Gravity and Levity*
Gitta Mallasz (Transcription) – *Talking with Angels*
C.A. Meier – *Healing Dream and Ritual*
      – *A Testament to the Wilderness*
Laurens van der Post – *The Rock Rabbit and the Rainbow*
R.M. Rilke – *Duino Elegies*
Miguel Serrano– *C.G. Jung and H. Hesse: A Record of Two Friendships*
Susan Tiberghien – *Looking for Gold*
Ann Ulanov – *The Wizards' Gate*
Ann & Barry Ulanov – *Cinderella and Her Sister: Envy and the Envying*

Jungian Congress Papers:

Jerusalem 1983 – *Symbolic and Clinical Approaches*
Berlin 1986 – *Archetype of Shadow in a Split World*
Paris 1989 – *Dynamics in Relationship*
Chicago 1992 – *The Transcendent Function*
Zürich 1995 – *Open Questions in Analytical Psychology*

Available from your bookstore or from our distributors:

In the United States:

Continuum
P.O. Box 7017
La Vergne, TN 37086
Phone: 800-937 5557
Fax: 615-793 3915

Chiron Publications
400 Linden Avenue
Wilmette, IL 60091
Phone: 800-397 8109
Fax: 847-256 2202

In Great Britain:

Airlift Book Company
8 The Arena
Enfield, Middlesex EN3 7NJ
Phone: (0181) 804 0400
Fax: (0181) 804 0044

Worldwide:
Daimon Verlag   Hauptstrasse 85   CH-8840 Einsiedeln   Switzerland
Phone: (41)(55) 412 2266   Fax: (41)(55) 412 2231
e-mail: Daimon@compuserve.com
Internet: http://ourworld.compuserve.com/homepages/Daimon/